FOUNDATIONS OF TEACHING AND LEARNING

ROBERT R. DUNWELL
Professor of Education
University of Hawaii

and

ROBERT L. WENDEL
Professor of Education
Miami University, Ohio

PRAEGER PUBLISHERS • New York

Published in the United States of America in 1976
by Praeger Publishers, Inc.
111 Fourth Avenue, New York, N.Y. 10003

© 1976 by Robert R. Dunwell and Robert L. Wendel

Library of Congress Cataloging in Publication Data

Dunwell, Robert R.
  Foundations of teaching and learning.
  Includes bibliographies and index.
    1. Education—Addresses, essays, lectures.
2. Teaching—Addresses, essays, lectures. 3. Educa-
tion—United States—Addresses, essays, lectures.
I. Wendel, Robert L., joint author. II. Title.
LB41.D88   370'.973   73-21347
ISBN 0-275-84830-2

Manufactured in the United States of America

FOUNDATIONS OF TEACHING AND LEARNING

To
Ernest E. Bayles
A Professor

Preface

The substance of *Foundations of Teaching and Learning* has been deliberately selected and organized to do something that the authors very strongly feel needs to be done.

We have chosen to address ourselves to teaching and learning because these should be the primary thrust of educational programs. This does not mean that we do not believe that other matters, such as classroom management and discipline or the organizational structure of American education, are not important; it does mean that we do not believe them to be *as* important to professional teachers as the basic questions we have addressed here.

We have chosen to emphasize human teaching and learning for at least two very important reasons. First, we do not deny the significance of the efforts of many theoretical and experimental psychologists to explore learning as an abstract or laboratory science involving various organisms and species. We assume and hope our audience is acquainted with the traditional topics of general psychology and even the more esoteric topics of parapsychology, including biofeedback and E.S.P. Our primary concern is the process of human interaction in actual learning situations in actual learning environments, the factors that affect that process, and how that process can be made more effective and more satisfying to all participants. Second, we have a basic commitment to "humanizing" this process, but not as some vague, ambiguous, warm, fuzzy, nonverbal feeling or affectation. We are sensitive to what happens when organizations and programs fail to take a stand against depersonalization: they become sterile and meaningless, inconsequential and cold. We have found the human condition exciting and meaningful; we have found human teaching and learning exciting and meaningful; and we want others to share this kind of experience.

We have chosen to address the most significant problems and issues in teaching and learning today because they are problems that all teachers will have to confront sooner or later and because they are problems that deserve full exposure and intimate attention. Our approach is neither cynical nor pessimistic. We gave up tilting windmills long ago, at least as a primary endeavor. We believe these are problems that can be solved, and we believe that each professional has an appropriate role in obtaining a solution regardless of his or her prior experience or present status. We believe it is detrimental—even dangerous—if we delay or avoid taking on these problems. More beginning teachers have been disillusioned because the situation was not as they were told it would be than discouraged because they were candidly advised that it would be tough, challenging, and demanding.

Because the problems are complex, and because the source of many of these problems is found in the confusion of assumptions and the lack of clarity among consequences, our approach has had to be analytical, specific and detailed. We hope that we have made the discourse and the logic as clear, simple, and direct as is possible. If we have not succeeded, and it is quite possible that we have not always done so, we hope the reader will view it more as a fault in our expression than a matter of the cruciality of the issue.

We have chosen to address the areas of (1) sociocultural foundations, (2) philosophic foundations, and (3) psychological foundations. Some may find this arrangement, particularly the inclusion of psychological foundations, uniquely different from the traditional foundations text. We have done so for several reasons. First, teacher-education programs suffer the same problem as many other disciplines, namely, that of too much separation and specialization. We have chosen to emphasize the interrelatedness of socio-philosophic-psychological views. We do not intend this to be a substitute for a course in educational psychology; we do see it as an excellent preliminary to the specific study of educational psychology. Second, we have set out to help students regard the educational enterprise as a system of mutually related variables rather than a happenstance collection of unrelated bits and pieces. Individuals have no recourse in an irrational situation except to strike out blindly. When they come to believe that they can analyze and organize disparate facts and events, they can begin to design effective interventions. Finally, there is a logical relationship among these fields based on an individual's belief system. Although individuals are not always logical or absolutely consistent, they do try to view different categories of events in a sensible, organized way. What an individual thinks about a social issue, such as capital punishment, is related to his view of man's moral nature and to his notion of what constitutes a desirable approach to the schooling of man. We have tried to demonstrate the interrelationship among foundational areas, and the inclusion of psychological foundations is a logical part of this effort.

The main body of the text is organized into units of three chapters on each of the foundational areas. Initially, we have described each of the major positions, the functional distinctions among these alternate positions, and the bases on which these distinctions are founded. We have tried in each case to emphasize the significant differences, the distinctions that result in differing practices when they are applied or put to work in concrete situations. In the second chapter in each unit, we have examined the implications these alternate belief systems have for classroom teaching. The substance of these chapters can be taken as a carefully thought out, step-by-step approach an individual teacher can use to clarify many of the discrepancies and confusions in teaching practices. We have also included an annotated list of sources the reader may use for further examples of the suggested approach. In the third chapter of each unit, we have presented a selected set of readings that are representative of the range of belief systems described in the text. They elaborate these positions and validate both the descriptions we have made and the implications we have drawn.

Comprehensive in scope, *Foundations of Teaching and Learning* attempts to bring into consideration the major issues confronting professional teaching in a complex society in a challenging if not critical time. It proposes realistic, reasoned, and tested approaches the individual teacher may take. It does not propose these as final pat answers, but as a beginning. And that is what we think is most important.

R.R.D.
R.L.W.

Contents

FOUNDATIONS OF TEACHING AND LEARNING

CHAPTER 1

The Dilemma
of Education

American education does not suffer from a shortage of critics. There are critics on the left and on the right. There are external critics and internal critics. There are critics who exploit the weaknesses of education to promote ends other than effective learning. There are some who do not seek to remedy but to destroy. And there are some who still believe in education, who have some notion of what education could possibly become, and who are committed to ameliorate what they criticize.

To many of us the educational enterprise seems a fascinating anachronism, so fraught with error and mischief that it should succumb to its own frailties. We wait for the senile bureaucracy to topple, for the staff of uncommitted mercenaries to tire or retire.

But this does not happen. Our educational system persists in spite of its faults, seemingly impervious to all attempts to reform it, continually increasing in complexity and cost and confusion. One innovation follows another, reaching a zenith and quickly fading, resulting in no fundamental change. All we have is another set of patent remedies to add to the list.

Before generalizing further, let us consider a few phenomena of the seventies.

Teacher militancy has never been so prevalent or so strident. Teacher strikes, once considered unacceptable or unprofessional because of the threat they pose to public welfare and safety, are now commonplace. Teacher organizations that once limited themselves to sanctimonious pronouncements have become hard-nosed advocates and even agitators. However, some suggest that the demand for better salaries and duty-free lunch periods is symptomatic of the fundamental dissatisfaction of the classroom teacher, born of a sense of powerlessness (Lieberman, 1972).

Student militancy has never been higher. Buoyed by the success of student strikes on university campuses, secondary school students have enthusiastically entered the arena of activism. However, the few well-publicized incidents of violent confrontation overshadow the continuing guerrilla tactics of vandalism. Consider the tragedy of a social agency reaching out to youth who respond by tossing a brick through a window. Consider the specter of multitudes of disinterested, disgruntled, disenchanted, disheartened, discouraged students who expect something significant in life but fail to find it in their schooling (Stutz and Jesser, 1970; Parker, 1971).

The demand for cost-efficiency in education has never been higher. State legislatures annually require more and more cost-analysis studies. Although local school boards publicly endorse educational quality, in executive session they often seek the cheapest means to operate. Some public school districts have been forced to close as early as April, March, or even February because bond and tax levies failed to obtain the support of voters. Private schools throughout the nation have declared bankruptcy, forced to abandon their ideological commitment because it generated no financial commitment. Behind the rhetoric of such innovations as flexible modular scheduling, differentiated staffing, and year-round schools is the conviction that they provide cheaper ways to run schools (Lessinger, 1969).

Public dissatisfaction with schools has never been more apparent or more vehemently expressed. A quibbling federal educational policy has become snagged on the issue of the means for achieving racial desegregation. The involvement of state and federal courts is not simply evidence of regard for educational matters; they are expressly concerned with political matters that happen almost incidentally to be sited in the schools. In local districts the advocacy of "neighborhood schools" has often been a thin veil for social apartheid, an implicit bigotry that has led to the dynamiting of entire fleets of school buses. Undoubtedly these acts of violence were done by men who want the best possible education for their children. Federal and state efforts to produce effective change have been paralyzed by bickering. Stutz and Jesser (1970) maintain that "the serious consequences of the inadequacies in educational opportunities provided are clearly evident in virtually every state and local school district."

Professional dissatisfaction with the schools has never been so pronounced, yet obviously the profession remains ineffectual in its efforts to remedy its complaints. Weingartner (1972) observes:

> It is tempting to elaborate on the curious staff subculture in the schools. Perhaps just one observation is appropriate at this point—that schools are psychopathically devoted to trivia. They reveal an incredible devotion to the task of elevating the trivial to the level of the crucial and then go on to expend most of their energy and resources on the witless task of enforcing the "rules and regulations" that derive from this self-sterilizing process.

Having expelled all school administrators to achieve organizational purity, teacher associations are waiting for a leadership to emerge that is mature enough to be concerned with other than "bread and butter" questions. Administrators, for their part, have yet to recover from their collective shock. The response of professional schools of education has generally been insipid; their only successes have come in the defense and preservation of their rather archaic presumptions and pretensions. Many professionals, overwhelmed by the enormity of the problem, have either devised effective rationalizations about the seriousness of the situation or retreated to blithe truisms. Others continue a kind of academic gamesmanship that sidesteps the problem in the guise of confronting it effectively. Confusion remains the prime characteristic of curriculum theory (Taba, 1962).

To preservice or beginning teachers, the situation must be perplexing. They want to become good teachers, yet almost everything seems to contradict or prohibit fulfillment of this aspiration. Teacher-preparation programs continue to expend great effort on training the wrong people in the wrong way for the wrong reasons. Although meticulous records are kept of courses taken to fulfill certification requirements and cumulative grade-point ratios, significant personal data on students entering teacher-preparation programs is scarce, and no follow-up study reveals how they perform as teachers (Haberman, 1971). Many young people who could contribute much to remedying the dilemma of education are never encouraged to consider the problem as one that merits their concern. Few of those who are extremely bright and competent in their chosen discipline ever think of teaching in our present school system. Little, if any, attention is devoted to identifying or recruiting those who possess the potential to become excellent teachers or to produce significant changes in the system. Indeed, persons who are most able to tolerate ambiguity as they work toward creative problem solutions are effectively screened *out* of teaching (Harvey et al., 1966). In employment interviews we consistently select those who most agree with our views, notions, and biases (Merritt, 1971). The system is most effective in perpetuating itself, not in remedying itself.

Even more astonishing and disturbing is the fact that nearly half of those who do survive the traditional teacher-education program quit after only three or four years, well before they have had sufficient experience to become skilled practitioners or the chance to become effective change agents. Here again, teacher education carefully avoids systematic assessment of the experiences, feelings, and frustrations of these dropout teachers. It also avoids appraising the beliefs, attitudes, and values of those who remain in the classroom year after year without making a single significant contribution beyond "keeping school."

Our brief examination of these unrelated phenomena does not enable us to determine a more appropriate course of action. We can bemoan the fact that schools are not what they should be, that teacher preparation is not as effective as it needs to be, that students suffer from these defects. But more is needed if we are to comprehend the nature and scope of the problem and to discriminate the points where it is most vulnerable to attack. What we offer is a brief but inclusive examination of the American educational system and the people and processes that comprise it, to serve as a base from which to project alternative courses of action.

The American Educational System

The educational system of the United States today encompasses several thousand school districts, hundreds of thousands of schools, millions of teachers, administrators, counselors, curriculum specialists, audio-visual technicians—and not a few students. Public and private, nonprofit and profit, sectarian and nonsectarian, general, vocational, technical, nursery, higher, adult—formal education serves a wide range of specific but only generally related purposes.

Education, in a technical sense, is nonetheless a system, an aggregate of elements that function in a more or less integrated manner.

The full implication of this concept is elusive. The system of public education has an obvious congruency of purpose and an interrelatedness of elements. But do cooperation and regularity exist in fact? And what forces or factors, moreover, cause the system of American public education to function *as* a system? Although certain federal regulations require a degree of conformity, as in establishing eligibility for aid to federally impacted areas or school-lunch-program subsidies, a federal "system" of education exists not by statute but by cooperation and social convention. Among the fifty states are fifty widely differing subsystems dedicated to achievement of the goals of public education. Similarly, within each state, local subsystems demonstrate similarities and dissimilarities. Both similarities and dissimilarities can be understood as arising from perceptions of goals and means in differing sociocultural circumstances. Two students may each want to become an outstanding teacher, but one may be convinced that a private, sectarian, liberal arts college affords the best preparation, while the other seeks a large state university.

As a general definition, education may be seen as a system of less formally related institutions, organizations, compacts, agencies, schools, programs, commissions, and associations. The units coordinate their functions only to the degree that the ability of a particular unit to achieve its goals is dependent on other units within the system. To the degree that goal achievement is *not* dependent on the other units, a particular school can function autonomously. Thus, schools with widely differing aims and objectives may need to adopt such formal means of coordination and communication as exchanging transcripts indicating courses, hours, grades, and degrees or diplomas earned.

Education, then, is a system of very loosely related parts that are similar in some respects, very different in others. In such a system, a change in any element or in the relationship among elements produces a change in the way the system works. The degree and direction of change depend on the combination of forces in the altered system. To produce a deliberately planned change in education, we need a comprehensive and intimate understanding of the elements and the relationships among them.

The enormously large and complex system of American education clearly needs radical change, either in the nature of its current elements or in the way these elements function.

Such a change would require the expenditure of far more time, money, and energy than an individual or even a large association can typically generate. Reorganization of school districts is a common example of effort to produce change. But even though political bodies work diligently to redraw district boundaries, restructure administrative organization, or reallocate administrative tasks, little fundamental change actually takes place within the system. In fact, manipulating the administrative structure of school districts usually does not affect what goes on inside the classroom.

What is required—and what is possible—is a significant change in the teaching-learning functions that may be carried out within the existing organizational structure of districts, schools, classrooms, and curriculums (Bayles, 1960:31).

The Human Factor within the System

The educational system includes a wide array of job descriptions or *roles,* definitions of certain behavioral expectations for the various offices or positions in an organization. For each role there is a range of *role expectations* that others hold of the behavior of the person occupying that office. With varying degrees of clarity, the office holder is aware of these expectations; he has certain *role perceptions* of what others expect of him (Owens, 1970).

What exists is a complex system of interpersonal relations, based on the social interaction among organizational members and contributors. In classrooms, for example, each teacher holds a certain notion of what to expect from "students," and each student has a notion of what to expect of "teachers." These perceptions influence the process of social interaction and, in turn, are modified by the process. The same process of social interaction applies more generally to "society."

As one lives and interacts with others in a given social context, he or she develops a structured and identifiable belief system (Harvey et al., 1966). In a pluralistic society a broad range of values and attitudes influences or determines the expectations held for certain roles. When people join together in an enterprise, the congruency and discrepancy of their beliefs can be described in specific terms. The effectiveness of the group can be analyzed and means devised to increase it (Dunwell et al., 1971; Likert, 1961).

Common sense suggests that changing anyone's belief system is not a simple task, and it should not be undertaken without serious reflection on ethical considerations and the possible consequences. Both the efficacy and the morality of attempts to prescribe beliefs, attitudes, and values of a group demand justification.

Yet in the educational enterprise, teachers accept prescriptive roles that limit their effectiveness as people and submit to policies that limit their effectiveness as teachers. Variance is summarily suppressed. Students suffer much the same fate. They accept and conform, or they are identified as abnormal, unmotivated, or dyslexic (a refined but sinister kind of name calling). Or they are simply crossed off the school roster by administrative fiat.

Many in education have become entrapped in performing highly ritualized roles. The school principal is frequently seen as unable to allow himself to become intimate or even friendly with his staff if he is to supervise them effectively. Beginning teachers are warned never to become friendly with their students because the opportunistic little devils will take advantage of any display of humanity. Students devise their own codes of conduct regulating behavior in schools and classrooms and attitudes toward teachers and courses. But organizations do not change unless roles, role expectations, and role perceptions change. Dehumanization is a self-sustaining condition, an incipient and progressive disease attacking organizational health. The humanization of education will never be achieved by other than deliberate, purposive, articulated efforts.

We are not contending that attempts to make fundamental changes in human personality should be avoided, for the system will not change unless the basic attitudes, values, and beliefs of the participants effectively change. Nor is it a problem of whether basic personality changes can be effected. The evidence of mind manipulation, mind control, and "brainwashing" demonstrates this possibility. At the same time, evidence affirms the human potential to become fully functioning (A.S.C.D., 1962; Combs, Avila, and Perkey, 1971). What is required—and possible—is a deliberate approach to influence *individual* belief systems. Admittedly, this is more a question of ethic than of technique.

The Technical Nature of Teaching

In the vast establishment created to serve universal education, teaching has ceased to be an art—if it ever was—and certainly has not become a science, although many assert that they treat it in a "scientific" manner. Were teaching an art, it would not deny the expression of aesthetic principles, of what is beautiful, appealing, or of more than ordinary significance. It would give appropriate evidence of the truly creative. It would differentiate clearly between what is faddish and what persists over time. Its practice would never be marred by lack of inspiration or excitement.

Were teaching an art, it would demonstrate a more commonly accepted set of principles and methods than appear to govern practice today. Most teaching is founded on a jumbled mass of techniques and "methods" with little apparent concern for any unifying principle or "method." The distinction here between the plural "methods" and the singular "method" is crucial. A great many instructional means may be used, but frequently these techniques are employed with no real sense of purpose. Teaching as a result lacks focus and significance (Silberman, 1970).

Were teaching a science, it would demonstrate a much more systematic arrangement of the facts and phenomena associated with it. Efforts to treat teaching in a "scientific" manner include descriptive theories and research efforts that have been limited deliberately to a very narrow range of phenomena. But treating a narrow range of phenomena with a high degree of technical sophistication does not make the process "scientific"; exclusion of known data from consideration is in fact unscientific, if not antiscientific.

Were teaching a science, it would approach the disciplines of knowledge rather differently than it typically does. Something happens in the translation of the disciplines (biology, history, literature, for example) into school subjects. It's usually a fatal process, and the teacher winds up conducting a begrudging tour of an intellectual graveyard, reading a few epitaphs from the scattered tombstones. Most curriculum-revision projects resemble taxidermy more than resuscitation.

Typically, school subjects address only some of the characteristics of the disciplines from which they are derived. School subjects, including college-level courses, usually focus on the factual substance of the discipline, some of the ways in which this factual substance has been developed and verified, a rather superficial history of the development of the discipline, and a lot of vocabulary exercises.

Defining "discipline" as a community of persons committed to active inquiry and discourse, King and Brownell (1966) propose that the school curriculum be modeled directly on the fundamental characteristics of such a community. Were this to occur, our curriculum would probably have these characteristics (Dunwell, 1970):

1. Each classroom would give evidence that it is a flourishing enterprise of persons who have a common commitment to contribute positively to intellectual affairs. This spirit would assist each learner to become an active member of the intellectual community rather than a nonparticipant or passive consumer of its products.

2. The curriculum would deliberately demonstrate that school subjects are an expression of human imagination rather than collections of impersonal data. The curriculum would help the learner to understand how others have expressed their imaginations and would provide opportunities for him to experience intellectual challenge and appreciate his own imagination and creativity.

3. Because each discipline defines its own domain of inquiry, the curriculum would provide a range of experiences broad enough to allow the learner to discover its parameters and limits, what it is and what it is not. He would discover for himself how the discipline has been defined and developed.

4. Because each discipline is a psychological process of organizing, ordering, structuring, and limiting human thought, the learner would examine the historical development of the discipline. The learner would experience the dilemmas that faced earlier inquirers and the results of the choices they made. The traditions of the discipline would be verified or challenged in terms of the learner's experiences rather than accepted by prescriptive dogma.

5. Because each discipline has developed its own mode of inquiry, through sustained investigation the learner would adapt and invent techniques that put things together in a logical arrangement. By this process the learner would come to know why others have found some techniques useful and others not.

6. Rather than accumulate unrelated facts, the learner would be encouraged to develop a conceptual structure to organize ideas as they are developed. This would enable him to expand his personal conceptual structure toward congruence with the structure held by other members of the discipline.

7. Recognizing that the specialized language and system of symbols of most disciplines are barriers to the novice, the curriculum would be based initially on commonsense notions expressed in commonsense terms. With increasing complexity, the specialized language of the discipline would be invented or adapted to foster communication.

8. As the learner progresses, he should be able to identify and work with the literature and communication systems of the discipline and to

understand their function for the members of that community of discourse. In fact, the curriculum itself is an instrument of communication, a means of showing others what the discipline is all about.

9. Each discipline reflects a value stance relative to the affairs of the world. The learner should come to know the values held by other members of the community of discourse. The curriculum should represent the position the discipline takes on problems and issues within its domain.

10. The learner should be welcomed as a member of the community of discourse because a prime motive of each discipline is to instruct, to make its substance and syntax clear and understandable, more knowable, more teachable, and more learnable.

These are the characteristics the educational process ideally should display; obviously, it does not always do so. Closing the distance between what is and what ought to be is the prime concern of teaching.

The Educational Dilemma

American education finds itself in a dilemma today: aware of severe problems demanding immediate attention but unable to discern which of several available means offers the most effective solution. The dilemma arises because education and those who are intimately involved in education have not been able to find effective answers to the following questions:

1. What instructional practices are required by different concepts of the essential nature of man and the reasons for education? Can the full range of requirements be met? If it cannot, which purposes or practices will be given priority? If choice is necessary, are the consequences of a particular choice acceptable?

EXAMPLE: Most teachers agree that it is desirable to conduct classrooms humanely and insist that they are really going to do something about this at some time in the future. They would do it right now, of course, but at the moment their classes are too big, or their kids are just not ready for it, or—the ultimate teacher excuse—their principal won't let them. If teachers really believed in being humane, they would work at changing classroom practices by discovering and testing out workable alternatives. Humane teaching practices can be achieved, but not until the teacher becomes unwilling to put up with the consequences of being inhumane.

2. What teaching techniques are required by different concepts of the fundamental nature of learning and the means to acquire and employ knowledge? Are these differences real and significant, or is it simply a matter of differing terminology or semantic variation? How does the

teacher plan instructional strategies that are effective in producing significant learning?

EXAMPLE: Many teachers agree that learning is more effective when interest and motivation are supplied by the learner. They really would like to do something more with motivation theory, and they would do it right now, *but*–. The common excuses are that study of some topics is necessary for the students' own good, even if they are just plain dull and uninteresting. So we wind up with a doctrine of student interest that is observed most frequently in the breach, because we have failed to seek out ways in which the interests of students can be brought to bear on subject matter. Any subject can be made boring by ineffective teaching; it follows that any subject can be made more exciting and vital by skillful teaching. Good learning theory ought to make clear the strategies teachers can use to create better learning.

3. What educational programs are required by a given set of social or political beliefs? Does effective participation in a democratic sociopolitical system require particular skills, attitudes, and understandings? Does this system require a particular approach to teaching and learning? Do we or can we educate in a manner consistent with democratic principles?

EXAMPLE: Almost all teachers will assert their fundamental and unyielding allegiance to democracy and will acknowledge some measure of responsibility to prepare students for participation in American society— at some time in the future. The fact is that almost all classrooms are authoritarian in practice, founded on the conviction that young people are not yet to be trusted. Teachers continue to employ undemocratic means, do a lot of talking about democratic responsibilities, and hope that students will eventually come to appreciate and adhere to democratic precepts. It won't happen that way. Shared participation in decision making has to be practiced and learned and it has to take place with today's students in today's classrooms.

There is a tendency to view these questions as hypothetical issues without genuine significance to teaching. Prospective teachers may feel this way because they have not experienced the dilemmas on which the questions are based. Some teachers regard answering these questions as more difficult than beneficial. Some believe that certain other issues are of greater importance and urgency. These teachers insist that treating the "realities" of the classroom or of individual problem behavior is much more "practical" than treating "theoretical" questions.

Some teachers concede that the questions are real, that they may have some plausible answers, that confronting them will place us in a more advantageous position and perhaps even enhance our understanding of what we are about. Nonetheless, even to these teachers the advantage to be gained doesn't seem to justify the effort required.

The Alternatives before Us

We believe that better teaching and learning will result from disciplined, even arduous, examination of the assumptions and hypotheses of pedagogy. Modern teacher-training institutions, with their obvious absence of philosophic clarity and consistency, have led many teachers to believe that they are expected to pick and choose fragments from discordant schools of philosophy in a generally haphazard manner. As a result, the notion has unfortunately emerged that teaching is nothing more than a technical process dependent upon the accumulation of particularized skills. Thus in some teacher-preparation programs student teachers are mechanically drilled before a videotape recorder until they master the behavioral pattern of "asking a probing question" of an intellectual and pedagogical vacuum. The obvious advantage here is that, since the teachers are involved in microteaching, all their mistakes are little ones. The greater errors of educational misjudgment and curricular mismanagement are reserved for macroteaching, for the masses of students in the classroom.

One is not, of course, obliged to be philosophically consistent, but it helps. It helps in determining if the observed results are related to the observed variables in a manner that allows valid prediction. It helps in pointing out discrepancies or parallels in known data that may be clues to larger generalizing principles. In teaching, it helps us to deal with the often ephemeral and elusive phenomena of human learning by allowing us to bridge from time to time, from place to place, from circumstance to circumstance.

Many teachers have been led to believe that they must approach teaching and learning more "objectively" by restricting their examination to the obvious, ignoring everything else, and charging those who have broader concerns with being nonobjective. Seeking what they view as academic respectability, they fail to recognize that the decision to limit their sphere of concern to a particular class of phenomena traps them into the most subjective choice. Nothing is more subjective than an arbitrary choice of what will be included and excluded. From this beginning an array of faults has arisen, with the full endorsement of the "scientific" community.

There *is* an alternative open to American education. It is not easily attained, but it *is* attainable!

Teaching must become disciplined, not in the sense of pretentious ritual, but in the terms we have used earlier to describe a discipline as a community of discourse. Setting aside current or popular views of schooling, consider what it would be like—

IF learners became active, spirited participants in an intellectual process;

IF learners came to see school subjects as challenging, imaginative, creative activities;

IF learners encountered the outer limits of their present understandings with fascination instead of fear;

IF learners put things together in a way that made sense to them;

IF learners invented ways to verify what they were doing;

IF learners found themselves becoming increasingly competent in dealing with complex problems;

IF learners found themselves becoming increasingly skilled in communicating *their* ideas clearly;

IF learners developed good reasons for wanting some things and rejecting others;

IF learners came to share a sense of community, a realization of shared commitment;

IF learners came to understand, accept, and cherish their humanity.

This is what we seek in human teaching and learning.

Conclusions

Considerable evidence indicates that American education is unable to cope with increasing social disruption, politicizing of the academic scene, and dissatisfaction with the efforts of educational agencies to respond to these problems. We are convinced, nonetheless, that it is possible for education to confront, alleviate, and even remedy them.

Considerable evidence indicates that American education has failed to consider intelligently the wide range of information available on the nature of the learner, the nature of knowledge, the nature of knowing, and the nature of valuing, and from these considerations to derive a theory of schooling that can guide educational practice. We are convinced, nonetheless, that it is possible for education to become competent to this purpose, and that to continue to ignore the means of enhancement constitutes the gravest professional immorality.

Considerable evidence indicates that American education has failed to inform itself adequately of the state of behavioral sciences and to utilize this information in the construction of verifiable propositions about teaching and learning. We are convinced, nonetheless, that such a statement of principles is indeed possible and desirable, that classroom teachers can come to a clear understanding of what is involved, and that they can come to practice teaching in a fully effective professional manner.

Considerable evidence indicates that American education has failed to fulfill the requirements of its consumers. We are convinced that confrontation of this problem is vital to the sustenance of the American educational system and that it is possible as well as essential.

REFERENCES

Association for Supervision and Curriculum Development. *Perceiving, Behaving, Becoming: A New Focus for Education.* 1962 Yearbook. Washington, D.C.: The Association, 1962.

Bayles, Ernest E. *Democratic Educational Theory.* New York: Harper, 1960.

Bigge, Morris L., and Maurice P. Hunt. *Psychological Foundations of Education.* 2nd ed. New York: Harper & Row, 1968.

Combs, Arthur W., Donald L. Avila, and William B. Perkey. *Helping Relationships: Basic Concepts for the Helping Professions.* Boston: Allyn & Bacon, 1971.

Dunwell, Robert R. "On Revisiting a Neglected Model." *Educational Perspectives* 9 (October 1970):7–11.

————, et al. *The Assessment of Informal Factors Affecting Teaching and Learning in a Ghetto High School.* ERIC Document ED 052 281, February 1971.

Haberman, Martin. "Twenty-Three Reasons Universities Can't Educate Teachers." *Journal of Teacher Education* 22 (Summer 1971):133–40.

Harvey, O. J., et al. "Teachers' Belief Systems and Preschool Atmospheres." *Journal of Educational Psychology* 57 (1966):373–81.

Herndon, James. *The Way It Spozed to Be.* New York: Simon & Schuster, 1968.

King, Arthur R., and John A. Brownell. *The Curriculum and the Disciplines of Knowledge.* New York: Wiley, 1966.

Lessinger, Leon M. "Accountability for Results: A Basic Challenge for America's Schools." *American Education* 5 (June–July 1969):133–40.

Lieberman, Myron. "The Union Merger Movement: Will 3,500,000 Teachers Put It All Together?" *Saturday Review* 55 (June 1972):50–56.

Likert, Rensis. *New Patterns of Management.* New York: McGraw-Hill, 1961.

Merritt, Daniel L. "Attitude Congruency and Selection of Teacher Candidates." *Administrator's Notebook* 19 (February 1971).

Nash, Paul. *Authority and Freedom in Education.* New York: Wiley, 1966.

Owens, Robert G. *Organizational Behavior in Schools.* Englewood Cliffs, N.J.: Prentice-Hall, 1970.

Parker, Don H. "Revolution or Anarchy in Our Schools?" *Education Digest* 36 (February 1971).

Runes, Dagobert. *Dictionary of Philosophy.* 15th ed., rev. New York: Philosophical Library, 1960.

Silberman, Charles. *Crisis in the Classroom.* New York: Random House, 1970.

Stutz, Rowan C., and David L. Jesser. "Focus on People: Improving Learning Environments, Opportunities and Procedures." In *Emerging State*

Responsibilities for Education. Denver: Improving State Leadership in Education Project, 1970.

Taba, Hilda. *Curriculum Development: Theory and Practice.* New York: Harcourt, Brace & World, 1962.

Weingartner, Charles. "Communication, Education, and Change." In *The Radical Papers: Readings in Education,* edited by Harold W. Sobol and Arthur Salz. New York: Harper & Row, 1972.

CHAPTER 2

Readings on
the Dilemma of Education

We have not related distorted or excessively pessimistic views about the educational dilemma: The crisis in education is real. Before constructive alternatives can be proposed, it is essential to analyze the conditions of the educational scene and to note some of the trends that are taking place.

The articles in this chapter make it clear that the dilemmas of education are not abstract or distant; rather, they are fundamentally human concerns, easily found within one's own experience. No single article offers recommendations adequate to resolve these problems; however, taken together the articles provide indicators that can be used to synthesize a clearer understanding of the issue.

In the first article, Donald H. Parker, an experienced teacher and educational researcher, describes various student attitudes toward public schooling, revealing a deep and intense student opposition to traditional teaching-learning. His recommendation for correcting some of these dilemmas may seem inappropriate in light of the seriousness of the issues. Dealing effectively with these student concerns requires a full understanding of them. Parker's article serves effectively to initiate our search for greater clarity about educational issues.

Not only are students dissatisfied with their educational experience; teachers also are voicing their disapproval of conditions in the public schools. They continue to be critical of administrators who listen neither to students nor to teachers, of buildings that lack adequate space and equipment, and of a culture that views teachers simply as public servants, an image that teachers believe is an excuse for inadequate compensation. Teachers want to change this; they also want greater involvement in curricular matters and in safeguarding their profession against arbitrariness. They want a reason to feel that the bureaucracy does not necessarily dehumanize all who are in it. The article by Myron Lieberman, director of the Teacher Leadership Program, City University of New York, speaks about the growing power of teacher organizations and the effect it may have in the decade to come.

Concern over public education is not restricted to students and teachers. Parents and the general public are alarmed by high student-dropout rates, the low reading and math levels of graduates, and the soaring costs of public education. These concerns have led some educators to advocate cost-benefit analysis for the public school modeled after industry. One of the earliest advocates of this type of educational accountability was Leon Lessinger, professor of education at the University of Georgia, and formerly associate commissioner of elementary and secondary education, U.S. Office of Education. His views are expressed in the article reprinted here.

Since the proposals for accountability in education were first voiced in the 1960s, the systems approach to teaching and learning has developed, complete with specified performance criteria to measure student behavior and instructional objectives for teachers to use. The teaching process itself is based upon a conception of how people learn best. But too frequently, prospective teachers assume that a student learns only substantive content and that the teacher's role is to select material for direct presentation to the class. Carl Rogers, an experienced teacher, author, and lecturer, has reflected seriously on his own learning and teaching style. His article suggests his awareness that his personal experiences with learning may be typical of many people. Rogers is not anti-learning; he is not advocating the deschooling of society. Rather, he is proposing personalized, meaningful learning as an alternative to "traditional" teaching. His statements imply a method of teaching that describes learning as the process of verifying perceived meanings. How much of your own educational experience was meaningful learning, and what resulted directly from "teaching"?

The final article is a perceptive summary of the dilemmas in education. Arthur Combs, of the University of Florida, reviews many of the controversies mentioned earlier from a person-centered perspective. Seeing the needs of the individual as imperative, he makes meaningful suggestions for the resolution of many of the issues we have outlined, which he emphasizes as human problems.

Revolution or Anarchy in Our Schools?
Donald H. Parker

It's too late for evolution. We now either produce a revolution in schooling—or take the consequences: anarchy in our schools.

I base this conclusion on 1,000 tape-recorded interviews I made in a 33,000-mile sweep of thirty states across the nation, asking ten questions revolving around the central query: *Schooling for what?* While interviewees ranged in age from 6 to 82 years, 512 of them were of high-school and college age. Why did fewer than 10 percent of these young people think that our schools are even "satisfactory"? Why did the remaining 90 percent complain of lack of attention to individual differences, courses irrelevant to today's world, poor teachers, working for grades instead of for learning, and lack of opportunity for creative learning experiences? Why did so many tell me, "School is a bore"?

How did things get this way? What are the events and conditions leading up to growing student backlash which began in the universities and is now reaching down into the grades? Here is a distillation of what's bugging these young people, as told to me on tape:

1. Beginning with Sputnik in 1957, schooling has put students in a concentration camp. As one Phi Beta Kappa student shrugged, "It just wasn't worth it."

2. A 16-year-old interviewee called schooling "a mouse race that gets you ready for the rat race."

3. "Teach-'em-all-alike schooling" is no longer useful to a nation standing, dinosaur-like, ankle-deep in the rising tide of an ecological wasteland with so many of its people victimized by bigness, organizational crunch, and institutional paralysis.

4. Schooling seems based on the Seven Deadly Sins, rather than on the Seven Cardinal Virtues. The young are crying out for schooling that exemplifies love—the qualities of *justice, prudence, temperance, fortitude, faith, hope,* and *charity.* But, instead of promoting these "Cardinal Virtues," our present educational system seems to reinforce the "sins." Take *sloth* for example—the *disinclination to action or labor.* When you

Reprinted, with minor deletions, from *Illinois Education* 59, no. 3 (February 1971):100–103, by permission of the publisher.

look at what is going on in the vast majority of schools across our country, we teach, at best, only the middle one-third of all pupils. The lower third lacks the capacity to learn what is dished out, begins to tire of continual failure, gives up, and becomes "lazy." The upper third completes more work in less time, finds school a bore, and lapses into idleness. Since the young refuse to accept failure or boredom as a way of life (nor do you and I!) they simply drop out and take to the streets—even as we berate them for the indolence into which they have been forced.

Take "grades." We build *pride: inordinate self-esteem* among students who have naturally superior ability by giving them "good" grades. We produce *envy* by giving "bad" grades to those who have less ability. We could go on to *anger* (history taught as man's checklist of wars), *covetousness* (economic success as the end goal), *gluttony* (the U.S., with 6 percent of the world's population consumes 40 percent of the world's resources), and *lust* (turning natural sexual desire into mere lust through deprivation of sex education).

5. Schooling is leaping headlong into accountability. Accountability may be seen by school administrators as a salve for the parent-taxpayer, and an antidote to the current school bond strike across the nation. But from the student's standpoint, it is something else. Instead of oil on the troubled waters, applying accountability to an already rigid schooling structure is like flinging a match into highly combustible material.

6. Industry in schooling will soon come under the searching fire of the young, as it takes bigger bites of the instructional dollar. "Now the Establishment is being paid to 'make us learn'—and make a profit on it, too!" Nor does the new industrial "you're-going-to-learn-or-else" approach bid fair to become a model of Christian ethic. In the nation's first teaching-for-profit scheme, the industry contractor was caught cheating on the tests! (As if it were not enough that the company also gave prizes for making good grades.) So far this bastardization of learning is directed mainly toward elementary pupils. But secondary students are already eyeing this latest prostitution of schooling by the establishment and planning ways of dealing with it.

7. Schooling based on national assessment seems a first step toward a national curriculum. Instead of giving the student more self-responsibility for what he shall learn and how he shall learn it, now there will be an even more rigid lock-stepping to the tune of "the system."

8. Schooling is mainly training, rather than a balance between training and education—between mere animal-like rote learning and the opportunity for creative learning experiences. The curriculum of most schools consists of 90 percent training with a bare 10 percent of a student's time available for education.

9. Schooling seems to have as its main purpose to fit people into society the way it is now, instead of trying to improve that society.

Can any thinking person doubt the validity of these complaints? How can we answer these deadly serious critiques? What can we do to revolutionize schooling and avoid anarchy? We can begin with the word itself: revolutionize—*to cause to revolve, rotate, turn around.*

I heard these demands for revolution:

1. Literally turn schooling around from a teaching-oriented to a learning-oriented approach.

2. Turn our schooling around to begin with what the learner wants to learn, instead of with what society wants to teach.

3. Turn schooling around from being mainly a study of the past to a recognition of the *now,* out of which might grow a concern for the future, evaluating what is being done today to make that future worth living in. With "future shock" already a reality, what are we doing to inure the young to a world in which nothing is permanent but change?

4. Turn schooling around from something that can take place only within four walls to embrace the notion that school should be a living laboratory for learning. Schooling should be where the learning is, the kind of learning the student is looking for, out where things are happening—in the store, the shop, the factory; on the seas, in the air; in the arts, in the sciences; in government, in business; in our country and in others. And who are the teachers out there? Those now working in these various activities and places. Think what would happen to the generation gap if nearly everyone were to get into the act! Where are the days of apprenticeship and appreciation of learning with someone who really knows?

Where would all this leave the school? I suggest it be a headquarters vital to such an exciting enterprise. The school would: a) open up for students broad areas of knowledge; b) be a resource consultant (where to go to get the needed learning experiences); and c) act as evaluation consultant, helping the student evaluate his own learnings, and perhaps suggesting next steps toward broad or specific goals.

5. Reverse our passion for fact-packing and testing and, instead, offer each student the opportunity to generate knowledge to meet his or her own needs in building both a self-identity and a membership in the society of man.

Why not courses in sensitivity training, body awareness, yoga, or meditation? Why not studies in *humanics?* Here students would blend sciences and humanities in a search for self-identity and a concern for human growth potential. They would pursue answers to such questions as "Who am I?" and "What kind of person do I want to become?" Dealing with these Who? What? Why? When? Where? questions would be a turning away from the mere "how?"—a concern that seems to have spawned our over-weening technology. We might stop doing things (building an SST, for example) without inquiring into the possible side-effects (further deterioration of the environment) on the human race.

6. Turn our schooling around from teaching a producer-consumer life style, directed toward keeping the wheels of industry turning to pour more and more money into the pockets of the rich and the super-rich. Instead, let us set the goal of schooling as the development of responsible citizens, interested in avoiding the violent "have-have not" conflict now in the making. This rising tide could be turned through a more equitable distribution of work opportunities for people of all capacities.

Instead of developing more assembly-line robots to fit into the system we need schooling to develop people who are more self-responsive (rather than authority-responsive). Such humanistic, self-actualizing individuals will sense the constant give-and-take within themselves which can lead to a dynamic view of what it is to be both an individual and a member-of-society. In the working dynamism (at times, conflict!) between these two parts of the self, the individual forms his value system. If boys and girls are to develop in this direction, they will need more-than-lip-service provision for individual differences. They will also need a learning smorgasbord instead of a force-fed curriculum described by so many of the young as "all that crud."

7. Convert our schools from mere training pens to places where education is considered at least equally as important as training. Animals can be trained, but they cannot be educated. Yet we run our schools as though we were training animals without making available the kinds of diverse and creative learning experiences that distinguish man as a thinking human being.

Training is skill-getting; education is skill-using. The learning process in training is different from that of education. In the training process, the learner must experience stimulus-response-feedback, and reinforcement/redirection in as many repetitions as he requires to "learn" the skill. Skill learning can be measured. Skill learning can be accountable and the process conducted by the systems approach.

8. Turn our thinking around from school as a place for nine-to-three-o'clock learning, to an on-call community learning resource center available perhaps twenty-four hours a day.

9. Turn our thinking around from school as a nine- or ten-months' "program" to a year-round learning opportunity so arranged that the learner—of any age—may walk in and begin learning what he wants to learn through self-programing materials and technologies. He might also attend one or more short-term courses to be completed in a matter of weeks instead of semesters. Such courses may be designed for wide-ranging orientation to open up a broad area of knowledge. Others might be directed toward intensive learning in a given direction. The student takes only as many courses as he needs to move toward his goals as he perceives and re-perceives them. Through new multimedia technology, employed in learning centers of various sizes and types, boys and girls

and men and women of all ages can pursue learning individually, or in small action groups, or in large audience-type situations. Teacher and learner roles might be constantly shifting as the photographer attends the leather worker's class or vice versa—the model maker, the mathematician's class; the astronomer, the dramatist's workshop; etc. In this exciting new concept, a new "super teacher" would emerge to fill the vital new professional role of learning consultant, with a working knowledge of multimedia, community resources, and guidance techniques.

10. Turn our thinking around from school as a place where the six-year-olds are kept for twelve years or so, toward schooling as a learning, resource, and guidance center from very early childhood through the entire adult life span. Very early childhood training and education serves not only the more complex needs of children growing up in an increasingly technological world, but also the needs of adults who seek increasing involvement outside the home, and more freedom to pursue their own interests as individuals—especially women seeking to escape boredom and gain a measure of economic and psychologic independence. At the other end of the age continuum, to stop learning is to stop living. Continuation schooling for adults into their seventies and eighties and beyond can be the difference between continued living and walking death.

11. We must turn our schools around from being places that prepare the young for college—or "prove" they can't make it. Getting rid of high-school and college diplomas would be a good start, replacing them with certificates of proficiencies in specific areas. Such papers would be meaningful not only to the learner, but also to a prospective employer.

12. Reverse the domination of the colleges and universities over our high schools, and consequently over the entire school system. Institutions of higher learning should be open to anyone who wants to learn what their various departments have to teach. This does not mean diluting the quality of college offerings. Rather it means getting rid of overall entrance requirements which literally set each child on the same learning track at age six and threaten something more than 50,000,000 students with a degradated self-image or outright disenfranchisement of their right to learn.

True, anyone who wants to be a dentist, for example, should go through every available sequence of learning that will give him the best dental expertise possible. The entrance requirements for such a student should be the background he will need to become a student of dentistry. But why should he be forced into such "required courses" as foreign languages, math, humanities, etc., when he could be getting on with dentistry and completing his competency requirements in perhaps half the time? He might then go to work with a master dentist in an apprenticeship role. Without such force feeding he might even elect "broadening" courses and actually enjoy them. Certainly, if we conceive of schooling as a lifetime pursuit, he would be continually seeking new learnings, following his interests in new directions, and becoming a more fully functioning person both as an individual and as a member-of-society.

The Future of Collective Negotiations
Myron Lieberman

In December, 1961, the United Federation of Teachers, Local 2 of the American Federation of Teachers, won the right to bargain for New York City's teachers. The UFT gained bargaining rights only after a long and bitter election contest, the first of many that dominated the teacher representation scene in the 1960s. At the time of the election, opinion was divided as to whether the UFT or the Teachers' Bargaining Organization (the National Education Association affiliate in New York City) would win the election. There was even greater disagreement over the significance of the election. At one extreme, some observers thought that the election outcome would mean very little one way or another. At the other extreme, it was asserted that the election outcome would have a catalytic effect upon teacher organizations in this country. Today, it appears that even the latter group largely underestimated the impact of the New York City experience and of teacher bargaining generally, not just upon teacher organizations but upon many other aspects of education as well.

In a field notoriously subject to bandwagons and exaggerated predictions of one sort or another, teacher bargaining or negotiating has drastically modified the institutional structure of education within a relatively short period of time. By 1971, approximately 70 percent of the nation's teachers were covered by collective agreements. Thus in less than a decade personnel administration has been forced away from its historic orientation toward individual contracts and from an approach which emphasized relations between administrators and individual teachers, totally ignoring teacher organizations. Teacher organizations now play a crucial role in formulating and implementing personnel policies affecting

Reprinted from *Phi Delta Kappan* 53, no. 4 (December 1971):214–16, by permission of the author and the publisher.

teachers. At the school level especially, teacher organizations typically play a vital role in grievance procedures. The organizations are involved in defining grievances, setting the time limits for their initiation, determining the steps in the grievance procedure, identifying who can grieve, and setting the conditions of grievance arbitration.

Within teacher organizations themselves, sweeping changes have resulted from the advent of collective negotiations. The number of full-time professional staff members has increased at least tenfold. Significantly, a considerable proportion of the increase, especially in NEA affiliates, has been in local associations which previously lacked full-time staff. Collective negotiations thus reflect a basic shift away from a legislative approach to teacher welfare. Actually, the negotiations revolution has greatly strengthened the legislative and political capability of teacher organizations, but this greater capability is now exercised in conjunction with a much more effective representational capability at the local level.

Teacher organizations have changed in other significant ways. Administrators have left or have been excluded from NEA affiliates in enormous numbers, especially since the middle 1960s. In 1961, one could legitimately characterize the NEA as administrator-dominated; in 1971, such a criticism would be clearly unwarranted, although it might still apply to a few state and local affiliates not fully involved in collective negotiations. As a matter of fact, the proposed new constitution for the NEA would render anyone representing a school employer ineligible for NEA membership. Even the AFT has adopted more stringent provisions governing administrator and supervisor membership as a result of the collective negotiations movement.

The process of administrator exclusion and/or withdrawal from NEA and AFT has, therefore, brought about a realignment in administrator organizations. Although this realignment is still in process, it is clear that the upper echelons of administration are rapidly and unequivocally identifying themselves as management. At the same time, however, there is much ambivalence and uncertainty among middle management, especially principals and supervisors. Most organizations of middle management retain ties with the NEA and state associations, but there is no clear-cut resolution of the role of middle management in the negotiations picture. In some districts, middle management is becoming organized as an employee group, sometimes under the jurisdiction of the AFL-CIO. Some of the variations in the role of middle management are due to differences in state laws regulating collective negotiations in public education. It may be that unless and until federal legislation brings about a more consistent approach to their role, there will be no definitive resolution of the negotiations issues pertaining to principals and supervisors.

Collective negotiations have clearly resulted in a significant reorientation in the functions and budgetary priorities of teacher organizations.

The need for full-time staff to negotiate and administer contracts has created enormous financial pressures upon the organizations at local, state, and national levels. The number of teachers paying dues and the amount of dues paid have increased substantially, but the pressure on services and programs not directly related to negotiations and teacher welfare is unremitting. In fact, there is a tendency for teacher organizations to divest themselves of some of the so-called professional functions and services they formerly provided.

The pervasive changes in teacher organizations have inevitably led to some fundamental changes in educational administration. School districts have been forced to establish new administrative positions or graft negotiating functions upon previously established positions. For the most part, educational administrators were unprepared for negotiation, and many are still not prepared for it. Resort to outside negotiators is still common and is likely to continue indefinitely.

Of all the significant consequences of collective negotiations, perhaps the one which has received the least attention thus far is the gain in the power of administrators and the corresponding decline in the power of school boards. This shift has gone unnoticed because so much attention has been devoted to the increased power of teacher organizations vis-à-vis boards and administrators. There is no doubt that such a shift has occurred. It is not generally recognized, however, that equally important shifts of power and authority have been taking place within as well as between the employer and employee sides. Negotiators for school boards must have the authority to negotiate. If they must first secure the approval of their boards for each individual concession, negotiations are practically impossible. Furthermore, the dynamics of negotiations require that negotiators be in a position to make a deal at the appropriate time—and this literally may be any time of the day or night, when it may be virtually impossible to have a board meeting. Thus boards of education have increasingly found it necessary to delegate more authority to their negotiating teams; the latter have been making more and more of the crucial decisions governing school personnel relationships. This is a basic change from the pre-negotiations era, when a board of education could consider terms and conditions of employment as individual issues, on a schedule unilaterally set by the board. It is also significant that teacher negotiating teams, which are increasingly dominated by full-time professional staff, are playing the same decisive role on the teacher side.

Perhaps the most important outcome of the negotiations movement will be the increased political effectiveness of teachers. Such an outcome, although highly paradoxical, is almost inevitable. In the pre-negotiations era, teacher organizations were politically ineffective. One major reason was the ideology that education is or ought to be a nonpartisan activity of government. Another was the absence of full-time activists at the local level. As previously pointed out, however, collective negotiations are bringing about an enormous increase in the number of full-time staff of teacher organizations. These staff members are rapidly providing the political clout which teacher organizations lacked in the past. Thus, although the negotiations movement is itself due to the prior over-emphasis upon a legislative approach to teacher welfare, one of its most important consequences is a much more active and influential political role for teacher organizations.

Although all of the preceding consequences have yet to reach full maturity, they are clearly visible in developments to date. At this point, however, let us consider what are likely to be the major developments in the next decade. Like those previously discussed, some of these are already under way. In general, however, they can be considered the second generation of developments in the collective negotiations movement.

Without trying to list them in any particular order of importance, I suggest that the following developments will predominate in the 1970s.

1. The widespread acceptance of collective negotiations in higher education and in nonpublic schools.
2. A trend toward regional and statewide bargaining.
3. Greater scrutiny and public regulation of the internal affairs of teacher organizations.
4. An intensive effort to organize paraprofessionals in education.
5. Greater negotiating and legislative emphasis upon organizational security, especially agency shop clauses.
6. A major effort to enact federal legislation regulating collective negotiations by state and local public employees.
7. A tendency to avoid substantial organizational expenditures for curriculum, teacher education, and other activities not central to negotiations, and a corresponding effort to have nonrepresentational services financed by the government.
8. The clarification and resolution of issues relating to elected and appointed personnel of teacher organizations; the trend will be toward the election of full-time policy-making officers and the appointment of those below the policy-making and political level.
9. A growing concern with performance contracting, voucher systems, and other institutional changes that appear likely to undermine traditional employment relationships in education.
10. Widespread internal as well as external conflict over organizational activity intended to protect teachers from racial or sexual discrimination.

It is also my belief that the NEA and the AFT will merge in the 1970s. It is already evident that the major factors impeding merger are not ideological but political—who gets what job, or what staff and allied interests (e.g., insurance companies and attorneys) will prevail after the merger. It also appears that the 1970s will see teacher leadership achieve unprecedented levels of political influence at all levels of government. This will happen concurrently with a greater emphasis upon better management in school districts generally.

One of the most important but least predictable matters is who will exercise the dominant leadership roles in the years ahead. In the AFT, it seems safe to say that the dominant figure is Albert Shanker, the president of the UFT; as a matter of fact, probably no other organization leader commands as much respect in both NEA and AFT as Shanker does. With or without a merger, he will unquestionably be one of the teacher leaders in the 1970s.

Partly because it is a much larger organization, partly because no state or local affiliate in the NEA is as dominant as the UFT is in the AFT, and partly because of unresolved issues pertaining to the role of elected as distinguished from appointed officers, it is much more difficult to identify individuals who will play the critical leadership roles in the NEA in the 1970s. Top talent is certainly there among both elected and appointed officers, but the present NEA structure is not conducive to leadership accountability to the membership. If the NEA's new constitution successfully resolves this issue, some of the most important and exciting political contests of our time will be those to decide the national leadership of teacher organizations.

As our nation moves toward a new economic structure, it is essential that teachers be effectively organized if their needs and interests are to receive adequate consideration. In my view, and without endorsing any particular organizational position on specific issues, teachers are better organized and represented today than at any other time in the history of this country, and there is every reason to expect even higher levels of organizational representation and service in the 1970s.

Accountability for Results: A Basic Challenge for America's Schools

Leon Lessinger

Today, too many young Americans leave school without the tools of learning, an interest in learning, or any idea of the relationship of learn-

Reprinted from *American Education* 5, no. 6 (June–July 1969):2–4, by permission of the publisher.

ing to jobs. It is a mocking challenge that so many of our children are not being reached today by the very institution charged with the primary responsibility for teaching them. A Committee for Economic Development report issued in the summer of 1968 summarizes the indictment: many schools and school districts, handicapped by outmoded organization and a lack of research and development money, are not providing "the kind of education that produces rational, responsible, and effective citizens."

Now, the educational establishment—right down to the local level—is being asked ever more insistently to account for the results of its programs. This fast-generating nationwide demand for accountability promises a major and long overdue redevelopment of the management of the present educational system, including an overhaul of its cottage-industry form of organization. Many believe this can be accomplished by making use of modern techniques currently employed in business and industry, some of which are already being used in the educational enterprise.

Before America's schools can productively manage the massive amount of money entrusted to them—and the even greater amount they need—they must be armed with better management capability. If education is going to be able to manage its budget properly, it must devise measurable relationships between dollars spent and results obtained. Education, like industry, requires a system of quality assurance. Anything less will shortchange our youth.

Sputniks and satellite cities, computers and confrontation politics, television and the technology of laborsaving devices—all have placed new and overwhelming demands on our educational system. Americans could say with the angel Gabriel of *Green Pastures* that "everything nailed down is coming loose." How can we provide the kind of education that would assure full participation for all in this new complex technological society? How to prepare people to respond creatively to rapid-fire change all their lives while maintaining a personal identity that would give them and their society purpose and direction? How to do this when the body of knowledge has so exploded that it no longer can be stored in a single mind? How to do this when cybernetics is changing man's function? How to do this when the cost of old-fashioned education soars higher every year with little significant improvement?

In 1965 the passage of the far-reaching Elementary and Secondary Education Act gave the public schools of America a clear new mandate and some of the funds to carry it out. It was a mandate not just for equality of educational opportunity but for equity in results as well. In place of the old screening, sorting, and reject system that put students somewhere on a bell-shaped curve stretching from A to F, the schools were asked to bring educational benefits to every young person to prepare him for a productive life. Under the new mandate the schools were expected to give every pupil the basic competence he needed, regardless of his so-called ability, interest, background, home, or income. After all, said a concerned nation, what's the purpose of grading a basic skill like reading with A, B, C, D, or F when you can't make it at all today if you can't read?

In essence, this meant that education would be expected to develop a "zero reject system" which would guarantee quality in skill acquisition just as a similar system now guarantees the quality of industrial production. Today's diplomas are often meaningless warranties. In the words of one insistent inner-city parent, "Many diplomas aren't worth the ink they're written in." We know, for example, that there are some 30,000 functional illiterates—people with less than fifth grade reading ability—in the country today who hold diplomas. And untold more are uncovered each day as manpower training and job programs bring increasing numbers of hardcore unemployed into the labor market.

Instead of certifying that a student has spent so much time in school or taken so many courses, the schools should be certifying that he is able to perform specific tasks. Just as a warranty certifies the quality performance of a car, a diploma should certify a youngster's performance as a reader, a writer, a driver, and so on.

If, then, the new objective of education is to have zero rejects through basic competence for all, how can the educational establishment retool to respond to this new challenge? Developing a system of quality assurance can help provide the way.

The first step toward such a system is to draw up an overall educational redevelopment plan. Such a plan must first translate the general goal of competence for all students into a school district's specific objectives. These objectives must be formulated in terms of programs, courses, buildings, curriculums, materials, hardware, personnel, and budgets. The plan must incorporate a timetable of priorities for one year, for five years, ten years, and perhaps even for twenty years. Such a plan should be based on "market research," that is, an investigation of the needs of the students in each particular school. It should also be based on research and development to facilitate constant updating of specifications to meet these needs. Through the plan the school district would be able to measure its own output against the way its students actually perform. It would be able to see exactly what results flow from the dollars it has invested.

The purpose of the educational redevelopment plan, of course, is to provide a systematic approach for making the changes in educational organization and practice necessitated by the new demands on the education system. To assure that the plan will provide quality, it should use a mix of measurements that are relevant, reliable, objective, easily assessable, and that produce data in a form that can be processed by modern-day technology. As a further guarantee of quality, teams of school administrators, teachers, and modern educational and technical specialists competent to interpret the results should be available. The plan should also spell out a clear relationship between results and goals, thus providing for accountability.

In reality, this educational plan is only a piece of paper—a set of ideals and a set of step-by-step progressions which schools and districts can approximate. But it does provide a blueprint for the educational managers of the district—the superintendent, teachers, principals, and school boards—who must provide the leadership and the understanding to carry out educational change.

To be effective and to assure that its specifications remain valid, an educational redevelopment plan must set aside dollars for research and development. The Committee for Economic Development in last summer's report revealed that less than 1 percent of our total national education investment goes into research and development. "No major industry," the report said, "would expect to progress satisfactorily unless it invested many times that amount in research and development." Many private companies plow as much as 15 percent of their own funds back into research and development.

If 1 percent of the yearly budget for education was set aside for research and development, we would have a national educational research and development fund of roughly $500 million. Such money could attract new services, new energies, new partnerships to education. And they would inspire competition that would spur rapid educational development. This research and development money could be used to buy technical assistance, drawing on the expertise of private industry, the nonprofit organizations, the universities, the professions, and the arts. The administrative functions of a school system—construction, purchasing, disbursement, personnel, payroll—also demand business and management skills.

Why not draw on business for technical assistance or actual management in these areas? Or for that matter, in formulating the educational redevelopment plan itself? The final step in setting up a quality assurance system is providing for accountability of both the educational process and its products, the students. Do pupils meet the overall objectives and the performance specifications that the school considers essential? Can Johnny read, write, figure? Can he also reason? Can he figure out where to find a given piece of information not necessarily stored in his head? Does he understand enough about himself and our society to have pride in his culture, a sureness about his own personal goals and identity, as well as an understanding of his responsibilities to society? Does he have the various cognitive and social skills to enter a wide range of beginning jobs and advance in the job market?

The accountability of process, of classroom practice, is somewhat harder to get at. At the risk of mixing it up with ideas about educational hardware, we might call it the technology of teaching. To find out a little about it, we might start by asking whether things are being done differently today in a particular classroom than they were done in the past.

A host of disenchanted teachers and others—from Bel Kaufman in her *Up the Down Staircase* to Jonathan Kozol in *Death at an Early Age*— have been telling us over the past few years what has up to now been happening in many classrooms in America. In *The Way It Spozed to Be,* James Herndon, a California schoolteacher, describes one kind of advice he got from experienced teachers during his first year in an inner-city school: "This advice was a conglomeration of dodges, tricks, gimmicks to get the kids to do what they were spozed to do. . . . It really involved gerrymandering of the group—promises, favors, warnings, threats . . . A's, plusses, stars. . . . The purpose of all these methods was to get and keep an aspect of order . . . so that learning could take place. . . ."

Today, teachers often try to teach order, responsibility, citizenship, punctuality, while believing that they are in fact teaching reading or French or gym. If Johnny forgets his pencil, for example, he actually may not be permitted to take the French quiz and might get an F—presumably for forgetfulness, certainly not for French, for the grade does not reflect Johnny's competence in French.

In one state's schools, girls' physical education regularly chalks up far more F's than any other course. A study of the reasons indicated that gym teachers actually were attempting to measure citizenship by tallying whether Jane kept a dirty locker or failed to take a shower. The grade hardly reflected her competence in physical education. Requirements such as punctuality, neatness, order, and time served, ought not to be used to reflect school subject mastery.

Despite considerable evidence to the contrary, many schools and teachers are still grouping youngsters as good or bad raw material. What can you do with bad raw material? some teachers ask, much as some doctors once asked about the mentally ill. What we are searching for in place of a "demonology" of teaching is sensitive and sensible classroom practice—a practice that treats every child as a person and uses a variety of pleasurable techniques to improve his performance in anticipated and replicable ways. We are not sure this will result in more learning—though we think it will—but we do know that sensitive and sensible classroom practice is good in itself. As such it will pay off in human ways, even if it doesn't pay off in learning.

As teachers' salaries rise and their demands for rights and benefits are rightfully met by the communities they serve, those communities can expect that teacher responsibility will also grow. In fact, they can insist on it. They can insist that better pay, more rights, and more status bring with them better standard practice in the schools and classrooms. They can insist that teachers become accountable for relating process and procedures to results. And pupil accomplishment, though it may reflect some new hardware and construction, by and large reflects teacher and administrator growth and development. This is the true meaning of a new technology of teaching.

Thus the changes that result when the redevelopment plan has been carried out must be demonstrably apparent in terms of both teacher and pupil progress. In order to measure how these actual results compare to the detailed objectives of the plan, it makes sense to call for an outside educational audit, much like the outside fiscal audit required of every school system today. The school system could request an audit either of its overall program or of specific parts of that program.

This new approach could conceivably lead to the establishment of a new category of certified educational auditors whose principal job would be to visit school districts, on invitation, to help determine the success of local program planning in achieving prestated goals. One expert suggests that an educational audit need take only ten school days a year for a single school system. His idea is to send a completely equipped and staffed mobile educational audit van to visit about twenty school systems a year.

Educators should also be encouraged to describe and measure the behavior expected of each student upon completion of programs funded from federal sources. To reinforce accountability for results, contracts for federal funds might be written as performance agreements. Thus a proposal for funds to back a reading program might stipulate that 90 percent of the participating students would be able to satisfy criteria by demonstrating they had achieved a particular advance in grade level in the time proposed.

Furthermore, special financial incentives based on meeting performance criteria might be specified in these contracts. For example, a certain amount of dollars might be awarded to a school for each student who achieves a high school diploma (defined as a verification that sixteen credits have been attained in specific subjects with a credit defined as seventy-two hours of successful classroom study). Or a school might be given monetary awards for each student who has been employed for a year after leaving the institution.

Lest the idea of performance contracts strike anyone as novel or bordering upon the impossible, it should be pointed out that they have been formulated and applied with great success by both industry and the armed services for years. The fact that many results of education are subjective and not subject to audit should not stop us from dealing precisely with those aspects that do lend themselves to definition and assessment.

Most directors of ESEA [Elementary and Secondary Education Act] projects should have more training in how to manage large sums of money than they have had in the past. Anyone who knows business knows you don't run half-million and million-dollar programs without considerable expertise in management. Obviously, managers of these projects need technical assistance if they are to manage in the best and most modern sense. For example, there should be technical reviews of all successful programs, practices, and materials used in embryo experimental projects. Educational objectives should be translated into a clearer framework for the purposes of reporting, evaluation, and feedback. In most cases, schools would need outside technical assistance to carry out either of these tasks.

Greater educational management competence is also needed in an area that might be called "educational logistics." Many projects don't get off the ground because the equipment, personnel, and training they depend upon are not properly coordinated. The notion of staging, for example, to bring together all the elements that are necessary for a project to achieve performance, is very important. Virtually the only time you see this, in education in general as well as in ESEA projects, is in the school drama programs or on the athletic field.

Today formal education is the chief path to full citizenship. School credits and diplomas and licenses are milestones on that path. Schooling is literally the bridge—or the barrier—between a man and his ability to earn his bread. Without it a citizen is condemned to economic obsolescence almost before he begins to work.

If we accept competence for all as one of the major goals of education today, then we must devise a system of accountability that relates education's vast budget to results. It is a paradox that while our technologically oriented society is a masterful producer of the artifacts our civilization needs, it seems incapable of applying that technology to educating our young citizens.

We can change the way our educational system performs so that the desired result—a competently trained young citizenry—becomes the focus of the entire process. In the same way that planning, market studies, research and development, and performance warranties determine industrial production and its worth to consumers, so should we be able to engineer, organize, refine, and manage the educational system to prepare students to contribute to the most complex and exciting country on earth.

Personal Thoughts on Teaching and Learning
Carl Rogers

I wish to present some very brief remarks, in the hope that if they bring forth any reaction from you, I may get some new light on my own ideas.

I find it a very troubling thing to *think,* particularly when I think about my own experiences and try to extract from those experiences the meaning that seems genuinely inherent in them. At first, such thinking is very satisfying, because it seems to discover sense and pattern in a whole host of discrete events. But then it very often becomes dismaying, because I realize how ridiculous these thoughts, which have so much value to me, would seem to most people. My impression is that if I try to find the meaning of my own experience it leads me, nearly always, in directions regarded as absurd.

So in the next few minutes, I will try to digest some of the meanings which have come to me from my classroom experience and the experience I have had in individual therapy and group experience. They are in no way intended as conclusions for someone else, or a guide to what others should do or be. They are the very tentative meanings, as of April 1952, which my experience has had for me, and some of the bothersome questions which their absurdity raises. I will put each idea or meaning in a separate lettered paragraph, not because they are in any particular logical order, but because each meaning is separately important to me.

a) . . . My experience has been that I cannot teach another person how to teach. To attempt it is for me, in the long run, futile.

b) It seems to me that anything that can be taught to another is relatively inconsequential and has little or no significant influence on behavior. That sounds so ridiculous I can't help but question it at the same time that I present it.

c) I realize increasingly that I am only interested in learnings which significantly influence behavior. Quite possibly this is simply a personal idiosyncrasy.

d) I have come to feel that the only learning which significantly influences behavior is self-discovered, self-appropriated learning.

Reprinted from *Merrill-Palmer Quarterly* 3 (Summer 1957):241–43, by permission of the author and the publisher.

e) *Such self-discovered learning, truth that has been personally appropriated and assimilated in experience, cannot be directly communicated to another.* As soon as an individual tries to communicate such experience directly, often with a quite natural enthusiasm, it becomes teaching, and its results are inconsequential. It was some relief recently to discover that Søren Kierkegaard, the Danish philosopher, has found this too, in his own experience, and stated it very clearly a century ago. It made it seem less absurd.

f) As a consequence of the above, *I realize that I have lost interest in being a teacher.*

g) When I try to teach, as I do sometimes, I am appalled by the results, which seem a little more than inconsequential, because sometimes the teaching appears to succeed. When this happens I find that the results are damaging. It seems to cause the individual to distrust his own experience, and to stifle significant learning. *Hence I have come to feel that the outcomes of teaching are either unimportant or hurtful.*

h) When I look back at the results of my past teaching, the real results seem the same—either damage was done—or nothing significant occurred. This is frankly troubling.

i) As a consequence, *I realize that I am only interested in being a learner, preferably learning things that matter, that have some significant influence on my own behavior.*

j) *I find it very rewarding to learn,* in groups, in relationships with one person as in therapy, or by myself.

k) *I find that one of the best, but most difficult, ways for me to learn is to drop my own defensiveness, at least temporarily, and to try to understand the way in which his experience seems and feels to the other person.*

l) *I find that another way of learning for me is to state my own uncertainties, to try to clarify my puzzlements, and thus get closer to the meaning that my experience actually seems to have.*

m) This whole train of experiencing, and the meanings that I have thus far discovered in it, seem to have launched me on a process which is both fascinating and at times a little frightening. *It seems to mean letting my experiences carry me on, in a direction which appears to be forward, toward goals that I can but dimly define, as I try to understand at least the current meaning of that experience.* The sensation is that of floating with a complex stream of experience, with the fascinating possibility of trying to comprehend its ever-changing complexity.

I am almost afraid I may seem to have gotten away from any discussion of learning, as well as teaching. Let me again introduce a practical note by saying that by themselves these interpretations of my experience may sound queer and aberrant, but not particularly shocking. It is when I realize the *implications* that I shudder a bit at the distance I have come from the commonsense world that everyone knows is right. I can best illustrate this by saying that if the experiences of others had been the same as mine, and if they had discovered similar meanings in it, many consequences would be implied:

a) Such experience would imply that we would do away with teaching. People would get together if they wished to learn.

b) We would do away with examinations. They measure only the inconsequential type of learning.

c) We would do away with grades and credits for the same reason.

d) We would do away with degrees as a measure of competence partly for the same reason. Another reason is that a degree marks an end or a conclusion of something, and a learner is only interested in the continuing process of learning.

e) We would do away with the exposition of conclusions, for we would realize that no one learns significantly from conclusions.

I think I had better stop there. I do not want to become too fantastic. I want to know primarily whether anything in my inward thinking, as I have tried to describe it, speaks to anything in your experience of the classroom as you have lived it, and if so, what the meanings are that exist for you in *your* experience.

Can Education Be Relevant?

Arthur Combs

Can education be relevant? Everybody knows these days that education is engaged in a tremendous struggle trying to bring itself in tune with this generation. Our system has gotten badly out of touch. On the one hand with the needs of society, we find ourselves saddled with the wrong curriculum. If you don't think that is so, all you have to do is listen to hear what they have to say. It is clear that most of what we are doing does not meet the real needs of the students with whom we are working. Young people are demanding above all else, what they call, authenticity. If a thing is authentic, it is relevant. When our youth look around at our generation, they frequently find that we haven't been very authentic. We

Reprinted, with minor deletions, from *Colorado Journal of Educational Research* 9, no. 3 (Spring 1970):2–8, by permission of the author and the publisher.

have frequently talked a good game about the brotherhood of man, for example, while we engaged in segregation or the importance of peace while engaged in an immoral war. They find that many of the things we do in education are not very relevant too. Listen to the words of the songs they sing: "I've got to be me" or "I'm not really making it, I'm only faking it" or "I did it my way."

In education we've done very well in gathering information in books and libraries and the minds of intelligent people. We've also done very well in *giving* people information; we do it through books, libraries, demonstrations, lectures and with the whole new field of electronic gadgets, we can do it better than ever. We are experts at giving information, but where we are failing is in helping people to discover the *meaning* of the information that we provide. This is the problem of the dropout, for example. A dropout is not a dropout because he wasn't told. He is a dropout because he never discovered the meaning of what he was told. After awhile he decided that the system was not very relevant, so he did the intelligent thing: he dropped out. We have built a system primarily for the people who need it least. For example, 10 percent of the children in the ghettos drop out of school before they reach the tenth grade, 60 percent more drop out almost immediately thereafter. The schools we have are primarily for kids who probably would learn whether we sent them to school or not. They don't do this in other professions. In a hospital, for example, the best doctors, the best nurses, and the best care is reserved for the people who are the sickest. In education, you have to fight tooth and nail to get teachers to teach the sickest; they all want to work with the gifted. Nobody wants to teach the difficult ones. . . .

If any change is going to be made in education it is going to have to be made by teachers. You know and I know that when that classroom door is closed, nobody, but nobody, knows what's going on in that room except the teacher and the students. And sometimes the students aren't quite sure! There is a great deal more freedom to do things in our schools than any of us are willing to adopt. They tell me that the scientists have finally discovered what they believe is the missing link between the anthropoid apes and civilized man. It's us! And the missing link between the student and what makes education relevant is also us. . . . Here are some of my nominations about things that need to be done.

1. I think we need to change our way of approaching the problem of curriculum change. Generally speaking, there are two ways of approaching the problem of what and how to teach. One of these ways is the *logical* way. This is the method we use in industry and in science. It consists of deciding what the problem is, defining what ends you hope to reach, determining the variables involved, then, setting about doing them. This is the logical approach to dealing with human problems. It works fine in industry. It works fine with cattle, but it works very badly

with people. Earl Kelley once said about logic, "Logic is only a systematic way of arriving at the wrong answers!" We have a good example of how this approach fails to work in our attempts to make educational innovations in the ghettos. We sit in our nice, air-conditioned offices and figure out what "those" people need "down there." After we have decided we go down there and try to give it to them or do it to them. But they don't want to be done to and they don't want what we want to give them. Often we are astounded at how inadequately things work out and end up saying, "It is their fault." . . .

2. Industry is designed in the logical kind of approach and too many people currently assume that it applies to education equally well, that it will make us more efficient. As a consequence there is a great pressure on us these days to follow the industrial models. The attempt to industrialize much of what is going on in the schools is producing some of the dehumanizing problems we have. It did the same thing in industry. When industry began to find it was necessary to create greater and greater efficiency in the industrial revolution, they achieved greater efficiency by treating workers like machines. This so upset the workers that they revolted and went out on strike. Does that sound familiar to you in terms of student revolt? I think we need to ask ourselves if this is the price we want to pay. Too much of education is already terribly inhuman these days. We have created larger and larger schools so students would have a richer curriculum. But people get lost in large schools, so we set up a guidance department to find them again! Then, after a guidance department has been established, the teachers have a place to send people with problems and don't have to deal with them themselves. They can wash their hands of them, because a specialist has taken over. No wonder students are saying "don't fold, spindle and mutilate me." No wonder they are complaining about the inhumanity of much that we do. If we are going to use the "get with it" approach it seems to me that we are going to have to break down the walls between the schools and the community, between the students and the teachers, between tradition and current needs, in far better ways than we have to this point.

3. To make schools relevant we are going to have to begin by being willing to start where people are. My good friend Don Snygg once said, "The problem with American education is that we are all preoccupied with providing students answers to problems they ain't got yet." That's true—a great deal of what we are trying to teach is out of touch with where students are. We could hardly have done better in making education inhuman if we had purposely tried to move in that direction. I remember Dean Klein at Ohio State years ago commenting on this in a seminar I was in. One of the graduate students came in late from teaching a class. The dean said to him, "Where have you been?" The student replied, "Well, sir, I have been casting pearls before swine," and I will

never forget Klein's answer. The old gentleman just sat there a moment looking at him. Then he said, "Yes, young man, but remember they were *artificial* pearls and real swine." This seems to me to be what we are doing in many places. We are providing artificiality. We are asking to deal with problems that don't seem relevant to the consumers.

If we are going to make ourselves more relevant, we are going to have to learn how to let students be who they are. We are so anxious that they should become something different from what they are, that we start demanding that they be what we hope they will be someday, right now, this minute, *today*. Take, for example, what we do with the delinquent who, over a period of fifteen years, has learned "Nobody likes me. Nobody wants me. Nobody cares about me," and comes to the conclusion, finally, "Well, I don't care about nobody either!" Feeling so, he joins a gang because there is a place where he can be relevant. He comes sauntering into our office with a chip on his shoulder and we say to him, "Now look here, young man, sit up there and behave yourself. Be polite!" In his society, being polite would ruin him! Yet we insist that he be this thing, which we hope that schools will somehow, someday make him, but we demand it today! That's like going to the doctor and hearing him say, "You have a bad case here. Go away and get better, then come back and I'll help you." We are going to have to be willing to begin with people where they are. Some of them are in pretty bad shape, so we are going to have to give up our preconceptions about what they *ought* to be and begin at the place where they *are*. We are also going to have to stop saying to young people, "Ah, your problem is nothing"; to the girl with the broken heart, "Oh, you'll get over it." Or, to the child with a bad case of acne, "Stop being so silly about it. It's not an important problem."

4. Psychologists don't know very much about learning, but one thing they do know, that people learn best when they have a need to know. Most of what we do in school, however, is to give students information before they have a need. To become more relevant we are going to have to find ways of creating needs to know *before* we give them information. In order to do that we are going to have to be willing to listen to young people. Often we don't even approve of them. Earl Kelley has a lovely saying about this: he says, "Whenever you get to worrying about the present generation you ought to remind yourself that they were all right when we got them." We don't approve of our young people very much. We don't approve of their dress, or the way they grow their hair. We don't approve of the problems they think are important and we don't accept their needs or their ideas as valid. Now, if young people do not find their problems treated as valid in an adult society, it ought not surprise us if they attempt to build their own society. This is just what they have done. They have built a world with their own music, their own language, their own standards of dress, their own considerations of proper

behavior, their own codes of ethics, their own values, their own symbols of status and prestige. I would like to suggest that this is a consequence of the fact that we have made our schools almost totally irrelevant for them. Because we do not consider their problems valid, they learn to play the game and go along with tongue in cheek learning as little as possible. In many places the word "adolescent" is practically a cuss word. It is time we got over that because we can't afford not to love our youth, not if we really hope to act as significant people in their lives. If that isn't good enough, we'd better care lest we discover that later in their maturity they don't love us old folks either.

5. If we are going to make education more relevant, we are going to have to actively work for greater self-direction and responsibility in the students we work with. Relevance requires involvement but there is not much opportunity for real involvement in most schools today. Two or three years ago I had a sophomore class of young women education majors preparing to teach elementary school, thirty-five of them from upper middle class homes, your homes. One day I asked them, "How is it you don't get committed to the education process?" Here is what they told me: "Nobody ever listens to us. Nobody ever thinks that anything we have to say is worthwhile. All they ask of us is that we conform. Nobody permits us to be creative. All they want us to do is take in what other people have done and said. They feed us a Pablum diet; it's all chewed over and there isn't any life left in it. It's grades, grades, grades, as though they mattered. Teachers and students ought to be friends, but they're not; they're enemies." They ended their list on this note, which all thirty-five of them voted was true. *The things worth getting committed to don't get you ahead in school.* Now I'm not talking about somebody else's kids, I am talking about your young people, and, I submit, that is a chilling indictment. We need to ask ourselves, "How can we get these people involved?"

We created this dilemma and we ought to be able to reverse it. The way to do so, it seems to me, is to systematically examine what we are doing. Let each of us take a look at his class, his procedures, his requirements and how he operates, asking himself, "What are the things I am doing which are keeping my students from getting involved?" I think if you try that you will discover an extraordinary number of such things. . . .

6. To make education truly relevant means that you and I are going to have to get over being afraid that people will make mistakes. Education is a business built on right answers. We pay off on right answers. Yet the most important learning situations which most of us have had have occurred when somehow or another we have made a mistake. We generally learn more from mistakes than from all the right answers that people try to give us. In spite of this fact we are so fearful that students

may make a mistake that we rob them of opportunities to try in the first place. We surround ourselves with such entangling rules and regulations that we make ourselves afraid to risk anything. In a school I visited the other day a teacher wanted to take her children out for a field trip. When she went to the office and discovered what was involved: that the permission of every parent had to be obtained in writing, that special insurance had to be taken out on the children, that the bus drivers had to be specially paid and wage and hour laws had to be understood and dealt with and so on, she decided it was all too much and gave up the trip. Risking, being unafraid of making mistakes is the very heart of creativity. Creativity is daring to make mistakes. Someone once defined a genius as a guy who gets into trouble for the sheer joy of getting out again. But if we do not let people get into dilemmas, if we are so fearful that they might get into trouble that we rob them of opportunities, then we have made the program we are dealing with irrelevant for them.

Responsibility is learned from being *given* responsibility. You never learn to be responsible by having it withheld. Take, for instance, the teacher who has to go down to the office. She says to the class, "I have to go down to the office for a few minutes, I want you to be good kids until I get back." So she goes to the office and when she gets back the room is in bedlam. At this she sails in and says, "I will never leave you alone again!" And by this decision, she has robbed these children of their only opportunity to learn how to behave when the teacher isn't there. You can't learn how to behave when the teacher isn't there, IF the teacher never leaves you. I think, also, of a school I was in recently. I arrived just after an election for student body president in which a young man had gotten elected after running on a platform of, "no school on Fridays, free lunches, no detention hall, free admission for football games" and so on. The teachers were in a tizzy. They said, "Don't you think this is a travesty on democracy?" I said, "No, I think it is democracy at work." They said, "Don't you think we ought to cancel the election and start over?" I said, "Heck, no, how else can these kids learn the terrible price you have to pay for electing a jackass to office? Better they should learn that early. Look at the mess the rest of us are in!"

Responsibility is learned like any other subject. It is learned by success experience with simple problems which gives you the courage to tackle bigger ones. Students need such opportunities to make decisions, but somebody once pointed out to me that we let children make more decisions in kindergarten than any other time! There they can decide which student they are going to play with, which block they want to use, whether they go outdoors, or stay in, go to the bathroom or stay in the room. They make millions of decisions. But the older kids get and, presumably the more they are able to make decisions, the less they are permitted to make. By the time they get to graduate school, they have hardly any.

7. To make schooling relevant it will be necessary to deal with the importance of children's self-concepts. Psychologists have been studying the self-concept for twenty or thirty years and we now know that what a person believes about himself is perhaps the most important single thing which determines his behavior. It determines what he is likely to do or not likely to do, whether he is likely to be successful or unsuccessful, adjusted or maladjusted, criminal or saint. Each of us behaves in terms of what he believes about himself. This also produces one of the tragedies of our society. We have literally millions of people walking around today who believe they are only X much, and because they are only X much, that is all the much they do. And the rest of us seeing them do X much, say, "Well, that is an X much person." They are the prisoners of their perceptions. This is a major source of our problems of civil rights, of the Negro in the South, the Chicano in the Southwest, the poverty-stricken whites, the people in ghettos and thousands of other people including yourself. With the child in school we go one step further. Not only does he learn he can't read, but because he believes he can't read, he doesn't try. Because he doesn't try, he doesn't do very well. Because he doesn't do it very well his teacher says to him, "My goodness, Jimmy, you don't read very well," which proves that was what he already thought in the first place! Then, we add a further gimmick, we send home failing grades so his parents can tell him also! Such a child finds himself surrounded by a conspiracy in which all of his experiences tell him that he cannot.

We can't ignore the self-concept because a person's self-concept comes right along with him into class. What happens there is affecting self-concepts whether teachers are aware of it or not. You can't suspend the laws of learning. You can't say, "Well, I know that self-concepts are important, but I don't have time to think about that question. It isn't important in my class, I've got to get on with the subject matter." That's like a man saying, "I know my car needs a carburetor, but I'm going to run mine without one."

We can't ignore the self-concept. Here are some statistics from research done recently with children in third grade and eleventh grade. In the third grade 12 percent of the children said they were not very sure of themselves. In the eleventh grade, despite the fact that about a third of them had dropped out already, 34 percent of them said they were not very sure of themselves. Now, where do you suppose they learned that? In the third grade 84 percent of the children said they were kind of proud of themselves. By eleventh grade 43 percent said they were discouraged about themselves. It seems to me each of us has to ask himself, "What is my school doing, what am I doing, to change the perceptions of the people I'm working with in positive ways?"

You change a person's conception of himself in positive ways by experience of success, not by failure. The best guarantee we have that a person will be able to deal successfully with the future is that he has been successful in dealing with it in the past. That means that what we have to do with young people is to provide them with success experience in their early years. That also gives us the key to what we have to do. We can find what to do by asking ourselves, "How can a person feel liked unless somebody likes him? How can a person feel he is a person of dignity and integrity unless somebody treats him so?"

8. The next thing I'd like to mention that gets in the way of relevancy has to do with the grading system. After thirty-five years as an educator, I am thoroughly convinced that the whole business of grades is the worst millstone around the neck of American education. We spend more time talking about this question, more time worrying about it, more time fretting about it, as though it were important. Yet, everything we know about it, indicates that it is not. The grading system prevents us from getting on with the innovations we need to make things relevant. Grades are an illusion, an artificial reason for learning in place of a real reason for learning; that means irrelevant. Look what stupid things it does to us. Take my own area, human growth and development. I suppose in that field there are about twenty-five basic principles. Only trouble is there are fifteen weeks in the quarter with three lectures a week—forty-five lectures —and only twenty-five principles! But there are a million details. So what I do is I fill up my lectures with details. Of course my students, hearing me lecture on the details, think they must be important so they carefully write them down filling up their notebooks with details and missing the principles. Then, of course, the registrar comes along and says, "You have to give me a grade for these people." So we whip out the normal curve and give a test to determine the grades. Now, we've got the problem again— only twenty-five principles and, of course, if it's a mid-term exam it only covers thirteen. So we test them on the details and that spreads them out very nicely and so we obtain a curve in proper fashion. The only difficulty is, again they've learned that it's details that are important while the important ideas, values and principles are missed in the process. That's just one of the things that grades do to us. There are others.

People will tell you that grades are a great motivator, they make people work. Now any teacher knows that's not true, except two days before the grades come out and one day after. The rest of the time they don't motivate anybody. Grades are artificial motives in place of real motives. You don't have to motivate people when the thing you are asking them to do is something which interests them and seems like they have a chance of succeeding with it. If it interests them and they think they have a chance of succeeding, they will work like crazy. Did you ever try to get your kids to come home when they are working on the float for the parade? When it's something they want and see a need to do they work like mad. Motivation is always there. Everybody is always motivated. Nobody ever does anything unless he'd rather. Our problem, then, is to find some real motives rather than artificial ones.

We all know that grades don't mean the same thing to any two teachers. One teacher grades on the basis of whether the child completed his work, another grades on the basis of adding up the scores on a set of quizzes, another one grades on the basis of the growth the child made at the end of the quarter, another one grades on what family he came from. Everybody grades on a different basis. Everybody knows this, still, we all sit around piously in faculty meetings and behave as though grades meant the same thing. Young people are asking us, "Let's be authentic. Let's stop kidding ourselves."

I think we ought to be more concerned with what we're teaching when we grade people. I remember my son coming home from school some years ago. He was furious. I said, "What's the trouble, Pete?" He said, "This blankety-blank grading system, this business of grading on the curve! Dad, how do you put up with it?" I said, "What do you mean?" He explained, "It is teaching me that my best friend is my enemy, that it is to my advantage to destroy him." That was a shocker to me. I never thought of it that way before, but it is true. That is what a competitive grading system does to people. It is hardly a basis on which to build a democratic society.

Fortunately, I think we are getting rid of grades. I think there is a movement all over the country to eliminate grading. We've got ungraded primaries. We're getting rid of grading in high school. We've got pass-fail grading in college and so on. One college is even now trying to do away with their college entrance examinations, another step in the right direction. What you and I need to do is to hurry up. We need to use the communist technique of boring from within, tearing it down from the inside.

9. A further source of irrelevance is our firm belief that competition is a great and wonderful thing. This is a myth so deeply engraved in our social structure that I'm sure that just hearing me doubt it is already upsetting some of you. Competition, we have told ourselves, is a great motivator. But here is what we know about it. Psychologically, people are motivated by competition if they believe they have a chance of winning. If they don't believe they have a chance of winning, they sit around and watch everybody else beat their brains out. A good example of this may be found on any Saturday afternoon in the fall of the year. At any foot-

ball stadium you can find seventy thousand people who need exercise sitting there watching twenty-two people who don't need it get it. The first thing we know about competition is that it works fine as a motive, *but only for those people who can be seduced into the competition and who can somehow be fooled into believing that they have a chance of winning.* The second thing we know about it is when people are forced to compete and do not feel they have a chance of winning, they are not motivated. Instead, they are discouraged and disillusioned. We cannot afford a discouraged and disillusioned populace. A third thing we know is that when competition becomes too important, morality breaks down and any means becomes justified to reach the end. When it becomes too important for the cadets at Colorado Springs to get their wings, they steal the examinations. When it becomes too important for a basketball team to win, they start using their elbows. When it is too important, then any means becomes justified to achieve the end and that is a very dangerous philosophy. . . .

10. Finally, a major source of irrelevance in my book is to be found in the grade level myth. Back before 1900, education had a certain curriculum which it offered. Students came and took it. If they didn't do very well, you simply threw them out and nobody worried very much. The student had to fit the curriculum. Then, in 1900, we made a magnificent decision. We decided to educate everybody. No country in the world had ever tried it before, but we decided to try. The minute we made that decision, the old way was no longer enough. The minute you decide to educate everybody you have to fit the curriculum to the people, not the people to the curriculum. Nevertheless, we are still trying desperately to find ways of treating people alike. We are trapped in the grade level myth. Even my own student teachers come back from their observation sessions saying, "But Dr. Combs, she's teaching everybody with a different book!" It's a matter of earth-shaking insight to discover that there are teachers who do that. Somehow, we've got to break out of this idea that people can all be treated alike.

Unhappily we are currently confronted with an invasion from the industrial model. We have decided that industry is a great success so we ought to apply its techniques to education. I think there are some things that industry can help us with, but I'm not about to turn over education to an industrial magnate. A few years ago we had a group of people from the Ford Foundation visit us. After they had been on the campus a few days, they said, "You know, when we first tried to make an impact on education, we thought the way to do it was through television and teacher-aids and things like that, but the longer we work with the problem, the more we are convinced that we have to deal with the whole child!" I thought, "My God, that's where I came in." Industry can help us, but it isn't going to save us. We're going to have to find ways of facing up to really individualizing instruction. We're going to have to give up the idea that there is any kind of a group to solve our problem. Most research shows us that there is no method of grouping which can be clearly shown to be superior to any other method of grouping or to nongrouping. Yet we are still trying to find ways of grouping people in such a way that we won't have to pay attention to individual difference. . . .

CHAPTER 3

The System of Sociocultural Beliefs

When we attempt to analyze the values and attitudes that underlie American social and political conduct, we find a number of disparities between cherished ideals and reality. Individualism, dignity, and autonomy are frequently replaced by conformity. Cooperation and teamwork are countered by aggressiveness, wealth accumulation, and financial security. Although society extolls the idea of equality, it disregards the rights of minority groups and subcultures, viewing them as inferior. Basic ideals such as equality, freedom, and rights are undergoing reinterpretation.

In a world of mass population and scientific "progress," many of the fundamental concepts of American democracy, such as rugged individualism, must give way to the goal of cooperation among people, companies, states, and nations; yet many people continue to hold values appropriate to an earlier time. Traditional American social values, and their embodiment in governance and education, are challenged by science and technology, large-scale bureaucratic organization, increased leisure, the mass media, urbanization, population growth, nationalism, mobility, cultural pluralism, the movements for the civil rights of minorities and women, and ecology.

These are hardly short-lived fads. Of significant concern is whether America's political foundation is strong enough to support the diversity already present.

Assumptions of the American Cultural System

The translation of beliefs about "human nature" into political and educational systems is also a concern. Here we shall consider the most commonly accepted positions and influences.

Puritan Influences

The Puritan belief that man is innately evil, propelled to disregard the laws of God by strong natural inclinations, has been a powerful influence on Western culture. This view of man's nature necessitates almost constant control over the populace by the institutions of society—the state, the family, the church, and the school—to check man's inclination toward corruption. To impose strict guidelines for conduct with the threat of stringent punishments for those who were overcome by temptation became the legislative function (Bigge and Hunt, 1968, chap. 4).

Our governmental system continues to operate on the Puritan assumption that man's nature is basically weak and easily corrupted. The provisions for frequent elections, shared decision making among three governmental branches, and referendum and recall were designed both to check and to modify his behavior. The perceived need for safeguards against corruption led to duplications of function, expensive elections, friction among branches, and difficulties in fixing responsibility (Shermis, 1967: 207–8).

In education, belief in man's corrupt nature led to practices that borrowed heavily from the church: a curriculum laden with religious history and doctrine, a method emphasizing drill, harsh punishments, and constant regulation and supervision, and the indoctrination of socially prescribed values and beliefs.

Even today, teachers and administrators employ methods based on the assumption of man's evil nature. Some are now suggesting that this assumption be reexamined. A brief look at alternative views of human character may help us to understand the demands being made upon both government and education today.

Romantic Naturalism

The position popularized by Jean Jacques Rousseau in the eighteenth century holds that man is born good, decent, kind, and generous, but that society causes him to develop selfishness and corruption. It follows that governmental and educational institutions should interfere with the individual as little as possible, so that his natural instincts for righteousness can persist. While Rousseau's views had some effect on political philosophy, Puritan tenets were too well entrenched in American government for the concept of governmental laissez-faire based on the laws of supply and demand to prevail. Eventually, as corporations and cartels began to eliminate small producers, federal regulations had to be passed to guard competitive practices.

Rousseau, believing that children are innately good, suggested in his writings that teachers and other adults should encourage the activities spontaneously initiated by children (Ulich, 1945: 217–24). This position was popularized in the early nineteenth century by two European educators, Johann Pestalozzi and Friedrich Froebel, who advanced the concept of the kindergarten and early elementary education and emphasized construction of a curriculum around the child's natural interests and curiosities. The role of the teacher was to facilitate the learning process, avoiding the authoritarian tendencies regarded as necessary by the theory of human depravity.

Classicism

Developed by Plato and extended by Aristotle, the classical position maintains that man has a superior and an inferior nature, and that individual men have either one or the other (Brameld, 1971: 267–70). Historically, even up to the present, this position has been demonstrated in the form of racism, which is analogous to the belief that "superior" people have greater intelligence and are more capable of learning and of leading the "masses." Members of the "elite" came to be identified by their possession of wealth.

According to the American dream, anyone who works hard to become either knowledgeable or wealthy also becomes "superior." Our popular literature tells of people from humble surroundings who became superior in the eyes of others. However, these examples are sufficiently scarce to perpetuate the dualistic doctrine of classical human nature, which has been demonstrated in both governance and education. Usually, says the theory, those who have attended private schools with classical curriculums are best suited to govern. The masses need only study basic disciplines and participate in vocational training. While many educators decry this dualism, school programs still consist of a general college preparatory curriculum and a separate technical training discipline.

Pragmatism

Pragmatism defines human nature as neutral; it emerges in a dynamic culture that establishes social values. Moreover, a person constantly revises his outlooks according to his experiences and changing purposes in given circumstances.

Assumptions of the Democratic Process

The assumptions underlying the Puritan view of man's nature guide American political, economic, social, and educational practices.

Equality

Among these assumptions, the concept of equality is foremost—the idea that all men have "equal rights," regardless of inequalities in physical abilities, talent, education, and social status. Christian doctrine holds strongly that all men's souls are equal in the eyes of God. Another, less spiritual, view of equality holds that men have an equal right to compete, that talent and desire are the determinants of success. A third position states that all men should have equal opportunities to succeed, that race, religion, and national origin should not deny one the chance to succeed. This view has been embodied in the Head Start program and recently in several Supreme Court decisions in the area of minority civil rights.

Although the concept of equality remains fundamental in a democracy, varying interpretations cause confusion in practice. How can we determine, for example, whether educational opportunity is equal for all children? Can the schools deal effectively with individual differences rather than oblige children to conform?

Freedom

The early settlers in America were searching for freedom from restrictions on their "rights" to worship, work, and travel. Even today freedom is described as the absence of coercion, and the search for freedom causes dissent over issues from adding fluoride to public water supplies, saying prayers in school, to bussing students as a means of desegregation (Shermis, 1967: 217–21). The need for increasing controls at all levels in a modern industrial nation has been reluctantly accepted by the populace as the price of material progress.

Rights

In the model of religious doctrine, the Constitution guarantees certain "inalienable rights" to all men, irrespective of their condition. The founding fathers identified the right of self-government, for example, as absolute.

Recent events have shown, however, that under certain conditions—such as after criminal conviction or during periods of war or extreme civil upheaval—rights can be modified or taken away from citizens. These rights, then, are neither absolute nor inalienable in practice; rather, they are important values of the culture that are relative and subject to revision as the society constantly redefines their meanings (Shermis, 1966: 515–17).

Participation

Another assumption underlying democratic governance is that all members of the group must be free to participate in the decision-making process. Our present form of representative government is a logical extension of this idea.

This assumption is founded on the idea of respect for the dignity and worth of every individual citizen. The democratic principle asserts that the wisest decisions over time will come through involvement of all members of the group. However, the democratic process does not guarantee that all citizens *will* participate in decisions or that the decisions will be correct.

If all citizens of a democratic society are to have equal opportunities to participate in decision making, then once a decision is made, all citizens must be equally obligated to abide by it. The majority has the obligation to protect minority rights, not to allow the establishment of one set of rules for the majority and another for minorities. A minority may disapprove of the decision, but as long as that minority had an equal opportunity to act in the lawmaking, it also has the equal obligation to abide by the decision. Of course, the minority's disapproval may lead to a revision of a law, but democracy demands that the law be observed unless rescinded (Bayles, 1960: chap. 10).

Democratic Values

Growing out of the assumptions basic to democracy were practices valued by the citizenry. Historically, our nation was founded on the promise of greater personal freedom and greater opportunity for material comforts than existed in Europe. It was mandatory that a form of government be devised that would allow and encourage individuals to improve their status and standard of living. It was clear that rule by force could not be tolerated if the positions underlying democracy were to be taken seriously.

Honesty, responsibility, participation, open-mindedness, autonomy, and individual worth have been viewed as values fundamental to democratic process. The concept of honesty has found formal expression in politics and economics as well as religion. When citizens are deemed capable of reasoned judgment, their participation takes the form of voting for representatives, running for office, campaigning for others, or simply voicing political views in public. Open-mindedness remains a significant goal as we regard how well our society can tolerate change, test new procedures, and consider alternatives, although indoctrination is more present in our order than we often realize. Autonomy and individual worth have long been tenets of this society that calls itself open and class-less, allowing free movement up and down the ladder of success and so-cial acceptance.

To insist that the conventional descriptions of these values be incul-cated is to insist that these meanings are static, absolute truths, accept-able for all times. The teacher faces the exciting challenge of assisting students to discover for themselves what these values are and what rele-vance they have for a world society today and in the future. The teacher is obliged to help the student develop understanding and continuity be-tween his own interest and the norms that ought to be enhanced for the betterment of both himself and the social group. In *Schools for the Six-ties,* the National Education Association outlined what it believed were the critical values as embodied in criteria for both present and future school practices: "(1) respect for the worth and dignity of every indi-vidual, (2) equality of opportunity for all children, (3) encouragement of variability, (4) faith in man's ability to make rational decisions, (5) shared responsibility for the common good, (6) respect for moral and spiritual values and ethical standards of conduct" (N.E.A., 1963: 7–8). These values have come to be accepted because they contribute to the processes of democratic governance, which in turn function as an instrument of man's goal fulfillment.

Social Applications of Democratic Values

In a democratic society, citizens must ask themselves whether social, po-litical, economic, and educational institutions are performing consistently with democratic values, and what happens if these values are *not* being observed. In our pluralistic system, values are interpreted differently by various subgroups within the society. People often shift from one set of values to another, sometimes without being aware that they have done so. Frequently they hold two opposing values simultaneously. Teachers and school administrators, for example, talk about the fundamentals of democracy, but many practices in the schools are autocratic and arbi-trary; many educational administrators are examining closely the basis for what they require of students and teachers in a setting that should be preparing citizens for active participation in a democratic society.

The racial protests of the 1960s have today given way to more so-cially acceptable political and economic strategies for gaining equality. Society's attention is being drawn to another latent social concern—sexism. The main thrust of sexism is cultural stereotyping by sex that affects the social, economic, and psychological outcomes for women. Schools harbor, promote, and encourage the proliferation of sex stereo-types.

Sex-role stereotyping begins in early childhood and leads to an evaluation by both sexes that men are more worthwhile than women (Baumrind, 1972), and that women are less creative because they lack initiative and assertiveness. It is believed that women tend to be more dependent, affiliative, and obedient than men. Before school entrance, boys are supplied with toys that inculcate a socially construed masculine role, while a girl gets a doll to nurture and a toy kitchen to practice "cleaning up." A girl is permitted to adopt a "tomboy" attitude, but a boy who demonstrates some feminine identification is despised as a potential homosexual. Anderson (1972) describes sex-role typing as a popular misconception, for the real concern is perceptions of individual differences, not just sex differences.

Although psychological sex stereotyping begins at home, schools are a major contributor. Beginning reading texts still show boys and girls playing with different toys; sex-related activities are reinforced and exemplified by textbooks, teachers, and administration. As a student goes through school, the sex-linked concept that girls are unable to dissect frogs or unskilled in manual arts is reinforced by the curriculum. Additional school experiences create a shared expectation that girls will be docile, more verbal, less athletic, more interested in clothes, home, family, and not serious about careers.

However, the school has an obligation to provide for differences and to encourage divergent behavioral development (Taba, 1962); to require exploration of new roles and personality types. For a school to interpret the "self-fulfilling prophecy" as synonymous with sexism is undemocratic. It is also illegal in light of affirmative action legislation.

The issue, then, is not really sexism in the schools but how to provide children with optimum exposure to diverse experiences that are meaningful and relevant. Teaching must encourage the student's active exploration of varied roles in a manner that does not restrict or stereotype either sex. The school and the teacher should become more aware of their own subtle discriminations in responding to the intellectual and social achievements of boys and girls, and initiate ways to remedy these biases.

Capitalism and Education

The notion that man's self-interest produces a natural urge to collect and possess goods of value supported the acquisition of wealth in America at a time when it appeared that there was more than enough for all. The world of business came to have a powerful influence on the schools. It soon became the school's role to see that students were trained to step into the vocational world as potential producers-consumers.

Instead of industry expanding at its own expense through apprenticeship programs and opportunities for on-the-job training, schools were expected to offer a curriculum that enabled the high school student to develop his vocational skills. The economic cycle propelled the curriculum away from the goal of character and intellectual development toward vocational education. Under the influence of business, the schools acquired standards for quantifying intellectual performance. Today we have nationwide assessment programs that chart educational attainment according to standards that measure learning skills.[1]

This economic encroachment upon the school system creates yet another paradox for education. If education is to remain dedicated to the development of intellectual growth and character in the individuals it serves, it needs to reevaluate the compatibility of capitalism and democracy. If the schools are serving an economic function rather than assisting individuals in self-development,[2] and if economic considerations imply undemocratic practices for public schools, then we must consider the implications of a democratic education. If the democratic concept of equal opportunities for citizens to participate in decision making and equal obligations to abide by decisions democratically arrived at is to be realized, schools have the responsibility to help students improve their ability to make decisions, to think independently, and to consider available information intelligently. If our political system were a dictatorship, there would be no need for studying social issues as a means of developing problem-solving abilities. But our commitment is to a democracy, and that implies the need to educate for open-mindedness, trust, responsibility, and decision making.

The Role of Government

Shermis (1967:233) suggests that "government exists to provide opportunity for all to realize their inherent potential." Freedom *from* becomes freedom *to*—freedom to realize one's potential in a society that allows greater opportunities for citizens to accomplish their aspirations, made possible by the availability of great wealth, technological advance, and by renewed and sincere reevaluation of fundamental democratic values. Rather than limit individualism, a government ought to create opportunities for its citizens by governing in such a manner as to facilitate self-realization. In this sense, government is viewed as an instrument of good will and encourages individual self-enhancement. The government spends its energies creating programs that allow maximum citizen growth ac-

[1] See Raymond Callahan's *Education and the Cult Efficiency* (Chicago: University of Chicago Press, 1962) for an analysis of the relationship between education and theories of quantification.

[2] For further reading on this idea see Herbert Marcuse, *One-Dimensional Man* (Boston: Beacon Press, 1964).

cording to the values of a democratic government. If individual self-realization ought to be the goal of the government, what ought the goal of schools to be? Obviously, the same.

The Role of Schools

For schools to facilitate self-realization of students would require that current school policy and curriculum be altered drastically. To say that public schools practice the tenets of democracy is ludicrous. Students are declared not mature enough to engage in decision making, and many teachers and administrators refuse to acknowledge that students have even basic human rights; interestingly, many parents agree. Thus adults disavow the aim of democratic education: to help students develop their abilities for independent thinking.

To maintain this traditional system of adult domination, public schools train students principally for roles as consumers. They teach passivity, respect for arbitrary authority, rewards for right answers, and conformity. They think it unwise to trust students or to allow their extensive participation in learning because it usually creates discipline problems and noise. Although schools announce democratic aims, they design activities to reinforce conventional standards. Thus as students progress through the grades they are compelled to adopt behaviors that satisfy the teacher, the test, and the adult system.

The student has little choice but to play "Let's Pretend." This game, as described by Postman and Weingartner (1969:49), includes the following assumptions, which many teachers and administrators take too seriously:

> Let's pretend that you are not what you are and that this sort of work makes a difference to your lives; let's pretend that what bores you is important, and that the more you are bored, the more important it is; let's pretend that there are certain things *everyone* must know, and that both the questions and answers about them have been fixed for all time; let's pretend that your intellectual competence can be judged on the basis of how well you can play Let's Pretend.

An increasing number of authors express a similar theme; see, for example, the works of John Holt (1964, 1966), Herbert Kohl (1969), George Leonard (1968), Richard Renfield (1969), and more recently, Charles Silberman (1970).

Teaching in a Democracy

How does teaching in a democratic social system require considerations different from teaching in another sociocultural context? The assumptions of our political and economic heritage serve as guidelines for both present and future society. A critical exploration of the "old ways" should not mean rejection of traditional functions; instead, we should make investigations of conventional culture and its development in the light of present society. Examination of the traditional should enable us to propose renewed application of these democratic values to a modern culture committed in spirit to democratic principles (Bigge, 1971: chap. 6). Reconsideration of the status quo implies synthesizing traditional democratic beliefs with current cultural trends.

Democratic Decision Making

Education in a democracy has the responsibility to sensitize each citizen to democratic processes through careful and critical study of his obligation, as a thoughtful person, to voice reasoned opinions (Crary, 1951: 154–60). Many teachers believe that students can make decisions only if given large amounts of information. Certainly students need something to think about, but simply obtaining information is not thinking. Overemphasis on information gathering may even inhibit thinking. Teachers have failed to guide students to the use of information in a discerning, intelligent, and independent manner.

Trust

A democracy requires a school environment that encourages independent and reasoned behavior. Trust, one of the primary values allied with democratic principles, is frequently rejected by educators in the public schools. Many teachers trust students to do only what they are told, and even then the teachers doubt that the task will be performed to their satisfaction.

Absence of trust is apparent in the numerous regulations that govern students. Most schools allow little or no student participation in deciding the fate of rule offenders. The result is often cheating, disciplinary problems, and boredom. Teachers tend to employ disciplinary measures that teach students to respect arbitrary authority, to conform to narrow standards of conduct, and to exhibit behavior and thinking judged correct by the teacher. To be trusting means that teachers and administrators must allow greater student participation in an atmosphere that fosters cooperation.

Thought Control or Thought Guidance?

Whether he teaches in a democracy or in some other political system, the teacher desires to effect a change in his students' behavior and, more important, in their beliefs and attitudes. If there is no demonstrated change, we assume that the students have not learned. This statement implies a paradox. On the one hand, teachers must teach so as to change both the attitudes and the behavior of students. On the other hand, the attempt to change attitudes may mean indoctrination. Thought control is undemocratic, but the act of teaching demands a considerable amount of thought guidance. An emphasis on the processes of reasoning and decision making leads to thought guidance without thought control.

Freedom is essential to education in a democracy. The freedom to inquire into topics of their own choosing helps students to become more competent to make decisions on the critical issues that face national or international society. Teachers must also be free to suggest and discuss topics that appear inappropriate or distasteful to some (Nash, 1966: chap. 2).

Traditionally, teachers have evaluated student beliefs on the basis of their agreement or disagreement with the teacher's position. When the student agrees with the teacher, it is judged that the student is thinking well. A large amount of instructional time is taken up with activities that allow the teacher to judge student beliefs according to predetermined criteria. But this procedure constitutes thought control and is undemocratic, or even antidemocratic (Bayles, 1960:177–85).

When students are excluded from determining criteria, application of the criteria is autocratic. Some other, less dictatorial, basis is needed on which we can test opinions.

Some hold that teachers must advocate and teach democratic beliefs in order to maintain intellectual freedom. But deliberately to "teach" democracy is propagandizing and violates the fundamental assumption of democracy—that individuals must have equal opportunity to participate in decision-making processes. For the teacher to advocate one view over another deprives students of the opportunity to face a problem and think out their answer. Classroom learning activities designed to teach by telling imply that learning is probably not open to numerous interpretations or meaningful student inquiry. Whenever teaching is restricted to content, democratic educational values are replaced by prescribed learning, dictated content, and arbitrarily determined solutions.

The role of the teacher, then, is not to justify a single view by using the power of his position to compel agreement. The assumption in a democratic classroom is that both teacher and students ought to be allowed the freedom to inquire into issues or concerns mutually identified as relevant to the course of study. By engaging in the process of learning *how* to think, one is following procedures that are nonindoctrinative.

Democratic Adoption of Criteria

Disposing of the dilemma of thought guidance without thought control requires more than an impassioned argument that teachers not impose autocratic standards. We expect that classroom learning procedures will come up with a valid answer. The assertion that classrooms should be more democratic does not mean that we are willing to settle for classrooms where learning does not take place.

If teachers are not to tell students when they are thinking well or whether what they are thinking is "right," how should teachers help students appraise their thinking? First, when confronted with a problem, students should be assisted in stating the guidelines, policies, or criteria necessary to answer the question in their own minds. They decide what is necessary to establish standards or expectations of correctness. Second, the students should oblige themselves to employ these criteria in their inquiry until the need to revise or rescind them becomes obvious.

What happens in this process is often amazing. The inquirer works to test his tentative answer against the criteria he has adopted—*and* works to test his criteria against the facts of the case! He becomes more skillful not only at determining "truths" but also at determining the criteria that are most useful to him. He becomes more skillful at guiding his own thinking with increasing independence.

Although establishing criteria for thought guidance is time consuming, it is not a waste of time. If one is to teach democratically, opportunities for students to participate in the democratic process of decision making are essential; to evaluate the products of that process as right or wrong is another matter.

Delegated Authority

Does democracy in the schools mean that students should determine whether they will learn, what they will learn, and how they should behave? Obviously not. Although freedom and participation are fundamental to the concept of democracy, these terms have application *within* the democratic framework and do not stand for anarchy. Our description of democracy places sovereignty in all citizens equally. Often the larger body, the body politic of all citizens, enacts decisions that give designated subgroups or individuals jurisdiction in certain matters. Thus boards of education are delegated authority by the state, and principals of schools are delegated authority by the board or superintendent, on behalf of the body politic.

The process of delegation correlates with democratic decision making. The right to appeal a decision made by the delegated authority, who is responsible to the people as a whole and who must stand for reelection or review from time to time, is an integral part of this process (Bayles, 1960:168; Bayles, 1966:88–89).

As applied to the schools or to other bodies, the principle of delegated authority does not mean that students can establish any rules they wish. Certain regulations governing student behavior—prohibiting the destruction of school property, for example—are established by the community, and the object of these laws is not to deny the right of some but to ensure that the rights of all are recognized. In certain areas the student body has jurisdiction. Traditionally, for example, students have been offered choices in electives, extracurricular activities, offices in student government, the content of school newspapers and annuals, and school functions such as dances, plays, and concerts.

Unfortunately, student decisions in these areas are often overruled by school authorities. This is understandably disturbing to students. The same mockery of meaningful participation occurs in the classroom if a teacher allows students alternatives that are later overruled because they do not agree with the teacher's standards. Even the very act of classroom discussion between teacher and students often gives the impression that if the student cannot guess the teacher's answer, his judgment or participation has no value—so why even get involved? For some reason, many teachers do not realize that they negate the worth and dignity of the individual by denying him any real or meaningful opportunity to participate in decision making. If democracy is to mean anything to students, it must be an experience that makes students aware of the processes that define areas of jurisdiction, and that permits meaningful student involvement in choices that will not later be overruled.

Responsibility

A recent trend in American society has been to recognize students as citizens having rights guaranteed by our Constitution. These rights were formerly thought to be part of the authority delegated to the schools. The most obvious example is in the area of freedom of expression, specifically in physical appearance. Following numerous federal and state court decisions involving dress codes, schools are moving toward more student involvement in deciding about aspects of behavior that most directly affect the student body.

To provide students with experiences in responsibility, many schools are revising their daily schedules around the concept of flexible scheduling of both class and free time. The student has greater responsibility to select from electives, to engage in independent study, to learn to manage his time effectively. Although this system can be, and has been, criticized, it can offer opportunities for students to learn trust, cooperation, and responsibility. Teachers in such a system ought to help students identify the concerns relevant to an area of study and arrive at tentative solutions. Often these concerns, manifested within the school community, reflect larger social issues.

Teach Issues

Contemporary issues in race, religion, economics, politics, relations among people and nations, man and technology, environment and sex, to name a few, are often thought to be so conflict-laden that students should not be exposed to them. Such an attitude and the fear it instills in the teacher concerned about job security deflect the schools from their commitment to democratic education by causing them to avoid issues essential to the life of democracy. Ignoring issues will not make them go away. Schools have the obligation to encourage critical examination of issues that require the ability to think about the broader world.

Internationalism

The schools must expand their ethnocentric viewpoint to include development of a student attitude that is international, not just nationalistic (Massialas and Cox, 1966:190–97). Our culture is full of ironic incongruities, but perhaps none is so obvious as our attitude toward peace and war. Public and government officials express strong desires for peace, at the same time meeting each international crisis with a buildup of arms and even more strenuous competition for the world's limited resources. This attitude prevents the international cooperation that surely must be a prerequisite for a more peaceful world order.

Inconsistencies in the values held by a large portion of the citizenry widen the gap between the democracy teachers talk about and actual school practice. Obviously, curricular emphasis must change if we are to provide students with an understanding of comparative governments, economics, and cultural differences. If international cooperation is essential, the schools ought to stop attempting to foster nationalism by building contempt for other peoples. Our attitude toward conflict as a means of settling disputes is constantly supported by a culture that praises superior force and discourages attitudes favoring arbitration and compromise. In this respect, the media's emphasis on strife further influences the public toward acceptance of conflict.

These advocated changes in school curriculums and methods, as well as in the media and the government, are admittedly idealistic; however, they point out how most of our institutions act in a manner contradictory to democratic fundamentals that would allow our citizens to grow progressively through democratic experiences. To continue to foster double standards, conflicting values, and attitudes that act as though no inconsistency existed is to invite further development of narrow-minded sectionalism, devoid of opportunities for free, open, cooperative inquiry by students and citizens. If we are to educate citizens to participate actively and meaningfully in a democratic society, the school, as a social institution, must offer viable decision-making opportunities for its students.

Conclusions

The schools, as social institutions responsible for fostering democratic participation, ought to reject outright those practices that do not meet the criteria of democracy. Because the schools are for the most part undemocratic, they do not sensitize students to democracy. Teachers tend not to facilitate individual decision making because they distrust students and because they reject the principle that students ought to be allowed opportunities for rational, meaningful participation in solving common problems. Although outwardly opposed to thought control, teachers constantly engage in activities that require students to reach narrowly acceptable answers. As evaluators of student work, they impose their own or the textbook's answers on students and reject establishing criteria cooperatively as the basis of evaluation. Academic freedom for both students and teachers ought to be taken seriously. To indoctrinate in favor of democracy as a product is just as undemocratic as to regard the outcomes of student inquiry as invalid unless they are acceptable to the teacher.

If the schools are committed to democratic education, there is no substitute for offering students meaningful experiences, sensitizing them to the values of cooperation rather than competition, to openness of thought instead of restrictive indoctrination, to trust instead of fear, to freedom with responsibility delegated democratically instead of pseudojurisdiction. Democratic education rejects a teaching strategy that avoids reflective study of contemporary issues. Democracy depends upon an informed citizenry, a population that has experienced in school the reflective study necessary to an understanding of oneself, one's society, and one's relationship to the world community.

Schools, like democratic governments, must create opportunities for each student to realize himself. But self-realization cannot be at the expense of others; it is not just the survival of a government, a nation, or a culture that is at stake. The pressing concern is the survival of man in his ecological environment. The problem of man in his society and in the world society will not fade away. While we do not put forth a doomsday philosophy, we do assert that every man must accept the responsibility to study the issues and to commit himself to responsible action as he sees it. The schools, as an integral element of society, have the clear obligation to prepare students for democracy.

REFERENCES

Anderson, Scarvia, ed. *Sex Differences and Discrimination in Education*. Worthington, Ohio: Charles A. Jones, 1972.

Baumrind, Diana. "From Each According to Her Ability." *School Review* 80 (February 1972):161–97.

Bayles, Ernest E. *Democratic Educational Theory*. New York: Harper & Row, 1960.

————. *Pragmatism in Education*. New York: Harper & Row, 1966.

Bigge, Morris L. *Positive Relativism: An Evergoing Educational Philosophy*. New York: Harper & Row, 1971.

————, and Maurice P. Hunt. *Psychological Foundations of Education*. 2d ed. New York: Harper & Row, 1968.

Brameld, Theodore. *Patterns of Educational Philosophy*. New York: Holt, Rinehart & Winston, 1971.

Crary, Ryland. "Characteristics of the Good Democratic Citizen." In *Education for Democratic Citizenship*, edited by Ryland Crary. 22d Yearbook of the National Council for the Social Studies. Washington, D.C.: The Council, 1951.

Holt, John. *How Children Fail*. New York: Pitman, 1964.

————. *How Children Learn*. New York: Pitman, 1966.

Kohl, Herbert. *The Open Classroom: A Practical Guide to a New Way of Teaching*. New York: Random House, 1970.

Leonard, George. *Education and Ecstasy*. New York: Delacorte, 1968.

Massialas, Byron, and C. Benjamin Cox. *Inquiry in Social Studies*. New York: McGraw-Hill, 1966.

Nash, Paul. *Authority and Freedom in Education*. New York: Wiley, 1966.

National Education Association. *Schools for the Sixties*. New York: McGraw-Hill, 1963.

Postman, Neil, and Charles Weingartner. *Teaching as a Subversive Activity*. New York: Delacorte, 1969.

Renfield, Richard. *If Teachers Were Free*. Washington, D.C.: Acropolis, 1969.

Shermis, S. Samuel. *Philosophic Foundations of Education*. New York: American Book, 1967.

————. "A Redefining of Rights." *Phi Delta Kappan* 47 (May 1966):515–17.

Silberman, Charles. *Crisis in the Classroom*. New York: Random House, 1970.

Taba, Hilda. *Curriculum Development: Theory and Practice*. New York: Harcourt, Brace & World, 1962.

Ulich, Robert. *History of Educational Thought*. New York: American Book, 1945.

CHAPTER 4
Sociocultural Guides to Teaching

Nearly every teacher is confronted by conflicting demands from differing groups. One group of parents advocates a return to basics; a community group wants more vocational education. A professional teachers' organization adopts a program of moral education that merits attention, while the principal returns from a central office meeting infused with bright ideas about metrics. And the kids sit there every day expecting the teacher to come up with something that is interesting and fun. In the face of such demands, what is the classroom teacher to do?

Many of these demands are founded on notions that are probably worthwhile, if only the teacher had the time and energy to carry them out. But time and energy do not exist in unlimited quantity. So one problem—not a simple task—is to sort out the "better" things to do from the merely "good."

Obviously, some demands contradict other expectations. Some time ago one of the authors taught high school English. The influence of his university methods professor, a thorough modernist, lay heavily upon him. He was convinced that he was doing a good job until parents from the faculty of the nearby university asked at an open house when he planned to give up his "progressive" ways and teach their kids some formal grammar. Some kids even asked when they would study sentence diagraming, a skill they apparently had been trained to see as functionally related to going to college and achieving the good life.

The author persisted in his approach and is still convinced that what was covered that year was immensely more beneficial to those kids than anything else he could have done, although not all the parents or students would agree with him. In fact, the expectations of some were probably unfulfilled.

Because teachers have a direct and immediate contact with the people of the community, the expectations of others are real and intimate, and conflicts among expectations are not abstract social phenomena. These conflicts may present challenges to the personal and professional identity of the teacher who is aware and sensitive. A teacher with strong personal convictions about his social and political responsibility is at immediate odds with those who hold equally strong convictions that the teacher should be a mute and passive servant of society and the board of education and demonstrably grateful for having been given the opportunity to teach.

A teacher can spend a great deal of time trying to mediate among conflicting demands in a pluralistic society without ever obtaining effective reconciliation or even understanding what approach should be taken. Needed change can go wanting in a system contented with its own achievements and heedless of any deficiencies. The loss of psychic energy is every bit as real and damaging as uneconomic use of physical or economic resources.

Before seeking an approach congruent with the pluralism in American society, let us examine several differing views of the relationship of the school to society. Abundant descriptions are to be found in the social philosophy of education (e.g., Taba, 1962; Bayles and Hood, 1966). For our purpose, we will focus on the way in which traditional belief systems have described the role of the classroom teacher.

Traditional Views of the Teacher's Social Function

From what we have suggested about the nature of American society, we can expect that at any given time there will be several differing, even contradictory, notions about the ends education should seek and the instructional means most appropriate to their achievement. The belief systems current in a given society are intellectually related to alternate philosophies of education and psychologies of teaching.

Among traditional views of the teacher's role are the following three:

1. *The teacher as preserver and transmitter of the cultural heritage.* Very much in the English preparatory-school tradition of Mr. Chips, teachers are frequently seen as custodians of knowledge and social tradition. The future is assured if what has proved valuable to preceding generations is transmitted in unaltered form and substance. The teacher is mandated by society to be the instrument of transmittal, obligated to be a master of the academic particularities of the subject and responsible for the student's mastery of it. Because the teacher with proper credentials represents the finest traditions of the discipline, because the teacher has demonstrated that he is intellectually disciplined, it is just and proper for him to insist on the student's unquestioning acceptance of the rigorous demands of the process. Anything less and the individual and the society

would become less able to maintain good order and form and less able to provide for social necessities.

2. *The teacher as an instrument of individual growth and development.* Because much of America's social experience has focused on working through adversity, even on deferring one's personal desires to enhance opportunities for those to follow, children have frequently been treated with benevolent concern. Society wants them to enjoy the advantages we labored to provide for them. Giving them the opportunity to grow and develop unhindered is both the fulfillment of the earlier generation's dreams and the expression of man's faith in the individual's ability to benefit from and progress toward even more desirable ends. All that is expected of the teacher is that he foster or nurture this growth in every possible way for every student in his charge.

3. *The teacher as an instrument of planned social change.* Many critics of current society insist that the good life can be obtained only if schools treat real or anticipated social problems in a much more deliberate manner. The school's program is the product of expert analyses of current social problems; curriculums are designed and engineered to correct social ills.

As an agent of society, the teacher is committed to work for these socially mandated goals. Deviation from the prescribed program by teacher or student—especially as a personal idiosyncrasy—would constitute a violation of the social ethic. Participants must recognize that the future of the society is at stake and accept social responsibility for their acts. The role of the teacher becomes primarily that of a blueprint reader and technician in this scheme of human engineering.

Were any one of these traditional views the consensus, some questions would be eliminated, and efforts could be focused on implementing the accepted plan. But the reality of the American social situation is that, after nearly two hundred years, *consensus does not exist.* Is consensus possible? Is it desirable? To answer these questions requires a realistic assessment of current sociocultural trends.

Current Sociocultural Trends

Change produces sociocultural disorientation. Modern man is experiencing the continuing effects of an energy revolution and a communication revolution. Access to nuclear sources has multiplied available energy far beyond man's concept of possible application. In much the same manner, access to computerized electronic language has increased our technical ability to communicate far beyond our conceptual ability. And if a person is confused about the present, he certainly is unable to cope with more ambiguity and uncertainty in the future. Man finds himself lost in what Higman (1969) has called "non-time, non-cultural *anomie*," a state of disorientation and anxiety.

Cultural traditions have decreasing value. Not only is man unable to cope adequately with the present situation, but his present culture also offers few guidelines or clues about how to deal with change. An accelerating rate of change makes the cultural future increasingly uncertain, and norms, values, and social conventions inherited from the past become increasingly inappropriate. Whereas the cultural heritage once supported man during the stress of change, its lack of relevance for an uncertain future does little to relieve man's anguish and cynicism.

The absence of certainty creates a fear of what could happen. Not only does cultural prediction become more speculative in the face of increasing change, but we become more sensitive to and threatened by the inadvertent consequences of technological change. We cannot even guess what might happen, yet we are fearful that any further change in the ecosystem will destroy what little balance is left. We are not satisfied with the vertical growth of cities, but we are even more opposed to urban sprawl. The products are distrust, demands, anxiety, and alienation.

Competing social action groups add to social complexity. Lack of certitude and predictability, accompanied by increasing anxiety and alienation, generates new social organizations, frequently several organizations attempting to deal with the same problems. Hence, in the face of an increasingly complex cultural future, one must cope with an increasingly complex and confused present.

The ability of society to create stability is diminished. One's personality develops through interaction with other members of his social group, in a process usually called socialization and acculturation. But if society and culture are undergoing fundamental changes, they lose their central focus and their ability to develop cultural personality. Even though society may feel an urgent need to help its members overcome alienation, for example, it may not be able to do so. The school as a social agency may recognize the need to promote autonomy in its students but, because of its present institutional state, may limit instead of encourage their potential for personal growth.

The resultant confusion of values and beliefs threatens the integration of the individual personality and the organization of the social group. Emerging alternative life styles may be more symptomatic of this unrest in values than representative of solutions that can endure in the face of continuing stress. The insistence of welfare recipients that they have certain "rights" has embroiled American society in ethical-legalistic argument over whether such "rights" exist, diverting us from the effort to remedy hunger and poverty. Society frequently attempts to adapt to the existence of undesirable social conditions rather than acting deliberately to eliminate their causes.

Changing conditions require a reinterpretation of the meaning of traditional values. In American society, where education for citizenship in a democratic sociopolitical order has become a tenet of government, continuing reinterpretation of the values and beliefs that undergird democracy is essential. The process of reinterpretation may be observed in the continuing controversies over gun control, wiretap evidence, due process, capital punishment, and abortion laws. Traditional notions of democratic values are no longer equal to the complexities at hand; in the face of an increasingly complex cultural future, *any* given pronouncement of traditional social democratic values has at best only passing merit.

A Modern View of the Teacher's Social Function

Current sociocultural trends suggest that teachers will find traditional views of their social function inadequate to meet the complexities of their situation. Teachers cannot assume that transmission of the cultural past in unaltered form will enable learners to meet new problems successfully. Teachers cannot assume that the complex problems of the future can be solved by individuals, even exceptionally well-developed individuals, acting alone. Nor can teachers believe that their foresight is so keen as to enable them to predict the latent problems their students may confront in an increasingly unpredictable future. A more comprehensive approach is required if learners are to develop the knowledge, attitudes, and skills required to cope with current sociocultural changes.

The following teaching tasks and functions can be derived directly from the foregoing considerations:

Teaching about Social Relationships

1. Teaching can reduce students' alienation from society by dealing directly with cultural ambiguity and by building conceptual bridges between the present and the future. To achieve this, teaching must be directed to the development of a concept of total man and total society as an integral relationship instead of pursuing notions that produce further fragmentation and separation.

The teacher helps the student to understand social realities, to assess his own social group, the society of the class and the school, by involving the student in an analysis of critical questions and problems before him. Students are encouraged to identify from experience examples of social-system difficulties, such as prejudice, denied rights, arbitrary behavior, and segregation. From subject-matter content, issues in economics, government, social welfare, and biology, for example, can be studied. Students are helped to realize that solutions are not always readily available and that continuing effort is required to solve social problems effectively. The teacher helps the student to identify conflicts in which the "facts" appear to be inconsistent with the accepted views, thus necessitating further investigation.

Through inquiry into identified issues, the teacher helps the student to understand himself as an individual in relation to society and to develop an awareness of his own potential. As a member of a group analyzing social realities, the student comes to recognize that he can contribute to group decision making, that a number of choices are available, and that there are really more questions to be answered than may be supplied by textbooks alone. The teacher deliberately encourages each student to consider novel means to bridge apparent cultural gaps, such as ways to coalesce minority views. He supports the student by providing additional information and suggestions for inquiry when the student is confronted by ambiguous data or circumstances, especially about himself and his social responsibilities. The teacher encourages investigation, trust, responsibility, cooperation, and respect in the classroom and thereby demonstrates to each student the positive value of individual efforts; to the teacher this serves as an effective means to help the student attain personal integrity.

2. The school's socializing function can be emphasized by helping students become increasingly competent in dealing with the realities of social change. To achieve this, teaching must broaden its role by deliberately incorporating life orientation, self-concept, and value learning into the curriculum.

The teacher asserts, rather than denies, that learning is personal to the individual students. By accepting responsibility for the socializing role of the school, the teacher creates the potential for open analysis of its socializing influences. The teacher helps the student to understand the socializing influences that affect him. He promotes the student's awareness of the values and beliefs he holds, why he has come to hold them, and the consequences toward which they tend. The teacher purposely initiates discussion on issues that are significant to the subject matter being studied. Emphasis is placed on the human values and viewpoints that provide the underlying rationale for decision making. Alternate solutions to an issue are not the teacher's main concern at this point; instead, serious study is undertaken to discover what social values, customs, and mores and what personal experiences contributed to the students' way of thinking. The teacher demonstrates the character of learning and the disciplines of knowledge in terms of man's efforts to cope with uncertainty and change. He exhibits positive regard for each student as a means to the development of self-concept. The teacher helps the learner to become aware of self and to develop greater personal competencies. He involves the student in the active examination of alternative values and the development of means to judge the appropriateness of values.

3. Because the society in which the student lives is changing at an increasing rate, his social relationships become increasingly complex and unpredictable. Teaching must foster a new conception of the dynamics of social relations if the school and the learner are to become effective social-change agents.

The teacher encourages consideration of a broad range of social phenomena. He promotes careful analysis of these phenomena toward an understanding of how social relations work. He seeks an appropriate balance in the consideration of one-to-one interpersonal relations and more formal intergroup and interorganizational functions. The teacher assists the learner to search for new conceptions of social relationships. He creates a setting in which alternate courses of social action may be proposed, examined, and evaluated openly and realistically. In this way he fosters development of the skills required in the analysis of social and cultural change. The teacher promotes awareness of the potential of the individual to act effectively for social change. The teacher encourages the student to accept responsibility for social change.

Teaching to Develop Social Competence

1. If it is becoming increasingly difficult to predict the nature and consequences of social changes, the emphasis of teaching must shift from the development of knowledge of current social conventions to the development of social competencies that will serve the individual over an extended time span.

The teacher emphasizes the development of skills that will enable the individual student to cope with problems of living in a rapidly changing world. He assists the student to utilize available knowledge and understandings and to assess realistically the functional value and limitation of available information. The teacher encourages development of intellectual ability, not as an end in itself, but as a functional means of dealing with increasingly complex problems. The teacher fosters development of skills of inquiry and discovery appropriate to the analysis of social phenomena. The teacher helps the student determine the relative potential of correct answers versus correct procedures (products vs. processes). The teacher assists the student in discriminating the crucial from the trivial and selecting appropriate points of inquiry.

2. The outcome of social progress is highly unpredictable, yet the individual is required to maintain a functional relationship to a changing system throughout his life. Teaching must emphasize development of the

individual's ability to think independently and the disposition to utilize this ability.

The teacher works to develop desired skills as the most functional way to influence the future. He assists the student in developing an adequate self-concept and realistic self-expectations and encourages increasingly independent thinking by individual students. The teacher freely grants the student responsibility for planning and carrying out learning efforts, supporting the student as he works to fulfill these responsibilities and promoting the establishment of criteria to judge progress toward independence. The teacher encourages the student to search beyond modes of adjustment and conformity and demonstrates belief in the functional value of other modes of action. The teacher helps the student attempt experimental approaches, providing assistance and guidance only when necessary. The teacher helps the student develop an increasing sense of competency and encourages him to undertake problems of increasing complexity.

3. A social structure capable of dealing with increasingly complex problems must be developed. Teaching must emphasize the creation of organizational skills that enable individuals to focus their unique personal competencies on the achievement of collective goals.

The teacher helps the student recognize the degree to which human variables are involved in problems of social organization. He assists the student in developing appropriate skills in working with human variables that are largely nonobjective and helps to clarify individual goals, collective goals, and the interrelatedness of many goals. The teacher demonstrates group processes that protect, maintain, and encourage individual autonomy, encouraging the student to pursue personal motives through collective processes. The teacher provides opportunities for resolution of intrapersonal conflicts, helps individual students to develop skills in group participation and leadership, and demonstrates the value of focusing differing individual competencies on collective purpose. The teacher helps the student to see social organization as an ongoing, progressive process capable of innovation and increasing productivity.

Teaching to Develop Social Values

1. Confusion among personal values and beliefs prevents the development of an integrated personality, and confusion among social values and beliefs creates inter- and intragroup conflicts. The teacher must act deliberately to facilitate the individual's development and clarification of personal and social values appropriate to the demands of a changing society.

The teacher helps the student to identify and cope with his sensitivities.

The teacher helps the student to understand how values are learned and to understand, clarify, and resolve internal and interpersonal value conflicts. The teacher fosters the development of skills that enable the student to make more rational and defensible value choices, at the same time helping him to become more sensitive to the values of others. By demonstrating a willingness to consider alternative values, the teacher encourages reflective consideration of value conflicts as a means of making the valuing process conscious, rationally defensible, and more effective.

2. A continuing reinterpretation of democratic values and beliefs is essential to the survival of this form of social organization in the face of profound social change. Education has been given the responsibility for the preparation of effective citizens, and teaching must take an active role in reexamining and verifying these values and beliefs.

The teacher assists the student in analyzing the democratic process. The teacher facilitates identification of the values that undergird democracy, promotes understanding of the relationship of democratic values to democratic goals, and demonstrates the functional value of democratic processes. The teacher develops students' abilities to utilize democratic processes effectively. He helps students to determine issues arising from application of democratic principles to changing social conditions. The teacher encourages critical analysis and reinterpretation of democratic beliefs and values, demonstrating the ability of democratic processes to adapt to changing social values and beliefs. He also fosters commitment to demonstrated values.

Conclusions

The preceding analysis gives unmistakable indication of the complexity and scale of what is happening in American society today, and what needs to be done. We have heard teachers acknowledge that sociocultural conflict is a problem—even a crucial problem—but they don't think they should be expected to do anything about it. Some will assert that there simply isn't enough time; others will insist that they were hired to teach math or science, not to be concerned about other matters.

We see no reason to apologize for making a different assertion, because the facts of the situation seem to speak for themselves. *Because of the unique function of schools in a democratic society, each teacher in each subject area has an undeniable social responsibility.* Achievement of this responsibility is not possible without a significant reordering of teaching priorities. Admittedly, this is more fundamental than introducing a new set of "innovative" gimmicks or curricular materials.

Our sociocultural belief systems and their implications for teaching suggest certain basic concepts about the individual, whether teacher or student. First, it probably is not feasible to regard the individual as a discrete, singular, functioning organism. A more meaningful approach is to regard him as a fairly complex system of differing dynamic forces. Human beings are more than the sum total of their physiological and psychological components. It is difficult to explain the values and beliefs an individual holds, for example, without considering the variables that affected his development of these values and beliefs. True, we can assess the values *now,* but this does not help us to predict how they will affect what he does.

Second, our analysis suggests that we can better understand the person in the context of the social and cultural forces that act upon him, his relationship with these variables, his sociocultural history, and his relationship with this historical past.

Significant here is the individual's anticipation of what his future might be like and the effect this has on how he goes about preparing for the future. If we know what's on our appointment calendar for tomorrow, we can use today effectively to get ready for anticipated events. Even if some of the events seem unpleasant, we can go forward prepared to meet our doom. When we find ourselves with no way of knowing what to expect, our activity becomes confused, random, pointless, and frenetic.

REFERENCES

Bayles, Ernest E., and Bruce L. Hood. *Growth of American Educational Thought and Practice.* New York: Harper & Row, 1966.

Higman, Howard. "The Alienated in Education: A Sociological View." *Colorado Journal of Educational Research* 8, no. 3 (Spring 1969).

Taba, Hilda. *Curriculum Development: Theory and Practice.* New York: Harcourt, Brace & World, 1962.

Suggested Readings

Bayles, Ernest E. *Pragmatism in Education.* New York: Harper & Row, 1966.

First describes the psychological and philosophical rationale for reflective teaching and learning. The last chapter contains excellent illustrations of reflective-inquiry teaching episodes.

Brown, Bob B. *The Experimental Mind in Education.* New York: Harper & Row, 1968.

Presents an experimental approach to education, based on John Dewey's philosophy. Includes a guide for teacher (or self-) observation.

Brown, George. *Human Teaching for Human Learning: An Introduction to Confluent Education.* New York: Viking, 1971.

Contains examples of classroom applications of affective techniques with personal commentaries by the teachers involved. Filled with practical ideas for teachers who wish to experiment with merging cognitive and affective experiences.

Combs, Arthur, ed. *Perceiving, Behaving and Becoming.* Washington, D.C.: Association for Supervision and Curriculum Development, 1962.

A series of articles by the leading educational theorists on perception, self-concept, and self-actualization. Included are statements by Carl Rogers, Abraham Maslow, and Earl Kelley.

————, Donald L. Avila, and William B. Perkey. *Helping Relationships: Basic Concepts for the Helping Professions.* Boston: Allyn & Bacon, 1971.

Describes the various roles and attitudes essential to the helping professions. Emphasis is on exploring the meaning and growth of self-concept, motives, freedom, purposes, understanding, communication, and helping.

Gorman, Alfred H. *Teachers and Learners: The Interactive Process of Education.* Boston: Allyn & Bacon, 1969.

One of the best books for classroom teachers on human communication. Contains a minimum of theory, with the emphasis on application.

Hullfish, Gordon, and Philip Smith. *Reflective Thinking: The Method of Education.* New York: Dodd, Mead, 1961.

The authors stress the importance of the teacher as the prime mover in advancing learning and advocate a teaching process patterned on developing citizens who are free and independent thinkers. Essential reading for understanding the theoretical bases of reflective thinking and teaching.

Hunt, Maurice P., and Laurence E. Metcalf. *Teaching High School Social Studies.* 2d ed. New York: Harper & Row, 1968.

A thorough discussion of reflective-inquiry teaching theory and procedure, with numerous examples of conflict in social-studies content and models of teaching strategies applicable to these investigations.

Hunter, Elizabeth. *Encounter in the Classroom: New Ways of Teaching.* New York: Holt, Rinehart & Winston, 1972.

A valuable book that provides numerous activities to increase student involvement with learning and suggestions to improve classroom discussions, question asking, and work with others.

Kohl, Herbert R. *The Open Classroom: A Practical Guide to a New Way of Teaching.* New York: Vintage, 1969.

A delightful paperback describing how to humanize lesson plans, deal with discipline problems, and communicate with parents, teachers, and principals.

Maslow, Abraham. *Toward a Psychology of Being.* Princeton, N.J.: D. Van Nostrand, 1962.

Must be read if one is to understand the concepts of humanistic and affective education. Maslow has been said to be an influence in psychology equal to Freud.

Massialas, Byron, and Jack Zevin. *Creative Encounters in the Classroom: Teaching and Learning through Discovery.* New York: Wiley, 1967.

Provides a rationale for inquiry in the classroom and presents sample episodes showing the application of analytical, discovery, and valuing processes to content in the social studies.

Metcalf, Lawrence, ed. *Values Education.* 41st Yearbook of the National Council for the Social Studies. Washington, D.C.: The Council, 1971.

An excellent paperback outlining the objectives of value analysis, procedures for resolving value conflict, and a model of a programmed text on valuing.

Otto, Herbert, and John Mann, eds. *Ways of Growth.* New York: Viking, 1969.

Selected readings dealing with expanded states of human consciousness such as awareness through breathing, smell, touch, relaxation, group therapy, dreams, and meditation.

Pfeiffer, J. William, and John Jones. *Structured Experiences for Human Relations Training.* Vols. I, II, III. Iowa City, Iowa: University Associates Press, 1970.

A series of handbooks designed to provide a repertoire of ideas and exercises for human-relations workers. Some exercises are ideal for classroom teachers in any subject area.

Postman, Neil, and Charles Weingartner. *Teaching as a Subversive Activity.* New York: Delacorte, 1969.

One of the early books critical of traditional education. The authors suggest means of helping students "learn how to learn."

Raths, Louis E., Merrill Harmin, and Sidney B. Simon. *Values and Teaching: Working with Values in the Classroom.* Columbus, Ohio: Merrill, 1966.

Outlines a theory of values and a classroom methodology for the clarification of values. Has many practical activities that teachers can employ to help students clarify their values.

Rogers, Carl. *Freedom to Learn.* Columbus, Ohio: Merrill, 1969.

An excellent book which explains in considerable detail how classrooms should be organized to free students to learn. Rogers clearly points the direction of education in the years to come.

Schmuck, Richard, and Patricia Schmuck. *Group Processes in the Classroom.* Dubuque, Iowa: Wm. C. Brown, 1971.

Discusses the basic concepts of group dynamics, leadership training, communications, and development of group cohesiveness. Each chapter also presents suggestions that can be applied by the reader.

Schrank, Jeffrey. *Teaching Human Beings: 101 Subversive Activities for the Classroom.* Boston: Beacon Press, 1972.

Suggests innovative uses of a wide variety of multimedia materials, including games, encounters, and unique uses of books and films.

Scobey, Mary-Margaret, and Grace Graham, eds. *To Nurture Humaneness: Commitment for the '70's.* Washington, D.C.: Association for Supervision and Curriculum Development, 1970.

An analysis by many authors of what it means to be human, with implications and imperatives for education.

Simon, Sidney, et al. *Values Clarification: A Handbook of Practical Strategies for Teachers and Students.* New York: Hart, 1972.

A valuable book describing strategies for making students more aware of their own feelings, ideas, and beliefs, so that they might make more conscious and deliberate choices based on their own value system.

Simpson, Elizabeth L. *Democracy's Stepchildren*. San Francisco: Jossey-Bass, 1971.

Examines the relationship between basic human needs and attitudes, values, motivation, and behavior. What this relationship means for teachers and democratic education is discussed, and the elements leading toward democratic socialization identified.

Torrance, E. Paul. *Encouraging Creativity in the Classroom*. Dubuque, Iowa: Wm. C. Brown, 1970.

Suggests ways of encouraging creativity in students, building creative skills, heightening anticipation, and going beyond textbooks to stimulate learning.

Weinstein, Gerald, and Mario D. Fantini. *Toward Humanistic Education: A Curriculum of Affect*. New York: Praeger, 1970.

Describes innovations in affective education at the elementary and secondary levels.

CHAPTER 5
Readings on Sociocultural Foundations

Our review of the cultural foundations of education indicates at least three significant influences on how a teacher approaches his work: (1) his view of the basic nature of man, (2) the attitude toward students imposed by this view, and (3) the effect of societal beliefs on his individual teaching.

A dominant influence on schools continues to be the image of education as an institution for transmitting cultural and factual information in carefully prescribed packages. We have suggested that the school recommit itself to the values of democracy, encouraging the personal growth of students and teachers through reflective considerations of issues significant to them and to society.

The articles in this chapter elaborate on the dichotomies in our culture and also suggest alternative means to reevaluate the issues and possibly overcome the conflicts.

Before one can determine the degree to which schools are democratic, asserts Lynn Weldon, of Adams State College, Alamosa, Colorado, some standards must be established. Weldon considers such major "yardsticks" as governmental and cultural viewpoints, learning theory, levels of thinking, student abilities, academic freedom, teacher role, curriculum, and measures of evaluation. He finds that schools and teachers employ undemocratic means, and so regularly that this brand of pseudodemocracy assumes acceptance as a social model.

The idea of freedom is an essential underpinning of the concept of democracy. At least two descriptions of freedom are popular among educators. Carl Rogers examines both interpretations in his article "Freedom and Commitment." The behavioral view presents man as the product of external conditioning forces; thus man is not free. The humanist position views man as capable of making meaningful choices that grant freedom. The structure of teaching and learning in the classroom emerges from these views of freedom. The implications of each position are clear in the article. Is man free?

In Chapter 3 we described the increasing influence of economics on education. The view that man is motivated toward material acquisition becomes the rationale for renewed emphasis on government support for career education at all levels in the public school. So state Robert Nash and Russell Agne, both of the University of Vermont. They review the justification for career education advanced by the U.S. Office of Education and selected schools in the country. What is clearly questionable, they suggest, is the government advocacy of a model that has not yet critically examined the human elements affected by this proposal. Possible fallacies of career education are whether acquisition needs are basic to human motivation and the validity of the learning rationale on which the model is based. The article constantly reminds us of the need to place enhancement of man foremost among our goals, and asks whether this can best be accomplished through "power, profit, or prestige."

People continue to view the public school as the only institution capable of solving the domestic problems facing society. As the influences of the family and the church decline, the school is required to teach additional topics and to correct social ills. Many educators feel that the school is already overburdened, what with vocational education, sex education, and driver's education. During the 1960s reformers believed that the schools could be used to reduce racism and socioeconomic inequalities, as well as attack another growing social and human concern—sexism.

The school, like the larger society, reinforces the inferior status of women. Janice Trecker, a former secondary school teacher currently serving on the Organization of American Historians' Committee on the Status of Women in the Profession, discusses how the schools contribute to this sexist attitude, examining selected areas of the curriculum—vocational training courses, textbooks, physical and athletic programs, and teacher-administration—that discriminate against women. Removal of sexism in education not only requires revision of textbook content, but demands that teachers and administrators change their thinking about sex-biased curriculum. The secondary school curriculum, insists Ms. Trecker, is masculine.

To help develop "a new society," it was thought that the school should provide more and higher-quality education for all. Numerous projects and programs were established and funded with public monies to provide a head start and equal opportunity. But after extensive research, Mary Jo Bane, of the Center for Educational Policy Research, Harvard University, and Christopher Jencks, professor of education at Harvard University, conclude that these projects have been of little real benefit in raising either test scores or success levels. They explain their findings clearly and suggest future social and educational policies based upon the concept of socialism.

Instead of merely providing a list of the democratic goals for education, Ernest Bayles, now retired from the University of Kansas, provides some suggestions for translating that purpose into an instructional strategy. In addition to presenting a plan to make both teaching and learning more democratic, he introduces the "democratic-reflective" method of education. It becomes evident that democratic education involves the individual in a personal search for meaningful data to help him understand his concerns. What this means for enhanced teaching becomes clearer when one reflects on the esssential elements in democracy. If teaching is to be democratic, the teacher must have a democratic attitude toward people and must employ teaching methods that are extensions of the characteristics of democracy—involvement, meaningful participation, respect, responsibility, and authenticity. It is the teacher's obligation to sensitize students. Democracy cannot be taught; it must be experienced.

Are Our Schools Democratic?
Lynn L. Weldon

In order to determine whether or not, or to what degree, our schools are democratic, we must have some bases for judgment. We need standards, criteria, scales, gauges, or yardsticks against which current educational practices may be measured. I would like to suggest some yardsticks which might be used. The yardsticks are meant to indicate emphases, not totally isolated categories. The yardsticks do not and cannot mirror the complexities of actual educational practices, so I am open to the charge of overgeneralizing. My defense is that the yardsticks are not designed to be descriptions of actual practices, but standards against which such practices may be measured.

I. Governmental Yardsticks

A. *Totalitarian Processes.* Totalitarian governmental processes go by many labels, such as autocracy, dictatorship, totalitarianism, authoritari-

Paper delivered at Rocky Mountain Conference on Educational Foundations, University of Wyoming, December 9–10, 1966; reprinted by permission of the author.

anism, etc., but they all have one basic trait: opportunity to participate in the decision-making process is unequal. Specially privileged individuals or groups determine what the total population will do. It is the task of the masses to conform to and accept the decisions handed down to them. By implication, an educational system consistent with such totalitarian processes would be one which fostered conformity to and unquestioning acceptance of the values held by those in power. Emphasis is on unquestioning obedience to authority and acceptance of established institutions and values.

B. *Anarchistic Process.* Anarchy is an individualistic governmental process emphasizing individual freedom and liberty to govern oneself as desired. No binding group decisions are made. Each person may do as he pleases, a law unto himself. If so inclined, he may cooperate in group actions, but he is not required to abide by group decisions. By implication, an anarchistic educational system would emphasize student-centered permissiveness. Student individual freedom and liberty would be central.

C. *Democratic Process.* The democratic governmental process is a group governing process in which all members of society have equal opportunity to participate in determining the regulations under which they operate. Since it is assumed that no group has a monopoly on truth and that the masses are competent to govern themselves, the ability to question, examine, and evaluate alternative courses of action is of central value. By implication, instead of either indoctrinating specially privileged values, or fostering student abilities to do as they please, democratic schools should foster the ability to analyze alternative courses of action.

II. Cultural Yardsticks

A. *Perennialism (Regressivism).* Perennialists would go back to the eternal truths ("Great Ideas") of the classical cultures and would inculcate these specially privileged truths into students.

B. *Essentialism (Conservatism).* Essentialists would preserve, conserve, and transmit the essential enduring truths of our American heritage, such as free enterprise and rugged individualism, through indoctrination of these specially privileged values into all American youth.

C. *Progressivism (Liberalism).* Liberals emphasize gradual modification of the present culture. They believe in tolerance and open-mindedness. The Progressive education movement found support among many liberals. Progressivists foster student freedom to follow their own impulses in carrying out individual projects and activities.

D. *Reconstructionism (Radicalism).* Reconstructionists believe that a radical cultural upheaval, fostered through the indoctrination of collectivism in the public schools, will usher in an inevitable socialistic future-centered "new" social order.

E. *Analysis (Reflection)*. Analysts would set up, perpetuate, and change the culture on the basis of reflective analyses of cultural problems.

III. Learning Theory Yardsticks

A. *Stimulus-Response (Behaviorism)*. Behaviorists emphasize stimulus-response learning of right answers (responses) through conditioning or reinforcement by repetition or drill. A contemporary example is B. F. Skinner's concept of operant conditioning, which is the rationale for most linear programs.

B. *Cognitive-Field (Gestalt)*. Gestalt psychologists emphasize learning as a change in insight or in cognitive structure. Insightful learning is central to the reflective process of "sizing up" problem situations, in analyzing what actions would seem to lead most efficiently to recognized goals.

IV. Levels of Thinking Yardsticks

A. *Memory-Level*. Memory-level thinking is based on sheer recall. Right answers are recalled in their original form. Right facts or concepts are restated exactly as they were memorized.

B. *Understanding-Level*. General concepts or principles are understood, particularly in terms of their applications to situations not previously experienced. Recognition of the general import of a situation allows previous understandings to be brought to bear through appropriate actions.

C. *Reflective-Level*. Reflective-level thinking is based on attempts to develop meanings in problem situations, situations so novel that the person must pause and "think it over." Meanings are sought and pondered. Reflective-level thinking is a process of formulating meanings in situations in which meanings are not immediately clear.

V. Student Abilities Yardsticks

A. *Conclusion-Centered Abilities*. Students are to develop abilities to absorb, accept, and apply the authoritarian predetermined conclusions (right answers) transmitted to them.

B. *Student-Centered Abilities*. Students develop abilities to foster their own individually unique capacities, interests, and concerns. Each student is to develop abilities to satisfy his own spontaneous needs and desires.

C. *Analysis-Centered Abilities.* Students develop abilities to examine existing and potential problem conclusions. They are to learn how to arrive at the tentative problem solutions most warranted by available evidence.

VI. Academic Freedom Yardsticks

A. *Autocratic Academic Freedom.* Teachers are free only to indicate generally accepted truths and values. Students are free to be indoctrinated with "sound" facts and concepts.

B. *Anarchistic Academic Freedom.* Advocates of this permissive type of academic freedom appear to believe that teachers should have total freedom and liberty to teach whatever they please in any way they please. Students would be free to learn, if they please, whatever and whenever they please.

C. *Reflective Academic Freedom.* Teachers and students are free only to carry out the problem analysis method of modern science.

VII. Teacher Role Yardsticks

A. *Imposition.* Teachers impose, transmit, or hand out correct facts and concepts.

B. *Permissive.* Teachers are resource specialists assisting students to carry out whatever projects or activities the students desire.

C. *Analysis.* Teachers stimulate student investigations and explorations in raising and solving significant problems.

VIII. Curriculum Yardsticks

A. *Autocratic Curriculums.* Authoritarian curriculums are composed of specially privileged right answers. These right answers usually are organized in textbook chapters or in units, and often exhibit this form: (1) Statement of concepts (right answers) to be learned (often labeled as "Unit Objectives"). (2) Main body of facts to be assimilated. (3) Activities to foster learning of the correct facts and concepts. (4) Test questions to be used in determining whether or not the students have absorbed the right answers. An effective modification of this authoritarian curriculum is the Skinnerian linear program of right answers carefully sequenced in small steps.

B. *Student-Centered Curriculums.* In Progressive schools, the curriculum is determined by the spontaneous felt needs and interests of the individual student. In essence, each student determines his own curriculum. He purposes, plans, executes, and judges whatever projects or activities he desires.

C. *Problem-Centered Curriculums.* Since, in democratic schools, students are to develop analytical abilities to deal with appropriate problems or conflicts, it is fairly evident that the core of democratic curriculums would be problems or conflicts. Curricular materials and activities for raising and solving problems generally fall into these analytical steps: (1) Becoming aware of the problem. (2) Setting up hypothetical problem solutions. (3) Determining criteria or standards for choice between solutions. (4) Testing alternative solutions on the bases of the criteria. There are no specially privileged right answers or problem solutions, since all solutions, whether presented by teachers or students, have equal opportunity to be presented and then to be tested on the bases of accepted criteria. Solutions must stand or fall on their own merits, after critical analyses of available alternatives.

IX. Testing Yardsticks

A. *Totalitarian Testing.* Students are tested to see whether or not they have memorized and can hand back (recall) the right answers transmitted to them. During such "closed book" tests, student use of class notes, textbooks, or other sources of information is strictly taboo.

B. *Anarchistic Testing.* Students evaluate their projects, if they desire.

C. *Democratic Testing.* Students are confronted with problem situations which are so novel that they must stop and think. The adequacy of the ways students attempt to solve the problems is evaluated. Since students are to be tested not on their abilities to memorize right answers, but on their abilities to raise and solve problems, testing is "open book." Students are free to use any information, materials, and activities needed to demonstrate their reflective abilities.

X. Cheating Yardsticks

A. *Totalitarian Cheating.* Students hide and use basic information, instead of memorizing and recalling it.

B. *Reflective Cheating.* The problem-raising and -solving accomplishments of others are presented as the student's own.

In Conclusion

Most teachers I know appear to me to foster the totalitarian governmental process in their classrooms by: (1) Emphasizing unquestioning obedience to authority. (2) Adopting the essentialistic or conservative cultural position of transmitting generally accepted truths. (3) Using the psychological process of conditioning or reinforcement almost exclusively. (4) Fostering student thinking on the recall or memory level. (5) Emphasizing student abilities to absorb predetermined specially privileged conclusions. (6) Conforming to the principles of autocratic academic freedom. (7) Accepting the teacher role of imposing or handing out correct facts and concepts, particularly through lectures. (8) Transmitting autocratic right answer curriculums. (9) Testing for memorization of right answers by giving "closed book" tests. (10) Branding unauthorized student use of basic information as "cheating."

Every article I have ever read which dealt with cheating labeled student use of unauthorized basic information as "cheating." Student use of such information could be branded as "cheating" only by authoritarian teachers. To me, my past experiences with teachers and the articles on cheating are hints, perhaps even broad hints, that most teachers are using totalitarian teaching and testing procedures. It appears that most teachers teach what, not how, to think. They apparently follow the dictum that "Some people are born with the ability to think. A major task of the schools is to eliminate that ability." Since most teaching practices do not seem to fit our frequently stated "democratic" national objectives, I believe that most teachers are thwarting the reflective abilities needed in a democratic society.

Are our schools democratic?

Freedom and Commitment
Carl Rogers

One of the deepest issues in modern life, in modern man, is the question as to whether the concept of personal freedom has any meaning whatso-

This article first appeared in *The Humanist*, 1964, 24, no. 2, and is reprinted by permission of the author and the publisher.

ever in our present day scientific world. The growing ability of the behavioral scientist to predict and to control behavior has brought the issue sharply to the fore. If we accept the logical positivism and strictly behavioristic emphases which are predominant in the American psychological scene, there is not even room for discussion. The title of this article is then completely without meaning.

But if we step outside the narrowness of the behavioral sciences, this question is not only an issue, it is one of the primary issues which define modern man. . . . The issues of personal freedom and personal commitment have become very sharp indeed in a world in which man feels unsupported by a supernatural religion, and experiences keenly the division between his awareness and those elements of his dynamic functioning of which he is unaware. If he is to wrest any meaning from a universe which for all he knows may be indifferent, he must arrive at some stance which he can hold in regard to these timeless uncertainties.

So, writing as both a behavioral scientist and as one profoundly concerned with the human, the personal, the phenomenological, and the intangible, I should like to contribute what I can to this continuing dialogue regarding the meaning of and the possibility of freedom.

Man Is Unfree

Let me explain, first of all, that to most psychologists and workers in the behavioral sciences, the title of this article would seem very strange indeed. In the minds of most behavioral scientists, man is not free, nor can he as a free man commit himself to some purpose, since he is controlled by factors outside of himself. Therefore, neither freedom nor commitment is even a possible concept to modern behavioral science as it is usually understood.

To show that I am not exaggerating, let me quote a statement from Dr. B. F. Skinner of Harvard, who is one of the most consistent advocates of a strictly behavioristic psychology. He says:

> The hypothesis that man is not free is essential to the application of scientific method to the study of human behavior. The free inner man who is held responsible for his behavior is only a prescientific substitute for the kinds of causes which are discovered in the course of scientific analysis. All these alternative causes lie *outside* the individual (1953: 477).

This view is shared by many psychologists and others who feel, as does Dr. Skinner, that all the effective causes of behavior lie outside of the individual and that it is only through the external stimulus that behavior takes place. The scientific description of behavior avoids anything that partakes in any way of freedom. For example, Dr. Skinner (1964:90–91) describes an experiment in which a pigeon was conditioned to turn in a clockwise direction. The behavior of the pigeon was "shaped up" by rewarding any movement that approximated a clockwise turn until, increasingly, the bird was turning round and round in a steady movement. This is what is known as operant conditioning. Students who had watched the demonstration were asked to write an account of what they had seen. Their responses included the following ideas: that the pigeon was conditioned to *expect* reinforcement for the right kind of behavior; that the pigeon *hoped* that something would bring the food back again; that the pigeon *observed* that a certain behavior seemed to produce a particular result; that the pigeon *felt* that food would be given it because of its action; that the bird came to *associate* his action with the click of the food dispenser. Skinner ridicules these statements because they all go beyond the observed behavior in using such words as *expect, hope, observe, feel,* and *associate.* The whole explanation from his point of view is that the bird was reinforced when it emitted a given kind of behavior; the pigeon walked around until the food container again appeared; a certain behavior produced a given result; food was given to the pigeon when it acted in a given way; and the click of the food dispenser was related in time to the bird's action. These statements describe the pigeon's behavior from a scientific point of view.

Skinner goes on to point out that the students were undoubtedly reporting what they would have expected, felt, and hoped under similar circumstances. But he then makes the case that there is no more reality to such ideas in the human being than there is in the pigeon, that it is only because such words have been reinforced by the verbal community in which the individual has developed, that such terms are used. He discusses the fact that the verbal community which conditioned them to use such terms saw no more of their behavior than they had seen of the pigeon's. In other words the internal events, if they indeed exist, have no scientific significance.

As to the methods used for changing the behavior of the pigeon, many people besides Dr. Skinner feel that through such positive reinforcement human behavior as well as animal behavior can be "shaped up" and controlled. In his book, *Walden Two,* Skinner says:

> Now that we know how positive reinforcement works and how negative doesn't, we can be more deliberate and hence more successful in our cultural design. We can achieve a sort of control under which the controlled, though they are following a code much more scrupulously than was ever the case under the old system, nevertheless *feel free.* They are doing what they want to do, not what they are forced to do. That's the source of the tremendous power of positive reinforcement—there is no restraint and no revolt. By a careful cultural design we control not the final behavior but the *inclination* to behave—the motives, the desires,

the wishes. The curious thing is that in that case *the question of freedom never arises* (1948:218).

Another psychological experiment done by Dr. Richard Crutchfield at Berkeley (1955), again illustrates a way in which behavior may be controlled, in which it appears the individual is unfree. In this experiment five subjects at a time are seated side by side, each in an individual booth screened from one another. Each booth has a panel with various switches and lights. The subject can use the switches to signal his judgments on items that are projected on the wall in front of the group. The lights are signal lights which indicate what judgments the other four members are giving to the items. The subjects are told that they will be given identifying letters A, B, C, D, and E and are instructed to respond one at a time in that order. However, when they enter the cubicles, each discovers that he is letter E. They are not permitted to talk during the session.

Actually the lights in each booth are controlled by the experimenter and do not express the judgments of the other four members. Thus on those critical items where the experimenter wishes to impose group pressure, he can make it appear that all four members, A through D, agree on an answer which is clearly at variance with the correct answer. In this way each subject is confronted with a conflict between his own judgment and what he believes to be the consensus of the group. Thus, for example, the question may be, "Which of these two irregular figures is larger, X or Y?" The individual sees clearly that X is larger than Y, yet one after another the lights flash on indicating that all of the other four members regard Y as being the larger figure. Now it is his turn to decide. How will he respond? Which switch will he press? Crutchfield has shown that given the right conditions almost everyone will desert the evidence of his senses or his own honest opinion and conform to the seeming consensus of the group. For example, some high-level mathematicians yielded to the false group consensus on some fairly easy arithmetic problems, giving wrong answers that they would never have given under normal circumstances.

I think it is clear from all of this that man is a machine—a complex machine, to be sure, but one which is increasingly subject to scientific control. Whether behavior will be managed through operant conditioning as in *Walden Two* or whether we will be "shaped up" by the unplanned forms of conditioning implied in social pressure, or whether we will be controlled by electrodes in the brain, it seems quite clear that science is making out of man an object and that the purpose of such science is not only understanding and prediction but control. Thus it would seem to be quite clear that there could be no concept so foreign to the facts as that man is free. Man is a machine, man is unfree, man cannot commit himself in any meaningful sense; he is simply controlled by planned or unplanned forces outside of himself.

Man Is Free

I am impressed by the scientific advances illustrated in the examples I have given. I regard them as a great tribute to the ingenuity, insight, and persistence of the individuals making the investigations. They have added enormously to our knowledge. Yet for me they leave something very important unsaid. Let me try to illustrate this, first from my experience in therapy.

I think of a young man classed as schizophrenic with whom I had been working for a long time in a state hospital. He was a very inarticulate man, and during one hour he made a few remarks about individuals who had recently left the hospital; then he remained silent for almost forty minutes. When he got up to go, he mumbled almost under his breath, "If some of *them* can do it, maybe I can too." That was all—not a dramatic statement, not uttered with force and vigor, yet a statement of choice by this young man to work toward his own improvement and eventual release from the hospital. It is not too surprising that about eight months after that statement he was out of the hospital. I believe this experience of responsible choice is one of the deepest aspects of psychotherapy and one of the elements which most solidly underlies personality change.

I think of another young person, this time a young woman graduate student, who was deeply disturbed and on the borderline of a psychotic break. Yet after a number of interviews in which she talked very critically about all of the people who had failed to give her what she needed, she finally concluded: "Well, with that sort of foundation, it's really up to *me*. I mean it seems to be really apparent to me that I can't depend on someone else to *give* me an education." And then she added very softly: "I'll really have to get it myself." She goes on to explore this experience of important and responsible choice. She finds it a frightening experience, and yet one which gives her a feeling of strength. A force seems to surge up within her which is big and strong, and yet she also feels very much alone and sort of cut off from support. She adds: "I am going to begin to do more things that I know I should do." And she did.

I could add many other examples. One young fellow talking about the way in which his whole life had been distorted and spoiled by his parents finally comes to the conclusion that, "Maybe now that I *see* that, it's up to *me*."

Let me spell out a trifle more fully the way such choosings occur in therapy. An immature, highly religious sixteen-year-old high school girl, brought up in a very strict family, had rather obviously been patterning herself upon a masculine ideal of work and scholarly achievements which was almost certainly beyond her abilities. The previous year she had had a "nervous breakdown" which overwhelmed her. Some months after her break, she came to me for help. To take just one theme of the many which she pursued through the interviews, I will focus on her views about being a woman, as quite fully reported in my notes. During the early interviews she made it clear that she disliked children, that she did not wish marriage, that she wished she were a man, or could act like a man. These feelings were accepted.

Later on she says, "I admire masculine qualities so much that I wish I could be a man. Maybe somebody ought to set me straight and show me that I could be a fine young woman." This more ambivalent attitude was again accepted as being her own.

Two interviews later she talks about her dislike for small children but adds thoughtfully, "Maybe my dislike has been more or less forced. Maybe I just thought I'd be that way."

In a later interview she talks rather freely of her fear of childbirth, her fear that marriage would interfere with a career, saying that she is still mixed up on all these issues, showing very definite ambivalence.

In one of the closing interviews she says, "You know I've thought about that femininity thing again and I'm going to see if I can put it into words. I'm a girl. I'm going to accept it, not as fate, not in a spirit of submission, but as meant for the best. I can probably do a lot more good by being myself and developing my own talent rather than trying to do something different. I'm going to accept it as a challenge. I feel that I've almost lost that feeling that I wanted to be masculine. I just want to be myself. Maybe before I get through I'll really be glad I'm feminine. I'm going to learn to cook and be a good cook and make an art out of it."

Here again we see a slowly growing experience of personal choice which appeared to be basic to all of the change in personality and behavior which occurred. She chose, freely, to perceive herself in a different way, and out of that different perception there flowed many changes in attitude and behavior.

Or perhaps I could somehow communicate best the significance of free and responsible choice by quoting one sentence from a confused, bitter, psychotic individual who had been in a state hospital for three admissions, the last admission having lasted two and one-half years at the time I began working with him. I think the changes which gradually took place were based on and epitomized by one sentence in one of his interviews when he was feeling particularly confused. He said, "I don't know *what* I'm gonna do; but *I'm* gonna do it." For me, that speaks volumes.

For those of you who have seen the film *David and Lisa* . . . I can illustrate exactly what I have been discussing. David, the adolescent schizophrenic, goes into a panic if he is touched by anyone. He feels that "touching kills," and he is deathly afraid of it, and afraid of the closeness in human relationships which touching implies. Yet toward the close of the film he makes a bold and positive choice of the kind I have been describing. He has been trying to be of help to Lisa, the girl who is out of touch with reality. He tries to help at first in an intellectually contemptuous way, then increasingly in a warmer and more personal way. Finally, in a highly dramatic moment, he says to her, "Lisa, take my hand." He *chooses,* with obvious conflict and fear, to leave behind the safety of his untouchableness, and to venture into the world of real human relationships where he is literally and figuratively in *touch* with another. You are an unusual person if the film does not grow a bit misty at this point.

Perhaps a behaviorist could try to account for the reaching out of his hand by saying that it was the result of intermittent reinforcement of partial movements. I find such an explanation both inaccurate and inadequate. It is the *meaning* of the *decision* which is essential to understanding the act.

What I am trying to suggest in all of this is that I would be at a loss to explain the positive change which can occur in psychotherapy if I had to omit the importance of the sense of free and responsible choice on the part of my clients. I believe that this experience of freedom to choose is one of the deepest elements underlying change.

The Meaning of Freedom

Considering the scientific advances which I have mentioned, how can we even speak of freedom? In what sense is a client free? In what sense are any of us free? What possible definition of freedom can there be in the modern world? Let me attempt such a definition.

In the first place, the freedom that I am talking about is essentially an inner thing, something which exists in the living person quite aside from any of the outward choices of alternatives which we so often think of as constituting freedom. I am speaking of the kind of freedom which Viktor Frankl vividly describes in his experience of the concentration camp, when everything—possessions, status, identity—was taken from the prisoners. But even months and years in such an environment showed only "that everything can be taken from a man but one thing: the last of the human freedoms—to choose one's own attitude in any given set of circumstances, to choose one's own way" (1959:65). It is this inner, subjective, existential freedom which I have observed. It is the realization that "I can live myself, here and now, by my own choice." It is the quality of courage which enables a person to step into the uncertainty of the unknown as he chooses himself. It is the discovery of meaning from within oneself, meaning which comes from listening sensitively and openly to the complexities of what one is experiencing. It is the burden of being responsible for the self one chooses to be. It is the recognition of a person that he is an emerging process, not a static end product. The individual who is thus deeply and courageously thinking his own thoughts, becoming his own uniqueness, responsibly choosing himself, may be fortunate in having hundreds of objective outer alternatives from which to choose, or he may be unfortunate in having none. But his freedom exists regardless. So we are first of all speaking of something which exists within the individual, something phenomenological rather than external, but nonetheless to be prized.

The second point in defining this experience of freedom is that it exists not as a contradiction of the picture of the psychological universe as a sequence of cause and effect, but as a complement to such a universe. Freedom rightly understood is a fulfillment by the person of the ordered sequence of his life. The free man moves out voluntarily, freely, responsibly, to play his significant part in a world whose determined events move through him and through his spontaneous choice and will.

I see this freedom of which I am speaking, then, as existing in a different *dimension* than the determined sequence of cause and effect. I regard it as a freedom which exists in the subjective person, a freedom which he courageously uses to live his potentialities. The fact that this type of freedom seems completely irreconcilable with the behaviorist's picture of man is something which I will discuss a bit later. . . .

The Emergence of Commitment

I have spoken thus far primarily about freedom. What about commitment? Certainly the disease of our age is lack of purpose, lack of meaning, lack of commitment on the part of individuals. . . .

Let me say . . . what I mean by commitment in the psychological sense. I think it is easy to give this word a much too shallow meaning, indicating that the individual has, simply by conscious choice, committed himself to one course of action or another. I think the meaning goes far deeper than that. Commitment is a total organismic direction involving not only the conscious mind but the whole direction of the organism as well.

In my judgment, commitment is something that one *discovers* within oneself. It is a trust of one's total reaction rather than of one's mind only. It has much to do with creativity. Einstein's explanation of how he moved toward his formulation of relativity without any clear knowledge of his goal is an excellent example of what I mean by the sense of commitment based on a total organismic reaction. He says:

During all those years there was a feeling of direction, of going straight toward something concrete. It is, of course, very hard to express that feeling in words but it was decidedly the case and clearly to be distinguished from later considerations about the rational form of the solution (quoted in Wertheimer, 1945:183–84).

Thus commitment is more than a decision. It is the functioning of an individual who is searching for the directions which are emerging within himself. Kierkegaard has said, "The truth exists only in the process of becoming, in the process of appropriation" (1941:72). It is this individual creation of a tentative personal truth through action which is the essence of commitment.

Man is most successful in such a commitment when he is functioning as an integrated, whole, unified individual. The more that he is functioning in this total manner the more confidence he has in the directions which he unconsciously chooses. He feels a trust in his experiencing, of which, even if he is fortunate, he has only partial glimpses in his awareness.

Thought of in the sense in which I am describing it, it is clear that commitment is an achievement. It is the kind of purposeful and meaningful direction which is only gradually achieved by the individual who has come increasingly to live closely in relationship with his own experiencing—a relationship in which his unconscious tendencies are as much respected as are his conscious choices. This is the kind of commitment toward which I believe individuals can move. It is an important aspect of living in a fully functioning way. . . .

A part of modern living is to face the paradox that, viewed from one perspective, man is a complex machine. We are every day moving toward a more precise understanding and a more precise control of this objective mechanism which we call man. On the other hand, in another significant dimension of his existence, man is subjectively free; his personal choice and responsibility account for the shape of his life; he is in fact the architect of himself. A truly crucial part of his existence is the discovery of his own meaningful commitment to life with all of his being.

If in response to this you say, "But these views *cannot* both be true," my answer is, "This is a deep paradox with which we must learn to live."

REFERENCES

Crutchfield, R. S. "Conformity and Character," *American Psychologist* 10 (1955):191–98.

Frankl, V. E. *From Death Camp to Existentialism*. Boston: Beacon Press, 1959.

Kierkegaard, S. *Concluding Unscientific Postscript*. Edited by Walter Lowre. Princeton, N.J.: Princeton University Press, 1941.

Skinner, B. F. "Behaviorism at Fifty." In *Behaviorism and Phenomenology: Contrasting Bases for Modern Psychology,* edited by T. W. Wann, pp. 90–91. Chicago: University of Chicago Press, 1964.

———. *Science and Human Behavior.* New York: Macmillan, 1953.

———. *Walden Two.* New York: Macmillan, 1948.

Wertheimer, M. *Productive Thinking.* New York: Harper, 1945.

Career Education: Earning a Living or Living a Life?

Robert J. Nash and Russell M. Agne

The U.S. Office of Education is currently advancing a case for career education that will affect schooling at all levels. [Former] HEW Assistant Secretary for Education Sidney P. Marland [continues to] talk about a "school-based" model of career training that will expose all children to a full range of career opportunities. Every subject in the public school curriculum will be "refocused" to help students narrow their occupational choices. When a student has selected a career he will be provided with intensive training to achieve "marketable, salable" skills. The USOE [spent] $168 million in 1973 on career education experiments; Marland has even stated that the "central" mission of all community colleges (with a projected 1975 enrollment of 3.3 million) will be to equip students with the skills guaranteeing them "useful" employment.[1]

Obviously, there is much that is positive in the career education concept. To provide people with the training to enter and succeed in a career whenever they decide to leave the formal educational process is a humane way to ensure each person a modicum of economic independence and a personal sense of worth. Also, the desire to relate abstract academic experiences to actual field work can only be salutary. For example, teachers in Mesa, Arizona, and Pontiac, Michigan, are requiring that course work in social studies and science be related directly to on-site experiences in journalism, social work, x-ray technology, and oceanog-

Reprinted from *Phi Delta Kappan* 59 (February 1973):373–78, by permission of the authors and the publisher.

[1] Sidney P. Marland, Jr., "Education for More Than One Career," *World,* June 7, 1972, pp. 46–49.

raphy.[2] Finally, career education has the potential of obliterating forever the myth that only a college degree signifies personal worth; by shifting the emphasis from gaining a career through academic certificate to gaining a career through performance, there is the chance that involuntary attendance at colleges will disappear and that work will begin to take on the important function of helping a young person to develop personal meaning.

In spite of the above, what disturbs us most about the career education movement is the number of key assumptions left unexamined. Nowhere in an exhaustive review of the literature have we discovered a single word of caution or criticism concerning the possible misuses of the career education concept. Nowhere have we found an analysis of the ideological premises underlying career education proposals. Instead, we observe that the literature accepts as an unchallenged good the continued existence of a corporate social order and a concept of human behavior which is achievement-motivated. As a result, much of the pleading for educational reform toward a career perspective is a thinly disguised politics.[3] Also, the literature on career education conveys a theory of learning which is at least open to question. Not once, however, have we encountered an explicit discussion of the learning theory peculiar to career education, let alone an in-depth analysis of its possible limitations. And, finally, in spite of the frequent references to career education as a program designed to effect "radical" educational change, there is practically nothing in the literature that recognizes any weakness in contemporary American schooling other than its poor performance as a feeder of skilled workers into the occupational world. Therefore, because of its excessive claims and the absence of significant self-criticism, we believe that the career education prospectus must undergo careful, constructive examination.

The Corporate Reality Principle

At the heart of the career education movement is an ideological commitment to a corporate social order. In his writings, Marland stresses his belief that American society is moving inevitably toward a social order that developing industry and technology will transform substantially from the one we now know. No longer will people be trained for one lifetime job. Instead, because society is becoming increasingly "organizational" and "technical," each person will have to learn new skills through-

---

[2] John C. Rogers, "Where Job Training Starts in Kindergarten," *Parade,* April 9, 1972, pp. 18, 19.

[3] For example, see "Nixon Sees U.S. Work Ethic Reaffirmed," *Boston Globe,* September 7, 1971, p. 9.

out his life if he is to enter and reenter the different careers which will emerge and disappear in the future. In one article Marland maintains that America's expanding corporate society will necessitate such sweeping "pragmatic, theoretical and moral" changes in education and the business-industrial world that people will become "obsolete" unless they can learn new attitudes and work skills.[4]

What is disturbing about all this is that American educators are being urged to accept, as an unquestioned social idea, a type of corporate reality principle emphasizing high productivity; spiraling wages; automation; increasing economic growth; accelerating rates of social change; systematic administration; complex, large-scale organizations; and a technical approach to the resolution of human problems. Because Marland and others rarely challenge the direction toward which the corporate reality principle is pulling education in America, many career education programs are being constructed without the possibility of students' being exposed to alternative societal models. For example, in Pontiac, Michigan, career training begins in kindergarten; children are taught that their education is important only if it prepares them for "the varied world of employment." From kindergarten on, students are helped to perceive themselves as "productive workers"; third-graders are visited by leaders in industry; sixth-graders are interviewed by an employment agency for jobs in the cafeteria and library; preschoolers are taught that their parents' jobs are "of indispensable importance" in maintaining the family unit.[5] Nowhere in the Pontiac model, however, is a student allowed to speculate about such "utopian" possibilities as a society where a person's worth is not dependent on his being a productive worker who contributes throughout a lifetime to an expanding economy.

A reader searches the career education literature in vain for the slightest sign that its advocates have read any of the social or political critiques of the corporate reality principle—critiques that have been on the upswing in recent years.[6] The critics have shown that corporate life often has a bogus quality that overvalues expertise and performance. They warn that technique and bureaucratic manipulation must never substitute for risk-taking personal expression. Also, some of the more political critics have demonstrated that American schools traditionally have rewarded students who exhibit the characteristics of compliant, passive workers. These students learn to subordinate emotional modes of personal cognition to modes which are cerebral and achievement-oriented. What these critics emphasize most, however, is that the tracking struc-

---

[4] Sidney P. Marland, Jr., "Career Education 300 Days Later," *American Vocational Journal*, February 1972, pp. 14–17.

[5] Rogers, "Where Job Training Starts."

[6] For example, see Philip Slater, *The Pursuit of Loneliness: American Culture at the Breaking Point* (Boston: Beacon Press, 1970).

ture of formal education in the United States tends to reflect the structure of industrial production: Just as students cede control over their activities to career educators, so too are workers stratified within the industrial system. What results is a worker who can be motivated only by the promise of external rewards and status-enhancement.[7]

Another tendency on the part of some career spokesmen is to conceal their corporate biases beneath a gloss of "futuristic" prediction. For example, the editors of a national journal assume that because technological growth is inevitable, given current trend indices, then such growth is ipso facto desirable.[8] Underlying their injunction to prepare students for the "new technological realities" is the assumption that corporate systems of business, production, and technology, with their everexpanding growth potential, will be (ought to be) *decisive* in shaping human behavior and values and in determining the best possible future of American culture. Not once in their proposals do the editors build into programs for vocational education a unit detailing the present evidence of systematic failures that the corporate growth principle has left all over the world. The editors have virtually ignored the imminent danger (as a consequence of unfettered technological growth) that the world's minerals will soon be exhausted and the biosphere enveloped in the pollution.[9]

Marland assumes that career education is "a way of combatting apathy" because such a perspective teaches "the skills, the knowledge, and the attitudes necessary for our citizens to adapt to change . . . so that our society will continue not only to survive but to *flourish.*"[10] What he overlooks is the burgeoning group of young people who are questioning the moral validity of learning skills which continue only to perpetuate a laissez-faire, expansionist economy with the GNP as its central index of achievement. Many youths are resisting attempts to be siphoned off into careers, because their educational experiences do not allow them to challenge the whole structure of corporate capitalism. These youths believe that earning a living is always secondary to living a life; by implication, career education programs must begin to contest the long held assumption that in order to secure material well-being man's energies have to be channeled into the making of money.[11]

An economist, Frank Riessman, points out that the possibility of qualitative growth in the human services is minimized because the GNP

[7] Joel H. Spring, *Education and the Rise of the Corporate State* (Boston: Beacon Press, 1972).

[8] "Tooling Up the System from Kindergarten Through Community College," *Nation's Schools,* December 1971, pp. 36–38.

[9] See Donella H. Meadows, Dennis L. Meadows, Jorgen Randers, William W. Behrens III, *The Limits to Growth* (New York: Universe Books, 1972).

[10] Joseph Cosand, "OE on Career Education," *Change,* June 1972, p. 7, pp. 60, 61.

[11] See Richard Flacks, *Youth and Social Change* (Chicago: Markham, 1971).

as an evaluative economic norm legitimizes industrial-technological growth while devaluing growth in the "people services."[12] Much of the literature on career education conveys the impression that only through continuous industrial-technological growth, and through the new careers created as a spinoff, will economic growth continue to flourish in the United States. A representative of the Pontiac Division of General Motors has extolled the concept of career education because it "presents the free enterprise system and its opportunities so that students can prepare themselves." He has offered to send several General Motors executives into the Pontiac, Michigan, schools to explain, among other things, the automobile industry's contributions to the GNP.[13]

Where such an approach is deficient is in its one-sided view of contemporary social reality. Industrial-technological growth is resource-depleting and capital-intensive; such growth is resulting in widespread unemployment, underutilization of people's talents, and the steady deterioration of the world's natural resources. Meanwhile, there is a dearth of people who have the career skills necessary to resolve the crushing personal and social problems of drug abuse, alcoholism, estrangement, human despair and malaise, and pathological violence. The single greatest failure of career education programs would be to push people into the corporate (industrial-technological) growth sector, with its status and financial attractions, while underplaying the value of careers in the human services.

Achievement-Driven Man

Joseph Cosand, assistant commissioner of higher education, bases his prescriptions for career education reform in colleges and universities on the following:

> It seems obvious that if you begin making students aware in kindergarten of all the career opportunities that lie before them, you are going to have students who are motivated—alive, alert, and working students—by the time they enter college. They are going to college with a purpose, with goals to *achieve*.[14]

Marland subscribes to a similar concept of human motivation; he has gently scolded young people who reject "conventional economic motivations" in favor of "an avocational interest more attractive to them at the moment." In spite of his comment that he understands young peo-

[12] Frank Riessman, "Quantum Leap or More Foreplay for the Human Services," *Social Policy,* January/February 1972, pp. 3, 4.
[13] Rogers, "Where Job Training Starts," p. 19.
[14] Cosand, "OE on Career Education," p. 60.

ple's alienation from the achievement ethic of Western culture, Marland nevertheless considers youth's real needs to be achievement-based.[15]

Much of the program development in career education is rooted in a belief that people's economic needs are prepotent. For example, the Sonoma County public schools in California have developed a career curriculum which integrates subject matter at all levels. In the junior high schools, math and English teachers have designed a collaborative program to relate their subjects to students' "real interests"—an examination of occupations in the banking industry. Activities include visiting a local bank, buying a car, writing a contract for a loan, computing monthly interest, writing a play about the "banking and auto sales industry," and taking slides of a typical day's activities at the bank.[16]

What is open to question about the above is *not* the attempt to relate academic material to real life situations, but the obvious effort to fuel the achievement drives of students by appealing directly to their acquisitive needs. Another questionable assumption is one that educators often make: Students will respond enthusiastically to subject matter only when it is reduced to occupational relevance. A social scientist, David McClelland, has made the classical defense of the achievement motive as the most forceful drive in contemporary man. He maintains that leaders can exploit this achievement drive in order to accelerate economic growth. Among his suggestions, he urges the introduction of "ideological conversions" emphasizing individualistic achievements; reorganizing people's fantasy lives so that they can begin to daydream about what they have to achieve; and encouraging the emergence of a corporate class characterized by a vigorous drive for economic achievement.[17]

Almost daily, events demonstrate that the Sonoma school system's image of human motivation, like McClelland's, is splintered. Contrary to McClelland's hypothesis, young people need more than "conventional economic motivations" to feel fully human. Recently, in Detroit, assembly-line workers disrupted the automobile factories because of their conviction that they are becoming "nothing better than machines to turn out profits." Although highly skilled and salaried, they have turned to alcoholism, drugs, and high absenteeism to express their resentment toward numbing, unfulfilling work.[18] Similarly, a social scientist, Daniel Yankelovich, found in a study of college students' personal and political attitudes on 50 campuses that young people are becoming increasingly skeptical of economic well-being and achievement striving as an exclusive prescription for personal happiness. Instead, students value friend-

[15] Marland, "Education for More Than One Career," p. 48.

[16] Darryl Laramore, "Career Education Concept Filters Down," *American Vocational Journal,* September 1972, pp. 45–47, p. 78.

[17] David McClelland, *The Achieving Society* (New York: Free Press, 1967).

[18] Agis Salpukas, "Workers Increasingly Rebel Against Boredom on Assembly Line," *New York Times,* April 2, 1972, p. 40.

ship, privacy, freedom of opinion and emotional expression, the family, and nature.[19]

To view human behavior as predominantly achievement-driven, and then to develop curricula based on such a belief, is to risk a total misunderstanding of contemporary social realities in America. For example, it is at best a dubious assumption that members of minority groups after being socialized to consume in middle-class ways, and after being given the training in skills to pursue the white, middle-class, corporate careers, will actually be allowed equal opportunity to achieve those careers. Even more questionable, however, is the assumption that any young person ought to strive for a career at all. Because of the instability of the economy, careers go in and out of fashion, and an occupation that seems so attractive and permanent in 1972 might be nonexistent in 1978.[20] What is especially unsettling, however, is the inability of so many career educators to understand that the more a person achieves, the greater his need for further achievement. Achievement, like acquisition, is rarely self-limiting; to promise a person total economic satisfaction because he has developed "marketable" skill is to provoke intense personal disillusionment. Personal happiness based on economic success is a chimerical formula; the ultimate social consequence is to convert each person's need for potency into a sense of impotence, generating an estrangement so severe that the society itself is brought to the breaking point.

Learning Fallacies in Career Ed

In Marland's basic rationale for all career education programs, he also advances an implicit theory of learning. He believes:

> A major component of the reform we seek must be increased productivity—finding ways of getting more out of each dollar invested by turning away from obsolescent cottage-industry methods through a major reordering of our principal resources, including teaching talent, and wider reliance on technology, which is our principal hope for the effective development and implementation of high-quality, lower unit-cost learning.[21]

In his review of how a "school-based model" of career education will work, Marland specifies that throughout the first six grades a student will be made aware of the various clusters of occupations available to him. These include "business and office occupations," "marketing and distribution occupations," and "media and manufacturing occupations."

[19] Daniel Yankelovich, *The Changing Values on Campus* (New York: Simon & Schuster, 1972).

[20] Dennis Hale, "Careers and the Future," *Change*, Summer 1972, pp. 13–15.

[21] Sidney P. Marland, Jr., "The Endless Renaissance," *American Education*, April 1972, pp. 7, 8.

As in high school and college, academic subjects will be "refocused" so "that these classes are presented in terms of the student's career interests."[22]

One educator recommends the use of Occupacs, "multimedia packages of materials that can be used for presenting kindergarten through ninth-grade career-development activities." These modules help students study specific occupations via cassette recorders or simulated work experiences "for the purpose of learning vocabularies and skills." For example, the Secretary Occupac module enables children to code letters alphabetically and prepare masters.[23] Another educator recommends a curriculum including such activities as "role playing," "coloring, drawing, and pasting types of occupations," "vocabulary lessons," "discussions concerning attitudes and feelings about certain careers," and "requirements for success in various occupations." One of the objectives in these activities is to understand "the characteristics of good students and workers."[24]

In grades 7-10, a student will select a "job cluster" to explore in great depth. One New Jersey middle school model, the Introduction to Vocations Program, involves a study of local industry, employment trends, and professional opportunities, via field trips, visits to classrooms by successful professionals, and television and film productions.[25] Grades 11 and 12 will enable the student "to acquire the skills" to take a job immediately after graduation "or prepare himself for entering a post-secondary institution that would train him as a technician."[26] For example, August Martin High School in New York offers students a comprehensive program in airline occupations including pre-pilot and pre-stewardess training, air-traffic control ticket sales, and management.[27] Finally, higher education will provide students with "training . . . in technical careers," in order to become "more alert to the changing realities of the job market."[28]

Career programs like the above assume a theory of learning based on four interrelated fallacies. What follows is a brief examination of the false assumptions and our own generalized suggestions for redirecting present career education programs.

Specialism. Whenever educators create a perspective of knowledge that is exclusively functional—i.e., ideas are relevant only when they can

[22] "Marland on Career Education," *American Education,* November 1971, p. 26.

[23] Marla Peterson, "Occupacs: Simulated Career Development Experiences for Elementary School Children," *Business Education Forum,* February 1972, pp. 6, 7.

[24] George E. Leonard, "Career Guidance in the Elementary School," *Elementary School Guidance and Counseling,* December 1971, pp. 124–26.

[25] Albert J. Pautler, "Occupational Education in the Curriculum," *Educational Leadership,* November 1971, pp. 174–77.

[26] "Marland on Career Education," p. 26.

[27] "Tooling Up the System," p. 49.

[28] Cosand, "OE on Career Education," p. 61.

be used to promote success in a career—then the educational experience is reduced to a kind of specialized training or programming. Knowledge gets filed into a series of "pragmatic" activities, distributed in clusters and modules, so that students can cultivate one narrow sector of their abilities in order to achieve occupational competence.

What is most disconcerting about collapsing the learning experience into such specialized boxes as "occupational clusters" is that educators sell their souls for a view of life superficially utilitarian. This view is fragmented because students gain insight only into the nature of outer reality; they neglect their inner nature—the intuitive and emotional life dependent for its sustenance on the arts, humanities, and religion. Unfortunately, there is an inexorable logic to specialized education: When persons are locked into one mode of thought or specialty, they become impervious to new ideas and experience. Vance Packard has shown the dismal consequence of career specialization: People become "strangers," driven from job to job, often under terrible stress, impelled chiefly by the external goals of status, promotion, and financial power.[29]

As long as career education remains highly specialized, human beings will continue to be separated from the totality of their experiences. In the future, career educators will have to construct programs more sensitive to young people's needs to absorb and integrate all kinds of knowledge (liberal, spiritual, instrumental, sexual, expressive, political, scientific). This entails placing far less emphasis on restrictive vocational goals and specialized work skills, and helping young people instead to assess the potential of a career to develop the total self.

Sequentialism. Eli Ginzberg has a developmental scheme demonstrating that occupational choice is a slow, sequential process, and not the result of a single, isolated event.[30] Unfortunately, one gets the impression that often the emphasis on levels and progression is self-authenticating. An administrator decides that career education will become the mission of schooling in a local community. Therefore, as an operational convenience, training gets meted out in stages, over specifically planned periods of time. And because a "major component" of career education is "increased productivity" and the "development of lower unit-cost learning," it follows that career training is efficient—and concerned with performance criteria, precise measurement methods, and the behavioral evidence that signals the student to move from one level to another.[31]

Rigid sequencing, in conjunction with performance objectives, can be

[29] Vance Packard, *A Nation of Strangers* (New York: McKay, 1972).

[30] Eli Ginzberg *et al., Career Guidance: Who Needs It, Who Can Provide It, Who Can Improve It* (New York: McGraw-Hill, 1971).

[31] For example, see "Researchers Discuss Career Education, Performance Goals," *American Vocational Journal,* February 1972, p. 25.

a devastating learning block for some students. To train all children in an inflexible age and grade sequence is to risk swamping the special tempo and style of each person's unique rhythm for learning. According to recent research in group theory and human potential studies, learning can occur as the result of exposure to new experiences, active discovery, and a restless searching and questioning. As students who have interrupted their formal education often demonstrate, it is possible to grow through a variety of informal learning situations. Some students gather in urban collectives, some in rural communes; others staff free schools, travel, become migrant laborers, and work in day-care centers.[32]

These activities grant the individual the sovereignty to develop his skills and interests at his own pace, whenever the need to disengage from established structures strikes him. When career educators can resist the tendency to schedule every moment of a student's time for occupational awareness and technical training, then human beings may be able to frame their own purposes and create their own satisfactions; they may even become more competent, satisfied workers. First, however, educators will have to free students from the suffocating sequential modes in which they have traditionally been trained.

Fundamentalism. The current emphasis on vocabulary, mathematical, and attitudinal competencies in curricular packages is incomplete and shortsighted. It is becoming exceedingly difficult to designate any body of knowledge or behaviors as "fundamental" for *all* students, because workers in the world of the future will need a diversity of skills and attitudes—some of which are still unknown. For example, one social scientist has predicted that in the future people will require a greater variety of human services than at present. In addition to health, education, and welfare services, people will need help in becoming more artistic, religious, philosophical, and interpersonal.[33]

To counteract the current preoccupation with marketable skills typical of many career programs, educators will have to consider the value of skills which may be probing, questioning, noninstrumental, and confrontative. This might mean that teachers will have to become human relations leaders, helping students to explore, discover, and test a number of personal competencies usually suppressed in formal educational settings. For example, many students will need competencies in becoming political clarifiers and activists; they will have to develop skills to clarify their own purposes and values and the ability to relate these insights to

[32] See H. E. Schein and Warren Bennis, eds., *Personal and Organizational Change Through Group Methods* (New York: Wiley, 1965). Also John Mann and Herbert Otto, eds., *Ways of Growth* (New York: Viking Compass, 1971).

[33] See Arthur Pearl, "An Ecological Rationale for a Human Services Society," *Social Policy,* September/October 1971, pp. 40, 41.

systematic political participation. These nonoccupational skills will necessitate a curriculum that helps students to think about issues and problems, aids them in clarifying their value confusions, and urges them to consider and act upon workable alternatives to the corporate system as it is.

Credentialism. Mr. Marland has stated that entrance to the professions, trades, and unions should be based exclusively on a person's performance; not on whether he has accumulated formal credentials.[34] While Marland's inclinations are praiseworthy, career educators have yet to show how they can avoid converting a performance-based model of education to one that is exactly the opposite—namely, the selection, training, and certifying of workers for the corporate state. Students will be quick to see that when performance criteria are product-oriented, system-serving, and adult-imposed, then they are indistinguishable from the tyranny of a credential.

In the future, a performance-based curriculum must include more than functional career training. The most "useful" learning, like play, is intrinsic, spontaneous, and leisurely—subordinating technical competence to growth in personal, physical, aesthetic, social, and political awareness.[35] Consequently, career educators will have to learn how to designate performance criteria for expressive learning as effectively as they do for "marketable skill" learning. This type of learning confers superior career advantages on a person because it is evocative and heuristic. A student learns to discover for himself the worth and meaning of an experience, the methods for arriving at and assessing that experience, and the implications an experience has for his private and public worlds. Evocative education prepares students, *not* merely to make a living, but to live a full life, free from boredom and excessive striving after meretricious credentials.

Earning a Living and Living a Life

We suggest that, in the future, career educators will have to ask three kinds of questions concerning the purposes of their programs:

1. *To what extent is career education enhancing the principle of maximum possibilities in occupations?* Educators must begin to move their curricula away from the unilateral provisioning of skilled careerists for the corporate state and toward the enhancement of human possibilities. Careers will have to increase personal joy and hope; this will mean pre-

---

[34] See Sidney P. Marland, Jr., "Career Education—The Most Exciting Trend in Schooling Today," *Parents' Magazine,* September 1972, p. 108.
[35] Bruno Bettelheim, "Play and Education," *School Review,* November 1972, pp. 1–13.

paring persons to live comfortably and enthusiastically with the inevitability of multiple occupations during a lifetime. One approach might be to prepare people to experiment with diversification in their work. For example, the quality of a person's daily living could be intensified if he had shorter work periods, broken up by other forms of work, such as teaching, gardening, counseling, wood chopping, poetry writing, or machine tinkering. In the future educators will have to resist the temptation to rely on such subtle incentives as human greed and status climbing to motivate students to choose careers. Students will have to be helped to select careers on the basis of whether a profession promises them *human* enhancement, rather than enhancement through power, profit, or prestige. The type of career to be avoided will be the one where a credentialed hierarchy imposes restrictions on occupational diversity because it wants to maintain its special privileges.

2. *How can career education obliterate the distinction between work and leisure?* Career educators must help each individual find meaning and hope in a profession by pointing out its possibilities for being a sphere of consequential leisurely activity. This might mean helping people to evaluate a career according to the opportunities it offers for contentment, joy, challenge, and excitement—experiences people ordinarily seek *away* from their work. Perhaps this will necessitate a kind of "personal worth index" where an occupation is assessed, *not* on the corporate terms of the wealth it produces or the mobility it generates, but on the total impact a job has on human life. One function of the "index" will be to blur the false distinction we have created between work and leisure, and to enable persons to pursue competence and personal meaning in their careers as well as in their avocational activities.

3. *How can career education be more concerned with human services?* Educators will have to develop and emphasize innovative, labor-intensive "human service clusters" while minimizing capital-intensive clusters (such as "marketing and distribution" and "construction and manufacturing") grounded in an infinitely expanding technological base. We urgently require persons trained in helping us to improve the quality of our education, health services, food, leisure-time activities, air, and water. Likewise, we need people with the skills to help us expand our appreciation for the artistic, recreational, spiritual, aesthetic, philosophic, political, and experimental facets of contemporary living. Until career educators build programs committed to maximizing each person's fully lived experiences, his sense of personal and professional competence, and his affiliative relationships; and until each person is included as a decision maker in the human service process, then the corporate state will continue to exacerbate the destruction of the earth's nonrestorable commodities and the deterioration of human hope and vitality.

Sex Stereotyping in the Secondary School Curriculum

Janice Law Trecker

One difficulty of dealing with sex bias in the public schools is that the integration of male and female students in most curriculum areas has led to a belief in educational equality. While such blatantly separate and unequal departments as physical education and vocational preparation are rationalized on the grounds of physical and attitudinal differences, other forms of bias are sufficiently subtle to be ignored altogether. At least until quite recently, stereotyped and biased curriculum offerings and materials were complacently accepted as either factually correct or not important enough to make changes worthwhile. The hidden assumption has been that girls, who were after all fortunate enough to have been admitted to secondary facilities over 100 years ago, could be adequately served by materials designed for boys.

Thus the standard in our secondary schools, after decades of coeducation, is still male. Texts and programs are designed to enhance the male self-image, promote identification with male spokesmen and heroes, explore the developmental and intellectual growth of young males, and reveal masculine contributions to our culture. So far as the typical secondary school curriculum is concerned, humanity is masculine. This is evident whether one examines the literary style or graphic design of textbooks, the topics and individuals chosen for consideration and emphasis, the administration of the curriculum, the manner in which students are tracked, or the underlying assumptions of the course offerings. Current curricula and textbooks present perhaps the clearest demonstration of sex prejudice in our schools.

A look at current United States history textbooks, for example, raises the question of how our country has maintained itself with a 99 percent male population. These books consistently refer only to men, i.e., "our revolutionary forefathers," "the men who conquered the West," or "the men who built our nation." The pictures, photographs, and paintings chosen for inclusion are almost exclusively about male subjects. Women

Reprinted from *Phi Delta Kappan* 55, no. 2 (October 1973):110–12, by permission of the author and the publisher.

are rarely chosen as spokesmen, and even books with ample sections of documentary material allot women writers and thinkers no more than the most meager space—if any at all. A recent linguistic study of social studies texts, "Equal Treatment of the Sexes in Social Studies Textbooks," by Elizabeth Burr, Susan Dunn, and Norma Farquhar, details the more subtle manifestations of sex bias, including demeaning terms for women, exclusive use of male pronouns and generic terms, and a perpetuation of images of women as fragile and timid.

Nor are history and social studies texts the only offenders. Recently, the New York City Chapter of the National Organization for Women (NOW) prepared a *Report on Sex Bias in the Public Schools.* Josephine Milnar, a contributor to the report, examined a number of junior high school mathematics and science texts. She found that female mathematicians and scientists of note were ignored, and that illustrative and problem-solving materials were consistently characterized by sexual stereotypes. For example, while boys in mathematical problems show a variety of activities—gardening, building, sports, and painting—girls and women were virtually confined to sewing, cooking, and child care. In science books nonbiased texts were frequently accompanied by illustrations showing only males using scientific equipment or solving problems. Considering the large numbers of female students with scientific and mathematical potential who do not pursue careers in these areas, it seems unfortunate that texts and materials do not present young girls with positive female images and role models.

The exclusion of women from pictorial material, the stereotyped descriptions of those who do appear, and the linguistic conventions of the texts show how supposedly objective school texts subtly encourage female students to pursue their traditional roles—the home, silence, and subjection. Any doubt about this message is soon removed by a closer consideration of the topics emphasized in the various curriculum areas. Reviewing virtually any catalogue of supplementary texts and novels for secondary school students reveals how few novels and biographies feature female protagonists. While one can find a plentiful supply of novels built around the experiences of young men and boys from Alabama to Ankor Wat, one is fortunate to find even one-fourth as many dealing with young women. Supplemental texts typically include few biographies of outstanding women, and in volumes of collected lives, women receive only token representation. Both teachers and publishers seem to assume that males are involved in more interesting and important activities than females and that while girls are willing to read about boys, boys would be unconcerned about female protagonists.

Similar attitudes are evident in the social studies. Topics of particular interest to women are frequently omitted altogether, and the effects of sex bias and sex stereotypes on other problems and topics are ignored. How else can one account for the fact that, even today, young women are largely ignorant of their legal disabilities and of the prejudices they face in education, employment, and public policy, and that the general public remains uninformed about the role of sex bias in social problems? One reason is that very few social studies courses or text materials consider sex-role conditioning, women's current and historic legal status, social and philosophical attitudes toward women, or the connections between these attitudes and women's rights. It would be difficult to argue that citizenship courses are doing an adequate job when they fail to inform all students about the civic and legal disabilities affecting more than half of the student population.

Similarly, it seems difficult to justify the continuing neglect of the part that attitudes toward women play in other contemporary problems. Two-thirds of the adult poor are female, and the vast majority of the welfare population is comprised of women and children. For these reasons, it is impossible to discuss the problems of poverty without consideration of the status of women and of attitudes toward women and children. Similarly, now that 40 percent of the labor force is female, labor problems and unemployment cannot be explored realistically without consideration of the prospects of working women and of attitudes toward female employment. When women are trained virtually from birth to regard homemaking and child bearing as the primary and, in some cases, the exclusive "feminine" occupations, consideration of social attitudes and female roles would seem mandatory in any discussion of population control or ecology.

The same patterns of omission and neglect are evident in American history texts and courses, and it would be surprising if similar criticisms do not apply to European, Latin-American, and Afro-Asian history courses as well. Such topics as the evolution of the social and legal status of women, the importance of female and child labor in the industrial revolution, women's work in the wars and in social reforms, the women's movement, and the contributions of outstanding women are conspicuous by their absence. The typical U.S. history book generously devotes one out of its 500 to 800 pages to women, their problems, and their contributions. Looking at the typical history texts, the social studies programs, and the secondary school English and humanities reading lists, one must regretfully agree with the Pennsylvania report, "Sexism in Education." The authors, from the Pennsylvania Department of Education, the Human Relations Commission, and a state women's group, concluded that the Pennsylvania public school texts and library materials showed the following weaknesses:

> . . . underrepresentation of women; representation in limited stereotyped roles—wives, mothers, teachers, nurses, secretaries, and other service-oriented jobs; reinforcement of culturally conditioned sexist characteristics showing as *female* such traits as dependency, passivity,

noncompetitive spirit, and emotionality; and a very meager appreciation of women's contributions to history, literature, science, and other areas of American life. . . .

In light of current scholarly research on women's history and on the contributions of women to the arts, sciences, and ideas, it is simply no longer adequate to tolerate such weaknesses in American history texts.

Unfortunately, sex bias is not confined to the curriculum per se but extends to its administration and to the rationale of certain courses and procedures, especially with regard to athletics and vocational preparation courses. It would be difficult, for example, to defend most current athletic and physical education programs. In comparison with programs designed for male students, girls' athletic programs receive less money and equipment and show a narrower range in offerings. While some school systems offer no competitive programs for girls at all, many more show vast inequities in funding. *Let Them Aspire,* a report on the Ann Arbor (Michigan) schools, revealed that the budget for boys' interscholastic sports was 10 times as high as the corresponding female budget, a discrepancy by no means unique in this field. The view that boys' sports just happen to be more expensive is a frequent but inadequate justification. While school districts do not hesitate to introduce such costly boys' sports as football and ice hockey, the introduction of comparably expensive girls' activities as show jumping, horseback riding, or figure skating is almost beyond civic contemplation. It is not unusual for girls to be denied the opportunity for swimming, because pool time is limited, or for towns to reject funding for a girls' coaching staff, requiring talented young women either to abandon athletic excellence or to pay for private coaching.

In a number of cases, the neglect of female competitive athletics is paralleled by a neglect of physical education opportunities as well. Testimony from a 1971 New York City court suit against the administration of Junior High School 217 for sex bias included statements that girls were only rarely allowed to use outdoor recreation areas, that they were denied the opportunity to use the school's soccer fields, and that their indoor sports program was inferior in variety and quality to the corresponding boys' program.

Although there are glaring inequities in girls' physical education and athletic programs, they are of minor importance compared to the sexual inequities in vocational and technical education. It is still common practice to track students by sex for vocational training. Such tracking usually begins in the junior high school, where girls are steered into homemaking and boys into industrial arts. Even where sex prerequisites for these courses are absent, vocational training programs reflect rigid notions of appropriate masculine and feminine occupations. Thus females are an overwhelming majority in homemaking, health occupations, and business, while males predominate to an equally striking degree in agriculture, the skilled trades, and the industrial and technical fields. While as many girls as boys (indeed, more, if homemaking is included) receive vocational training on the secondary level, their training prepares them for a very narrow range of occupations, mainly in low-paying women's fields. Nonvocational homemaking courses received the lion's share of federal funds for home economics until very recently, but young women are not prepared in these courses for paid employment but for unpaid labor as housewives.

Whether or not female students are deliberately excluded from vocational schools and courses, these sex divisions are justified on the ground that young girls are not interested in the traditionally masculine fields. Considering the economic disadvantages of their vocational choices—the low wages and worsening economic position of the American woman worker—materials and programs which might enlarge the career possibilities and raise the aspirations of young women should be a high priority item in any responsible school program. In addition to the legal and administrative changes needed to end tracking by sex, young women and men need information about the status of women in the labor force and about the new career opportunities available to women. Both ERIC and the Women's Bureau distribute informative material on women in the labor force, and the new interest in career education and vocational training will certainly make such material especially pertinent and useful. In perhaps no other area of the curriculum is there more need for nonstereotyped information and for positive role models for young women than in vocational training and career education. There is little doubt that traditional stereotypes about the proper work for women have combined with overt economic discrimination to greatly restrict the aspirations and opportunities of the female secondary school student.

Removal of bias in vocational training goes beyond a simple revision of textbooks and materials. It requires new ways of thinking about the needs of girls and women and revisions in thinking about their capacities. This is true of the curriculum as a whole, as well as of its constituent parts. School programs need to be evaluated from the point of view of female as well as male needs, and the supposition should not automatically be made that these are the same. For example, should the educational program include some form of women's studies, self-defense classes, the inclusion of material on contraception in sex education courses, and nonstereotyped courses about the family and marriage?

The removal of stereotypes and the development of a curriculum which is appropriate for both female and male students is a complex procedure requiring the cooperation of teachers, administrators, counselors, and educational publishers. The role of teachers is especially important. While a few subjects, such as history or science, lend themselves to a relatively small number of standardized texts, other areas, such as the humanities, literature, family life, and sex education, use such diverse materials as to require the cooperation of several departments and teachers in researching material and evaluating textbooks. In research and evaluation, in creating alternative nonsexist books and materials, and in their dealings with the major textbook houses, policy-making bodies, and the public, teachers and teacher organizations can make major contributions to the elimination of sexual bias in the secondary schools. Hopefully, educators will begin to initiate and support efforts to evaluate school policies, curriculum, and educational materials with regard to sex bias and to work to eradicate stereotyping and bigotry in courses and programs.

The Schools and Equal Opportunity

Mary Jo Bane and Christopher Jencks

Americans have a recurrent fantasy that schools can solve their problems. Thus it was perhaps inevitable that, after we rediscovered poverty and inequality in the early 1960s, we turned to the schools for solutions. Yet the schools did not provide solutions, the high hopes of the early-and-middle 1960s faded, and the war on poverty ended in ignominious surrender to the status quo. In part, of course, this was because the war in Southeast Asia turned out to be incompatible with the war on poverty. In part, however, it was because we all had rather muddleheaded ideas about the various causes and cures of poverty and inequality.

Today there are signs that some people are beginning to look for new solutions to these perennial problems. There is a vast amount of sociological and economic data that can, we think, help in this effort, both by explaining the failures of the 1970s and by suggesting more realistic alternatives. For the past four years we have been working with this data. Our research has led us to three general conclusions.

First, poverty is a condition of relative rather than absolute deprivation. People feel poor and are poor if they have a lot less money than their neighbors. This is true regardless of their absolute income. It follows that we cannot eliminate poverty unless we prevent people from falling too far below the national average. The problem is economic inequality rather than low incomes.

Second, the reforms of the 1960s were misdirected because they focused only on equalizing opportunity to "succeed" (or "fail") rather than on reducing the economic and social distance between those who succeeded and those who failed. The evidence we have reviewed suggests that equalizing opportunity will not do very much to equalize results, and hence that it will not do much to reduce poverty.

Third, even if we are interested solely in equalizing opportunities for economic success, making schools more equal will not help very much. Differences between schools have very little effect on what happens to students after they graduate.

The main policy implication of these findings is that although school reform is important for improving the lives of children, schools cannot contribute significantly to adult equality. If we want economic equality in our society, we will have to get it by changing our economic institutions, not by changing the schools.

Schooling and Opportunity

Almost none of the reform legislation of the 1960s involved direct efforts to equalize adult status, power, or income. Most Americans accepted the idea that these rewards should go to those who were most competent and diligent. Their objection to America's traditional economic system was not that it produced inequality but that the rules determining who succeeded and who failed were often unfair. The reformers wanted to create a world in which success would no longer be associated with skin color, economic background, or other "irrelevant" factors, but only with actual merit. What they wanted, in short, was what they called "equal opportunity."

Their strategy for achieving equal opportunity placed great emphasis on education. Many people imagined that if schools could equalize people's cognitive skills this would equalize their bargaining power as adults. Presumably, if every one had equal bargaining power, few people would end up very poor.

This strategy for reducing poverty rested on a series of assumptions that went roughly as follows:

1. Eliminating poverty is largely a matter of helping children born into poverty to rise out of it. Once families escape from poverty, they do not fall back into it. Middle-class children rarely end up poor.

2. The primary reason poor children cannot escape from poverty is that they do not acquire basic cognitive skills. They cannot read, write,

calculate, or articulate. Lacking these skills, they cannot get or keep a well-paid job.

3. The best mechanism for breaking this "vicious circle" is educational reform. Since children born into poor homes do not acquire the skills they need from their parents, they must be taught these skills in school. This can be done by making sure that they attend the same schools as middle-class children, by giving them extra compensatory programs in school, by giving their parents a voice in running their schools, or by some combination of all three approaches.

Our research over the last four years suggests that each of these assumptions is erroneous:

1. Poverty is not primarily hereditary. While children born into poverty have a higher than average chance of ending up poor, there is still an enormous amount of economic mobility from one generation to the next. A father whose occupational status is high passes on less than half his advantage to his sons, and a father whose status is low passes along less than half his disadvantage. A family whose income is above the norm has an even harder time passing along its privileges; its sons are typically only about a third as advantaged as the parents. Conversely, a family whose income is below average will typically have sons about a third as disadvantaged as the parents. The effects of parents' status on their daughters' economic positions appear to be even weaker. This means that many "advantaged" parents have some "disadvantaged" children and vice versa.

2. The primary reason some people end up richer than others is not that they have more adequate cognitive skills. While children who read well, get the right answers to arithmetic problems, and articulate their thoughts clearly are somewhat more likely than others to get ahead, there are many other equally important factors involved. The effects of I.Q. on economic success are about the same as the effects of family background. This means, for example, that if two men's I.Q. scores differ by 17 points—the typical difference between I.Q. scores of individuals chosen at random—their incomes will typically differ by less than $2,000. That amount is not completely trivial, of course. But the income difference between random individuals is three times as large and the difference between the best-paid fifth and the worst-paid fifth of all male workers averages $14,000. There is almost as much economic inequality among those who score high on standardized tests as in the general population.

3. There is no evidence that school reform can substantially reduce the extent of cognitive inequality, as measured by tests of verbal fluency, reading comprehension, or mathematical skill. Eliminating qualitative differences between elementary schools would reduce the range of scores on standardized tests in sixth grade by less than 3 percent. Eliminating

qualitative differences between high schools would hardly reduce the range of twelfth-grade scores at all and would reduce by only 1 percent the disparities in the amount of education people eventually get.

Our best guess, after reviewing all the evidence we could find, is that racial desegregation raises black elementary school students' test scores by a couple of points. But most of the test-score gap between blacks and whites persists, even when they are in the same schools. So also: Tracking has very little effect on test scores. And neither the overall level of resources available to a school nor any specific, easily identifiable school policy has a significant effect on students' cognitive skills or educational attainments. Thus, even if we went beyond "equal opportunity" and allocated resources disproportionately to schools whose students now do worst on tests and are least likely to acquire credentials, this would not improve these students' prospects very much.

The evidence does not tell us why school quality has so little effect on test scores. Three possible explanations come to mind. First, children seem to be more influenced by what happens at home than by what happens in school. They may also be more influenced by what happens on the streets and by what they see on television. Second, administrators have very little control over those aspects of school life that do affect children. Reallocating resources, reassigning pupils, and rewriting the curriculum seldom change the way teachers and students actually treat each other minute by minute. Third, even when the schools exert an unusual influence on children, the resulting changes are not likely to persist into adulthood. It takes a huge change in elementary school test scores, for example, to alter adult income by a significant amount.

Implications for Educational Policy

These findings imply that school reform is never likely to have any significant effect on the degree of inequality among adults. This suggests that the prevalent "factory" model, in which schools are seen as places that "produce" alumni, probably ought to be abandoned. It is true that schools have "inputs" and "outputs," and that one of their nominal purposes is to take human "raw material" (i.e., children) and convert it into something more "useful" (i.e., employable adults). Our research suggests, however, that the character of a school's output depends largely on a single input, the characteristics of the entering children. Everything else—the school budget, its policies, the characteristics of the teachers—is either secondary or completely irrelevant, at least so long as the range of variation among schools is as narrow as it seems to be in America.

These findings have convinced us that the long-term effects of schooling are relatively uniform. The day-to-day internal life of the schools, in contrast, is highly variable. It follows that *the primary basis for evaluating a school should be whether the students and teachers find it a satisfying place to be.* This does not mean we think schools should be like mediocre summer camps, in which children are kept out of trouble but not taught anything. We doubt that a school can be enjoyable for either adults or children unless the children keep learning new things. We value ideas and the life of the mind, and we think that a school that does not value these things is a poor place for children. But a school that values ideas because they enrich the lives of children is quite different from a school that values high reading scores because reading scores are important for adult success.

Our concern with making schools satisfying places for teachers and children has led us to a concern for diversity and choice. People have widely different notions of what a "satisfying" place is, and we believe they ought to be able to put these values into practice. As we have noted, our research suggests that none of the programs or structural arrangements in common use today has consistently different long-term effects from any other. Since the character of a child's schooling has few long-term effects, and since these effects are quite unpredictable, society has little reason to constrain the choices available to parents and children. If a "good school" is one the students and staff find satisfying, no one school will be best for everyone. Since there is no evidence that professional educators know appreciably more than parents about what is good for children, it seems reasonable to let parents decide what kind of education their children should have while they are young and to let the children decide as they get older.

Short-term considerations also seem decisive in determining whether to spend more money on schooling or to spend it on busing children to schools outside their neighborhoods. If extra resources make school life pleasanter and more interesting, they are worthwhile. But we should not try to justify school expenditures on the grounds that they boost adult earnings. Likewise, busing ought to be justified in political and moral terms rather than in terms of presumed long-term effects on the children who are bused. If we want an integrated society, we ought to have integrated schools, which make people feel they have a stake in the well-being of other races. If we want a society in which people are free to segregate themselves, then we should apply that principle to our schools. There is, however, no compelling reason to treat schools differently from other social arrangements, including neighborhoods. Personally, we believe in both open housing and open schools. If parents or students want to take buses, expand the relevant schools, and ensure that the students are welcome in the schools they want to attend. This is the least we can do to offset the effects of residential segregation. But we do not believe that forced busing can be justified on the grounds of its long-term benefits for students.

This leads to our last conclusion about educational reform. Reformers are always getting trapped into claiming too much for what they propose. They may want a particular reform—like open classrooms, or desegregation, or vouchers—because they think these reforms will make schools more satisfying places to work. Yet they feel obliged to claim that these reforms will also reduce the number of nonreaders, increase racial understanding, or strengthen family life. A wise reformer ought to be more modest, claiming only that a particular reform will not harm adult society and that it will make life pleasanter for parents, teachers, and students in the short run.

This plea for modesty in school reform will, we fear, fall on deaf ears. Ivan Illich is right in seeing schools as secular churches, through which we seek to improve not ourselves but our descendants. That this process should be disagreeable seems inevitable; one cannot abolish original sin through self-indulgence. That it should be immodest seems equally inevitable; a religion that promises anything less than salvation wins few converts. In school, as in church, we present the world as we wish it were. We try to inspire children with the ideals we ourselves have failed to live up to. We assume, for example, that we cannot make adults live in desegregated neighborhoods, so we devise schemes for busing children from one neighborhood to another in order to desegregate the schools. We all prefer conducting our moral experiments on other people. Nonetheless, so long as we confine our experiments to children, we will not have much effect on adult life.

Implications for Social Reform

Then how *are* we to affect adult life? Our findings tell us that different kinds of inequality are only loosely related to one another. This can be either encouraging or discouraging, depending on how you look at it. On the discouraging side, it means that eliminating inequality in one area does not dictate inequality in other areas.

To begin with, genetic inequality is not a major obstacle to economic equality. It is true that genetic diversity almost inevitably means considerable variation in people's scores on standardized tests. But this kind of cognitive inequality need not imply anything like the present degree of economic inequality. We estimate, for example, that if the only sources of income inequality in America were differences in people's genes, the top fifth of the population would earn only about 1.4 times as much as the bottom fifth. In actuality, the top fifth earns seven times as much as the bottom fifth.

Second, our findings suggest that psychological and cultural differences between families are not an irrevocable barrier to adult equality. Family background has more influence than genes on an individual's educational attainment, occupational status, and income. Nonetheless, if family background were the only source of economic inequality in America, the top fifth would earn only about twice as much as the bottom fifth.

Our findings show, then, that inequality is not determined at birth. But they also suggest that economic equality cannot be achieved by indirect efforts to manipulate the environments in which people grow up. We have already discussed the minuscule effects of equalizing school quality. Equalizing the amount of schooling people get would not work much better. Income inequality among men with similar amounts of schooling is only 5-10 percent less than among men in general. The effect is even less if we include women.

If we want to eliminate economic inequality, we must make this an explicit objective of public policy rather than deluding ourselves into thinking that we can do it by giving everyone equal opportunity to succeed or fail. If we want an occupational structure which is less hierarchical and in which the social distance between the top and the bottom is reduced, we will have to make deliberate efforts to reorganize work and redistribute power within organizations. We will probably also have to rotate jobs, so that no individual held power very long.

If we want an income distribution that is more equal, we can constrain employers, either by tax incentives or direct legislation, to reduce wage disparities between their best- and worst-paid workers. We can make taxes more progressive, and we can provide income supplements to those who do not make an adequate living from wages alone. We can also provide free public services for those who cannot afford to buy adequate services in the private sector. Pursued with vigor, such a strategy can make "poverty" (i.e., having a living standard less than half the national average) virtually impossible. Such a strategy would also make economic "success," in the sense of having, say, a living standard more than twice the national average, far less common than it now is. The net effect would be to make those with the most competence and luck subsidize those with the least competence and luck to a far greater extent than they do today. Unless we are prepared to do this, poverty and inequality will remain with us indefinitely.

This strategy was rejected during the 1960s for the simple reason that it commanded relatively little popular support. The required legislation could not have passed Congress, nor could it pass today. That does not mean that it is the wrong strategy. It simply meant that, until we change the political and moral premises on which most Americans now operate, poverty and inequality will persist at pretty much their present level. Intervention in market processes, for example, means restricting the "right" of individuals to use their natural advantages for private gain. Economic equality requires social and legal sanctions—analogous to those that now exist against capricious firing of employees—against inequality within work settings. It also requires that wage rates, which Americans have traditionally viewed as a "private" question to be adjudicated by negotiation between (unequal) individuals or groups, must become a "public" question subject to political control and solution.

In America, as elsewhere, the long-term drift over the past 200 years has been toward equality. In America, however, the contribution of public policy to this drift has been slight. As long as egalitarians assume that public policy cannot contribute to equality directly but must proceed by ingenious manipulations of marginal institutions like the schools, this pattern will continue. If we want to move beyond this tradition, we must establish political control over the economic institutions that shape our society. What we will need, in short, is what other countries call socialism. Anything less will end in the same disappointment as the reforms of the 1960s.

The Purpose of Democratic Education

Ernest E. Bayles

We have already noted the imperative placed by democracy (as defined) upon public education: viz., reflective teaching, and basing criticism always on criteria that are suited to each occasion as it occurs, that are clearly understood by the participants, and that apply equally to all (the teacher included). This is educational *program*—the way in which educational purpose is to be achieved. Corresponding *purpose*—end-in-view, or goal—is to develop intellectual independence; capacity to do one's own thinking while working with one's fellows in reaching decisions "on matters deemed to be of group concern"; independent learning ability.

When it is said that democracy requires teaching people how to think as well as, if not rather than, *what* to think, it is *reflective* thinking that must be meant; otherwise, the logic is violated. This point, we hope, has previously been made clear, so we need not explain it again; we reiterate merely for emphasis, because of its great importance. Democracy, of course, is crucially dependent on the "straight thinking" of the body politic. But, educationally, the premises on which such thinking is to be based must be developed via democratic-reflective process. If not, it is indoctrination, failure to encourage and promote intellectual independence. Regardless of the subject-matter field involved in the instruction and regardless of whether the teacher is seeking to develop knowledges, skills, or attitudes, or any combination of these, the *method* should, in overall context, be reflective. To seek, for example, to promote "creativity" in the so-called appreciation-type subjects (such as art, music, and literature) and in actuality not teach reflectively is gross self-contradiction, prelude to failure. And to develop "skills" in dogmatic, authoritarian fashion is to develop slaves to routine; to deaden the intellect and entail inefficient, low-quality workmanship. A heads-up, mentally alert athlete has a built-in advantage over one who functions routinely, unimaginatively, and thoughtlessly.

Our assumptions regarding democracy, then, establish the *method* of teaching. It is to be reflective, the teacher serving more as moderator or chairman of an investigational body than as promoter of a point of view. Teaching is to be exploratory rather than explanatory. This is the imperative of democracy.

But what of *content?* What imperative covers the subject matter of study? *What* is to be taught? On this question, a teacher is not to be neutral even though he is to be nonpartisan or nonindoctrinative. School time is to be well spent, not to be frittered away. What is given place in the curriculum must be educationally significant. Whimsicality in curriculum construction is to be avoided, whether it be the whims of students, of teachers or other school personnel, or of local communities and the school boards that represent them. Basic principle must be evoked and followed in the choice of subject matter of instruction, and this can only be effected by a trained body of professionals who when needful are able to put their theory on the line and report clearly and honestly the foundations on which it is based, and who adhere to it in practice.

Basic principle to be employed in the choice of subject matter should seemingly be expressed in terms of insights to be gained. This in no wise denies that skills and attitudes ought also to be sought; it is merely recognition that changes in attitude consequentially *follow* changes in insight[1] and that, in accordance with the principle of least action, per-

---

[1] Ernest E. Bayles, *The Theory and Practice of Teaching* (New York: Harper & Row, 1950), pp. 71–74; 77–78; also Ernest E. Bayles, *Democratic Educational Theory* (New York: Harper & Row, 1960), chap. 8, esp. pp. 126–27.

formance in any given situation and toward any given end is the consequence of insightful design.[2] Though we admit and indeed insist that education should be concerned with both the cognitive and the conative, we recognize that changes in the cognitive are precedent to and entail changes in the conative; hence, to repeat, *what* is to be studied should be expressed in terms of insights to be gained.

To delineate curricula, however, in long lists of itemized specifics is to ignore relationalism—the principle of psychological configuration, an essential tenet of pragmatism. Relationalism implies always a search for a single, unifying principle or generalization, from which by logical deduction the multifarious details of particular cases can be derived. This, incidentally, is the reason why logical learning is so much more easily achieved and so much longer lasting than learning by rote, a principle that enjoys virtually unanimous recognition by psychologists. How can this be attained in democratic curriculum theory?

Betterment of Student Outlooks

By Expansion

An expression that can serve to encompass all one's insights would be one's *outlook,* on life or on the world of which one is a part. We may also designate such an outlook as one's *world of insight.* In contradistinction, we can designate the "world" that pushes and pulls one about—regardless of one's knowledge or one's wishes about it—as one's *world of effect.* Obviously, one's world of effect will greatly exceed one's world of insight, and expansion of one's world of insight toward greater coverage of one's world of effect would doubtless receive close to universal approval as at least one criterion for judging improvement of the former. Upon entering school, each and every child brings with him a sizeable life outlook, or world of insight; none starts from scratch. And it is presumably the business of schooling continually to seek betterment or improvement of student outlooks. The pragmatic next-question is, therefore, "What constitutes betterment?" Since this is an axiological (value-packed) question, it is taken pragmatically to be a humanly personal one; in that sense, arbitrary. It is, of course, to be dealt with as thoughtfully, or reflectively, as possible, but the answer that we must reach as a working principle cannot be a scientific one; it is not an epistemological matter.

In the preceding paragraph, we already have noted one way by which to judge betterment or improvement of life outlook: make it bigger, cover more territory, include additional insights or broaden those already possessed. In other words, a *more adequate* outlook on one's world of

2 Bayles, *Theory and Practice of Teaching,* pp. 67–70.

effect will be almost universally approved as a better one, so our fifth criterion—widespread agreement on the part of prospective users—may well be satisfied. Moreover, addition of new insights and enhancement of old ones has, from the beginning of recorded educational history, been a major objective of instruction and often the only one. If what already is taught doesn't seem to be accomplishing what it should, concoct a new course to take care of the seeming fault.

By Harmonization

Bigness, however, is far from an unmitigated virtue, as the reader doubtless already has been thinking. Consider the dinosaurs, who got too big for their brains, or the several hundred pounds of dead weight that has to be carried about by the 600-pound fat man. School curricula tend also to gather "dead weight," as is so neatly depicted in *The Saber-Tooth Curriculum*.[3] As we note (elsewhere), Dewey warned us against flooding a child's mind with information that he cannot grasp. And, in *Democratic Educational Theory*,[4] we have documented one of Bode's continuing inveighments against the confusion in our thinking that is engendered when we fail to ask whether a given *addition* to life outlook (a new insight) harmonizes with what is already embodied therein. Apparently, whenever we add something new, we need to ask what it may do to the old. If it fits into the overall pattern of the old and thereby furnishes additional support, well and good. But if it does not—if it knocks a glaring hole in the pattern or introduces an incompatibility—then reconstruction is seemingly in order.

Whether bigness is a virtue seems to hinge, therefore, on how well the matter under scrutiny hangs together, on how well each and every part contributes to and helps promote the outworkings of each and every other part. When a given item or aspect of a given pattern tends to work contrary to the remainder of the pattern, it is to that degree a drain upon the pattern. It tends in that degree to undo what the rest of the pattern is tending to do. Moreover, in the degree to which a given aspect or item tends neither to help nor to hinder the general tendency of the pattern as a whole, it is useless baggage and in the interests of efficiency is better done without. Thus it appears that whether something is better because it is bigger is vitally dependent upon the exclusion of anything that is incompatible or disharmonious. Harmony, compatibility, consistency: these are names for a characteristic or property that apparently must be possessed by anything that may justifiably be deemed as possessing or evincing highest quality, or perhaps even high quality.

---

[3] J. Abner Peddiwell, *The Saber-Tooth Curriculum*, foreword by Harold Benjamin (New York: McGraw-Hill, 1939). Available in paperback.
[4] Bayles, *Democratic Educational Theory*, pp. 211–12.

Betterment Defined

Consequently, improvement or betterment of one's world of insight or one's outlook on life would seem to require (a) increase in coverage or greater adequacy, provided there is no loss in consistency, or (b) increase in consistency or harmony, provided there is no loss (or, at most, little loss) in coverage, or, better still (c) increase in both coverage and consistency (adequacy and harmony). In other words, *betterment of student outlooks on the world of which the students are a part* means that such outlooks must become *more adequate and more harmonious;* they must gain in either without sizeable loss of the other or, preferably, gain in both.

As an objective for democratic education, this is *not* taken to be a philosophic absolute—something laid down in the very nature of things and not subject to human tampering. It is recognized as a human concoction; hypothetical; subject to human frailties, hence continually open to reconsideration and reappraisal; taken to be the best we have for now and the basis for present planning and design, but open to modification whenever such seems justified. This very characteristic, however, makes the objective compatible with democracy. Hence, to that degree it satisfies our third criterion for a definition; viz., avoidance of self-contradiction. Moreover, it furnishes a distinct and definite basis for curriculum design, hence satisfies our first criterion; viz., indicates a definite line of action. And, by being explicit in this respect, it satisfies our second criterion, differentiation among various alternatives. Finally, it is concise and, in light of the foregoing discussion, it would seem to accord in high degree with the thinking of people who give the matter serious consideration, thus satisfying our fourth and fifth criteria.

A further matter of importance is that, as an educational objective, the idea that subject matter chosen for study should be such as will promote more adequate and more harmonious student outlooks on the life of which they are a part is thoroughly compatible with the modern scientific criterion for determining what is true; viz., adequacy and harmony of outlook or conclusion in light of obtainable data. . . . Thus, the open-endedness of democracy, and of science as well, is incorporated. And when it comes to the brutally hard and necessary facts of life, to what way of obtaining truth other than the scientific are the American people genuinely and practically committed? It is quite true that there are many who *claim* allegiance to "higher" ways of obtaining "truth." But should we not suggest that it is personal *belief* that such persons really have in mind when they so speak—not honest-to-goodness truth? Belief is axiological, not epistemological. Belief is personal; it represents human conviction or choice; it represents the "self" speaking on its own; it does not depend on the principle of interaction wherein the nonself is called upon for corroboration, as does science. But to rely upon scientific investigation as much as possible in arriving at beliefs is certainly a pragmatic behest, and our proposed educational objective obeys it.

Summary Statement of Purpose

Curriculum content—what we are to study—must thus be promotive of more adequate and more harmonious student outlooks on the life of which they are (and probably will be) a part. Coupled with the previously noted behest of democracy—to promote independent learning capacity—we arrive at the proposition that the overall objective (or covering-end) of democratic education should be to *promote more adequate and more harmonious student outlooks on the life of which they are (or foreseeably will be) a part, and heightened capacity to reconstruct outlooks independently.* This means that American school personnel are presumably commissioned by the body politic to seek (a) to expand each student's world of insight toward progressively fuller coverage of his world of effect, going as far as possible in the time and under the conditions that are provided; (b) to harmonize, first, student outlooks; then, as studies reveal incompatibilities and shortcomings in the world of effect, to help students attain more harmonious and more adequate (hence more tenable) ideas as to how the world of effect may in turn be improved; and (c) to foster heightened capacity to participate, when they become full-fledged members of the body politic, in progressive reconstruction both of personal outlooks and the world of effect as it progressively confronts them.

CHAPTER 6

The System of Philosophic Beliefs

The Relevance of Philosophy to Schooling

Let's begin by examining a few commonplace differences among popular beliefs:

> CITIZEN A: I was really glad to see the governor make it tough for those slobs on welfare. You've got to show them that they can't expect something for nothing, or they'll never get off their duffs and go to work!
>
> CITIZEN B: I don't blame them one bit! The way big business exploits the little guy, I think he's justified in getting every penny he can any way he can.
>
> CITIZEN C: Nobody wants to be on welfare. We have more responsibility than just dole out a minimal level of subsistence. What about providing programs that will help them find jobs and become self-sufficient?

Are there different opinions, different philosophies, or different beliefs about the basic nature of man and what motivates him? Try an example more directly related to classroom teaching:

> STUDENT TEACHER: I'm really excited about trying to individualize the reading program to really help each student attain a feeling of self-worth.
>
> TEACHER A: That kind of idealism is great, but don't be too disappointed when you find it doesn't work. Some kids will just never make it.
>
> TEACHER B: I've got one real loser. He shouldn't even be in school. I had his older brother last year and he was the same way.

Before you assume that we have contrived these examples to prove that basic differences exist, consider the distinction McGregor (1957) has made between two contradictory views of management. Theory X, the conventional view, assumes that:

1. Management is responsible for organizing the elements of productive enterprise—money, materials, equipment, people—in the interest of economic ends.

2. Without active intervention by management, people would be indifferent—even resistant—to organizational needs. They must therefore be persuaded, rewarded, punished, controlled—their activities must be directed to fit the needs of the organization.

3. The average man is by nature indolent—he works as little as possible, lacks ambition, dislikes responsibility, and prefers to be led. He is inherently self-centered, indifferent to organizational needs, resistant to change, gullible, and not very bright, the ready dupe of the charlatan and the demagogue.

Theory Y is based on "more adequate assumptions about human nature and human motivation":

1. Management is responsible for organizing the elements of productive enterprise—money, materials, equipment, people—in the interest of economic ends.

2. People are *not* by nature passive or resistant to organizational needs. They have become so as a result of experience in organization. Motivation, potential for development, the capacity for assuming responsibility, the readiness to direct behavior toward organizational goals are all present in people. It is a responsibility of management to make it possible for people to recognize and develop these human characteristics for themselves.

3. The essential task of management is to arrange organizational conditions and methods of operation so that people can achieve their own goals by directing their own efforts toward organizational objectives.

McGregor concurs that people are often passive, indolent, self-centered, and resistant, but he takes issue with the attempt to develop reasons for these observed behaviors that mistakenly attributes them to something in the nature of man, as opposed to something in the nature of organization.

The Theory X–Theory Y argument, and all its implications, demonstrates the ability of philosophy to raise open-ended, troubling questions. Our intent is to establish by illustration the basic premise of our inquiry into philosophy: that individuals appear to hold fundamentally different notions, views, or beliefs regarding the nature of and reasons behind differing events or phenomena.

One of the most troublesome tasks imaginable is to verbalize one's beliefs. An individual's philosophy of life or of education is quite abstract, therefore making it difficult to find precise words or phrases that communicate one's perceptions or views (Kneller, 1966:171). Two individuals who actually hold similar life views might produce two radically different statements.

One way to find out something about a person's philosophy is to obtain his reaction to a deliberately constructed set of statements (Roscoe, 1968; Dunwell et al., 1971), such as: "Man is born basically bad; hence, education has the responsibility of attempting to purge the evil from students by any means that seem appropriate." We can ask the individual to indicate how strongly he agrees or disagrees with this.

We can include in our list statements that represent philosophic belief systems that contradict each other. For example:

8. Developing students who know the "right answer" is the prime function of education.
19. Getting the right answer is not as important as knowing how to arrive at a solution and inventing new ways of approaching and solving problems.

Such an inventory provides a good indication of the views of individuals and groups, even though the respondent has to react to someone else's statements, which may not fit his own meanings. Too, the respondent's statements may not reflect what he actually does in behavioral situations.

In administering philosophic inventories to groups of teachers, the authors have found:

1. A surprisingly high degree of concurrence on *certain* items, even within a relatively large group of teachers (N = 264). For example, 97 percent agree with the statement, "Learning is a process by which students are able to raise, explore, and solve problems on their own."

2. A high degree of consistency in accepting-rejecting *some* sets of statements deliberately constructed to represent opposing views. For example, 96 percent agree that "getting the right answer is not as important as knowing how to arrive at a solution and inventing new ways of approaching and solving problems," and 90 percent disagree with the statement that "developing students who know the 'right answer' is the prime function of education."

3. A number of glaring contradictions in responses to *other* sets of statements. While 97 percent agree that learning is an open process of student exploration and problem solving (item 1 above), 80 percent *also* believe that "the mind can be trained and strengthened by presenting problems which will exercise it, *such as any other muscle of the body*" (italics added). The first statement is constructed to reflect development of the fully functioning person, the second to reflect mental discipline, a prescientific notion dredged up from education's mythological past.

4. A *wide division* of opinion on *certain* questions that appear crucial to effective conduct of teaching. Among these are questions of whether the student can be "trained" in matters of aesthetics (truth, goodness, and beauty); whether competition for grades is desirable; and whether "indoctrination" of students with the ideals of democracy is appropriate.

Although these findings obviously do not give us a comprehensive picture of the teaching practices and the learning environment of a particular school, they do expose a fundamental characteristic of teaching: There is no clear agreement among teachers about what the school can best do to serve its students because there is no clear agreement on the fundamental nature of the human individual.

There is no clear agreement among teachers about *how* learning takes place. This results in a perplexing admixture of generalizations about learning: (1) some students learn better one way, others another way; (2) some things are learned better one way, other things in some other way; (3) at some times students learn some things better one way, at other times the same students learn better some other way.

Before you accept these generalizations, think about what they offer you. Do they tell you anything about how you ought to teach? Do they give you any clear directions for the development of competent teaching practice? What they represent is a pretty poor theory of teaching, because the theory does not generate anything more than what was known initially. We are left with the feeling that a clearer understanding of teaching/learning principles is not only possible, but esential. And that is precisely what philosophy tries to give us.

Earlier we extracted a rather simple observation about the way people view the circumstance of life:

1. Individuals appear to hold fundamentally different notions, views, or beliefs regarding the nature of and reasons behind differing events or phenomena.

Now we are ready to add several other observations which may at first seem rather simplistic, but nonetheless provide a sound working base for our inquiry into philosophy as a foundation for education:

2. Individuals form notions or beliefs regarding different events or phenomena as they experience and consider them. No one individual is likely to encounter every possible event or phenomenon.

3. Although each person tends to form *patterns* of beliefs, frequently an individual arrives at an observation or conclusion without regard for its consistency with prior observations and conclusions.

4. In the development of an educational program, the effectiveness of goal setting and means determination is dependent upon the degree of clarity and consistency present.

Especially in matters of knowledge and wisdom, upon which teaching is evidently predicated, it is essential to be clear and consistent. If one of the prime needs of education today is clarity and consistency, and if philosophy promotes this, teaching practice can be improved by gaining an understanding of the issues and approaches offered by the discipline of philosophic thinking.

Philosophic Issues in Education

Let us now look at some of the ways in which formal philosophy treats the general issues of educating man. These general issues have to do with: (1) the relationship between man and the world; (2) the relationship between man and knowledge; and (3) the relationship between man and goodness, truth, and beauty. We should be able to demonstrate how each of several alternate philosophic belief systems influences specific teaching practices used in dealing with these general educational problems.

(Teachers frequently reject philosophy because they do not see a progressive bridging from the general to the specific, and often fail to differentiate among teaching practices that appear similar but in fact are not. Chapter 7 is concerned specifically with teaching practices derived from different philosophies.)

The Relationship between Man and the World

One area of philosophy, called metaphysics or ontology (see Table 6–1 for the derivation of formal terms and the organization of typical philosophic questions) is concerned primarily with the nature of the world, in the most comprehensive sense, and of man, in the most particular sense. The physical world may be viewed as subordinate to the "real" world (Idealism) or as precisely equivalent (Realism). This relationship may be regarded as nondetermining (Relativism) or as nonconsequential (Existentialism).

We can describe the relationship of man and the physical world in similar terms. Man may be viewed as superordinate to other physical things (Idealism) or precisely equivalent to all other physical things (Realism), or this relationship may be regarded as determined by the interaction between man and the physical world (Relativism). One's view of this relationship is based upon one's conception of man's actional nature. Man may be seen as possessing free will and capable of autonomous independent action (Idealism), as passively controlled by events over which he has no influence (Realism), or as capable of interacting with and influencing the course of events (Relativism). The various philosophic positions hold fundamentally different views of man's actional nature, granting or denying that man inherently possesses a motive force, the old Theory X–Theory Y dichotomy.

But man's actional nature by itself is not sufficient to understand or predict *how* man will act or behave. To obtain a functional understanding of behavior, we need to know whether or not man is capable of action and, if he is, what direction this action may take. This is a moral ques-

TABLE 6-1: THE ORGANIZATION OF PHILOSOPHIC QUESTIONS AND TERMS

	Being or Existence	Knowledge and Knowing	Values and Valuing
TYPICAL PHILOSOPHIC QUESTIONS	What is the world really like? What caused the world to be as it is? What are things in the world including man, really like? What caused these things, including man, to be as they are? What are all possible things really like? What caused all possible things to be as they are?	How do we really know? How dependable is what we know? How do we go about obtaining knowledge? How do we go about verifying knowledge? What knowledge is of greatest value to us? What can we do with knowledge?	Of what we know, how can we discriminate between what is good and what is bad? What value do we assign to certain things? Why do we give them this value? What value do we assign to certain ways of acting? Why do we give them this value? How can we set criteria to judge the goodness, truth, beauty, or other value of all possible things?
PHILOSOPHIC TERM AND ITS ORIGIN	Ontology [< Gk *ont-*, to be + *ology*, study.] synonymous with Metaphysics [< Gk *ta meta ta physika*, lit. the works after the physics, referring to the arrangement of topics in Aristotle's writing.]	Epistemology [< Gk *episteme*, knowledge + *ology*, study.]	Axiology [< Gk *axios*, worthy + *ology*, study.] The study of value, how it comes about, how criteria for judging value are established. Ethics [< Gk *ethos*, custom, habit, character.] The study of the value of certain acts or behavior, and how they are judged. Aesthetics [< Gk *aisthetikos*, to perceive, perception.] The study of the value or beauty of all manner of things, and how they are
DEFINITION	The study of being or existence, the theory of what causes something to exist.	The study of knowledge, how it comes about, how it is structured, and how it is verified.	

TABLE 6–2

PRINCIPLES OF BEHAVIOR DERIVED FROM NOTIONS
OF MAN'S ORIGINAL NATURE

Man's Moral Nature	Man's Actional Nature	Resultant Principles of Behavior
Good	Active	Neutral-Active
		Bad-Active
		Good-Active
Bad	Passive	Neutral-Passive
Neutral (capable of becoming good or bad)	Interactive	Neutral-Interactive

tion, a matter of good or bad. Does man start off good and become better, or does he start off bad and become worse? Man's moral nature may be viewed as directed toward eventual attainment of good or, alternately, of evil, or man may be considered capable of attaining either good or evil depending on what he himself does about the question of morality.

The possible combinations of man's moral and actional natures are displayed in Table 6–2. It is immediately apparent that certain possible combinations have no logical consequence. If man is taken to be passive by nature, incapable of influencing the course of events that befall him, his original moral nature or inclination make no difference. Similarly, if man's original actional nature is taken to be interactive, it makes no sense to ascribe an original moral inclination to man because potentially he may become either good or bad.

What we have is only an indication of the divergence among philosophic belief systems, as demonstrated in Table 6–3. These distinctions are fundamental and powerful enough to generate widely different schools of psychology. Here is where the sorting out, like some huge intellectual scrabble game, becomes both fascinating and frustrating.

Without getting too involved in analyzing the complexities of these positions, we can derive some valid propositions about the nature of the educational process required by each of the moral/actional principles (Bayles and Hood, 1966):

1. *Neutral-Active Principle.* If man is capable of attaining either good or bad, and if we *also* assume that his original nature enables him to reason through to the ultimate scheme of things, education must deliberately lead him to consider those ideas which best contribute to the development of disciplined thought. Ultimately man will arrive at the absolute ideals of truth, beauty, and goodness, and he can start his search by considering the most rational thinking available in classical form and text.

TABLE 6-3

PSYCHOLOGICAL/PHILOSOPHIC POSITIONS DERIVED FROM DIFFERING
NOTIONS OF MAN'S ORIGINAL NATURE

General Philosophic Position	Man's Moral/ Actional Nature	Derived Psychological/ Philosophic Positions
Idealism	Neutral-Active	Classicism
	Bad-Active	Puritanism
	Good-Active	Romantic Naturalism
Realism	Neutral-Passive	Apperception or Herbartianism
		Connectionism
		Behaviorism
		Operant Conditioning
Relativism	Naturally Active	Gestalt
	Neutral-Interactive	Goal-Insight
		Cognitive-Field
Relativistic Humanism		Third-Force
Existentialism	Neutral-Interactive	Existential Psychology

2. *Bad-Active Principle.* If man's original nature actively propels him toward evil ends, his natural tendencies must be deliberately countered by an opposing force for good. Schools and other social agencies must join the church to serve as an active instrument of society. Direction is obtained from moral prescription, particularly the Scriptures.

3. *Good-Active Principle.* If man's original nature actively propels him toward good ends, his natural tendencies must be deliberately protected from any corrupting or perverting forces. Rather than adopt a passive role, schools must work actively to protect and nurture the development of the individual's natural propensities.

4. *Neutral-Passive Principle.* If man's original nature is passive, any motive force or direction must be obtained from some external source.

A pool ball does not move by itself; it moves at the speed and in the direction imparted by the cue stick. Man is subject to the same laws of nature and of physics as any other element in the scheme of things. The school facilitates man's understanding of the natural laws that govern the forces acting on him in order to promote his adjustment to them.

5. *Neutral-Interactive Principle.* If man's original nature makes him a participant in the shaping of events, he needs to determine what he can and cannot do. His knowledge of an event is not dependent on some external a priori meaning, but on the meaning he himself makes of the event. To behave effectively, he must become perceptive and skillful in structuring and utilizing the meanings he obtains through interaction. The school's responsibility is then to assist man to experience and make intelligent use of his experience.

In this last instance we have used the term "interaction" in a particular way. If man is passive and responds to an external force, he is *re*-acting rather than acting. A series of such events is best denoted as *alternating reaction* (Bigge, 1971:73). If man is *interactive,* he does not merely react but sees himself in a mutual relationship with his environment, obtains meanings, and uses these meanings in an advantageous manner (Bigge, 1971:74). The relationship is *simultaneous, mutual, and interactive.* (Bigge describes this relationship as the "SMI concept.")

Obviously there are differing degrees or levels of interaction. The interest of a child in watching a bug crawl around differs from that of an entomologist analyzing aspects far beyond the child's perceptual and cognitive abilities. However, they are doing the same thing at different levels of sophistication.

This same interrelationship is useful in handling the active-passive dualism. The concept of interaction does not mean that *all* men are *always* active, or *always* passive, but that individuals may become more one than the other, depending on the nature and quality of their experiences.

The Relationship between Man and Knowledge

The term *epistemology* denotes the study of knowledge—how it comes about, how it is structured, and how it is verified. Knowledge (the product of knowing) and knowing (the process by which knowledge is attained) are so closely related that it is difficult to talk about one without referring to the other. It is also apparent that anything we have to say about knowing carries direct implications for learning, learning theory, instruction, and educational psychology.

Knowledge may be viewed as: (1) existing within man and hence entirely dependent upon the nature of man for its development and function (Romantic Naturalism); (2) having a discrete existence separate and apart from man and hence entirely independent in its nature, organization, and structure (Absolutism); or (3) an integral function of the interaction of man and his environment and hence directly related to a multivariate system (Relativism).

1. *Knowledge within Man.* If knowledge is inherent within man, it must be inborn, or innate, in potential form, and would have to grow or emerge naturally in the same manner as any other human trait. Variations in knowledge potential among men would have to be explained like other human differences, primarily on the basis of genetically inherited traits.

With this set of assumptions, the central purpose of schooling would be to ensure the natural development of the individual and prevent anything that might inhibit or retard it. The condition of knowledge would be attained through maturation and would be the same for individuals of the same inherited genetic pattern.

Certain genotypes must obviously possess greater natural endowment, greater knowledge potential, greater capacity to rule. The efficiency of schooling could thus be vastly improved by creating schools based upon social class, and caste systems designed to assure the survival of the species.

2. *Knowledge Independent of Man.* If knowledge has an existence independent of man, its existence does not depend upon the existence of man. Knowledge would exist as a given before being known by man and even if it were not known by any individual. Granting knowledge an existence independent of man asserts that its nature and structure are unchanging and fixed; hence the notion that knowledge is a given, or an absolute.

It would remain then to describe the nature and structure of knowledge and how it came to exist in that form. For knowledge to have a nature and form external to man, it must have been created or established by some force, power, or being external to man. This may be attributed to the absolute power of ideas (Idealism), the absolute power of a divine being (Religious Realism), or the absolute power of nature (Natural or Scientific Realism).

How does knowledge that exists external to man come to be known by man? What portion of the total sum of knowledge can man come to know? If ideas have an existence apart from mere physical reality, as Idealism asserts, it is doubtful that physical man can ever transcend the physical world and come to the ultimate reality of the ideal world. However, through the exercise of his powers of reason he can catch glimpses of what must exist "out there." From these images man can make successive approximations toward ultimate reality. Thus man can come to know something of what is real, but his knowledge will never be absolutely free of inaccuracies and imperfections.

Religious Realism grants that man can attain knowledge of perfect order through observation of the Divine Being's work, but only to the extent that the Divine Being wills it so. Scientific realism grants that man can attain knowledge of nature's order through scientific observation of the physical reality that is the world.

In each instance the elements of knowledge are ordered and arranged in an unchanging structure that has an existence of its own. Although each of these alternate views maintains a different rationale for the way its particular structure came into being, they view the organization of knowledge in similar ways. Knowledge is arranged into disciplines; the disciplines fall into a hierarchical order from fundamental to esoteric; each discipline is discrete and complete in its own right; within each discipline knowledge can be arranged from the general to the specific. Given such an order, man can catalog the elements of knowledge—facts, ideas, and concepts—with a high degree of certainty.

3. *Knowledge Interdependent with Man.* If knowledge comes into existence through the interaction of man and his perceived environment, the nature and structure of these meanings are psychologically rather than externally determined. Knowledge is focused or directional because it is related to man's focus or direction; it is orderly because it is given order by purposive interaction; it is structured because man gives structure to it.

Giving structure to knowledge is essential if man is to deal with the ever-increasing number of meanings arising through his interaction. To avoid a clutter of meanings, a person attempts to economize intellectual effort by imposing order on his field. Based on certain identities among different but related experiences, the individual forms unified regions of his psychological reality, or categories (Phenix, 1964). The individual's choice of a particular categorizing scheme among the infinite number possible is that which is most appropriate to him.

It might seem that the world consists of individuals each with his own particular set of knowledge structured in his own particular way. To some degree this is true. However, there are a great many similarities among the structures of knowledge held by different individuals, because the processes of experiencing, making meanings, and structuring knowledge is fundamentally the same for all individuals; individuals interacting in similar environments tend to form similar meanings, and we determine the validity of our meanings or insights in part by checking them against those held by other persons. What emerges is a set of insights individually obtained and verified and commonly shared or concurrently held by a number of individuals.

As the process becomes more specific, formal, highly structured, commonly shared, and comprehensive, we obtain formal knowledge, or a discipline of knowledge.

We are able now to define a discipline as a way of knowing, a way of making knowledge. As such, a discipline is characterized first by domain, an area of human experience or phenomena for which members of the discipline take responsibility; second as a set of rules that has to do with how "truth" is established, conceived of, and stated within the discipline; and third as having a history that may be described and presumably known by the inquirer (Foshay, 1962).

The Relationship between Man and Goodness, Truth, and Beauty

Goodness, truth, and beauty, the concerns of axiology (see Table 6–1), are more particular extensions of alternate beliefs about ontology and epistemology. We can expect goodness, truth, and beauty to be treated like other areas of philosophy. Standards for goodness, truth, and beauty may be regarded as inherent in the nature of man (Romantic Naturalism), external to and independent of man (Absolutism), or a function of the process of interaction (Relativism).

The nature and structure of a system of values—whether it pertains to ethical conduct or to artistic merit—are logically derived.

1. *Intrinsic within man's nature.* Following the premises of Romantic Naturalism, if man is allowed to develop according to his natural propensities, he will *naturally* become good, behave appropriately, and discriminate beauty. This development can be facilitated, but its course and direction are internally determined.

2. *External and independent existence.* Man must acquire knowledge of these standards by deliberate observation and analysis of that which best represents ultimate goodness. Ethical conduct is obtained in terms of conformance to external standards. The worth of any act can be judged in terms of these standards, an accurate knowledge of which is prerequisite to effective behavior.

3. *A function of interaction.* To the relativist, man acquires the knowledge of truth, goodness, and beauty through a process of mutual interaction. He obtains meaning situationally and designs behavior to achieve the ends sought most effectively. He judges what is appropriate or inappropriate and becomes progressively more skillful in designing behavior. He creates art to obtain the most meaningful satisfaction of his desires. He holds to be true those meanings which he has found to be most dependable.

The Topics of Formal Philosophy

Because the range of possible topics about the universe is as large as the universe, any attempt to create understanding is facilitated by the grouping of these topics according to apparent similarities and dissimilarities. Grouping similar questions together makes it easier to sort out and verify possible answers. Often the justification of an answer is found in its context. Second, since philosophic questions are usually stated in universal terms so as to obtain universal answers, inquiry is directed toward related sets of phenomena. All that is known about existence, for example, is brought together for analysis; explanations of what is not known are tested in terms of how well they fit what is known.

As is shown in Table 6–1, typical philosophic inquiries or questions include topics dealing with: being or existence (ontology or metaphysics); knowledge and knowing (epistemology); and values and valuing (axiology). This categorization of philosophic topics is functional rather than merely traditional.

Table 6–4 displays the basic categories of philosophic concerns across the horizontal axis and the major philosophic theories down the left side. As stated earlier, these different systems are based on fundamentally different conceptions of what phenomena make up reality, or different answers to the ontological question of what is real.

Metaphysical/Ontological Questions and Answers

Idealism. In attempting to determine the true nature of the world, the Idealist is struck by two apparently immutable conditions. First, although real, physical, substantive things exist, including his own physical being, they do not account fully for all of what is known about reality. The true nature of "tree-ness" cannot be determined by viewing a single tree and cannot be found in any given tree. The essence of "tree-ness," the ultimate reality of "tree" as an idea, does *not* exist in physical or substantive reality (Shermis, 1967:51). A physical reality exists, but it cannot be taken as ultimately real.

The second condition is that apart from the substantive or physical nature of the world, there must exist a second domain made up of the ultimate ideas or idea essences. This aspect of world must be *really* real, with the physical aspect merely a reflection of the ultimate idea of the thing. Because this reality is ultimate, by definition it is absolute. Nothing exists beyond this final reality (Shermis, 1967:65).

The true nature of man also demonstrates this dualistic reality. Man's physical being is real and substantive. But man is more than merely physical. The essence of man must be a real, nonsubstantive spirit or soul, which is housed in but capable of transcending the physical being. For early philosophers the explanation of a soul-spirit conveniently dealt with their observations of mental functions: consciousness-unconsciousness, cognition-intuition, logic-fantasy (Butler, 1966:42).

If we grant that man has an inherent or innate spirit or soul, he be-

TABLE 6-4

A TAXONOMY OF PHILOSOPHIC CONCEPTS

	Ontology	Epistemology	Axiology	
CLASSIFICATION OF PHILOSOPHIC THEORIES	The study of what has caused something to exist; a theory of being.	The study of how knowledge and knowing come about; how knowledge is organized and validated.	The study of how value is ascribed to certain things; a theory of valuing.	
			Ethics	Aesthetics
			Applied to how certain acts or behaviors are judged.	Applied to how beauty is judg in all manner things.
IDEALISM (Idea-ism)	Dualistic reality of absolute ideals (ideas) and soul-spirits.	Absolute truth independent of soul obtained through reason.	Judged by congruence with absolute ideal.	Judged by refl tion of absolut ideal.
RELIGIOUS REALISM	Unitary reality created by absolute God.	Absolute truth obtained through God's work revealed.	Judged by congruence with God's will revealed.	Judged by qua of Divine insp tion; creative i tuition as God will.
SCIENTIFIC REALISM	Unitary reality created by absolute nature.	Absolute truth obtained through scientific observation.	Judged by congruence with observed natural law.	Judged by con gruence with natural form.
RELATIVISM (Relation-ism)	Pluralistic worlds caused by variant experiences of man.	Truth a function of effective relations man has developed and tested.	Judged by community through tested experiences; the public tests.	Judged by com munity on accepted criteria the public tast
EXISTENTIALISM	Pluralistic worlds caused by experiencing one's own existing.	Truth a function of man's choice of alternatives he has experienced.	Judged by individual forced into existential choice.	Judged by indi vidual independ ent of public prescription.

comes capable of many other functions or self-initiated actions. He has mind and is capable of reason. He is endowed with a spirit of the ultimate and is capable of achieving ultimate goodness. If he is not himself Divine, he nonetheless possesses at least a touch of divinity. Man is inherently good; man is inherently active.

This dualistic description further establishes direction in life functions: *from* the inferior, representational, physical reality *toward* the superior, spiritual, ultimate reality of ideas. The substitution of *ideal* for *idea,* and *Idealism* for *Idea-ism,* is a logical consequence of striving for ultimate reality (Bayles, 1960:69).

Realism.   Confronted by the same question of the nature of reality, some are troubled by the Idealist's dismissing the substance of physical reality in favor of an abstract notion of mind-essence. By what manner can superiority be granted to mind-essences or ideas when they are nonsubstantive, largely nonverifiable, and often apparently capricious? Is not physical reality substantive, verifiable, objective in and of its own self?

Abetted by the rise of scientism, philosophic Realism abandons the Idealist notion of ultimate reality vested in the "idea" of a thing and focuses on the thing itself, its substance and nature (Shermis, 1967:83). A tree *is* a tree, nothing more, nothing less. All that is "tree" about a tree can be determined by precise, objective analysis of a tree. "Tree" can be deductively analyzed into its constituent parts or elements, which can be synthesized inductively back into "tree." The whole is equal to the sum of the parts; the sum of the parts is equal to the whole. Nothing more; nothing less.

Again, one realizes the absoluteness of this concept. "Nothing more; nothing less" is not to be taken as rhetoric but as principle, and the principle is immutable. In fact and practice, these principles are regarded as so absolute as to be called "laws"—laws of nature, laws of motion, laws of learning—*governing* all existence.

The existence of man is explainable in terms of this same set of laws as part of this unitary reality. Man is one of several variant classes of organisms. At birth he exhibits all the characteristics of others of the same phylogenetic origin; any variance can be described by the appropriate laws of genetics. His moral nature is, like all nature, unburdened by moralistic judgments, unless of course you accept the Religious Realist notions of man's fall from grace and conception in sin. Man's actional nature is determined as all other action is determined; it is the result of forces exerted upon the object by an external source. Nothing more; nothing less.

The Realist conception of life is not without consideration of force and direction; however, determination of force and direction is external to man and beyond his individual control. Man is impelled by the external forces that act upon him. If these forces happen to bring him closer to concordance with the existing order of nature and he obtains "appropriate" or "adequate" response sets, "good" is achieved. Disharmony, discordance, maladjustment to nature are "bad." Man is capable of becoming either good or bad, but, because of the accident of arbitrary causes, not through his own will.

Relativism, or Pragmatism.   Some are still not satisfied with the Realist explanation of reality as a unitary absolute. They observe that man does not *always* appear to be a passive reactor to external forces; in some instances man appears to initiate action. They observe that man does not *always* view the same phenomenon in precisely the same way; at differing times and in differing circumstances differing meanings are attached to apparently similar happenings. They observe that the moral nature of man is not *always* determined by the accident of arbitrary causes; man may indeed play a role in determining what he may wish to become.

From this they *infer* that man is not dominated by an external, unitary, absolute reality but rather that he functions in relationship with events of which he is an integral part, in accordance with the meanings he ascribes to these events (Bayles, 1966). From this emphasis the philosophic theories of relation-ism, or Relativism, and functionalism, or Pragmatism, are developed. It is not that a tree is a tree, but that what I take to be a tree is a tree.

As a philosophic theory, Relativism views the world in a systematic, orderly, structured, focused manner (Bayles, 1966:54). The Realist would not be able to accept this proposition simply because its bases are radically different from those he has constructed.

The Realist sees change in any element as determined absolutely within a system of absolutes. Some would suggest that the Relativist or Pragmatist views change as constant and inevitable, resulting in a world view that is an ambiguous mass of confusion and chaos. This is scepticism or irrationalism, not Relativism. The Relativist views change as caused and understandable, occurring as a change in meaning or relationship occurs. To make change absolute would be to contradict a basic premise of Relativism.

Hence the nature of the world is neither singular nor absolute but systematic and orderly as a *function* of the meanings man attributes to world events (Bayles, 1966:54). Albeit pluralistic, these alternate world views may be differentiated into meaningful relationships.

Man himself, then, need not be singular and absolute to be understandable. Obviously, men differ widely, most in how each perceives himself, how each perceives himself in relation to his perceived world, and how each sets about making sense of this relationship. But these differences are understandable because they are founded in the meaning each has made of his interactions within his world.

Some men become "good," some become "bad," but they are not compelled to goodness or condemned to badness. As a matter of fact, they have much to say about the conceptions of both "goodness" and "badness" and how they will relate to those conceptions.

Existentialism.   The Existentialist sees something more in the nature of the relationship between man and world. This has little to do with the question of the world's finiteness or infiniteness; it has much to do with the fact that existence *is* as man knows it; it is specifically finite. Existence is real; it is intensely personal and singular; it is expressly limited by the fact of death. Confronted by his own mortality, man does not have the time to consider anything else; he is compelled to deal with the significance of his own existence before it comes to its inevitable conclusion.

More than any other philosophic theory, Existentialism eludes formal analysis (Morris, 1966:12). Among Existentialists, recognition of the fact of death ranges from positive affirmation of the need to make one's existence meaningful to a preoccupation with death itself. The emphasis on personal awareness of the condition of existence—"I" exist for "me" to create "my" essence—deliberately precludes verification of the meanings derived. What is real to you can only be real in your terms (Morris, 1966:14).

Man's moral nature, then, is subject to no external value judgment. What is "good" is "good" only in terms relative to the individual; what is "bad" is "bad" only in the same sense. Concern is directed to helping the person achieve enhanced awareness of his being and of the existential choice that confronts him. What he makes of this *is* what it is.

Epistemological Questions and Answers

Idealism.   Having conceived an absolute and ultimate world of idea-essences, Idealist philosophic theory focuses on: (1) the nature of this knowledge, how it is ordered and structured; and (2) the nature of knowing, how man achieves knowledge. The explanations are surprisingly simple.

Ultimate knowledge or absolute truth exists independent of and superior to the physical world and physical man. Knowledge or truth exists ultimately; it exists absolutely. Because it is fixed and unchanging, it exists only in an absolute state of perfection or ideal form. Ultimate knowledge is absolute truth existing in perfect form and order. Perfect knowledge is structured in perfect form. Knowledge is verified in terms of its conformity to this perfect form and order. Given this fixed ideal toward which perfection may be directed, one must deal only with what is necessary to move from imperfection to perfection, transcending physical man and substantive mind to the nonsubstantive essence of spiritual man/mind (Butler, 1966:65).

Here man is fortunate, for ultimate truth must be the product of the disciplined application of ultimate reason, and man is capable of reason. In the perfection of substantive mind toward perfect form, he has at hand those forms that most nearly represent perfection—e.g., the classics. The disciplined analysis of these forms yields a disciplined substantive mind capable of reasoning toward perfection. Development of the substantive mind accrues from disciplined exercise applied to any form; the greater development of the power of reason accrues from disciplined exercise applied to the more perfect forms or disciplines. Both content and process for learning are proscribed by the existence of absolute truth.

The Idealist, who ascribes a theistic origin to ultimate truth, believes that it is possible for him to "dis-cover" something of God's will in His revealed work. With devout humility, he carefully studies God's handiwork and the works of others divinely inspired to "dis-cover" or reveal the will of God hidden from the unrighteous.

Realism.   In much the same manner, Realist philosophic theory seeks to answer the same sort of epistemological questions. But here the distinction between Religious Realism and Scientific Realism becomes more significant.

The Religious Realist "knows" that absolute truth, absolute form, absolute order, absolute perfection exist. He *knows* they were established by his absolute God "in the beginning." He *knows* that these can be revealed to him ultimately on his ascension to paradise. He *knows* that by living a more perfect life he becomes a more likely candidate for Divine revelation, Divine inspiration, and ultimately Divine salvation.

The Scientific or Natural Realist also knows that absolute truth, absolute form, absolute order, absolute perfection exist. He knows they were established "in the beginning" by the nature of things, which he absolutizes, or have evolved following a natural order.

He believes that it is possible for him to "dis-cover" something, if not everything, of this absolute natural order through the analysis of that which exists in this physical reality. He believes that knowledge of this preexisting perfect natural order may best be achieved by the more perfect, "scientific" observation and analysis of natural phenomena. He strives to determine each fact of nature and to order it into the ultimate form or structure to which it naturally belongs.

Knowing, to the Realist, is simply cognition of that which already exists external to the observer. The increase or improvement of knowing depends naturally on either: (1) increasing the number of opportunities for exposure to external stimuli (enrichment); or (2) improving the technical quality of the observation itself, usually through instrumentation (Butler, 1966:73; Bayles, 1960:71).

Knowledge is considered verified by *replication*. Application of a known principle must demonstrate its ability to produce precisely the same results previously observed under controlled conditions.

Relativism, or Pragmatism.   It was noted earlier that the Relativist views the world in a systematic, orderly, structured, focused manner, but a manner radically different from the preceding philosophic theories. The Relativist does not assert the preexistence of knowledge in some absolute form. Rather, he asserts that the function of man in his world may be more clearly understood only in terms of the particular meanings or insights a particular man has made of his particular experiences.

How man views a tree, to return to that example, depends precisely on the meanings/insights he has acquired, his purposes, and the potential function/insight he ascribes to the tree. He may seek shelter, shade, food, firewood, lumber, a log for a raft or canoe, or a place to hang a hammock, purpose being situational. Reciprocal interaction of ends sought/means utilized/ends attained results generally in the formation of insights or knowledge. The process is coming to know; the products are insights or knowledge.

For the Relativist, the entire set of epistemological questions and answers shifts focus from externally determined and structured absolute knowledge to internally acquired and structured relative knowledge. This knowledge is relative because it is derived from the interactional relationship and conditionally limited by the dimensions of the interactional events.

As man acquires more insights, he generalizes according to the functional relationship among them. He structures his knowledge, not in accordance with some external form but in accordance with the scheme that seems to him most reasonable and meaningful. He structures knowledge to enhance its instrumental value to him.

Knowledge is focused for the Relativist because it focuses on man's interaction with world (Bayles, 1966:45). It is systematic because it gives consideration to reciprocal means/ends relationships. It is orderly because of its focus upon a given end. It is structured because man gives structure to it.

Knowledge is verified by the pragmatic test. A principle or insight must demonstrate its ability to predict results with accuracy. This may not be replication, for the conditions of relationship need not be identical as long as variations are taken into account in the predictive validation (Bayles, 1966:49).

Existentialism. The Existentialist approach to epistemological questions and answers is even more elusive of analysis. Having granted man free choice—even compelling him to choose because of the imminence of his own death—the philosophic theory must then accommodate the full range of possible alternatives. The world *is* what each man makes it. Conceivably the range of beliefs held by Existentialists could run from absolute knowledge through relative knowledge through absolute scepticism. Truth—if there is a concern for truth getting—is obtained in confronting the dilemma of finite existence with some kind of choice required. Truth is in the act of choosing, not necessarily in the particular choice.

Validation of knowledge or verification of beliefs against some external criterion comes to be meaningless. What is relevant to each person is the essence of his own existence. It does not require verification except that which he requires in making a choice; the judgment of another would be both impertinent and destructive of the essence of the other person's existence (Morris, 1966).

The Existentialist concern for learning—learning the significance of one's own existence—is obvious. It is also obvious that learning in this sense precludes or opposes formal institutionalized schooling as it is currently conceived.

Axiological Questions and Answers

Idealism. The Idealist deals with the questions of beauty and ethical conduct in a manner consistent with Idealism's theory of ontology and epistemology. Perfect form exists as an ideal in the nonphysical world of ideas (Shermis, 1967:120). Reflections or representations of perfect form exist in the physical world. These available physical forms are products of substantive mind striving toward perfection. They represent ideal beauty to the degree that substantive mind is able to achieve disciplined reason (Butler, 1966:74).

Representations of ethical conduct are similarly obtained. The disciplined substantive mind is better able to conceive of the absolute ideals of virtue, honesty, and purity and to behave in ways that are virtuous, honest, and pure.

Realism. As suggested earlier, the Religious Realist seeks to determine and emulate God's will revealed. Perfect beauty is attainable only through Divine perfection. God is beauty. God's will is revealed in two ways: (1) through His work, or the natural world He has created; and (2) through the work of man that He has divinely inspired. Man can come to know beauty through careful observation of all that is beautiful in nature. In art, man seeks to reflect perfectly the beauty of the sunrise, the flowers, of the human formed in God's image. Man can come to know beauty through the careful study of products of divinely inspired artists, particularly those whose works are the product of religious passion, fervor, even suffering in God's name.

Ethical behavior is similarly derived. Man seeks to know God's will and to discipline himself to perform God's will. Given an absolute definition of good and evil, the prescription of behaviors and thoughts can be spelled out by doctrine and dogma specifically and absolutely.

Scientific Realists derive axiological answers in much the same way as they derive epistemological answers. Given an absolute nature, the source of absolute beauty must reside within this nature. That which is most beautiful is that which most realistically reflects the true nature of things. That which is to be made more beautiful must be made more natural, more congruent with natural form. Axiological laws are derivations of natural laws and are directly applicable to the creation of art forms.

The same is true of ethical behavior. Absolute natural laws prescribe those behaviors that provide best for the accommodation of and adjustment to natural order. Those behaviors that are congruent with natural order promote good; those that conflict with natural order promote maladjustment, disharmony, disequilibrium. Because natural order is absolute, ethical behavior is observable, attainable, verifiable.

Relativism, or Pragmatism.   As the Relativist seeks knowledge or insight from reciprocal interaction of ends sought/means utilized/ends attained, he finds meanings appropriate to the axiological questions of beauty and ethical behavior. Because he deliberately avoids absolutes, pluralistic meanings of beauty will exist at any given time. A given person may find many different meanings for beauty, each of which are functional and meaningful at a given time, or one that predominates, or none. Some meanings of beauty and ethical behavior are intimately personal, even arbitrarily chosen (Bayles, 1966:58); other value meanings are commonly shared and generalized. Thus, among Relativists *both* community standards for what is beautiful and individual tastes will be found. Rather than being fixed and unchanging, these standards of beauty will change as the meanings change with experience over time (Shermis, 1967).

Ethical behavior is considered in much the same way. Those behaviors that promote the achievement of ends sought will come to be seen as having instrumental value. However, the definition of what is ethical will not be singular or fixed over time, precisely because it is what one deems to be situational and experiential. In a social climate that values individualism and social change, tolerance is extended to some widely divergent behaviors, although some are given preference (Bayles, 1966: 58). Standards may vary from community to community and from time to time, not randomly, but systematically.

Existentialism. Having placed emphasis on the individual's self-determination of what is meaningful to him, the Existential theory would place the same requirement for choice in axiological matters. As in the case of Pragmatism, one must determine what is beautiful and ethical in one's own terms through the experience of one's own existence. The judgment of another person can have no relevance or pertinence to this choosing (Morris, 1966; Shermis, 1967).

Philosophical Alternatives Summarized

1. *Metaphysical/Ontology*
   a) The Idealist postulates a dual universe of mind/soul and matter/substance. Of these the mind is controlling and superior. Man is an actor and he is good.
   b) The Realist has a single universe of matter/substance. Man is passive within a cosmos of universal and operant principles. He is neutral in inclination.
   c) The Pragmatist perceives a plural universe involving human purposiveness. It is a fluid phenomenon—one of relative change. Man is interactive, although he is neutral before the interactional state.
   d) The Existentialist understands only his own existence and struggle for essence. He is good, as no other alternatives exist in the confrontation of self and an end to self. The world of mankind may have no meaning at all except in the individual presence.
2. *Epistemology*
   a) Idealism recognizes knowledge as a distillation of human experience toward perfection. It is an embodiment of the noble and virtuous, the ideal. The ultimate is inherent within the soul/mind, to be nurtured through discipline in the struggle to attain.
   b) Realism understands knowledge as a set of operative universal absolutes which are deduced from empirical evidence. The mind can be trained to reason. Adaptation is the reason for knowing.
   c) Pragmatism perceives knowledge as experience to which meanings are ascribed for utility within purposive seeking. This seeking of insight within the situation field is the means of gaining meaning.
   d) The Existentialist must perceive knowledge as events and happenings which are either relevant to self-appropriation or not.
3. *Axiology*
   a) Representational perfection of the ideal form is beauty to the

Idealist. His behaviors are disciplines from the ideals of the noble and virtuous.

b) Replications or extractions of the very thing itself are beauty to the Realist. His behaviors are disciplined responses to principles derived empirically.

c) Functional meanings which satisfy are beauty to the Pragmatist. His behaviors are interactional seeking of means to ends with consequences that are also perceived as beneficial. A truth is the workability of a means.

d) The Existentialist must choose what is beautiful and ethical in terms relevant to his own existence/essence.

The Implications for Teaching

Earlier we made the commonsense observation that different people appear to hold fundamentally different views of the nature of and reasons behind certain events or phenomena. This occurs not only in particular instances—two Monday-morning quarterbacks with two entirely different interpretations of what should or should not have been done to ensure a win—but also in the larger sense, leading to a range of alternative philosophic explanations.

Generally, alternative philosophic explanations arrange themselves into differing patterns or schools of thought. Yet within each philosophic school are many variant patterns or individual belief systems that diverge to some degree. Because certain beliefs are mutually exclusive, these philosophic schools do not represent points on a continuum, as one might expect, but tend to form separate belief systems distinguished by these fundamental differences.

Alternative philosophic explanations differ primarily in the nature of the basic phenomena that are taken into account and the explanation of the cause of these phenomena—that is, in ontology or metaphysics, the question of what causes something to exist as it exists. The metaphysical question is basic because, as shown earlier, it leads to other considerations: how do we know this exists, how do we verify our knowledge, how do we differentiate good and bad? So the metaphysical question is basic both to the other philosophic inquiries grounded in it and to the differentiation of various schools of philosophic thought.

To summarize, philosophic alternatives have come into existence because of: (1) fundamentally different conceptions of what phenomena make up reality (substantive structure); and (2) fundamentally different ways of treating and verifying this particular set of phenomena (syntactical structure).

The dilemma of education persists to a large degree because it is difficult to obtain agreement as to what the schools should be doing (Taba, 1962:16). In turn, the lack of agreement on educational purpose stems from a lack of agreement on the precise nature of the student and how he learns. What we are attempting to do now is obtain a functional description of different ways of viewing man, knowledge, and knowing so as to determine the implications of these views for schooling. We are attempting to establish the relevance of philosophy as a foundation for educational practice—nothing more; nothing less.

REFERENCES

Bayles, Ernest E. *Democratic Educational Theory.* New York: Harper & Row, 1960.

————. *Pragmatism in Education.* New York: Harper & Row, 1966.

————, and Bruce Hood. *Growth of American Educational Thought and Practice.* New York: Harper & Row, 1966.

Bigge, Morris L. *Learning Theory for Teachers.* 2nd ed. New York: Harper & Row, 1971.

Butler, J. Donald. *Idealism in Education.* New York: Harper & Row, 1966.

Dunwell, Robert R., et al. *The Assessment of Informal Factors Affecting Teaching and Learning in a Ghetto High School.* ERIC Document ED 052 281, February 1971.

Foshay, Arthur W. "Education and the Nature of a Discipline." In *New Dimensions in Learning: A Multidisciplinary Approach,* edited by Walter B. Waetjen. Washington, D.C.: A.S.C.D., 1962.

Kneller, George S. *Logic and Language of Education.* New York: Wiley, 1966.

McGregor, Douglas. "The Human Side of Enterprise." *The Management Review* 46 (1957):22–28; 88–92.

Morris, Van Cleve. *Existentialism in Education.* New York: Harper & Row, 1966.

Roscoe, John T., et al. "American College Student Values: Preliminary Report of a Nationwide Survey." *Colorado Journal of Educational Research* 8 (Fall 1968).

Shermis, S. Samuel. *Philosophic Foundations of Education.* New York: American Book, 1967.

Taba, Hilda. *Curriculum Development: Theory and Practice.* New York: Harcourt, Brace & World, 1962.

Suggested Readings

Brown, Bob Burton. *The Experimental Mind in Education.* New York: Harper & Row, 1968.

Bruner, Jerome S. *The Process of Education.* Cambridge: Harvard University Press, 1960.

Dewey, John. *Democracy and Education*. New York: Macmillan, 1916.

———. *Essays in Experimental Logic*. Chicago: University of Chicago Press, 1917.

———. *Experience and Education*. New York: Collier, 1938.

Elam, Stanley M., ed. *Education and the Structure of Knowledge*. Chicago: Rand McNally, 1964.

Ford, G. W., and Lawrence Pugno. *The Structure of Knowledge and the Curriculum*. Chicago: Rand McNally, 1964.

James, William. *Pragmatism*. New York: Longmans, Green, 1919.

King, Arthur, and John Brownell. *The Curriculum and the Disciplines of Knowledge*. New York: Wiley, 1966.

Martin, William O. *Realism in Education*. New York: Harper & Row, 1969.

May, Rollo, ed. *Existential Psychology*. New York: Random House, 1961.

CHAPTER 7

Philosophic Guides to Teaching

We have arrived at the issue that is a critical weakness of most teacher-education programs. What can be done to derive a sensible approach to teaching in view of the effort of philosophy to encompass, categorize, and rationalize everything, which nevertheless results in a range of alternate explanations founded on widely differing assumptions? Do teachers have time to get seriously involved in philosophy? How do teachers select from among available alternatives? Teacher-education programs have approached these questions in the following ways.

A Laissez-Faire Approach

Teacher-education programs are free to adopt any philosophic theory they choose. A program might be clearly identified with a particular philosophy (e.g., Religious Realism, Existentialism). The elements of the program—courses, policies, practices—might be planned as a systematic part of the total program design. Every program element could contribute to the whole, with all elements carefully articulated and coordinated.

But in spite of the fact that teacher-education programs are free to do this, most do not. Few programs can be identified with a particular philosophic school, and these few are usually associated with highly ethnocentric language and culture schools, sectarian schools with dominant theological belief systems, and an even smaller number devoted to specific pedagogical doctrine, such as Montessori schools. One also finds a variance from "hard line" to "soft line," programs with a high degree of internal consistency, and programs with a measured tolerance of the espoused doctrine.

The effect of these programs on prospective teachers is frequently minimal. The inability of education to influence an individual's beliefs, attitudes, and values has often been pointed out (Lieberman, 1960;

Coleman, 1966; Jencks, 1972). Other factors usually have a greater effect on the development of the individual. We acknowledge the major impact of socialization and acculturation but seem to ignore what influences the student in the school. The formal program of the school has less effect than the informal influence of the peer culture. It is not that the student is *not* influenced by the culture of the school, but that the culture of the school *is* the culture of the students. This is another way of asserting that the school culture can serve as a "planned addendum and a corrective to the socializing processes" (Taba, 1962:66) while acknowledging that it usually does not.

In higher education, where schools of a broad range of size, type, location, and character are available, even less change is apparent in the student's philosophy from start to finish. However, this probably is not because of the influence, or lack of influence, of the schools. Roscoe's massive study of the attitudes and values of college students (1968) suggests that different types of schools exhibit different philosophic belief systems; the individual student appears to select a school that agrees with beliefs he already holds. In substance, the individual does not want his beliefs or values changed; he wants them supported and validated. Higher education's influence on student values *is* significant, despite the fact that it produces no apparent change.

Perhaps the worst thing that takes place within a laissez-faire system is that the learner is exposed to a wide range of unrelated bits and pieces of philosophy. Each course is based on a different set of philosophic assumptions; each faculty member is allowed to present his pet notions and beliefs and to use them as performance criteria. Students quickly learn that the most rational approach to this irrational process is to "psych out" the prof and ignore whatever other logic there may be. The entire process is rationalized by both student and faculty as a necessary part of the academic game and is often defended as a perverse interpretation of the academic freedom of the faculty member. Few are concerned about protecting the student's academic privilege.

We assert that there can and should be a mutual accountability—between teacher and student, between academe and the "real" world, between what can and what cannot be verified. If there is any area in which this accountability should be obtained, it is philosophy.

An Authoritarian Approach

It was asserted at the outset that American public education is a non-system, or at best is systematic only because of some interstate accommodations of mutual convenience. Nevertheless, consideration ought to be given to the possibility of a nationalized federal public education system.

This proposal generates much the same skepticism that San Franciscans have for their Bay Area Rapid Transit (BART): there is evidence that most of the elements of the system actually exist, there is a belief that such a system would probably eliminate most of the city's present problems, but nobody is convinced that the thing will ever really work.

It is possible to speculate about the form such a federal system of public education might take. The "philosophy" of this educational enterprise would become a uniform national policy modeled after the European system of centralized ministries of education. All units would be governed by standardized operating practices. The coordination and effectiveness of the system would be ensured by the control exerted by some central ministry. Any haggling over policy questions would be done at a national level, thus relieving school-level teachers and administrators of these onerous problems.

Many Americans, haunted by the specter of George Orwell's *1984* and Big-Brotherism, believe this solution would be undesirable. While we might accept a clear statement of educational purpose, direction, and practice as advantageous, there is tremendous concern about the process by which these might be achieved. It is doubtful that we would want to submit Skinnerian operant conditioning versus Rogerian student-centered practice to the vagaries of political popularity. Even if we were able to work out the mechanics of establishing educational practices by polling the public, we would still have trouble dealing with the issue of appropriateness of philosophical politicking.

It may not even be possible to attain national consensus on how schools should be operated, much less the sophisticated means to put such a system into effect. Historical evidence demonstrates that the success of such organizations is abnormal; they fail more frequently than they succeed. Even if it were possible to govern teacher education in America by the adoption of an official philosophy of education (and it probably is not possible), it seems less than desirable (and probably it is undesirable).

A Pluralistic Approach

It is possible to enjoy the advantages of a clearly structured approach to education without making the grave error of accepting a unitary scheme whose consequences are not yet discernible. We can make deliberate provisions for several approaches with careful attention to the outcomes and consequences of each. We can commit ourselves to act without committing ourselves to a particular course of action. We can observe where we are going without plunging blindly into inescapable consequences.

Such an approach has much to offer as a means of establishing and clarifying the role of teacher-education institutions and their philosophy or beliefs about how teaching should be carried out in a democratic society. It really is not a matter of "electing" a particular philosophy to guide education, nor is it a matter of adverse competition among alternate belief systems. What is important to the democratic system is the regard for "minority" views, how they are treated, and what privileges are assured them. If a particular philosophy were ever to obtain "majority" support, it would likely enjoy this status for only a limited time, subject to reopening and reconsideration of the issue. The same "privilege" would be accorded any previous "loser," for minority views would still have the right to seek additional support and similarly be subject to reexamination and reconsideration (Bayles, 1966).

Democratic principle requires pluralism, but it certainly is not a laissez-faire approach. Consideration of the widest possible range of ideas offers the best chance to develop the best answer available at this time under these circumstances. However, if this process is to have any significance, the examination has to be deliberate, disciplined, and thorough, even exhaustive. We seek something more than mere acceptance of the possible correctness of a notion—the considered conviction that this *is* the best possible answer available.

Even though we may adopt and believe in a particular philosophy of education, even though we may have examined the evidence that supports other views, if we do not hold ourselves open for further examination of the issues we may be less than correct and less than secure in our position. Not to do so would require more energy to defend one's beliefs than is required by reexamination of the alternatives.

Other evidence lends support to the notion that students should be expected to conduct an honest investigation of available alternate views. Our earlier description of the characteristics of the disciplines (King and Brownell, 1966) provides the guide for approaching philosophy as a discipline. One does not have functional knowledge of a discipline until one knows each of its identifiable aspects—domain, substantive structure, and syntactical structure among them. Since philosophy possesses several concurrent structures, competent knowledge must mean knowledge of the particular characteristics of each, especially the differing beliefs and values that form their basis.

In a teacher-education program, each educational philosophy should be examined thoroughly. The consequences that may be anticipated from each should be considered before any individual is encouraged to commit himself to a particular choice.

This requires an approach rather different from what we usually find. Individual faculty members would be required to enter into an honest discourse. Because their professional beliefs have been personalized, they usually are not willing to submit them to examination by other members of the community (peers or students). Educational policy should promote substantive interaction among all members of the community. Often policies are established that prevent students from participating fully, with faculty members protected from accountability before the larger community. The result has been a vast accumulation of academic minutiae and policies that serve someone's clerical convenience more than the educative function of the academic community.

The suggestion that such an approach is appropriate to teacher education is not made casually. The educator in a subject discipline has an even greater responsibility to know and understand each concurrent structure than the practitioner, who has the obvious luxury of adhering to a singular point of view. The educator, who knows that some notions become popular because of their simplistic explanations, must press the learner to consider some matters more deeply than some practitioners believe necessary. The educator, even more than the practitioner, must distinguish what is objective and what is nonobjective in the discipline. We are not suggesting the easiest way to teach or to apply philosophy to education, merely the most reasonable and responsible approach.

We intend at this point to demonstrate the application of this approach to philosophy, to analyze each of the major categories—ontology, epistemology, axiology—and to derive the specific instructional acts that best fulfill the requirements. Although few teachers actually see themselves as philosophy teachers, clearly each subject area has a direct relationship to the encompassing structure of philosophy. We intend to demonstrate that philosophy has a natural, functional, sensible, and completely understandable relationship to classroom teaching practices.

Guidelines Derived from Ontological Propositions

Existence

Idealism, Realism, Relativism, and Existentialism have emerged as alternate structures of philosophy to describe the nature and order of all that exists. This includes alternative descriptions of all objects, events, happenings, and phenomena. As learning progresses and the range of included substance increases, it becomes increasingly difficult to comprehend, organize, and remember all that has occurred, and to determine the direction or tendency of developmental patterns, especially when alternate descriptions and assumptions are utilized. Skillful teaching in each subject discipline is essential to promote the most adequate view of reality.

Because younger learners are in the process of obtaining initial experience and meaning from the world in which they find themselves, the teacher encourages them to examine carefully all aspects of that world.

The question "What is it?" is fundamentally ontological. The skillful teacher will use this question to arouse initial interest or puzzlement that can lead to interest. The teacher asks "What else do you see?" to develop an inquisitive attitude that elicits more elaborate descriptions. The teacher expands the area of concern by asking the learner to consider items that have gone unnoticed to this point. Initially the teacher accepts verbal descriptions without judgment or intervention. But when the learner is without terms adequate to express his ideas or feelings, the teacher assists in developing language appropriate to the requirements of communication.

As the learner is required to deal with phenomena and events of greater number and complexity, the teacher helps identify similarities and differences and assists in finding the apparent order of things in the world, including alternate ways to organize and structure reality. The epistemological concern for the structure of knowledge necessitates that every effort be made to ensure that the learner's views are always as clear and coherent as possible. The teacher encourages the learner to relate alternative structures to alternative assumptions: "If we use this notion as the criterion for our description, what kind of order is obtained? If we use an alternative base, what is obtained? Which approach seems clearer and more logical?"

As the learner becomes increasingly mature, he grows more aware of the distinction between real and unreal, between what is imaginary and what is comprehensible. The teacher provides means, both personal and technical, to help the learner understand these distinctions. Each subject treats different aspects of reality and has different ways of defining reality. The teacher promotes the development of skills to test the relevance and validity of each of these different views of reality. The teacher encourages the learner to attempt larger conceptualizations of events, moving from the here and now to questions of larger, perhaps universal, significance. The teacher, as a representative of the discipline, works to establish the substance of the discipline as a reliable base for the continuing growth of knowledge.

The teacher actively helps the learner to sort out those things in reality (objects, events, happenings) that are part of self and those things that are part of all else about him, or nonself. The teacher encourages the learner to expand his concept of self to encompass all appropriate elements, particularly those within assigned subject disciplines. The teacher suggests means for the learner to distinguish among physical, social, emotional, and intellectual aspects of self, how they are related to each other, and how they are related to external elements. The teacher provides support and security while the learner experiences and learns to cope successfully with the awareness of and sensitivity to self.

The teacher promotes the learner's awareness of and sensitivity to others; assists the learner in assessing the expectations he has of others and others have of him; and encourages the learner to examine and analyze interpersonal relationships. The teacher provides access to available knowledge that helps expand the individual's understanding, particularly through subject matter. The teacher helps the learner to distinguish differing concepts of man's relationship to man and to the world. The teacher requires consideration of the discrepancies that become apparent when we look at different descriptions, pressing for clarification and understanding of the existence of differences before attempting to reconcile discrepancies.

Causation

Different descriptions of what exists lead to different explanations of what causes things to come into existence and different expectations of what we may find to exist. Possible responses to the question "Why is this so?" or "What caused this to be so?" differ substantively from one another and do not necessarily relate to a known antecedent. As one attempts to move from awareness of the existence of something to knowledge of the causes—from effect to insight—any earlier confusion among the alternate descriptions is compounded. Skillful teaching is required in each subject discipline to help distinguish alternate explanations of causes and to obtain adequate understanding of cause-effect relationships.

For all learners, young and old, the question that most logically follows "What is it?" is "Why is it that way?" or "What made it that way?" The skillful teacher will use these questions to sustain or expand the learner's initial interest. Recognizing the potential learning that lies just beyond initial awareness, the teacher deliberately looks for the opportune moment to enlarge the scope of consideration to include causal elements. Starting with a student-described event, the teacher asks "Why did it happen that way?" both to clarify the student's awareness of what happened and to initiate consideration of causes. The teacher demonstrates a phenomenon before a group of students, listens to their various observations, and initiates the question "What could possibly have caused it to happen in that way?" The teacher's concern is to see that learners become aware of alternative explanations before an effort is made to verify any specific explanations. At this point the teacher deliberately holds matters open for consideration and avoids pressing for the "right" answer or even the best available answer. The teacher remains sensitive to the fact that an even better answer may be obtainable just around an intellectual corner.

As the learner experiences more and more possible alternate explanations of causality, he becomes increasingly aware of what is plausible and what is logical. The teacher encourages consideration of an increasing range of explanations as a means of broadening the base for verification.

The teacher assists learners to broaden consideration by presenting new opportunities, providing means for resolving matters, and providing support while ambiguities and uncertainties are being examined. If this is not done, learners grasp simplistic explanations prior to thorough consideration, avoid dealing with ambiguities and uncertainties, and become increasingly less able or less willing to approach novel situations.

As the learner grows in sophistication, he becomes more aware of the events for which at least one plausible explanation exists and the events for which he has no plausible explanation at present. The teacher helps the learner organize and keep track of these distinctions, determine the points where explanation seems more relevant to the total scheme of things, and assign priority to efforts that are most productive. The teacher encourages the learner to develop more adequate theories of causality, moving from immediate, simple explanations toward larger ones. The teacher, as a representative of the discipline, works to establish awareness of the alternative means utilized by the discipline to test cause-effect relationships.

Having helped the individual learner become aware of and sensitive to the range of events that affect him, the teacher actively assists him to understand why they affect him as they do. The teacher helps the individual determine changes within himself and relate these changes to known events or possibly unperceived causes. The teacher encourages the individual learner's search to identify what influencing factors may or may not be controlled or altered. The teacher promotes development of personal skills, adjustive and adaptive behaviors, and coping mechanisms, and provides personal support and resource to the learner as this personal growth progresses.

The teacher promotes consideration of influences on groups of individuals and determination of the causes of changes in group behavior. The teacher encourages examination of a wide range of relationships, seeking, for example, the degree to which geographical factors influence patterns of living and the degree to which individual and group preferences influence choice of geographic locale for residence. The teacher provides access to available knowledge of cause-effect relationships through the subject, emphasizing the need to reexamine and reverify this knowledge in light of current conditions. The teacher confronts the individual learner with the necessity to consider apparent discrepancies as a potential means to fill in perceived gaps in available knowledge of group behavior.

Human Vector

Alternate descriptions of existence and causation result in different descriptions of the nature and capability of man in relation to all other reality. Different descriptions of the nature and appropriate role of man result in conflicting role perceptions and role expectations. During youth and adolescence, this lack of clarity or certainty contributes to role ambiguity, ambivalence, and alienation from reality. Skillful teaching is essential to foster development of an integrated sense of self and reality.

In considering existence and causation, the teacher emphasizes the significance of alternate descriptions of reality for the individual and for man in general. In coming to understand the substance of historical events, the teacher helps the student clarify each interpretation of the events and asks "What did this mean to the people at that time?" The teacher assists the learner to clarify the nature of the events, the effect these events had in that time and place, and the influence of man in determining the course and nature of the events. The teacher promotes concern for and assessment of the human variables—emotions, feelings, beliefs, attitudes—that must have been a part of this influence. The teacher requires consideration of the alternative courses available to man at that time and the possible consequence of an alternative course of action.

In assessing the current state of affairs, the teacher asks "What does this mean to us now?" The teacher encourages expression of the full range of feelings, emotions, concerns, and beliefs among various learners and helps the individual learner to clarify his feelings in relation to the event he has derived. The teacher demonstrates the existence of a range of alternative descriptions, beliefs, and feelings within the current context of the learning group. The teacher promotes consideration of the possible effect of the emotions and feelings of others on the choice of available alternative courses of action. The teacher encourages individuals to explore the effect alternative choices could have on the course of their own lives.

In promoting consideration of future possibilities to prepare persons to deal effectively with future probabilities, the teacher asks "If this continues or happens again in the future, what will it mean to people then?" The teacher promotes consideration of the widest range of alternatives and their probable consequences if adopted as a course of action. The teacher asks the learner to consider both objective and nonobjective factors in the situation and the effect these could have. The teacher encourages the individual to consider the alternatives available to him, the personal preferences that may influence his perception and choice, and their implications. Rather than emphasize agreement with a set of prescriptions, the teacher emphasizes development of views and skills of analysis and effective problem solving that are widely transferable. The teacher fosters development of a sense of confidence in one's ability to meet the demands of the future. The teacher fosters development of a sense of the alternative courses of action available to the larger society, and something of the appropriateness of each alternative.

Guidelines Derived from Epistemological Propositions

Knowing

Major philosophic schools assert opposing descriptions of the process by which man obtains knowledge of reality. The way knowing is treated is determined by fundamentally different conceptions of the nature of reality and the availability of knowledge about that reality. If we take "knowing" to mean identifying and accepting independently existing, authoritative knowledge, then anything of which we are less than absolutely certain may be discredited and ignored. If we assert "knowing" to be a matter of arbitrary personal choice of any possible meaning, we deny any means to share, communicate, or verify meaning unless we happen to be communicating on the same frequencies.

The answer to this philosophic dilemma is, logically enough, to treat the problem philosophically. The fundamental question that should be raised in the classroom is "How do we know?"

One primary set of skills/attitudes a teacher should strive to develop is the ability to assess a problem situation competently. The teacher helps the learner identify what is known and, from what is known, to determine what is appropriate to the situation. The teacher helps the learner to plan and develop means of identifying what is not known in a learning climate free of inhibiting feelings of anxiety, frustration, or incompetency. The teacher encourages the learner to "find out." If knowledge cannot be "found out," the teacher assists the learner in planning alternative approaches to problem solutions, including the making of "new" knowledge.

The teacher suggests that the learner "invent" knowledge, and then helps the learner to develop appropriate means to appraise the reliability of these inventions. The teacher assists the learner to identify what procedures are effective in the discipline and to become skillful in the employment of these methods of verification. Realizing that the younger learner may not possess sufficient background to judge the significance of newly obtained skills, the teacher provides contextual cues representing the larger dimensions of the discipline. As the learner progresses, the teacher fosters increasing independence by encouraging the learner to verify and reverify his procedures.

The teacher assists the learner in distinguishing and developing different ways of knowing appropriate to different classes of knowledge. The teacher demonstrates that facts, ideas, concepts, thinking, attitudes, values, sensitivities, feelings, and behaviors are different forms of knowing, obtained by differing means, and verifiable against differing standards and procedures. The teacher demonstrates that knowing is an ongoing process requiring and meriting the attention and concern of all learners.

Knowledge

Major philosophic schools assert fundamentally different descriptions of the nature, order, substance, and structure of knowledge, ranging from the notion of a complete, perfect, comprehensive structure of absolute knowledge that exists independent of man to the notion that knowledge is absolutely dependent upon the individual's unique experience.

Although teaching gives primary emphasis to the process of knowing, knowledge products are made more useful if they are organized for fluent acquisition, retrieval, application, display, comparison, and reexamination.

Enhancement of knowledge immediately follows acquisition of knowledge. As soon as the younger learner has made initial appropriation of a meaning, the teacher begins to ask "What can we do with that?" Some meanings have immediate application. The learner quickly senses how they can be used now and in similar future situations. In other circumstances the teacher may know of this particular meaning's potential use, but the learner does not, so an entirely different strategy—perhaps "Let's leave that for now and come back to it later"—is required. The teacher deliberately avoids "knowledge for the sake of knowledge" as a motive, for that is not the natural motivation for knowing even at the highest level of abstraction, and more often it becomes demotivating. The teacher encourages the learner to seek applications for his meanings, to identify "growth points" where new knowledge may be added, and to reexamine meanings continually for further possible use.

As the learner matures and becomes more skillful in ordering and structuring his acquired knowledge, the emphasis shifts to the larger structure—its comprehensiveness, its completeness, and its discrepancies, if any. The teacher demonstrates an attitude of nonjudgmental acceptance to encourage the learner's examination of knowledge "gaps" without fear or defensiveness. The teacher provides the learner with skills and means of analysis to assist him in testing the adequacy of the knowledge structure. The teacher encourages development of alternative means of assessment leading toward independent judgment. The teacher promotes inquiry into the adequacy of parts of the structure of knowledge by analogy to other parts or structures. The teacher emphasizes the manner of organization that the larger community has found useful, but encourages critical analysis rather than passive acceptance. The teacher leads the learner to the limits of knowledge as quickly as is feasible and demonstrates "stepping-off places" or "growth points." The teacher demonstrates the skills and attitudes of the inquirer and researcher and encourages the learner to adopt these as functional behaviors.

Guidelines Derived from Axiological Propositions

Valuing

Axiology, as an integral category of knowledge, inherits the same set of problems faced by epistemology. Major philosophic schools assert opposing descriptions of the manner in which man obtains knowledge of values. The process of valuing is determined by fundamentally different notions of what values are, how knowledge of values can be acquired, and how one uses values. Valuing may be treated as the application of absolute standards that exist independent of the process and unchanged by their use. Valuing may also be seen as an interactive process in which value meanings are derived, verified, and altered by the process of application. For the purpose of guiding teaching, teachers should involve learners in the meaningful study of valuing procedures to determine which of the several available notions is most defensible.

One of the primary sets of skills/attitudes a teacher should strive to develop is the ability to assess value meanings competently; this may also be called appraisal or appreciation. The teacher deliberately includes appreciation studies as integral with other studies. The teacher helps the learner identify currently held individual and societal values. From this knowledge the teacher helps the learner determine what still needs to be appraised or reappraised. The teacher encourages the learner to consider the merit of things not previously considered. The teacher helps the learner develop skills of appreciation, refine his existing skills of appreciation, "invent" new ways of determining or assessing value, and verify the adequacy of these "inventions."

The teacher assists the learner in identifying valuing processes employed by others in the discipline, determining how successful these processes have been, and acquiring the skills appropriate to these methods of valuation. The teacher suggests contextual cues that may assist the younger learner to determine the importance of the matter under consideration relative to the larger dimensions of the discipline. As the learner progresses, the teacher fosters increasing independence by encouraging continual verification of methods of appraisal.

The teacher helps the learner to distinguish among different ways of determining value. The teacher helps the student determine the effectiveness and appropriateness of alternative ways of valuing. The teacher helps the learner develop different ways of valuing appropriate to different classes of value. The teacher demonstrates that aesthetics, ethics, attitudes, feelings, sensitivities, and behaviors are different forms of valuing, obtained by different means, and verified against different standards and procedures. The teacher demonstrates that valuing is an ongoing process requiring and meriting the attention and concern of all learners.

Values, or Value Products

Major philosophic schools assert fundamentally different descriptions of the nature, order, substance, and structure of values as a special category of knowledge. This ranges from the notion of a complete, perfect, comprehensive structure of absolute values that exists independent of man to the notion that values are absolutely dependent upon the individual's unique assignment of value. Although primary emphasis is given to the process of valuing, value products are made more useful by organizing and structuring them for fluent acquisition, retrieval, application, display, comparison, and reexamination.

As is true of other forms of knowledge, valuing/values are integral relationships more than separate categories. As the process of valuing begins, initial products become available for examination and analysis. The teacher helps the learner become aware of the values at work in a problem situation and the effect of these values on the proceedings. The teacher encourages the learner to ascertain how one's values influence the way one approaches a problem situation. The teacher assists the student in becoming aware of how values affect the process and the resulting situation. The teacher strives to help the learner develop value sets which appear more appropriate to the conduct of learning processes in predicting desired results.

The teacher avoids seeking acceptance of a set of values without subjecting them to careful examination and analysis. The teacher does not state "This (value, behavior, ethic, art form, whatever) is most appropriate" but asks "What (value, behavior, ethic, art form, whatever) seems most appropriate?" This approach does not deny the particular philosophic belief system of any individual, nor does it affirm a belief system to which an individual might object. It does—and this is its heuristic value—require individuals with differing belief systems to reconsider and substantiate the bases for their beliefs.

As the learner matures, the emphasis shifts to the larger structure of his value system—its comprehensiveness, its adequacy, and its discrepancies, if any. The teacher encourages the learner to consider situations in which value conflicts are apparent and situations in which existing values are not adequate to the complexities of the problem. This analysis proceeds best in a nonjudgmental climate in which the teacher assists the learner to appraise rather than by appraising for the learner. The teacher is a continuing resource of alternate value systems, emphasizing the value structures others have found appropriate and the circumstances in which they were found appropriate. The teacher leads the learner to autonomy, encourages the acceptance of responsibility for value choices, and supports the learner in his efforts toward independence.

REFERENCES

Bayles, Ernest E. *Pragmatism in Education.* New York: Harper & Row, 1966.

Coleman, James S., et al. *Equality of Educational Opportunity.* Washington, D.C.: Superintendent of Documents, U.S. Government Printing Office, 1966.

Jencks, Christopher, et al. *Inequality: A Reassessment of the Effect of Family and Schooling in America.* New York: Basic Books, 1972. Summarized in *Saturday Review* 55, September 16, 1972, pp. 37–42.

King, Arthur R., Jr., and John A. Brownell. *The Curriculum and the Disciplines of Knowledge.* New York: Wiley, 1966.

Lieberman, Myron. *The Future of Public Education.* Chicago: University of Chicago Press, 1960.

Roscoe, John T., Carolyn E. Ritter, Steve Teglovic, Jr., and Jerome D. Thayer. "American College Student Values: Preliminary Report of a Nationwide Survey." *Colorado Journal of Educational Research* 8 (Fall 1968).

Taba, Hilda. *Curriculum Development: Theory and Practice.* New York: Harcourt, Brace & World, 1962.

Suggested Readings

The references listed below provide additional points of view and stress the application of philosophy to teaching and learning. Many of the Suggested Readings in Chapter 4 are also relevant to this chapter.

Bayles, Ernest. *Democratic Educational Theory.* New York: Harper & Row, 1960.

One of the earliest and clearest discussions available on learning, existence, value theory, knowing, and democracy. Deliberately suggests democratic reflective education is essential to a free society of individuals.

Bayles, Ernest, ed. Philosophy of Education Series. New York: Harper & Row. Volumes include: Ernest Bayles, *Pragmatism in Education,* 1966. Morris Bigge, *Positive Relativism,* 1971. J. Donald Butler, *Idealism in Education,* 1966. John Magee, *Philosophical Analysis in Education,* 1971. Wm. Martin, *Realism in Education,* 1969. Van Cleve Morris, *Existentialism in Education,* 1966.

Each volume presents an authentic contemporary philosophy. How each philosophy views reality, truth, knowledge, values, and their implications for teaching is clearly discussed.

Belok, Michael, O. R. Bontrager, Howard C. Oswalt, Mary S. Morris, and E. A. Erickson. *Approaches to Values in Education.* Dubuque, Iowa: Wm. C. Brown, 1966.

Written by practicing teachers, describes many approaches to using valuing exercises with traditional content.

Bloom, Benjamin S., ed., *Taxonomy of Educational Objectives. Handbook 1: Cognitive Domain.* New York: McKay, 1956.

Paperback, one of the best sources for a complete listing of the cognitive level of thought. Also included are chapters dealing with applications and uses of the taxonomy to curriculum and instruction.

Brameld, Theodore. *Patterns of Educational Philosophy.* New York: Holt, Rinehart & Winston, 1971.

Presents each of the major educational philosophies—Progressivism, Essentialism, Perennialism, and Reconstructionism—and describes clearly how each views reality, knowledge, and value. These concepts are discussed in relation to education and the implications each has for curriculum and classroom instruction is presented.

Bruner, Jerome. *On Knowing: Essays for the Left Hand.* New York: Atheneum, 1966.

Collection of essays exploring the philosophical and psychological roots of knowing, intuiting, and creating. Discusses how one's concept of reality influences action and commitment, with suggestions for new approaches to teaching and learning.

Drews, Elizabeth, and Leslie Lipson. *Values and Humanity.* New York: St. Martin's, 1971.

A thorough investigation of values—their origin in man and their relationship to the person, the society, and changing universal hierarchies. Particularly beneficial to the person examining his personal life styles and the philosophies on which they are based.

Ford, G. W. and Lawrence Pugno, eds. *The Structure of Knowledge and the Curriculum.* Chicago: Rand McNally, 1964.

A collection of essays each describing the structure of knowledge in selected areas of study—natural sciences, math, English, and social studies. Each essay describes the implications of knowledge in that subject to curriculum and instruction.

Hipple, Theodore, ed. *The Future of Education: 1975–2000.* Pacific Palisades, Calif.: Goodyear, 1974.

A collection of essays by outstanding educators whose responses range from closing down the schools (Illich) to the exploration of transcendental meditation in the future curriculum (Weingartner).

Hunkins, Francis P. *Questioning Strategies and Techniques.* Boston: Allyn & Bacon, 1972.

One of the best and most recent books describing the uses of questions as a method of instruction. Describes the application of questioning to the discovery of knowledge and the relationship of questioning both to cognitive and affective thought processes. Besides providing numerous illustrations, the book presents a model for student and teacher evaluation of this approach.

Krathwohl, David R., Benjamin S. Bloom, and Bertram B. Masia. *Taxonomy of Educational Objectives. Handbook 11: Affective Domain.* New York: McKay, 1964.

Provides a thorough treatment of the five levels of the affective domain. Included in this treatment are examples of instructional objectives and test objectives for each of the levels and their subcategories.

Nash, Paul. *Authority and Freedom in Education*. New York: Wiley, 1966. Designed to help the reader arrive at a synthesis by examining crucial dialectics existing in education. The implications for education are clearly present as the author discusses work vs. play, groupness vs. oneself, determinism vs. choice, excellence vs. equality.

Parker, J. C., and Louis Rubin. *Process as Content*. Chicago: Rand McNally, 1968. Distinguishes between knowledge being process or content and establishes a basis for process as a method of instruction. Especially helpful are the numerous illustrations of process instruction in the fields of English, math, physics, and social studies.

Purkey, William. *Self-Concept and School Achievement*. Englewood Cliffs, N.J.: Prentice-Hall, 1970. Explores the growing emphasis on the student's subjective and personal evaluation of himself as a dominant influence on his success or failure in school. It explains how the self-concept develops in social interaction and what happens to it in school. It also suggests ways for the teacher to reinforce positive and realistic self-concepts in students.

Raths, Louis E., Selma Wasserman, Arthur Jonas, and Arnold M. Rothstein. *Teaching for Thinking*. Columbus, Ohio: Merrill, 1967. Shows how to encourage thinking within the framework of the present curriculum. Besides discussing theory of thinking, the authors provide examples of practical applications of techniques to foster thinking at the elementary and secondary levels. The chapter describing the teacher's role and responsibilities in this process is particularly valuable.

Richards, Fred, and Anne C. Richards. *Homonoyus: The New Man*. Boulder, Colo.: Shields, 1973. Projects a new concept of man by examining mythology, scientific tradition, modern literature, technology, and existential man himself. The time of the book is Maslow's self-actualizing man.

Sanders, Norris. *Classroom Questions: What Kinds?* New York: Harper & Row, 1966. An excellent book that shows teachers clearly the value of questioning as a teaching strategy. Provides numerous examples of questions at different thought levels. A good resource for teachers who want to initiate inquiry learning.

Shermis, S. Samuel. *Philosophical Foundations of Education*. New York: American Book, 1967. Excellent book, examines the central concerns of metaphysics, epistemology, axiology, and social philosophy as they apply to education.

Venable, Tom. *Philosophical Foundations of the Curriculum*. Chicago: Rand McNally, 1967. Examines the strengths and weaknesses of each major educational philosophy as applied to the learner, subject matter, processes of learning, and teaching.

CHAPTER 8

Readings on
Philosophic Foundations

If philosophy teaches one to consider the nature of man, knowledge, and reality, then the study of philosophy must relate practically to teacher preparation. A teacher's view of man, knowledge, and reality becomes a basic tool for guiding learning activities.

In this chapter we elaborate selected philosophic concepts and their applications to teaching. The article by S. Samuel Shermis of Purdue University presents a clear picture of how philosophy can guide teaching. It points out typical conflicts between teaching theory and practice and identifies questions that could reduce these conflicts in educational practice. Teachers should consider these questions seriously; education could then move more directly toward enriching the lives of students.

In Chapter 6 we contrasted the views of the Idealist, the Realist, the Pragmatist, and the Existentialist, and gave consideration to the "newest" recognized movement in educational philosophy, Humanism. In the public school one can find various applications of these philosophic concepts, each of which implies a different emphasis for teaching and learning. A more detailed description of the humanistic position is essential to understand how the humanist views of reality, truth, the nature of man, goodness, and science influence teaching and learning.

Michael Littleford of Auburn University elaborates these concepts and translates them into a promising view for man's future. Education is a process that can be facilitated when its purposes are clearly defined, understood, and perceived as appropriate. The teacher needs to evaluate whether he agrees with these assumptions. If he does, he must begin to formulate some ideas about what is meant by helping students learn. After reading this article, recall the message of Carl Rogers in Chapter 2, where he concluded that he is not interested in "traditional teaching by telling." Does the Littleford article provide a rationale for Rogers' beliefs, a basis for his statements?

There are various views of human potential. Willis Harman of Stanford University and the Stanford Research Institute predicts that a new science of subjective experience is rapidly developing. This view presents a much broader image of man, stressing the importance of enhancing the actualization of one's capacities. The consequences of this revolution in thought, he says, may be more profound than those of the revolutions fostered by Copernicus, Darwin, or Freud.

The humanist philosophy is an optimistic view of education helping man to discover his potential. This discovery depends upon the school's identifying its aims clearly and dedicating itself to their achievement. The study of philosophy invites a search for purpose. Educational philosophy tries to clarify educational purpose to keep educators from losing sight of their goals and to help them reevaluate these aims continuously.

After an extensive review of education, journalist and scholar Charles Silberman published his findings in *Crisis in the Classroom* (1970). Silberman was appalled by the dehumanizing effect of the public schools, due mainly to what he calls "mindlessness" in education, a failure to give serious consideration to the purpose of education, which results in needless conflicts that weaken the entire system. He suggests that educators have lost their sense of purpose or have conflicting purposes that falsely appear to be in harmony. It is not that teachers do not try to do their best, says Silberman, but that education in general is confusing because educators are mindless of what they are doing.

In our abstract from his book, Silberman urges educators and the general population to think seriously about the purposes of education. If you agree with Silberman that educational purpose needs reconsidering, the concepts and processes of educational philosophy are essential for this review.

Philosophy and education are both means of enhancing the person. Schools hold as one of their highest goals the encouragement of creativity. Creativity, like truth and goodness, tends to be a personal quality viewed subjectively, and teachers have not always known how to teach for creativity. They have emphasized instead the more obvious factual content, overlooking the purposeful development of creative potential. In so doing they have often created a classroom climate and procedure that threaten and suppress creativity.

Paul Nash of Boston University describes creativity as a process best advanced by balancing authoritarianism and freedom. He suggests methods that should encourage creativity in the student and elimination of those conditions that threaten creativity. Interestingly, Nash lists as threats to creativity motivation, technology, fear, and the low expectations teachers usually have of their students. Unless educational philosophy becomes the vehicle for integration of man and his world, Nash believes that education will continue to produce immature people lacking well-balanced perspectives.

Chapter 6 presented a thorough discussion of the nature and structure of knowledge. How one perceives the processes of coming to know is important for the teacher. Depending on one's view, teaching may be seen as transmitting the findings of others or as assisting students in identifying and solving problems. Psychologist Jerome Bruner elaborates on the nature of knowledge and its applications to instruction. His article considers the nature of subject matter—the facts, principles, concepts—the *what* of teaching and learning. Concurrent with the examination of the substantive nature of knowledge is a review of the method by which one comes to know a subject. Thus, for the teacher, a clear understanding of the nature of knowledge provides guidelines for determining both what and how to teach.

The articles presented in this chapter are intended to clarify educational philosophy, to show the relationship among the philosophic elements, and to suggest practical applications of philosophy to teaching. Rather than advocating acceptance of a particular view, the crucial concern is challenging the student to structure a philosophy of teaching and learning for himself that is harmonious, applicable, dynamic, and humane.

What Can Philosophy Do?
Samuel Shermis

Forces pointing in different directions and having their origins in many parts of our culture pull and push a teacher. As a result, instead of possessing sufficient knowledge to select a goal, an appropriate set of methods to reach that goal, and a means of evaluating the goal, the teacher often either perceives no goals, methods, or means of evaluation, or perceives them in such numbers that their meaning is likely to be unclear. The body of theory that is supposed to guide teaching practice is crowded with contradictions, often unperceived by practitioners and teachers of practitioners alike.

Such contradictions can lead to serious problems. A teacher at any time has his choice of assuming that children are passive objects whom

Reprinted from *Philosophic Foundations of Education* (New York: Van Nostrand Reinhold, 1967), pp. 275–79, by permission of American Book Co., Div. of Litton Educational Publishing, Inc.

he is to "shape" by mechanical means, or that they are essentially goal-oriented beings with purposes. He can believe passionately in democracy and yet preside over the classroom as an authoritarian. He can know that, because of the structure of our society, individuals must unite effectively and enforce collective demands before they can get what they want, and yet feel that collective action and demands seem unprofessional. At any given time he may read and accept the fact that *the* most significant value of education is a social value that can be satisfied only when all children learn what they must know. Or he can choose to believe that the most significant value in education is the individual development of persons and self-fulfillment of individuals. Or he can prefer to believe that the goal of education is met only when students become proficient in a certain subject matter.

What happens when all these attitudes—and many more—overlap in the teacher's consciousness? The results are ambiguous and difficult to evaluate. Perhaps it is the strain of incompatible beliefs that generates a vitality in American education unmatched in the world. But education is also pulled in different directions, energy is dissipated, support is difficult to obtain,[1] and the quality and quantity of education vary enormously through the country. Some of the consequences of theoretical confusion include the following: teachers who verbalize in one way and practice in quite another; teachers who undergo internal conflict because they do not really know what to do;[2] teachers who engage in mutually conflicting practices for dimly perceived goals, alternating between "strict" and "permissive" classroom control for the goal of "self-discipline"; teachers who require aimless busywork of their students— filling in page after page of workbooks, watching movies and filmstrips only distantly related to the matter at hand; school systems which vaguely sense that the curriculum is meaningless and attempt to compensate for curriculum inadequacies with grades, prizes, material bribes, punishments, and rewards; students who, sometime after the fourth grade, miss the joy of learning and bend all their energies to preparing for an acceptable college; parents who willingly collaborate by first talking about the importance of self-fulfillment and then force their children to take courses toward a college major or an occupation seen as appealing only by the parent;[3] schools and colleges that require courses in art appreci-

---

[1] There is evidence that communities are becoming more and more reluctant to pass school bond issues.

[2] This is seemingly most evident about grading time. The teacher who believes in the stern dictum that grades are objective measures of a student's progress agonizes about giving a failing grade to the pleasant, cooperative, hard-working, but dull student. Duty pulls one way but personal feelings push another.

[3] This is illustrated by the parents who tell their child, "We want you to choose an occupation that will make you happy. We feel you will be happiest as a doctor, lawyer, or a CPA."

ation and then build a campus in an architectural style that can only be called Early Penitentiary;[4] high-school superintendents and teachers who verbalize about the necessity for something called "meeting needs" and then wonder why three-fourths of their lower-class minority students drop out in the sophomore year.

This list could be expanded almost indefinitely. The point is that the many self-defeating, ineffectual, and superficial educational practices in our culture are the result, ultimately, of lack of understanding at the theoretical level. Improvement will come only when those responsible for education understand the philosophical meaning of what they do. It is a fallacious notion that all educational problems can be solved or lessened if we but spend more money, offer more courses in college, or load classrooms with more sophisticated machines. Better financing, more education, and better use of technology may be necessary conditions, but they are clearly not sufficient. The complex process of education will be improved only when we begin to understand the nature of the complexity involved. And whatever useful information psychologists, sociologists, and financial experts may tell us about education, all educational issues are ultimately philosophical.

What is needed are teachers, principals, curriculum consultants, boards of education, parents—those who make decisions about education—who understand, at the deepest level, what the problems and the decisions are really about. Certainly part of the responsibility for developing this understanding devolves on those who call themselves educational philosophers.

Educational philosophers can teach how to ask the right questions. What *is* it that is being proposed? What assumptions support the proposal? What evidence supports the proposal? What consequences are likely to flow from the proposal? What alternatives are there?

An important intellectual skill is the realization that theory is not divorced from practice. When those responsible for education stop belittling theory as irrelevant abstraction and pay attention to the consistency and adequacy of their theory, the first step to the improvement in practice will be taken.

One critical skill is the development of sensitivity to conflicts. Any educational practice ought to be evaluated in the light of the following questions: What values does this particular practice enhance? What values does it tend to endanger? In the light of the values enhanced and

---

[4] In almost all institutions of higher education can be found verbalizations about the need for teaching students to appreciate beauty. But the architecture is ugly because the trustees fear the wrath of citizens who will object to spending public money on "frills." The implications for the students about the "value" of beauty are clear.

the values harmed, is the practice worth it? It is important to realize that values are not easily seen or measured. Whatever the cost of a certain program, class, or building, what kinds of values can be expected at what time in the future? How will we know if these values have come about? What instruments or means exist to evaluate the results? The assumption here is that only to the extent to which one's theory—one's map of the future—is clear and coherent will one be likely to realize the desired values.

Educational philosophy ought also to teach tools of understanding, not just in the sense of comprehending structure and process, but in the sense of seeing what lies beyond the immediate. No teaching method, school architectural plan, extracurricular activity proposal, textbook, or test is a self-sufficient, independent entity. To choose a book or give a test commits one to a range of values that go beyond the classroom or the school environment. When one makes an educational decision—any kind of educational decision—one is, in a sense, affirming or denying a universe of values. For a teacher to station himself in a classroom during an examination for the purpose of erecting barriers against cheating is not merely for him to conduct an examination. It is to commit himself to a certain position regarding human nature: that human beings need constant guarding to repress their natural evildoing. Similarly, for him to refuse to deal with a controversial issue in class is to commit himself to a theory of human nature: that students are not capable of reaching a decision on important matters.

To teach a subject is not simply a matter of presenting subject matter to a class of live bodies. One does not learn merely by being in contact with something. Effective teaching requires that one possess a theory of learning, a body of conceptual tools concerning the definition of learning and beliefs about how learning takes place, about the meaning of motivation, and the meaning of forgetting or nonlearning. This statement appears to be beyond serious doubt, and all departments of education teach learning theory in some sense. But what must also be realized is that any learning theory presupposes a philosophical position. To make an assertion about learning commits one to a theory of reality, a theory of knowledge, and a theory of human nature. Fully to understand one's own learning theory requires understanding the philosophical foundations on which it rests.

More specifically, as we have tried to point out, a learning theory involves beliefs about the meaning of knowledge. When one becomes acquainted with theories of knowledge, it becomes fairly obvious that the verb "to know" includes a large number of meanings—that knowing the multiplication tables is not the same as knowing that crayfish moult, and that neither of these kinds of knowledge is the same as knowing that good

children do not push or shove in a lunch line. When the teacher begins
to see the implications of this, he is in a better position to improve the
learning process in the classroom.

Finally, anyone who has ever engaged in fruitless argument with another or who has ever failed to teach a child is in a position to appreciate the insights of metaphysics. Apparently, opposites in a dispute must
be perceiving reality somewhat differently. The same must be true of the
nonlearning child and the teacher. If so, matters might be helped if the
disputant or the teacher understood how the other perceived reality. If
this position is valid, then theories of reality may be a conceptual tool of
use in understanding. What we are suggesting here is that an extremely
abstract subject—metaphysics—has considerable practical use.

That education is necessary for the constant renewal of a culture is
granted by all. That education is an enterprise which can enrich the lives
of all who engage in it is equally conceded to be true. But before a
teacher can derive the immense satisfaction from teaching that many
have claimed, he must first know what he is about—what teaching is and
how best to teach. To this end, he will spend his life asking questions.

Some Philosophic Assumptions
of Humanistic Philosophy
Michael Littleford

In the past thirty years or so a group of psychologists, broadly identified
as the Humanists, have launched an attack on . . . hitherto mostly unquestioned (at least by scientists) assumptions. Every human endeavor,
insists the Humanist, involves values and philosophical presuppositions.
This is true whether or not we make them explicit. It should be obvious
that this is particularly applicable to psychology and other disciplines
which study human beings. In nearly every activity one makes certain
assumptions about such things as the nature of reality and man, the good
life, the nature of truth and knowledge, and the like. These assumptions
exert a very strong influence on the questions the psychologist asks in his
pursuits, the means by which he attempts to get at his data, and the interpretations he places on his findings. Indeed, if he made no assumptions,

Reprinted, with deletions, from *Educational Theory* 20, no. 3 (Summer 1970):
229–44, by permission of the author and the publisher.

if he held no values, he would have no questions to ask nor any goals to pursue. Thus, it is as Abraham Maslow has so aptly stated: "The issue is thus not over whether or not to have a philosophy of psychology, but whether to have one that is conscious or unconscious."[1] The Humanists, believing that psychology and philosophy could not really be divorced from each other, have attempted to make their philosophical assumptions explicit. It has been their assertion that each current psychology has its own philosophical presuppositions and that much harm and very little good can come from obscuring or denying these basic beliefs.[2] It is the purpose of this paper to examine and analyze some of the philosophical ideas of the twentieth-century American humanistic psychologists.

Reality, in its most fundamental sense, is internal. True reality lies in the perceptual field or private world of the individual. It is the meanings of events to the person which are real to him and which are crucial to his behavior.[3] Behavior is always in response to the reality as perceived by the individual.[4] Thus, existence exists nowhere except in the individual's point of view. The way a man defines his situation constitutes reality for him.[5]

The above comments reveal that for the humanistic psychologist, basic reality is subjective. It is contained within the experience of the organism and all experience is subjective, even that which we call "objective."[6] This does not mean that the Humanists would dogmatically deny that such a thing as objective reality may exist. What they are saying, however, is that the only reality man can truly know is his own subjective experience. They would agree with the existentialists that this is the only avenue to a firsthand description of reality. The nature of the world "as it really is" and the subjective experiences of others can only be known indirectly through inference.

It can be seen that the nature of reality is in a sense relative. It differs somewhat from one individual to the next. Moreover, it is not the same to men of different periods and cultures. Thus, to a large extent we create our own reality. Reality is subjectively lived from moment to moment

[1] Abraham Maslow, "A Philosophy of Psychology: The Need for a Mature Science of Human Nature," in *Humanistic Viewpoints in Psychology,* ed. Frank T. Severin (New York: McGraw-Hill, 1965), p. 23.

[2] Rollo May, *Psychology and the Human Dilemma* (Princeton: D. Van Nostrand, 1967), p. 134.

[3] Arthur W. Combs, "Intelligence From a Perceptual Point of View," in *The Self in Growth, Teaching and Learning,* ed. Don E. Hamachek (Englewood Cliffs, N.J.: Prentice-Hall, 1965), p. 134.

[4] Carl Rogers, *Client-Centered Therapy* (Boston: Houghton Mifflin, 1951), p. 484.

[5] Gordon Allport, *Becoming* (New Haven: Yale University Press, 1955), p. 84.

[6] J. F. T. Bugental, "The Challenge That Is Man," in *Challenges to Humanistic Psychology,* ed. Bugental (New York: McGraw-Hill, 1967), p. 6.

and changes to the individual as his experiences and perceptions change.
. . . Reality does not exist apart from or prior to man. It is not an ultimate something which is "out there" only waiting for him to discover
and get in harmony with.

It should be evident that a basic feature of reality is change. It is not
fixed or static. The universe is an open system. Its nature is not teleological. Reality is a constant state of flux and becoming. Growth and change
are ever-present aspects of it. However, there is also a basic stability or
tendency to maintain organization in the universe and its component
parts. Everything is not lawless flux or in complete disorder. Hence, the
world at its most basic level consists of stability in change. . . .

Much of the work of the humanistic psychologists has dealt with the
question of man's basic nature. A general consensus among all of them
seems to be that the nature of the human being has been critically over-
simplified by academic psychologists, particularly the behaviorists and
the Freudians. The modern Humanists protest that in its view of man,
psychology has deprived him of essential humanity and made gross errors
regarding his potentialities. The Humanist maintains that man cannot be
understood at all if we see in him only what our studies of nonhuman
organisms allow us to see, if we reduce him to mechanical determinism
or fragment him into separate instincts and isolated drives. He rejects
the position that man is to be described almost wholly as an adaptive
organism whose behavior is stimulus-bound, habitual, and tied to the
past.

The Humanists do not deny that man is, in part, what the behaviorists
and the Freudians say he is. When viewed externally, he does exhibit behaviors which can be labeled conditioned responses. He does, at times,
seek to reduce unpleasant drives or tensions and an outside observer
could certainly describe this by saying that the organism is seeking ho-
meostasis or to return to equilibrium. Moreover, he is certainly capable
of behaving in what we commonly call an irrational manner.

The point is, however, that this is not all. Man is much more than this.
He is a being who seeks to maintain himself, who has a drive for organization, but he goes beyond mere self-preservation. He is also a being
who seeks enhancement and self-actualization at considerable disequilibrium and sustained tension.[7] Therefore, man is not an organism
merely seeking equilibrium with himself and his environment, but is a
purposeful, striving being. His personality is not governed merely by
outer stimuli, but is also governed by a disposition to realize his potentialities. It is not just the stimulus that is important, but how the individual defines and interprets the stimulus. Man's one basic motive in life
is actualizing and enhancing his capacities. His nature is essentially

[7] Gordon Allport, "The Open Personality System," in *Varieties of Personality
Theory,* ed. Hendrik M. Ruitenbeck (New York: Dutton, 1964), p. 157.

active and spontaneous, not passive and reactive. He is always tending toward what he is not yet. He has the tendency never to be satisfied with things as they are. This ceaseless striving seems to be one of the outstanding characteristics of man. Hence, since man is always in the process of becoming he cannot be viewed as a fixed object. The human self in its most fundamental sense is a fluid self-actualizing process.[8] The human personality is in no way a closed or static system. It is never finished, but is always in a transitive process. It has a certain stability in its organization, but like reality, it is a stability in change. There is no such thing as complete fulfillment or reaching some ultimate final goal. Irrespective of his culture, man seems to carry on constantly in some purposeful way. Man has interests and commitments which are insatiable. He strives toward long-range goals which require sustained tensions and in which each success raises aspirations.

In order for the individual to move effectively and constructively in the direction of self-actualization, however, he ordinarily must have a basic physical and psychological security. In other words, one needs to be sufficiently secure in order to set forth upon new experiences which require courage and determination. Once this security is attained, humans continuously seek to enrich and enlarge the quality of their experience. They are free to become; they never fully adapt, . . .

The Humanists consistently maintain that the manifest uniqueness and individuality of each person is not an idle poetic dream, but a reality confirmed in their experiences in psychotherapy and elsewhere. Finally, it should be obvious by now that the human being is an irreducible unit. He is more than the mere sum of all his parts. Thus, the humanistic psychologist not only views human nature in an individualistic sense, but also maintains that each individual can be understood adequately only when viewed as an indivisible whole. . . .

Man is tied to the animal kingdom by his physical requirements, his finiteness, and other limitations, but can also transcend these through self-awareness, imagination, and creativity.[9] He is a being who is aware of himself and his experience and aware that he has a world. He knows that he has both possibilities and limitations. Due to this awareness, he is constantly seeking to make sense of his own existence. Meanings make life bearable and purposeful. However, life does not come fraught with meanings awaiting the individual to partake of them. It is a condition of human existence in today's modern scientific world that each individual must find his own meanings within himself. There is no power transcend-

8 Carl Rogers, "The Place of the Person in the New World of the Behavioral Sciences," in *Humanistic Viewpoints in Psychology*, pp. 401–2.
9 Erich Fromm, "The Creative Attitude," in *Creativity and Its Cultivation*, ed. Harold Anderson (New York: Harper & Row, 1959), p. 51.

ing man that can solve his problems for him or bring purpose to his life.[10] Meanings come only from full involvement in life. All of this is quite consistent with the humanistic ideas concerning reality which imply that meanings are not intrinsic to the stimulus, but lie in the perceptual field of the person.

Because he is aware of himself and the world, man, at least subjectively, experiences the reality and necessity of choice. Since reality at its most fundamental level is subjective, the phenomenon of choice is something with which we must deal. It is true that from the point of view of the acting scientist the individual appears to have no choice. However, according to the Humanists, this is a paradox with which we must live. Choice is a core experience in a person's internal life and it is quite irrelevant to him how it seems to others.

Freedom, in the humanistic viewpoint, is an internal state and is tied up with the experience of choice. It is a concept which describes an individual's opportunity to choose wisely and to experience the consequences of these choices. Man can only be free when he is secure enough to move in the direction of self-actualization. Regardless of external circumstances, if an individual is nonthreatened in his internal life and open to his experiences he will be able to choose wisely in terms which will facilitate his own growth and the welfare of those around him. Freedom, in the last analysis, is the freedom to realize what one potentially is and when free to do this, "men will find their own best ways."[11]

Since choice is part of our subjective existence as human beings, responsibility is another reality with which we are confronted. We respond to the world, we act upon it, and consequences for ourself and others flow from our actions. . . . We feel responsible when we choose. . . .

Thus, guilt, anguish, despair, and anxiety are ontological conditions. They are imminent aspects of our existence as human beings. Human existence inevitably involves its tragic side. These aspects are as real as the joyous loving aspects of life. Being in the world means having both possibilities and limitations. The Humanists contend that if psychology could and did eradicate these conditions, this would make men less than human. In this case, we could not experience the consequences of our own choices; we would not be aware of our limitations or possibilities, but would live docilely and contentedly with a minimum of growth. The idea, then, is not to ignore these conflictual realities, but to be able to deal with them constructively and not be crippled by them. The ability to do this defines, in part, the healthy person.

Another inescapable aspect of our human existence is the necessity of

[10] Erich Fromm, *Man for Himself* (Greenwich, Conn.: Fawcett, 1947), p. 53.
[11] Arthur W. Combs, "What Can Man Become?," in *The Self in Growth*, ed. Hamachek, p. 573.

association with others. The human self is "essentially a social product arising out of experience with other people."[12] "The reality of the self is validated by its participation in the world of other selves." "Man finds his fulfillment and happiness only in relatedness to and solidarity with his fellow man."[13] Thus, the Humanists contend that even though each man is a unique individual and distinct from all other men, he is not separate from them. There is no dualism involved here, but a sense of the oneness of all mankind. Moreover, this unity is further emphasized by the humanistic view that love of self and love of others is an indivisible whole. The conditions of human existence make men continuous with and a part of all of mankind as well as a part of and existing within their universe or environment. . . .

Man has an inherent drive for growth which is really only another name for self-actualization. Despite its sometimes painful and almost always uncertain nature, "in the overwhelming majority of individuals, the toward direction of growth is more powerful than the satisfactions of remaining infantile."[14] Growth is a process, a direction toward which healthy people are moving. It is its own end, not an unfolding toward some fixed goal or ultimate state of being. Growth has process goals, not teleological ones. It has no final consummation and the goal behavior is not separated from the object of that behavior. Growth is not something which is done to people, but something which they do.

Since growth is the natural direction in which people move, blockages of growth are abnormal. People are unable to assume this very natural process when they are too threatened to take the risks involved; when their tensions are crippling rather than serving as a readiness to act constructively. Such tensions or emotions are destructive rather than helpful in the growth process.[15]

The kind of knowledge which is possible depends upon one's conception of reality. According to the Humanists' view, "truth exists for the individual only as he himself produces it in action."[16] Ideas and truth do not exist outside of and independent of man.[17] "An event is true because it has been subjectively lived."[18] Thus, all true knowledge is based upon concrete experience. It does not exist apart from and prior to human experience. Likewise, it is not something "out there" complete in itself

---

[12] Arthur Combs and Donald Snygg, *Individual Behavior*, 2nd ed. (New York: Harper & Brothers, 1959), p. 134.
[13] Fromm, *Man for Himself*, p. 23.
[14] Rogers, *Client-Centered Therapy*.
[15] Combs and Snygg, *Individual Behavior*, p. 231.
[16] May, *Psychology and the Human Dilemma*, p. 129.
[17] Fromm, *Man for Himself*, p. 247.
[18] Hubert Bonner, *On Being Mindful of Man* (Atlanta: Houghton Mifflin Co., 1965), p. 21.

and only waiting for us to discover. It is not a fixed entity to be possessed as an end in itself, but consists of meanings existing in man's active experience to be used by him to further his development.

There is no such thing as objective truth, at least insofar as man is concerned. This does not mean, however, that every truth is equally as good as another. The Humanist does not contend that each person's conception of reality and truth is as valid as anyone else's. . . . The test of the validity of truth is in the field of action. It is the effectiveness of one's behavior which determines the validity of one's knowledge. This behavior in turn depends upon the adequacy of perceptions or meanings available to the person at any given moment.[19] The knowledge and "truths" held by a healthy, growing, or self-actualizing person will be more valid than those of a less healthy individual because the former will be more open to his experience and will have less need to distort information in order to protect himself. The difference will be apparent in the behavior of the two individuals. . . .

Since knowledge comes only through subjective experience, it should be apparent that there is no such thing as an objective science. The Humanistic psychologists have probably done more than any other group to dispel us of the myth that science is value-free. They have done much to show us that value judgments are involved in science from beginning to end. . . . Furthermore, subjective assumptions not only determine our goals and procedures, but also influence the interpretation of the results of our research. Contrary to popular belief, the facts do not speak for themselves.

However, the fact that science cannot be value-free is by no means something to be regretted. Values belong with science because without them you have a crippled, amoral, and nonhuman science.[20] . . .

They [the Humanists] are calling for a science of man which is more urgently human and will not be afraid to deal with such ever-present themes of human existence as love, hate, the fear of death, the search for enhancement and meanings, the attainment of selfhood, creativity, and the like. These things are a part of reality and psychologists, in ignoring them, merely succeed in getting a distorted and incomplete view of man. This means that psychology can no longer afford to deny the subjective life of man and should not try to separate itself from the purposes of men because when it does it becomes trivial and irrelevant.

A unique element in this emerging science of man is the idea that it is as valuable to study healthy people as it is to examine those who are sick. If one studies only crippled people one will have a cripple psychology.[21]

[19] Combs, "Intelligence From a Perceptual Point of View," pp. 135–36.

[20] Abraham Maslow, *Religion, Values and Peak Experiences* (Columbus: Ohio State University Press, 1964), p. 17.

[21] Abraham Maslow, "A Theory of Motivation and Personality," in *Varieties of Personality Theory,* ed. Ruitenbeck, p. 310.

There is a need to study healthy, self-actualizing people in order to get a complete view of man. These people reveal the central meaning of human experience as much or more as people who are ill.[22] The Humanists have begun putting this idea into action. Of special interest are Maslow's studies of self-actualizing people as his research is, at the present time, the most extensive. It is apparent that this new dimension of psychology is consistent with and based upon the Humanistic psychologist's philosophical assumptions concerning the nature of man.

One can sense from all of this that there is something terribly exciting and challenging in this emerging philosophy of science. One gets the impression that the aim is as complete a description as possible of what it means to be alive as a human being. Science will be freed to be far greater in scope than it has been in the past. Countless new variables will emerge to be researched. Hence, it is as though a whole new world is emerging in the science of man which will find room for both internal and external frames of reference.[23] . . .

Consistent with their conceptions of truth and reality, the Humanists hold that there is no such thing as absolute Good which exists apart from or transcends man and to which he must be subservient. Valuing is an act or process and there is no value except as one commits himself to it. This does not mean, however, that values and ethics are completely relative. It simply means that the sources of norms of ethical conduct are to be found in man and his nature, not gained from a power superior to him. The criteria for such an ethical system is man's welfare and it is not relative because when violated the result is mental and moral disintegration.

One extremely important aspect of this ethical system is the idea that each individual is an end in himself. He is not an object to be manipulated or used by himself or others, an object for conditioning nor an object for calculation and control. Following from this we find that self-love or affirmation of self is a supreme value in humanistic ethics. . . .

Only those capable of loving their own selves can truly love others. According to Combs, two of the most important characteristics of more self-actualizing people are a positive view of one's self and a broad identification with and acceptance of others.[24] Hence, the more adequate an individual feels the more he cares for himself and the more he cares for himself the more he becomes one with all of mankind. When an individual views his self positively, "in seeking his own maintenance and enhancement he will be seeking that of others as well."[25] . . .

---

22 Maslow, "A Philosophy of Psychology," p. 27.
23 Carl Rogers, "Toward a Science of the Person," in *Behaviorism and Phenomenology—Contrasting Bases for Modern Psychology,* ed. T. W. Wann (Chicago: University of Chicago Press, 1934), p. 119.
24 Combs and Snygg, *Individual Behavior,* p. 239.
25 Ibid., p. 247.

An idea implicit in the entire philosophical thought of the Humanistic movement is that man is definitely not basically evil or asocial. It would appear that good is more basic to the human personality than evil because when a human being is able to grow in a normal way, when he is able to progress properly toward self-actualization, he exhibits behaviors which are "good" in the sense that they are constructive and facilitating to himself and others. Thus, the nature of evil is that it is a secondary phenomenon, the sources of which are the conditions which block growth. The result of such conditions is indifference to one's self or self-mutilation and possibly harm to others. Hence, evil is crippling of man's powers. It follows that the worst crime that can be committed against man is to rob him of his possibilities for positive growth or self-actualization. This will ultimately make a vegetable of him. Man basically is human potentiality and when you deny him the opportunity to actualize it, you virtually rob him of his humanness. . . .

One question with which a philosophy must ultimately concern itself is what is possible for man? What can he become? It is evident from many of the previous comments that to the Humanist, man is an organism of unknown potential. He is viewed as being at an early stage in his evolutionary history in which hardly a minute fraction of his potential has been tapped.

Combs' discussion of intelligence sheds some light upon the possibilities for man's improvement. Mind or intelligence is not an object which is stored in the brain in isolation from one's surroundings and experiences. Intelligence is the effectiveness of one's behavior. It is a process, the adequacy of which depends upon the availability of perceptions or meanings at the moment of action.[26] Obviously, unless we are dead we are continually making new differentiations in our perceptual field. We never stop discerning new meanings. Intelligence never ceases to develop in the living human. Hence, the limitations on man are not irrevocable hereditary factors, but are limitations which it is possible to overcome. These variables include such things as social environments, self-concept, goals and values, physical conditions, etc. The Humanists, of course, do not mean to imply that it will be a simple matter to remove these limiting factors. However, the possibilities are there and they are vast. There is as yet no limit in sight.

Thus, human nature and capacities are not fixed and can be improved. We have no idea as to what the limits are to man's progress, but we are able to catch a glimpse of the possibilities for such improvement in Maslow's studies of self-actualizing people. He believes that these individuals represent the highest reaches of human nature.[27] Of course, it must be

[26] Combs, "Intelligence From a Perceptual Point of View," pp. 135–36.
[27] Abraham Maslow, "Cognition of Being in Peak Experiences," in *The Self in Growth,* ed. Hamachek, p. 171.

kept in mind that no utopias are envisioned in which all human problems have been solved or other ultimate goals have been achieved. Consistent with their other philosophical assumptions, the Humanists consider the continuous process of perfection as the aim rather than setting up a fixed standard as an end goal. Self-actualization is a matter of degree.

The Humanists' point of view about the nature of man and his possibilities has a very hopeful quality about it. . . . It is precisely the image of man [as] capable of being a free and responsible organism that the Humanists believe in and seek to further. . . . Of course, in order to achieve these wonderful possibilities man must be free to become, to achieve the fullest possible fulfillment of his potentialities.[28] Once he is free, he will continually seek to surpass himself in constructive ways. He will not seek . . . to become . . . the "average Joe," because, . . . as Professor Combs has remarked, "Who, after all, wants to be average?"[29] In this statement, with all that it implies about man, he seems to sum up the humanistic view of the possibilities for the human race.

[28] Combs, "What Can Man Become?," p. 565.
[29] Ibid., p. 563.

The New Copernican Revolution
Willis W. Harman

As future historians look back on our times what will they conclude to have been the most significant event of the [1960s] in terms of its impact on the future? The hippie movement? The riots in the cities? The Vietnam War? The Great Society programs? Student protest? Technological and scientific advances? Man on the moon?

None of these, I would make bold to guess. Nor any of the events or trend discontinuities which the in-vogue forecasters are picking out with their current methodologies. I will suggest below that it will be something quite different from any of these, an event perhaps well symbolized by an obscure scientific conference . . . held in Council Grove, Kansas, in April 1969.

What follows is a report on research in process. It does not pretend to present demonstrated conclusions. Rather, it raises questions and ad-

Reprinted from *Stanford Today* (Winter 1969), series II, no. 1, with permission of the publishers, Stanford University. Copyright © 1969 by the Board of Trustees of the Leland Stanford Junior University.

vances possible interpretations which are so momentous in their possible implications for the future that the fullest possible amount of responsible dialogue is called for.

Let us suppose for a moment that we are back in the year 1600, concerned with forecasting probable future trends. In retrospect it is clear that one of the most significant events in progress was what came later to be called the Copernican revolution. Would our futurist researches have picked this up? They might have, if we were looking at the right things. What was the essence of this remarkable transformation that started with the brash suggestions of Nicholas Copernicus and Giordano Bruno and led to consequences as diverse as a tremendous acceleration in physical science and a decline in the political power of the Church? One useful interpretation is that a group of questions relating to the position of the Earth in the universe and the nature and significance of the heavenly bodies passed out of the realm of the theological and philosophical and into the realm of empirical inquiry. No longer were these questions to be settled by referring to this or that ecclesiastical or scholarly authority; rather they were to be subjected to illumination by systematic observation and experiments. The consequences of such a shift are manifold. New research activities are started; familiar phenomena are given new interpretations; educational approaches are altered; power structures in society undergo change; new bases for consensus are applied to conflicts between belief systems.

A later similar event occurred with the work of the geologists, paleontologists, and biologists of the nineteenth century culminating in the controversial evolutionary hypotheses. Questions relating to the origin of the earth and of man were relabeled "empirical" instead of "theological." Again the consequences reverberated throughout the worlds of research, education, and politics.

I believe there is good reason to suspect that we are in the midst of another such situation today. Much evidence suggests that *a group of questions relating to the commonality of an interpretation of man's subjective experience, especially of the "transcendental," and hence to the bases of human values, are shifting from the realm of the "philosophical" to the "empirical." If so, the consequences may be even more far-reaching than those which emerged from the Copernican, Darwinian, and Freudian revolutions.*

The evidence is of various sorts. The most obvious kind, of course, is simply the indications that scientists—that is, persons with recognized scientific training, on the staffs of research organizations and universities with high standards, and holding membership in good standing in recognized scientific associations—are manifesting more and more interest in developing an adequate science of ordinary and extraordinary subjective experience. This is not completely new, of course. The phenomena of hypnosis have been studied in a scientific way, off and on, for at least a century and a half. Phenomenology has been a sometime influence in psychology. Freud's psychoanalysis and its offshoots have attempted to probe the unconscious processes. Pioneering books in the exploration of supraconscious processes include F. W. H. Myers' *Human Personality and Its Survival of Bodily Death,* Richard Bucke's *Cosmic Consciousness,* William James' *Varieties of Religious Experience,* and Pitirim Sorokin's *The Ways and Power of Love,* the first three being approximately two-thirds of a century old. . . . The April 1969 Council Grove (Kansas) conference on "voluntary control of inner states," cosponsored by the Menninger Foundation and the American Association for Humanistic Psychology, represents an unprecedented assemblage of scientists working with altered states of consciousness through such techniques as autohypnosis and group hypnosis, aural feedback of alphawave signals, and psychedelic drugs.

In the field of clinical psychology several scientists are proposing to formulate through their researches "a natural value system, a court of ultimate appeal for the determination of good and bad, of right and wrong" (A. H. Maslow), "universal human value directions emerging from the experiencing of the human organism" (Carl Rogers).

An ever-increasing number of students, now in the millions at least, are involved with "awareness-expanding" activities in free-university courses and elsewhere. This concern is intimately related to student demands for a person-centered, rather than scholarship-centered, education.

The science of man's subjective experience is in its infancy. Even so, some of its foreshadowings are evident. With the classification of these questions into the realm of empirical inquiry, we can anticipate an acceleration of research in this area. As a consequence there is new hope of consensus on issues which have been at the root of conflict for centuries (just as earlier there came about consensus on the place of the Earth in the universe, and on the origin of man). The new science will incorporate the most penetrating insights of psychology, the humanities, and religion. These developments will have profound impacts on goal priorities in society, on our concepts of education, on the further development and use of technology, and perhaps (as in the case of the Copernican revolution) on the distribution of power among social institutions and interest groups.

Young and incomplete as the science of subjective experience is, it nevertheless already contains what may very well be extremely significant precursors of tomorrow's image of man's potentialities. Space does not permit documenting them here; however, the following three propositions have accumulated an impressive amount of substantiating evidence:

1. The potentialities of the individual human being are far greater, in extent and diversity, than we ordinarily imagine them to be, and

far greater than currently in-vogue models of man would lead us to think possible.

2. A far greater portion of significant human experience than we ordinarily feel or assume to be so is comprised of unconscious processes. This includes not only the sort of repressed memories and messages familiar to us through psychotherapy. It includes also "the wisdom of the body" and those mysterious realms of experience we refer to with such words as "intuition" and "creativity." Access to these unconscious processes is apparently facilitated by a wide variety of factors, including attention to feelings and emotions, inner attention, "free association," hypnosis, sensory deprivation, hallucinogenic and psychedelic drugs, and others.

3. Included in these partly or largely unconscious processes are self-expectations, internalized expectations of others, images of the self and limitations of the self, and images of the future, which play a predominant role in limiting or enhancing actualization of one's capacities. These tend to be self-fulfilling. Much recent research has focused on the role of self-expectations and expectations of others in affecting performance, and on the improvement of performance level through enhancing self-image. On the social level research findings are buttressing the intuitive wisdom that one of the most important characteristics of any society is its vision of itself and its future, what Boulding calls "organizing images." The validity of the self-fulfilling prophecy and the self-realizing image appears to grow steadily in confirmation.

Assuming that the evidence substantiating these propositions continues to mount, they have the most profound implications for the future. For they say most powerfully that we have undersold man, underestimated his possibilities, and misunderstood what is needed for what Boulding terms "the great transition." They imply that the most profound revolution of the educational system would not be the cybernation of knowledge transmission, but the infusion of an exalted image of what man can be, and the cultivation of an enhanced self-image in each individual child. They imply that the solution to the alienation and widespread disaffection in our society is not alone in vast social programs, but will come about through widespread adoption of a new image of our fellow man and our relationship to him. They suggest that the most pervasive illness of our nation is loss of the guiding vision, and the cure is to be found in a nobler image of man and of a society in which his growth may be better nurtured. They reassure that an image of fully human man and of a new social order need not be built of the gossamer of wishful thinking, but can have a sound foundation in the research findings of the most daring explorers of the nature of man and his universe.

It is perhaps not too early to predict some of the characteristics of the new science. Preliminary indications suggest at least the following:

1. Although we have been speaking of it as a science of subjective experience, one of its dominant characteristics will be a relaxing of the

subjective-objective dichotomy. The range between perceptions shared by all or practically all, and those which are unique to one individual, will be assumed to be much more of a continuum than a sharp division between "the world out there" and what goes on "in my head."

2. Related to this will be the incorporation, in some form, of the age-old yet radical doctrine that we perceive the world and ourselves in it as we have been culturally "hypnotized" to perceive it. The typical commonsense-scientific view of reality will be considered to be a valid but partial view—a particular metaphor, so to speak. Others, such as certain religious or metaphysical views, will be considered also, and even equally, valid but more appropriate for certain areas of human experience.

3. The new science will incorporate some way of referring to the subjective experiencing of a unity in all things (the "More" of William James, the "All" of Bugental, the "divine Ground" of Aldous Huxley's *The Perennial Philosophy*).

4. It will include some sort of mapping or ordering of states of consciousness transcending the usual conscious awareness (Bucke's "Cosmic Consciousness," the "enlightenment" of Zen, and similar concepts).

5. It will take account of the subjective experiencing of a "higher self" and will view favorably the development of a self-image congruent with this experience (Bugental's "I-process," Emerson's "Oversoul," Assagioli's "True Self," Brunton's "Overself," the Atman of Vedanta, and so on.)

6. It will allow for a much more unified view of human experiences now categorized under such diverse headings as creativity, hypnosis, mystical experience, psychedelic drugs, extrasensory perception, psychokinesis, and related phenomena.

7. It will include a much more unified view of the processes of personal change and emergence which take place within the contexts of psychotherapy, education (in the sense of "know thyself"), and religion (as spiritual growth). This view will possibly center around the concept that personality and behavior patterns change consequent upon a change in self-image, a modification of the person's emotionally felt perception of himself and his relationship to his environment.

John Rader Platt has argued in *The Step to Man*—as have Kenneth Boulding and Teilhard de Chardin before him—that the present point in the history of man may well, when viewed in retrospect by some future generation, appear as a relatively sudden cultural step. The portentous impact of the new technology is the heady yet sobering realization that we have the future in our hands, that man recognizes his role as, to use Julian Huxley's phrase, "a trustee of evolution on this earth." The new man, "Homo progressivus" in Teilhard de Chardin's words, is described by Lancelot Law Whyte as "unitary man," by Lewis Mumford as the "new person," and by Henry A. Murray as an "ally of the future." The challenge of our time is whether we make "the step to man" or our Faust-ian powers prove our undoing and the whole vast machine goes off the track through the strains of internecine conflict and degradation of the environment.

To become the new man and to construct the new moral order require a guiding image which is worthy of the task. Man's highest learning has seemed to comprise, in C. P. Snow's terms, not one culture but two. And the noblest of the images of man is to be found in the culture of the humanities that appeared somehow alien to the culture of the sciences. The preceding arguments suggest that this state of affairs is probably a temporary one. For example, Ernest Becker proposes that the two cultures can be joined in a true science of man through admission of the universal value statement that that which estranges man from himself is unwholesome. Whether this or something else becomes the unifying principle, the reconciliation may soon take place. On the one hand, we will come to use comfortably many pluralistic images of aspects of man—one for his biochemical functioning, another perhaps for dealing with his pathologies, still another for encompassing his most fully human actions and proclivities. But on the other hand we will find nothing incompatible between any of these and an overarching image of what man can be, or perhaps more accurately can come to realize that he is already.

The social significance of our dominant basic assumptions regarding the interpretation of subjective experience can be made more specific. At the surface level, so to speak, the nation is beset by numerous social problems which we point to with the terms poverty, crime, racial discrimination, civil disorder, unemployment, pollution, and the like. Experience with attempts to deal straightforwardly with these problems—to tackle discrimination with civil-rights legislation, to alleviate the ills of poverty with minimum-wage laws and welfare payments, to eliminate ghettos with urban-renewal programs, to deal with civil disorders by increasing police power—indicates that such direct measures typically have unexpected and unintended outcomes. It is as though an "ecology of situations" were upset by a piecemeal approach.

The reason appears to be intrinsic. It seems that these manifest problems are in a sense symptoms of underlying conditions that are more pervasive and less easy to objectify. At another level these problems reside in the institutions of the society, in built-in power distributions, in the traditional roles to which persons are trained, in the time-hallowed structures and processes. At a still deeper level they involve the most basic assumptions, attitudes, and felt values held by the individual and promoted by the culture. The most carefully designed social measures will not achieve their desired goals unless they involve not only rationally designed programs and structures, but also changes in deeply rooted beliefs, values, attitudes, and behavior patterns, both of the individuals who constitute "the problem populations" and of the self-righteous others who assume they are not implicated.

An analogy with the process of psychotherapy may reassure that in attending to these underlying conditions we are dealing with that which is more, not less, real and relevant. In the end the neurotic discovers that he was divided against himself, and in a sense lying to himself to conceal that condition. So it may be with our social problems that the significant constructive change is first of all an inner one rather than outer, and in the direction of recognizing the hidden lies and resolving the hidden divisions. To put it in somewhat different terms, just as it is possible for a person to have a pathological set of beliefs about himself, so it may be possible for our society to possess a dysfunctional belief and value system.

In fact, much of today's student unrest centers around the accusation that the society's operative assumptions about man's deepest desires are indeed not consistent with individual inner experience nor in the long-term interest of man or society. A dominant theme among disaffected students is that the American corporate capitalist system manipulates and oppresses the individual.

Thus it is not solely in an idealistic vein that the new science of subjective experience is hailed as having profound significance. It has survival value as well.

Several recent scholars of the future such as Robert Heilbroner, Kenneth Boulding, and Fred Polak have made much of the concept that it is the image of the future which is the key to that future coming into realization. . . . As previously noted, much evidence has been accumulated to indicate that the power of the image may be far greater than we have heretofore suspected.

To whatever extent the science of the past may have contributed to a mechanistic and economic image of man and a technocratic image of the good society, the new science of subjective experience may provide a counteracting force toward the ennobling of the image of the individual's possibilities, of the educational and socializing processes, and of the future. And since we have come to understand that science is not a description of "reality" but a metaphorical ordering of experience, the new science does not impugn the old. It is not a question of which view is "true" in some ultimate sense. Rather, it is a matter of which picture is more useful in guiding human affairs. Among the possible images that are reasonably in accord with accumulated human experience, since the image held is that most likely to come into being, it is prudent to choose the noblest.

It is strange to observe that at this point in history when we literally have the knowledge and material resources to do almost anything we can image—from putting a man on the moon, to exploring the depths of the oceans, to providing an adequate measure of life's goods to every person on earth—we also seem the most confused about what is worth doing. The great problems facing us are a sort where we need belief in ourselves and will to act even more than we need new technologies, creative social program concepts, and program budgeting. At a time when the nation may well be in its gravest peril in over a century, and Western civilization may hang in the balance, it could even come to pass that a new "Copernican revolution" might provide a missing balance in some four-century-old trends started by the first one.

REFERENCES

Assagioli, Roberto. *Psychosynthesis: A Manual of Principles and Techniques.* New York: Hobbs, Dorman, 1965.

Becker, Ernest. *Beyond Alienation.* New York: Braziller, 1967.

Boulding, Kenneth. *The Meaning of the Twentieth Century.* New York: Harper & Row, 1964.

Brunton, Paul. *In Quest of the Overself.* New York: Dutton, 1938.

Bucke, Richard M. *Cosmic Consciousness.* New York: Dutton, 1923.

Bugental, James F. T. *The Search for Authenticity.* New York: Holt, Rinehart & Winston, 1965.

Fromm, Erich. *The Revolution of Hope.* New York: Harper & Row, 1968.

Harman, W. W. "Old Wine in New Wineskins." In *Challenges of Humanistic Psychology,* edited by J. F. T. Bugental. New York: McGraw-Hill, 1967.

Huxley, Aldous. *The Perennial Philosophy.* New York: Harper, 1945.

Maslow, A. H. *Toward a Psychology of Being.* Princeton, N.J.: D. Van Nostrand, 1962.

Platt, John R. *The Step to Man.* New York: Wiley, 1966.

Teilhard de Chardin, P. *The Future of Man.* New York: Harper & Row, 1964.

Education for What?
Charles E. Silberman

What we teach reflects, consciously or unconsciously, our concepts of the good life, the good man, and the good society.

Reprinted, with deletions, from *Crisis in the Classroom: The Remaking of American Education* (New York: Random House, 1970), pp. 5–11, by permission of the publisher and of William Morris Agency, Inc., on behalf of the author. Copyright © 1970 by Charles E. Silberman.

But if our concern is with *education,* we cannot restrict our attention to the schools and colleges, for education is not synonymous with schooling. Children and adults learn outside as well as—perhaps more than—in school. To say this is not to denigrate the public schools: as the one publicly controlled educating institution with which virtually every child comes into close and prolonged contact, they occupy a strategic, perhaps critical, position in American society. Nor is it to denigrate the colleges and universities, which for different reasons occupy a position of great and growing importance. It is simply to give proper weight to all the other educating institutions in American society: television, films, and the mass media; churches and synagogues; the law, medicine, and social work; museums and libraries; the armed forces, corporate training programs, Boy Scout troups. From Plato to Rousseau to Jefferson to the early John Dewey, as Lawrence A. Cremin points out in *The Genius of American Education,* almost everybody who wrote about education took it for granted that it is the community and the culture—what the ancient Greeks called *paideia*—that educates. The contemporary American is educated by his *paideia* no less than the Athenian was by his. The weakness of American education is not that the *paideia* does not educate, but that it educates to the wrong ends.

To study American education, therefore, means, in part, to study American society and culture. But only in part. The traditional Platonic or Jeffersonian notion of education as *paideia* is inherently ambiguous; carried to its logical conclusion, "education" all but disappears, for the definition makes education synonymous with what the anthropologists call enculturation. This would have condemned us to study every one of the myriad ways by which American society and culture shape the individual. . . .

In the view taken here, therefore, education is defined . . . as the deliberate or purposeful creation, evocation, or transmission of knowledge, abilities, skills, and values. To emphasize the deliberate and the purposeful is not to deny that nondeliberate influences may be more powerful; it is to assert that man cannot depend upon a casual process of learning. Unless men are to be forced to rediscover all knowledge for themselves, they must be educated, which is to say that education, to be education, must be purposeful.

It is one thing to say that education must be purposeful; it is another to say what those purposes should be. . . .

I thought I *knew* what the purpose of education should be: namely, intellectual development. "The United States today is moving away from progressivism," I had argued in 1961, and still believed when I started the study, "not because it is 'false' in some absolute sense, but because it badly serves the needs of our own time. The growing complexity of organization and the explosive pace of technological and social change are creating an enormous demand that is without historical precedent. Society has always needed a few men with highly developed and disciplined intellects; industrial society needed masses of literate but not necessarily intellectual men. Tomorrow requires something that the world has never seen—*masses of intellectuals.*"[1] . . .

I was wrong. What tomorrow needs is not masses of intellectuals, but masses of educated men—men educated to feel and to act as well as to think. . . .

What educators must realize . . . is that how they teach and how they act may be more important than what they teach. The way we do things, that is to say, shapes values more directly and more effectively than the way we talk about them. Certainly administrative procedures like automatic promotion, homogeneous grouping, racial segregation, or selective admission to higher education affect "citizenship education" more profoundly than does the social studies curriculum. And children are taught a host of lessons about values, ethics, morality, character, and conduct every day of the week, less by the content of the curriculum than by the way schools are organized, the ways teachers and parents behave, the way they talk to children and to each other, the kinds of behavior they approve or reward and the kinds they disapprove or punish. These lessons are far more powerful than the verbalizations that accompany them. . . .

Most of all, however, I am indignant at the failures of the public schools themselves. "The most deadly of all possible sins," Erik Erikson suggests, "is the mutilation of a child's spirit." It is not possible to spend any prolonged period visiting public school classrooms without being appalled by the mutilation visible everywhere—mutilation of spontaneity, of joy in learning, of pleasure in creating, of sense of self. The public schools —those "killers of the dream," to appropriate a phrase of Lillian Smith's —are the kind of institution one cannot really dislike until one gets to know them well. Because adults take the schools so much for granted, they fail to appreciate what grim, joyless places most American schools are, how oppressive and petty are the rules by which they are governed, how intellectually sterile and esthetically barren the atmosphere, what an appalling lack of civility obtains on the part of teachers and principals, what contempt they unconsciously display for children as children.

And it need not be! Public schools *can* be organized to facilitate joy in learning and esthetic expression and to develop character—in the rural and urban slums no less than in the prosperous suburbs. . . .

What makes change possible, moreover, is that what is mostly wrong with the public schools is due not to venality or indifference or stupidity, but to mindlessness. To be sure, teaching has its share of sadists and

[1] Charles E. Silberman, "The Remaking of American Education," *Fortune,* April 1961.

clods, of insecure and angry men and women who hate their students for their openness, their exuberance, their color, or their affluence. But by and large, teachers, principals, and superintendents are decent, intelligent, and caring people who try to do their best by their lights. If they make a botch of it, and an uncomfortably large number do, it is because it simply never occurs to more than a handful to ask *why* they are doing what they are doing—to think seriously or deeply about the purposes or consequences of education.

This mindlessness—the failure or refusal to think seriously about educational purpose, the reluctance to question established practice—is not the monopoly of the public school; it is diffused remarkably evenly throughout the entire educational system, and indeed the entire society. . . .

If mindlessness is the central problem, the solution must lie in infusing the various educating institutions with purpose, more important, with thought about purpose, and about the ways in which techniques, content, and organization fulfill or alter purpose. And given the tendency of institutions to confuse day-to-day routine with purpose, to transform the means into the end itself, the infusion cannot be a one-shot affair. The process of self-examination, of "self-renewal," to use John Gardner's useful term, must be continuous. We must find ways of stimulating educators—public school teachers, principals, and superintendents; college professors, deans, and presidents; radio, television, and film directors and producers; newspaper, magazine, and TV journalists and executives—to think about what they are doing, and why they are doing it. And we must persuade the general public to do the same.

Education for Creativity
Paul Nash

An education that is designed to produce sound, mature people cannot fail to include an aesthetic component. Today in the West we are generally aware of the need to nurture in young people an appreciation of the *true* and the *good* but are more likely to forget the importance of the *beautiful*. Not only are all three vital, but they need to be related to each other through the educational process so that the individual can integrate

Adapted and reprinted, by permission, from *Authority and Freedom in Education,* by Paul Nash. Copyright © 1966 by John Wiley & Sons, Inc.

the rational, the ethical, and the aesthetic within himself. Without this integration we are in danger of producing the narrow intellectual snob, the preaching moralist, or the affected aesthete, none of whom can be considered mature or soundly educated people, because they lack perspective and breadth of vision. . . .

It is a mistake to think that certain activities—such as poetry, literature, art, music—touch the aesthetic and creative part of man, while others—such as science, mathematics—do not. Creative imagination is important in all fields, although not equally so at all levels. In recent years its importance in science has been increasingly recognized, and certainly one of the earliest lessons in aesthetic education can be taught by insisting on clean arithmetic papers.

Nonetheless, all fields are not equally valuable in nurturing creativity and aesthetic sensitivity. The great enemies of creativity are fear and passivity, and these reactions are often engendered in children as a result of their growing realization of the vastness of the universe and its limitless power. The consequent feeling of personal powerlessness carries the danger of the dissipation of energy. One way of combating this danger is to give children the opportunity to deal with material that is tractable and malleable, on a scale that is comprehensible to them, so that, at one level, they can experience the feeling of mastery and control. Hence, of outstanding value in this educational process are painting, pottery, woodwork, metalwork, sculpture, and all work that gives the child the chance to alter the material form of the world. . . .

Creativity cannot be taught. Nevertheless, the environment can be arranged so that enabling rather than disabling conditions operate on the creative potential of the individual.[1] What guidelines can be laid down that will make the educational process one that nourishes rather than destroys the potential creativity of all men and women? The basic challenge that presents itself to parents and educators arises from the phenomenon that almost all children are promising, from a creative point of view, but very few adults are functionally creative. Between the promise and the performance is a gap that can be reduced by the skillful parent or teacher. Instead of hastening the apparently inexorable process by which the potentially creative child grows into the dull, uncreative adult, the wise and ingenious teacher can help the child to release the creative forces within him and to mold them into effective performance.

The surest way of nurturing this creativity lies in leading the child through an experience of harmonious balance between the qualities of

---

[1] "We do not need to be taught to *think:* indeed . . . this is something that cannot be taught. Thinking processes actually are automatic, swift, and spontaneous when allowed to proceed undisturbed by other influences. . . . What we need is to be educated in how not to interfere with the inherent capacity of the human mind to think." Lawrence Kubie, *Neurotic Distortion of the Creative Process* (New York: Noonday Press, 1961), pp. 142–43.

discipline and *freedom*. Creative activity is the product of an appropriate blend of restraint and flexibility, conservatism and progressivism, control and experiment. Creative ideas are essential but insufficient: there must also be discipline and skill to translate the idea into reality. . . . How much control and pressure is suitable to evoke the creative response of which a child is capable? The fault of most traditional education has been to apply too much control and pressure, on the assumption of the wickedness and laziness of children, thus effectively discouraging the potential creativity of slow or unconfident children and producing mental breakdown in sensitive ones. The fault of some types of progressive education has been to apply insufficient control and pressure, on the assumption of the goodness and self-direction of children, thus producing a large number of complacent, self-satisfied, uncreative nonentities. The solution to this dilemma lies in distinguishing between two types of pressure. The first type presents a problem or challenge that the individual can solve—or try to solve with a good chance of success—with the ideas, skills, background, and knowledge that he possesses or can foreseeably gain. The second type presents a problem or challenge that the individual cannot, or feels he cannot, possibly solve or overcome with his own resources. The first type is often the stimulus to creativity; the second is often the cause of passivity and despair. . . .

The skillful teacher will realize that the kind of discipline that nurtures creativity has little connection with mere external control. This kind of control has served in the past largely as a means of stamping out creativeness; discipline should be used as a means of controlling those forces that impede creativeness, thus making possible a release of creative energy. Fundamentally, the discipline required involves a mastery of the *self* in relation to the *material* or to other *people*. Gradually the child should become aware that the discipline necessary for the productive expression of creativity takes the form of self-control, unabating effort, deep concentration, renunciation of transient but interfering pleasures, sacrifice of time, leisure, and material goods, vigorous and honest self-examination, and self-criticism.

Discipline is related to order in the life of the creative person. It is easy to underestimate the importance of material and mechanical factors in the nurture of creativity. The painter needs physical space, the writer a clean desk, the child space and time, uncluttered with trivia, if they are to perform as they might. A regular place and time of work and a tidy arrangement of workthings are often aids to creativity. It is a fallacy to think that the creative worker needs to be untidy, disorganized, chaotic, and temperamental. This is a popular stereotype that has done much harm. . . .

Interwoven with these manifestations of discipline in the creative process there must be at the same time manifestations of freedom. There must be freedom for the child to penetrate deeply into his experiences and to absorb them. This means above all that the teacher must give the child *time*—time to sit quietly and reflectively before knowledge and events to gain real insight into them, instead of memorizing facts, quickly using them, returning them to the examiner, and forgetting them. There is a crucial need for more reflection and contemplation in school. Instead of always insisting on quick answers, the teacher should sometimes ask the children to sit in quiet contemplation of a question before attempting to answer. Freedom for the child to become deeply involved in his studies means also that the teacher must not teach too much, not cover too much ground, not teach too many subjects, not be afraid of leaving gaps. Only by concentrating on depth in whatever is studied can the teacher give the child time to penetrate below the superficial level. . . .

Another important freedom that creativity demands is the freedom to *feel*. If children are to be creative they must be enabled to experience their *own* genuine emotions and to be unafraid of them. Only through recovering our deep emotional life can we escape the stifling influence of the artificial sentimentality that pervades our society. . . . Too often our education teaches us *what* to feel, what is respectable or fashionable to feel, thus hindering the process by which the person frees himself from conventional sentiment and gains the courage of his own spontaneous, creative feelings.

Freedom from inflexibility is yet another aspect of creative freedom. Its nurture is always difficult and is probably impossible with inflexible teachers. To help the individual's creativeness we must teach him how to be *ready*—ready to take advantage of the unexpected, the unforeseen, the unusual. This means encouraging a certain skepticism toward things as they are, an eager readiness to entertain new ideas, to see familiar things in unusual ways, to be on the lookout for unusual analogies and patterns of relationships. Needless to say, only the secure teacher can afford to maintain a classroom atmosphere in which such flexibility can flourish. . . .

Education for creativity is especially important in a technological age: the machine affords us more leisure in which creativity can blossom; but it also destroys creativity by increasing the use of repetitive, simple, fractured operations, often devoid of meaning and context. Meaninglessness, atomization, interruptions, noise—these are all prime threats to creativity that are aggravated by the machine. . . . Unfortunately, many of the destructive features of industrial life have been carried into the home and school. In the home, creativity is impeded by the constant noise and kaleidoscope of confusing experiences presented by the ubiquitous television and radio. In the school it is impeded by short periods of work, frequent bells, rigid timetables, and enforced gregariousness, all of which militate against the deep and sustained concentration and periods of reflective solitude that are necessary to bring the creative spirit to the surface.

Another threat to creativity stemming from the assumptions of an acquisitive, technological society is the predominant emphasis on material productivity. . . .

In the schools and universities, this dominance of productivity takes the form of a concentration on examinations and marks, the outward signs in the academic world of successful production. Oscar Handlin, among many others, has deplored this development in American colleges, whose students, he has claimed, are so grade-hungry that they have no time for genuine education. The ablest, potentially creative, young people secure an admirable training in what he called "the techniques of the right answer. They learn to remember; to be accurate, neat, and cautious. But they are rarely called on to use their ability autonomously or speculatively, to deal with situations in which the answers are not known but must be discovered. . . . With what pain, if ever at all, will they learn how to know what they do not know, how to probe alone beyond the limits of what is handed to them, how to be creative original thinkers."[2] . . .

Teachers who are concerned to encourage creativity among their pupils must resolutely oppose the concept of education as information-feeding. It is, of course, wasteful for children to have to rediscover for themselves everything that has already been discovered. And it is necessary to gain some basic knowledge to use it as a springboard for creative work. The problem is how to help children to gain this knowledge without, in the process, killing their creative drive because of the *way* in which the knowledge is assimilated. We know that spoon-feeding and mechanical, ground-covering[3] methods are most likely to kill creativity. Teaching children thoughts rather than how to think is one example of this approach. Readymade thoughts that have to be absorbed into the memory work against the encouragement of originality. If we insist that children memorize hundreds of isolated scraps of information, we must be prepared for the fact that, with their time totally taken up with absorbing mountains of data, there will be no time or energy left for thinking. If we insist on continually hurrying to cover the curriculum, to complete the book or assignment, we must be prepared to sacrifice those vital moments of insight that are so rare that everything needs to be stopped to assimilate and cultivate them.

We must view with caution and use with care the range of audiovisual

[2] Oscar Handlin, "Are the Colleges Killing Education?," *Atlantic,* May 1962, p. 43.

[3] Riesman has cited the history of the development of psychoanalysis as an example of the fact that the ideas of inclusiveness, of eclecticism, of covering the ground, are hindrances to creativity. David Riesman, *Constraint and Variety in American Education* (New York: Doubleday, 1958), pp. 112–14.

techniques that technology is making available to us. While these have many valuable uses, they often tend to nurture a passivity in the student that is a severe threat to creativity. A prime example is the use of television, which tends to capture and satisfy the imagination rather than stimulate and liberate it. A good teacher, like Socrates, should make us feel a little uncomfortable, should prod us into creative activity. Television, with its rich supply of visual images, tends by contrast to saturate us, to fill in all the gaps, to provide the missing pieces, so that there is little or nothing left for us to do.

Closed-ended pedagogical techniques of all kinds are impediments to creativity. This includes objective examinations,[4] true-false tests, and a host of minor techniques, most of which have the "virtue" of keeping energetic children busy. Busyness is itself not only a misleading sign of the degree of genuine activity going on in the classroom, but a major obstacle to creativeness. . . .

One of the commonest ways in which we, as adults, suppress the creative freedom of children is through what I would call the *authority of expectations*. We limit the creativity of many children by holding unduly low expectations of what they can become. Children arrive at their own evaluation of themselves partly through their perception of what we expect of them. In large measure they docilely become what we appear to expect them to become. We can help children by showing that we have faith and confidence in them, without making our expectations so specific in terms of role or performance that we in effect mold them according to our preconceived notions. And there is a mutuality between this concern for the creativity of children and our own creativity: parents who help children to solve their problems creatively are themselves strengthened. Just as teachers who suppress children's creative endeavors must pay the cost of this suppression in terms of their own personal development, so teachers who help children to become more creative will themselves benefit in terms of the growth of their own creative powers.

Finally, we must not ignore one of the commonest and most serious obstacles to creativity—fear. In the family, the primary enabling conditions of creativity are parental love and loving family relationships. The primary disabling conditions are parental and family relationships that breed fear and insecurity. In the school, it is necessary to arrange the environment with extreme delicacy, if we want the emotional and unconscious life of the child to feed the springs of creativity. It is unlikely that high-quality creative work can be nourished from these sources if there

---

[4] For a criticism of objective examinations as enemies of creativity, see Paul Nash, "The Assumptions and Consequences of Objective Examination," *Canadian Education and Research Digest* 1, no. 1 (March 1961):42–50; and "Objective Examinations and the Process of Education," *Canadian Education and Research Digest* 11, no. 2 (June 1962):99–103.

is a harsh, unsympathetic, authoritarian teacher who motivates by fear. Creative work should be expected only in a warm, supporting, secure atmosphere. We shall never get children to frame important questions for themselves, to wonder deeply, or to play with ideas—all ways of releasing creative energies—unless we can reduce their fears. There is a case to be made for removing much of the personal risk from education, for encouraging children to play with ideas in a largely risk-free situation. But we have a long way to go in this respect. John Holt, who has vividly documented the failure of schools to nurture creativity in children, has maintained that our substitution of fear for creativity is deliberate. It is no accident that the child in school is afraid, he has charged. "We have made him afraid, consciously, deliberately, so that we might more easily control his behavior and get him to do whatever we wanted him to do."[5] . . .

Is it enough to educate for creativity and leave it at that? Certainly, the parent or teacher who succeeds in freeing the latent creative urges of the child, and in disciplining them into functional creative power, might justifiably feel that he had done more than most adults do for the children in their care. But even this is insufficient. Just as we need to examine more carefully the link between the aesthetic and the ethical, so we need to study the link between creativity and values.

On the practical level, we need to show children that their creative gifts should be used not for selfish or destructive ends but for the service of their fellow men. We have already seen examples of the ghastly possibilities for the abuse of creative power in the fiendish ingenuity used to destroy, torture, and experiment on the inmates of Nazi concentration camps. Closer to home, we must be prepared to raise and examine the case of the creative research scientist who puts his talent at the disposal of his government to create more efficient ways of destroying his fellow human beings through atomic, bacteriological, and chemical weapons. It is clear that we cannot afford to raise and educate creative but conscienceless men and women.

How, then, are we to help people to distinguish between productive and destructive creativity, between positive and negative creativity? As an initial guide, we might suggest that the kind of creativeness we want to encourage will be characterized by the two criteria of *love* and *joy*. If the creative worker works in a spirit of love—love for life, love and respect for himself, his work, and his fellow men—we can be happy if we have helped to nurture this creativity. If, on the other hand, a research scientist says, "If you're doing the kind of creative work you want to do, you can't afford to enquire too closely into where the money comes from or how your work will ultimately be used," then we are justified

---

[5] John Holt, *How Children Fail* (New York: Pitman, 1964), p. 68. See especially pt. II, "Fear and Failure."

in doubting whether this is the kind of creative worker we should like to have produced. For these are the men who create cancers in the body of the world. "Cancer," wrote Karl Stern, "is life created by parthenogenesis, new life created without love . . . cancer is a case of loveless creation, a paradox. A paradox right out of hell."[6] In the end, there is no positive, productive creativity except in a spirit of love.

[6] Karl Stern, *Through Dooms of Love* (New York: Farrar, Straus & Cudahy, 1960), p. 400.

What Education Is
Jerome S. Bruner

Education seeks to develop the power and sensibility of mind. On the one hand, the educational process transmits to the individual some part of the accumulation of knowledge, style, and values that constitutes the culture of a people. In doing so, it shapes the impulses, the consciousness, and the way of life of the individual. But education must also seek to develop the processes of intelligence so that the individual is capable of going beyond the cultural ways of his social world, able to innovate in however modest a way so that he can create an interior culture of his own. For whatever the art, the science, the literature, the history, and the geography of a culture, each man must be his own artist, his own scientist, his own historian, his own navigator. No person is master of the whole culture; indeed, this is almost a defining characteristic of that form of social memory that we speak of as culture. Each man lives a fragment of it. To be whole, he must create his own version of the world, using that part of his cultural heritage he has made his own through education.

In our time, the requirements of technology constrain the freedom of the individual to create images of the world that are satisfying in the deepest sense. Our era has also witnessed the rise of ideologies that subordinate the individual to the defined aims of a society, a form of subordination that is without compassion for idiosyncrasy and respects only the instrumental contribution of a man to the progress of the society. At the same time, and in spite of ideologies, man's understanding of himself

Reprinted by permission of the publishers from pp. 115–17 and 120–24 of Jerome S. Bruner, *On Knowing: Essays for the Left Hand* (Cambridge, Mass.: The Belknap Press of Harvard University Press, 1962). Copyright © 1962 by the President and Fellows of Harvard College.

and of his world—both the natural and social world—has deepened to a degree that warrants calling our age an intellectually golden one. The need is now to employ our deeper understanding not only for the enrichment of society but also for the enrichment of the individual.

It is true, as Dewey said, that all education proceeds by the participation of the individual in the social consciousness of the race, but it is a truth with a double edge. For all education, good and bad alike, is of this order. We know now to what degree this is so. To take but one example, the very language one speaks conditions the style and structure of thought and experience. Indeed, as we have seen, there is reason to believe that though processes themselves are internalizations of social intercourse, an inner colloquy patterned by early external dialogues. It is this that makes education possible. But education, by giving shape and expression to our experience, can also be the principal instrument for setting limits on the enterprise of mind. The guarantee against limits is the sense of alternatives. Education must, then, be not only a process that transmits culture but also one that provides alternative views of the world and strengthens the will to explore them. . . .

The Subject Matter of Education

The issue of subject matter in education can be resolved only by reference to one's view of the nature of knowledge. Knowledge is a model we construct to give meaning and structure to regularities in experience. The organizing ideas of any body of knowledge are inventions for rendering experience economical and connected. We invent concepts such as force in physics, the bond in chemistry, motives in psychology, style in literature as means to the end of comprehension.

The history of culture is the history of the development of great organizing ideas, ideas that inevitably stem from deeper values and points of view about man and nature. The power of great organizing concepts is in large part that they permit us to understand and sometimes to predict or change the world in which we live. But their power lies also in the fact that ideas provide instruments for experience. Having grown up in a culture dominated by the ideas of Newton, and so with a conception of time flowing equably, we experience time moving inexorably and steadily, marked by a one-way arrow. Indeed, we know now, after a quarter of a century of research on perception, that experience is not to be had directly and neatly, but filtered through the programmed readiness of our senses. The program is constructed with our expectations and these are derived from our models or ideas about what exists and what follows what.

From this, two convictions follow. The first is that the structure of knowledge—its connectedness and the derivations that make one idea follow from another—is the proper emphasis in education. For it is structure, the great conceptual inventions that bring order to the congeries of disconnected observations, that gives meaning to what we may learn and makes possible the opening up of new realms of experience. The second conviction is that the unity of knowledge is to be found within knowledge itself, if the knowledge is worth mastering.

To attempt a justification of subject matter, as Dewey did, in terms of its relation to the child's social activities is to misunderstand what knowledge is and how it may be mastered. The significance of the concept of commutativity in mathematics does not derive from the social insight that two houses with fourteen people in each is not the same as fourteen houses with two people in each. Rather, it inheres in the power of the idea to create a way of thinking about number that is lithe and beautiful and immensely generative—an idea at least as powerful as, say, the future conditional tense in formal grammar. Without the idea of commutativity, algebra would be impossible. If set theory—now often the introductory section in newer curriculums in mathematics—had to be justified in terms of its relation to immediate experience and social life, it would not be worth teaching. Yet set theory lays a foundation for the understanding of order and number that could never be achieved with the social arithmetic of interest rates and bales of hay at so much per bale. Mathematics, like any other subject, must begin with experience, but progress toward abstraction and understanding requires precisely that there be a weaning away from the obviousness of superficial experience.

There is one consideration of cognitive economy . . . that is paramount. One cannot "cover" any subject in full, not even in a lifetime, if coverage means visiting all the facts and events and morsels. Subject matter presented so as to emphasize its structure will perforce be of that generative kind that permits reconstruction of the details or, at very least, prepares a place into which the details, when encountered, can be put.

What then of subject matter in the conventional sense? The answer to the question, "What shall be taught?" turns out to be the answer to the question, "What is nontrivial?" If one can first answer the question, "What is worth knowing about?" then it is not difficult to distinguish between the aspects of it that are worth teaching and learning and those that are not. Surely, knowledge of the natural world, knowledge of the human condition, knowledge of the nature and dynamics of society, knowledge of the past so that it may be used in experiencing the present and aspiring to the future—all of these, it would seem reasonable to suppose, are essential to an educated man. To these must be added another: knowledge of the products of our artistic heritage that mark the history of our aesthetic wonder and delight.

A problem immediately arises concerning the symbolism in terms of which knowledge is understood and talked about. There is language in its natural sense and language in its mathematical sense. I cannot imagine an educated man a century from now who will not be largely bilingual in this special sense—concise and adept in both a natural language and mathematics. For these two are the tools essential to the unlocking of new experience and the gaining of new powers. As such, they must have a central place in any curriculum.

Finally, it is as true today as it was when Dewey wrote that one cannot foresee the world in which the child we educate will live. Informed powers of mind and a sense of potency in action are the only instruments we can give the child that will be invariable across the transformations of time and circumstance. The succession of studies that we give the child in the ideal school need be fixed in only one way: whatever is introduced, let it be pursued continuously enough to give the student a sense of the power of mind that comes from a deepening of understanding. It is this, rather than any form of extensive coverage, that matters most.

The Nature of Method

The process and the goal of education are one and the same thing. The goal of education is disciplined understanding; that is the process as well.

Let us recognize that the opposite of understanding is not ignorance or simply "not knowing." To understand something is, first, to give up some other way of conceiving of it. Confusion all too often lies between one way of conceiving and another, better way. It is one of our biological inheritances that confusion produces emergency anxiety, and with anxiety there come the defensive measures—flight, fright, or freezing—that are antithetical to the free and zestful use of mind. The binding fact to mental life in child and adult alike is that there is a limited capacity for processing information—our span, as it is called, can comprise six or seven unrelated items simultaneously. Go beyond that and there is overload, confusion, forgetting. As George Miller has put it, the principle of economy is to fill our seven mental-input slots with gold rather than dross. The degree to which material to be learned is put into structures by the learner will determine whether he is working with gold or dross.

For this reason, as well as for reasons already stated, it is essential that, before being exposed to a wide range of material on a topic, the child first have a general idea of how and where things fit. It is often the case that the development of the general idea comes from a first round of experience with concrete embodiments of ideas that are close to a child's life. The cycle of learning begins, then, with particulars and immediately moves toward abstraction. It comes to a temporary goal when the abstraction can then be used in grasping new particulars in the deeper way that abstraction permits.

Insofar as possible, a method of instruction should have the objective of leading the child to discover for himself. Telling children and then testing them on what they have been told inevitably has the effect of producing benchbound learners whose motivation for learning is likely to be extrinsic to the task—pleasing the teacher, getting into college, artificially maintaining self-esteem. The virtues of encouraging discovery are of two kinds. In the first place, the child will make what he learns his own, will fit his discovery into the interior world of culture that he creates for himself. Equally important, discovery and the sense of confidence it provides is the proper reward for learning. It is a reward that, moreover, strengthens the very process that is at the heart of education —disciplined inquiry.

The child must be encouraged to get the full benefit from what he learns. This is not to say that he should be required to put it to immediate use in his daily life, though so much the better if he has the happy opportunity to do so. Rather, it is a way of honoring the connectedness of knowledge. Two facts and a relation joining them is and should be an invitation to generalize, to extrapolate, to make a tentative intuitive leap, even to build a tentative theory. The leap from mere learning to using what one has learned in thinking is an essential step in the use of the mind. Indeed, plausible guessing, the use of the heuristic hunch, the best employment of necessarily insufficient evidence—these are activities in which the child needs practice and guidance. They are among the great antidotes of passivity.

Most important of all, the educational process must be free of intellectual dishonesty and those forms of cheating that explain without providing understanding. I have expressed the conviction elsewhere that any subject can be taught to anybody at any age in some form that is honest. It is not honest to present a fifth-grade social-studies class with an image of town government as if it were a den of Cub Scouts presided over by a parent figure interpreting the charter—even if the image set forth does happen to mesh with the child's immediate social experience. A lie is still a lie—even if it sounds like familiar truth. Nor is it honest to present a sixth-grade science class with a garbled but concrete picture of the atom that is, in its way, as sweeteningly false as the suburban image of town government given them the year before. A dishonest image can only discourage the self-generating intellectual inquiry out of which real understanding grows.

CHAPTER 9
The System of Psychological Beliefs

What's the Matter with Learning Theory?

Something is the matter with learning theory. All teacher-education programs require the study of educational psychology and learning theory; however, the study doesn't seem to have much effect on teachers and what they do.

This assertion requires some common-sense support:

1. Many teachers do not grant much credibility to education courses in general and to learning-theory courses in particular (Luchsinger, 1969). The most frequent advice given student teachers by their professional counterparts is "Forget all that stuff they talked about in your education courses; out here in the classroom you have to deal with realities." If you accept this as evidence of a problem, you recognize that these teachers are not anti-intellectual or antieducation. They probably are reporting their own experience and frustration in trying to make sense out of instructional problems.

2. Many teachers do not really know how children learn and do not apply concepts learned in educational psychology courses to their teaching practice. When teachers are asked to state in their own words how children learn, even after having taken an educational psychology course, they most frequently use terms like "absorption," "drill and repetition," "imitation," and "hard work." In some informal samplings, Weber (1965) reported that one-third of the teachers replied that they did not know how children learn, that they had not really thought about it. If you accept this at face value, it is an appalling indictment of persons who don't know much about the essential nature of their practice. Can you imagine asking a surgeon how he is going to operate and getting a response like "I don't know; I've never really thought about it"? If you consider the situation analytically, it appears to indict teacher educators more than teachers.

3. Teachers manifest a lack of both clarity and consistency when they are asked to agree or disagree with descriptive statements of different learning theories. Within a given school faculty, the writers have found that 94 percent of the teachers generally agreed with the statement "Learning is a process by which students are able to raise, explore, and solve problems on their own" (Humanistic learning theory), but that 81 percent also agreed that "The mind can be trained and strengthened by presenting problems which will exercise it, much as any other muscle of the body" (faculty psychology) (Dunwell *et al.*, 1971). If there is little clarity and consistency at this level, we can predict that there will be little clarity and consistency in the instructional program. We are even more perplexed by the question of how teachers got this way, having gone through a professional training program and been certified as teachers, and yet knowing so little about learning.

We conclude that something is the matter with learning theory as it is currently taught. Let us, therefore, focus our attention on what may need to be done differently.

One major problem in the attempt to utilize knowledge from psychology arises from the character of the relationships between this subject and other disciplines (Figure 9–1). It is a long way from formal philosophy to instructional principles, and a lot gets lost in the journey. We suggest that educational psychology has a lot to offer teachers, but only when the assumptions upon which educational psychology is founded are clearly understood, and only when the implications and consequences of the learning principles are clearly translated into valid, practical knowledge for teachers.

In the teacher-education bureaucracy, jurisdictional jealousies and academic parochialism force the student to sample unrelated courses taught by unrelated departments with almost no regard for sequence or articulation. The most difficult intellectual task—developing a comprehensive framework within which to integrate diverse disciplines—is thrust upon the student, the person least experienced and least competent to attempt it. This happens in most other disciplines as well, but that does not justify the situation in teacher education.

The second major problem is that what is typically taught as learning theory is not that at all. Students are exposed to long lists of topics *about* educational psychology, but these add up to little more than a partial coverage of: (1) the history of educational psychology; (2) the specialized language of educational psychology; (3) some of the literature of educational psychology; (4) something about the structure of educational psychology; and, on rare occasions, (5) something about the mode of inquiry employed by some educational psychologists.

This does not make a discipline, or at least not an adequate description of a discipline. What is required, especially if teachers are to be able

FIGURE 9-1

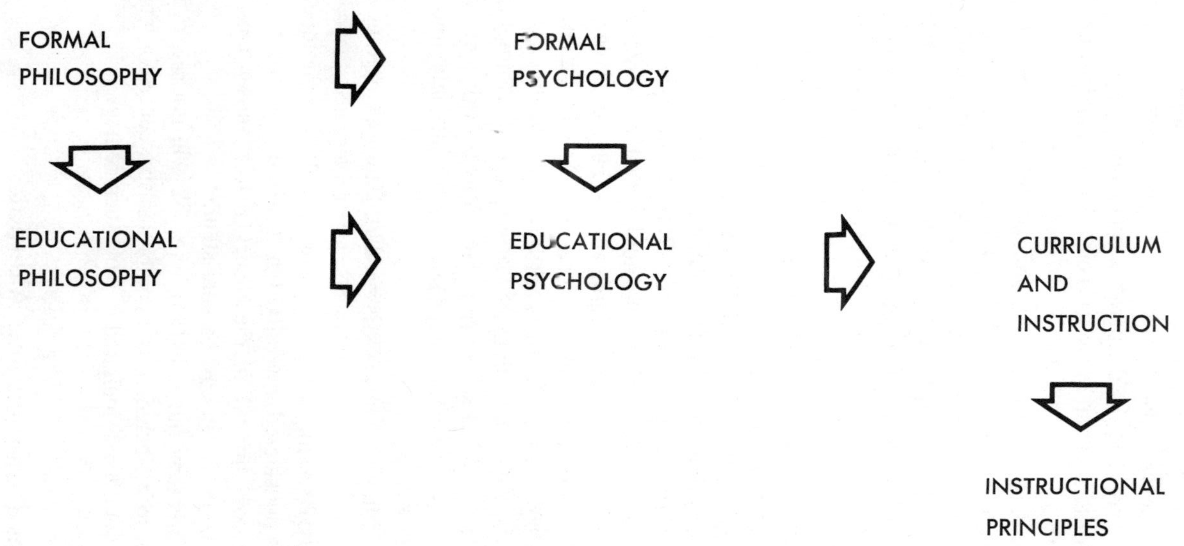

FORMAL PHILOSOPHY EDUCATIONAL PHILOSOPHY

FORMAL PSYCHOLOGY EDUCATIONAL PSYCHOLOGY

CURRICULUM AND INSTRUCTION INSTRUCTIONAL PRINCIPLES

to use educational psychology effectively, is something about: (6) the nature of the community of educational psychologists; (7) educational psychology as an expression of human imagination; (8) the domain of the educational psychologist and the means he uses to establish this domain; (9) the valuative and affective stance taken by educational psychologists; and (10) the deliberate structuring of educational psychology to promote its acquisition by learners (King and Brownell, 1966; Dunwell, 1970).

As if accommodation of these dimensions were not enough of a problem, the situation is compounded by the fact that educational psychology, like most other disciplines, does not have a single, commonly accepted, integrated structure. Instead, it is made up of different structures, each dependent upon a particular set of assumptions. Functionally, there are several educational psychologies in existence at the same time.

The student of education is in the unenviable position of having to learn reliable operational principles from an array of data that can be viewed in alternative ways, or having to make sense out of different operational principles that have been constructed using entirely different sets of assumptions. It is little wonder that teachers have come to view learning theory skeptically, and to accept the unsophisticated statements of eclectic methodology; they have not been offered much else.

The fallacies that beset learning theory have even been sustained by some of the most distinguished writers in the field, among them Jerome Bruner (1968), Ernest Hilgard (1956), and William Burton (1944). To *avoid* dealing with differences in structuring assumptions, each has attempted to derive a set of generalizations to which all theories could ascribe. The results of this approach have been ambiguous, vague, and misleading.

Quite a different approach is needed: The assumptions employed by each alternative theory need to be clearly identified, each theory needs to be analyzed using pertinent criteria, and the consequences of each need to be considered carefully. On this basis, the teacher can make a functional commitment to the theory that promises most in practical application and can at least be consistent.

This is precisely our intention here. We will not set forth a digest of what ought to be included in a comprehensive course in learning theory, but rather what is *not* included in most such courses.

Questions Distinguishing Alternate Psychological Approaches

Our earlier consideration of philosophy established a number of concepts significant to the structure of psychology.

First, the assumptions of the causes of being presented a number of alternate explanations of the nature of man and his world. Psychology is a precise derivation of that knowledge which emphasizes the mind of man (*psyche*). It leads logically to a consideration of man's nature and an explanation of man's behavior.

Second, the study of knowledge and knowing leads directly to the psychological topics of thinking, learning, and intelligence. It implies, as well, alternate views of what constitutes knowledge and how knowledge may be organized and structured.

Axiology has direct implications for the psychological explanation of personality, character, and ethical behavior. It also suggests reasonable explanations of why man values certain beliefs more than others and why he seeks certain ends as opposed to others.

The relationship between philosophic knowledge and psychology is direct and, in most instances, clear. Differing psychological positions can therefore be analyzed and compared on the basis of the major questions they seek to explain:

1. What are the assumptions about the moral and actional nature of man on which the psychological theory is based? Do these assumptions adequately describe the moral and actional nature of man? What consequences come from these alternate assumptions? Are these consequences acceptable in terms of what we wish to obtain through education?

2. How does the theory define psychological phenomena? What does it include in their domain, what does it exclude, and how does it arrive at this distinction? Is this treatment consistent with what we know about man? Is it adequate? What are the consequences to which each alternate description leads? Are these consequences acceptable in terms of what we believe education and schooling should be?

3. How does the theory define and treat intelligence? If "intelligent" man is the end sought by education, is this definition and treatment appropriate and adequate to what we know about our social circumstance and what we desire that social circumstance to become?

4. How does the theory define and treat thinking? Is this treatment consistent with what we know about man? Is it an adequate description? Are the consequences and implications of this description acceptable in view of what we know and believe about education and schooling?

5. How does the theory treat the process of learning and the role of the learner? Since these functions carry direct implications for the conduct of school, are these alternate positions appropriate to what we have come to believe about schooling? Are there consequences and implications that are not acceptable in terms of what we believe?

6. If the instrumental value of learning resides in what it enables the learner to do, how does the theory regard and treat transfer of learning? Toward what purposes is learning directed? Do these appear to be appro-

priate and adequate to the purposes we ascribe to education? If not, what further consideration is required?

Analysis of Alternate Psychological Theories

Each major psychological theory and its approach to each of the distinguishing explanations are shown by the categories in Table 9–1. It is immediately apparent that these categories do not always result in simple, clear delineation. This is not necessarily a fault of the philosophic system, nor is it a fault of the categories of questions posed. It may not even be a fault. Although perplexing, movement between nonexclusive categories seems characteristic of the way the human intellect functions. These categories are generalizations or central tendencies of diverse philosophic positions; in many instances some degree of overlap exists among them. Table 9–1 distinguishes among exclusive categories (single and double lines) and nonexclusive categories (broken lines).

Faculty Psychology

Philosophic interpretations of the nature of man and of mind came into existence long before science and scientific explanations. This does not mean that these descriptions are irrational, or that scientific explanations are more rational. In fact, they were the most rational descriptions possible.

Having categorized reality into a dualistic system of absolute ideals and soul-spirits, the early Idealist required a plausible explanation of the interface between the two: how mind comes to know, or hold an idea. Having granted ideas an existence in and of themselves, it was essential to grant mind an *active* character if it were to acquire knowledge of the external reality of the world of ideas.

Without any better explanation of the distinction between physical reality and the reality of ideas, *by analogy* the mind was separated from the physical body to become some sort of intermediary between the two. Mind was granted a real, if unknown, substantive existence. From this supposition, characteristics or traits of the mind were quickly derived, again by analogy with the physical body. If parts of the body had separate functions, parts of the mind must have separate functions (faculties). If the desired state of physical well-being was harmonious and complete development of the body, the desired state of mental well-being must be harmonious and complete development of the mind. We have little difficulty in acknowledging the Greek ideal of "a sound mind in a sound body," for the mind was vested locus there.

The fundamental assumptions of faculty psychology are apparent: an active mind made up of discrete faculties requiring harmonious development to deal with what existed in the separate world of ideas. The implications of these assumptions become clear. The continuing development of an active mind is achieved through further activity or exercise. The most appropriate activity or exercise for the mind would be: (1) that which has the greatest effect in strengthening the faculties of the mind; and (2) that which enables it to correspond most adequately with that external absolute. Since the world of absolute ideas is external, the active mind by itself does not possess direction; direction must be externally imposed. Hence, if learning man is not capable of guiding his own learning, he is dependent upon external guidance provided by learned man; an intellectual hierarchy of learner-teacher is established and at once justified. Further, since the internal exercise of a given faculty of the mind is independent of the external end sought, it follows that the nature of the exercising makes little difference as long as strengthening results. By analogy, it makes little difference what you lift to strengthen the lifting muscles as long as it is heavy. And heavy is precisely what curriculum became: Ancient History, Greek, Latin, Classical Literature.

How man acted could be compared with the external, absolute idea of reason. The degree to which he had come to know reason determined directly the degree to which his action was reason-able. Intelligence became the degree to which the intellect or the several mental faculties had been developed, and thinking corresponded to a particular faculty, the power to reason or the power of reason.

Of particular concern to learning theorists is consideration of how a trained or educated person transfers learning from one situation to another, particularly from the context in which learning originally occurred to a different context. In terms of the assumptions of Faculty Psychology, reality is absolute and independent of context or situation, and the trained intellect is also independent of context or situation. Transfer therefore becomes the *automatic* application of developed mental faculties to the new problem and requires no special consideration.

Throughout the development of these suppositions, philosophy struggled to obtain a plausible explanation of the original source of the external absolute or ultimate reality. The notion of a theistic creation offered one explanation, but it introduced alternate religious views of the nature of man. Theistic Idealism could accept an order of both the physical and spiritual world Divinely created, an order in which man actively sought to attain correspondence with God's will, but the *neutral-active* notion of man's moral and actional nature assumed that all men would strive for absolute goodness.

To many this did not appear to be an accurate or adequate description of what they observed of man's actions or how they conceptualized divine order. The supposition that not all men were moved to strive for a

TABLE 9-1

A TAXONOMY OF PSYCHOLOGICAL CONCEPTS

General Philosophic Position (Chapter 6)	General Psychological Position	Derived Psychological/ Philosophic Positions	Man's Moral/ Actional Nature	Psychologica Activity
Idealism	Faculty Psychology	Classicism	Neutral-Active	Determined by c respondence with solute reason
		Puritanism	Bad-Active	
		Romantic Naturalism	Good-Active	Detetmined by m original nature
Realism	Tabula Rasa	Apperception, or Herbartianism	Neutral-Passive	Determined by e sure to appercept
	Behaviorism	Connectionism	Neutral-Passive	Determined in ac cordance with sc tifically derived l and principles by prior conditionin
		Behaviorism		
		Operant Conditioning		
Relativism	Developmental Psychology	Psychology of Cognition	Naturally Active	Natural stages o velopment deter mined by nature stimulation from ternal environme
	Field Theory	Gestalt		Determined by s tures formed in a cordance with natural laws
		Goal Insight	Neutral- Interactive	Validly predicta as the function o interaction of dis cernible variable
Relativistic Humanism		Cognitive-Field		
		Third-Force		
Existentialism	Existential Psychology		Neutral-Active	Behavior accoun able only to self

Learner/ Learning	Intelligence/ Wisdom	Transfer of Learning	Thinking
ctive exercise of ental faculties to engthen mind	Degree to which intellect or mental faculties have been developed	Automatic application of developed mental faculties	One faculty of the mind: the power of reason
eservation of original ture; negative edu- tion	Degree to which origi- nal nature has been preserved	Innate capability of mind	Innate function of mind
nsory receptor for perceptions: ap- ceiving	Size of apperceptive mass	Available apperceptions link to new ideas	Mechanistic link- ing of related apperceptions
ssive subject to ex- nally determined con- ioning program	Number of correct con- ditioned responses ac- quired	Elements acquired through earlier condi- tioning apply to identi- cal elements in new situation	Mechanistic linking of simple responses into more complex linear chains
ntinuous transforma- n of the structure of ironment	Formal operations ac- quired as natural out- growth of preceding developmental stages	Operational applica- tion of range of skills and competencies ac- quired at that stage of development	Natural growth from simple opera- tions to formal operations
al-directed reorgani- ion to form organic ght	Process of acquiring meaningful sets or patterns	Application of insights to form new patterns of understanding	Purposive process of developing under- standing of inner relations
eracting with per- ved environment to- rd building, modifying looks	Span or scope of in- sights/ability to act with dependable foresight	Insights purposively applied toward goal achievement in new situation	Purposive process of clarifying and en- hancing outlooks
nanced awareness re- ing from imposed ices	Extent of knowledge of self	Significance limited to current existence	Clarification of im- posed choices

state of grace, or that not all men were intended to achieve a state of grace, required the notion either that some were elected to achieve grace while others were not (divine ordination) or that all men had fallen from grace and some would achieve return to grace while others would not.

By this rationale Idealism obtained a religious motive, but divided as to whether man was *neutral-active* or *bad-active*. Although this had little influence on the basic theory of faculty psychology, the altered conception of the learner and his motivation did affect instructional practice tremendously and extends into the current conduct of schools. Once the necessity to oppose man's actively evil nature directly has been established, rote memorization, recitation of prescribed forms, and severe discipline including corporal punishment become essential to achieve the ends sought.

The alternate philosophic *good-active* principle of Romantic Naturalism provides a significant clue to the inadequacy of the assumptions underlying faculty psychology. If we suppose man's essential nature to be active, is it not just as plausible to suppose his moral nature to be innately good instead of either neutral or evil? Assuming man to be innately good *and* active endows him with all that is essential to achieve the ends he seeks if only his *original* nature could be preserved. Here no elaborate psychological theory is needed, for all that is required is assumed to exist innately. These requisites are transferred from one generation to another genetically. At the same time, the logical consequence of these assumptions provides its own negation, each human variable—personality, intelligence, and so forth—must now be explained in terms of inborn traits, a complexity that confounds modern genetics.

Faculty psychology, then, fails on several significant counts. The fundamental assumption that man is innately *active* is not sufficient to our observations, for not all men appear inherently motivated all the time. To assume that men are usually motivated is semantic quibbling unsatisfactory as a commonsense explanation. The fundamental assumptions that active man is either good or bad, or that some men are good and others bad, lead us into religious arguments that can be resolved only in terms of knowledge available through sources not common to all men (Divine revelation). If resolution of the argument is not available, the argument is not productive.

Faculty psychology fails as well because the philosophic assumptions identify the existence of a system of external absolutes—absolute reason, absolute truth, absolute beauty—that are categorically separate and apart from man. Explanation of what is necessary for man to transcend this epistemological gulf is at best labored and cumbersome; it may not even be possible.

The failure of faculty psychology as an adequate description of mental functions rests in its prescientific origins. There are no such things as discrete mental faculties. Modern neurological science gives evidence of a few sites of gross motor functions. The function of the intellect appears to be not only general, but highly generalizable. Man appears able to overcome neurological dysfunctions by developing alternative neurological functions. Despite this, the mythology of faculty psychology persists, as witness the recurrence of Bacon's epigram "Reading is to the mind what exercise is to the body."

The consequences of faculty psychology, particularly in the form of educational puritanism, do not seem to require rebuttal by logical arguments, even if such rebuttal were an effective way of altering personal convictions. Some teachers will continue to view some students as innately evil, their natural inclinations requiring the severest possible prohibition and punishment. There is little reason to ask these teachers to examine the effect this has on students, for they will view docile conformity as success and anything else as proof of the flaw they presumed. As Bayles asserts, "Perhaps an educationally justifiable comment on today's schools is not that they have departed too much from 'time-honored' practice, but rather that *they have not departed enough*" (Bayles and Hood, 1966:19).

Apperception, or Herbartianism

Given the Idealistic conceptualization of a dualistic world of man and ideas, an alternate epistemological answer arose to explain how man came to know external reality. If ideas possessed a motive force of their own, they could determine independently how knowledge was acquired. If man or mind were *passive,* active ideas could have an impact upon man, giving him cognition or knowledge of the external idea. The mind then must be a passive repository for the ideas that exist externally and independently. The notion of mind as *tabula rasa,* the shaven wax tablet upon which ideas are inscribed, was granted some credence.

This explanation avoids the problem of whether or not man is possessed of an innate motive force; if man is passive he cannot by himself seek or obtain salvation or avoid damnation. He must then be morally neutral, his fate determined by the nature and number of ideas that happen to impinge upon him. Variations among men must be due to exposure to certain ideas or capricious circumstance. Thus man is relieved of responsibility for his fate. This explanation also deals with the problem of whether or not man carries innate qualities. The wax tablet bears no prior imprint; man at birth possesses potential, but not a predetermined or instinctive nature.

But, as is the case with many explanations, the notion of *tabula rasa* has several disadvantages, most important its failure to deal with the manner in which active ideas form interrelationships. Rather than random exposure, there must be some explanation of why some ideas "make an impression on the mind" and others don't. And rather than random impact on a two-dimensional surface, ideas seem to need some space in which they can move around.

With only rudimentary notions of how man's senses function, a pseudoscientific explanation developed. Mind became a vessel holding ideas that had been *apperceived,* taken *through to* some place. (Apperception is more than simply becoming aware of the idea; it is depositing it in a place from which it can be recalled.) So ideas could enter through the level of consciousness and form an apperceptive mass, and apperceived ideas could rise to the level of consciousness, link with newly apperceived ideas, and form a concept, or combination of ideas.

Given the notion of active, discrete ideational elements and a passive receptacle for ideas, analysis of psychological activity focused on the process by which ideas enter the mind and the nature of logical relationships among "active" ideas. Understanding the behavior of an individual was dependent upon: (1) assessment of the number of ideas acquired or the size of his apperceptive mass through achievement testing; (2) measurement of the individual's ability to receive sensory inputs through physiological tests of sight, hearing, and so on; and (3) measurement of the individual's native ability to store apperceptions, or mental *capacity,* through IQ tests (the kid who was as full of ideas as he was supposed to be was given a score of 100).

Transfer of learning was possible because the individual brought his accumulated wisdom to the new situation. Elements in the new situation attracted appropriate elements from among those available, and a new relationship was formed.

At the outset, assessment of this line of reasoning must recognize the impact it has had on educational practice. Apperception provided the infant discipline of education with a methodological approach at a time when it suffered from a lack of structuring concepts. It fostered concern for the media of instruction which anticipated the development of educational technology.

At the same time, several associated notions have persisted into modern instructional practice, evidence of the maladaptation that occurs when practices are separated from the assumptions upon which they were based.

1. Although apperception abandoned its arguments about instinct theory, it fostered the notion that man at birth does possess a predetermined and fixed capacity or potential for learning, and that different men can be distinguished by their different mental capacities. The consequence of this assumption is that ultimately human potential is treated as though it were predetermined, immutable, and quantifiable.

2. By treating mind as a passive receptacle for ideas, apperception placed responsibility for what man becomes on external factors. Man is not *causal;* man is *caused.* Man does not determine his fate; his fate is determined by external, often extraneous, circumstances which he cannot hope to control or affect.

3. By treating active ideas as independent of mind, curriculum development focused on the clarification and categorization of ideas as a completely separate step in instructional planning. As the learning process assumed that these ideas were deposited without alteration, that they were discrete and fixed, the primary focus of instructional methods became mechanistic projection of the idea into the mind. While this may have led to increased technical proficiency, it did not necessarily lead to more effective learning because it treated the learner only as a sensori-motor receptor. Pedagogy focused on the act of teaching, not on the process of learning.

4. If the notion of transfer of learning is limited to the application of the ideas one possesses, effectiveness of transfer becomes dependent upon the specific ideational elements available and how well they link up with elements in the new situation. The theory explains away creative solutions as new or unique relationships among ideas, not as the function of a creative man.

5. Because the theory was prescientific, it is not at all congruent with elements of scientific knowledge.

Behaviorism

The rise of philosophic Realism resolved the problems inherent in a simple explanation of the relationships between the dualistic worlds of physical reality and spiritual notions by the arbitrary decision to consider only that which was directly observable. Although Realism was divided on the question of whether the physical world was created and set into motion by a divine force (Religious Realism) or a natural force (Scientific Realism), both factions viewed the world as a unitary reality. Scientific Realism directed its efforts toward discovery of the absolute principles that described natural phenomena; Religious Realism, to the discovery of God's will, revealed through His works.

To provide consistency within this system, it was necessary to relegate man to a position no different from that of any other organism within the real physical world. Like apperception, this denied man an original nature other than that which could be explained by natural laws. Having assumed natural law to be absolute, it was not plausible to assume further that some will or volitional nature might contravene this natural law. Again, these assumptions fix the nature of man: He must be *neutral-passive.*

Having chosen categorically to confine scientific analysis to observable phenomena, the science of psychology focuses on: (1) what the organism does as a part of the larger physical system; and (2) what causes the organism to do what it does. One determines cause-effect relationships for the observable behavior of man in precisely the same manner as for any other class of observable phenomena. This makes psychology just as scientific and objective as any other discipline.

The line of reasoning is logically simple, or simplistically logical, as the case may be. If man does not possess the innate ability to cause his own behavior, and there can be no behavior that is not caused, all behavior must be caused by the effect of some natural factor external to man but within the system of observable physical events. Understanding even complex behavior becomes possible by the analysis of the whole into its constituent parts. Hence, all behavior may be described in terms of simple cause-effect events, or stimuli and response linked together in some way.

If all behavior can be determined by connected causes, then the total behavior of man must also have some cause in man's historical past. Although these past causes are not directly observable or retrievable, their effects are, and the nature of causes can thus be established by inference. This process is not unique to psychology; many discoveries in physics and chemistry are based on inferences rather than direct observation even though the supposition has been made that they are directly observable, which confuses some people.

In any event, man's behavior is caused and, to the degree that we have knowledge of his prior conditioning, it is predictable. It also becomes possible to cause man to behave in certain predictable ways. And because we can refer to absolute natural law, it is possible to determine with certitude how man *should* behave and to condition him to behave in these ways.

Behaviorists assert that a valid educational program can be derived directly from these suppositions. The purpose of education becomes to condition man to adjust effectively to the natural scheme of things, to *fit into* the real world in which he exists. Effective man, or intelligent man, is the man who has acquired responses congruent to the way things really are. Learning is being conditioned or acquiring correct responses. Thinking, in much the same manner as the apperceptionists described it, is the development of linear chains of correct behaviors by linking together simple correct responses. Transfer of learning occurs when a correctly conditioned person is stimulated by old elements in a new situation, and correct response behavior is evoked. Learning and transfer of learning in man are analogous to animal learning because all the elements, including the behaving organism, are analogous.

This system of beliefs forms the basis for such current educational practices as programed instruction, diagnostic and prescriptive teaching, behavior modification, and the specification of behavioral objectives.

If behaviorism is to be accepted as the most adequate explanation of psychology, it must stand before the same kind of assessment that we have applied to other theories:

1. The fact that behaviorism restricts its concern to observable behavior suggests an inadequacy of this system. The assumption that the reason for all psychological activity can be inferred from direct observation has not been validated. Neither has the assertion that inferences drawn by the behaviorists are more "scientific" than inferences drawn by other systems. For example, it may be possible to analyze the effect of emotions on physiological functions, but a cause-effect relationship is not *proved* by this; an increased respiratory rate does not *cause* emotion. This is supported, at least in part, by the dictum of the undergraduate: "Don't mistake asthma for passion!"

2. As in the case of other systems that assume man to be *neutral-passive,* the behaviorist must accept that man is simply the product of his historical past and that there is nothing man can do about it. This predicates the practice of personal counseling to be nothing more than assisting the person to adjust to reality, to accept his lot in life. And it assumes that man will find satisfaction and fulfillment in this fatalistic proposition. We mark this treatment of motivation theory insufficient.

3. Like other part-whole systems which attempt to explain the complex in terms of the addition of simpler elements, behaviorism's efforts to explain complex mental functions and creative thought process are deficient. The attempt to describe the human mind as analogous to an electronic computer is a simplistic mechanism of the same class as the discredited notion of neurological connections across synaptic arches. We know more about the way the mind works than explanations of electrical circuitry can accommodate.

4. If transfer of conditioned behaviors is to be at all effective, the assessment of man's future needs must be precise and certain. Time must be allowed for the translation of these precise behaviors into instructional programs, which must be disseminated, installed, and implemented. To do so, needs assessment must be extended far into future time. If the effects of the program are to be evaluated in order to make necessary revisions, the process must be projected even further into the future. Behaviorism does not answer satisfactorily how this is to be done or who is to do it. At best this process is uncertain, if not completely unachievable. At worst, it can be controlled by elitist groups of scientists. Behaviorism provided no safeguards against this sort of complication.

5. A notion fundamental to American democracy is that man is capable of governing himself. The *neutral-passive* principle, upon which behaviorism is founded, takes the premise that man is governed by external

forces and achieves a degree of self-regulation only after he has been properly conditioned. Thus the assumptions of behaviorist psychological theory are not congruent with the assumptions of American sociopolitical theory.

6. Behaviorism attempts to reduce man to the level of simple mechanistic functions; many people resent this.

Gestalt Psychology

Despite an extensive experimental base focused heavily on learning theory, gestalt psychology seems to have had little general impact on American education and educational psychology. Nonetheless, credit must be given for several significant contributions of gestalt to educational practice.

Many of the principles of gestalt arose from research on the psychology of visual perception. Working with visual elements, gestalt psychology identified the effort of the individual to generalize beyond particular parts to form larger patterned wholes. These patterns, or gestalts, represent something more than the sum of the separate elements. The notion that the whole is greater than the sum of its parts obviously contradicted the suppositions on which Realism was founded. It also placed most of the explanations of gestalt outside the realm then accepted by scientific practice. The formation of a gestalt requires the creation of something more than exists in the stimuli present, more than external impact on a passive organism; it requires that the organism actively develop a sense of pattern, of completion or need for completion, of closure or continuation. Gestaltists accepted this as a natural tendency of psychological activity and developed a theory incorporating an *active* principle of human nature.

Gestalt psychology provided an understandable explanation of visual phenomena which exceeded the capability of behaviorist theory, but its application to cognitive phenomena—meanings, concepts, thought patterns—required a theory of knowledge radically different from all previous epistemologies. It required an explanation of the formation of cognitive patterns larger than the factual elements upon which they were based. It required a nonmechanistic approach at the time when most approaches, including that of science, were limited to mechanism.

At a time when behaviorism was explaining initial behavior in terms of random actions of the organism, gestalt psychology was emphasizing purposive, goal-directed efforts to form meaningful patterns of understanding. At a time when behaviorism was emphasizing objective observations of human behavior, gestalt psychology appeared to accept subjective views and interpretations of meanings. At a time when behaviorism based its descriptions of behavior on natural law, gestalt psychology credited man with an entirely different kind of nature. For several decades the uses of gestalt psychology were limited principally to descriptive studies. It was not translated into educational theory and descriptive principles of classroom practice. Currently, however, gestalt has found acceptance and elaboration as a therapeutic counseling model, almost exclusively as a result of the perceptive work of the late Fritz Perls and the Esalen group (Perls, 1969a; 1969b). Gestalt psychology *as such* has not been used directly as a model for the derivation of teaching strategy and the development of instructional materials. However, it has made possible the emergence of many later, more productive notions. The acceptance of many gestalt principles, especially in the later Third-Force movement, is apparent.

Developmental Psychology

Analysis of the development of human mental activity gave rise to the field of developmental psychology. Developmental psychologists extended the notion of perceptual patterns advanced by gestaltists and applied it to observable similarities in the development of cognition and thought. They describe the growth process from simple responses of the young child to complex intellectual acts of the intelligent adult as following an orderly evolution, described by Piaget and others (1950) in the following manner:

SENSORIMOTOR STAGE:
(*Birth to age 2*)

1. Development of sensorimotor intelligence through coordination of sense impressions and movements.
2. Formation of habits, or fixed ways of responding to satisfying behaviors.
3. Cumulative reorganization of habits toward more generalized behavior.

THE STAGE OF
CONCRETE OPERATIONS:
(*Age 2 to 7*)

4. Establishment of preconceptual symbolic thought by creating symbols.
5. Development of intuitive thinking by extending, differentiating, and combining action images.

(*Age 7 to 11*)

6. Development of concrete operations or the ability to think while manipulating objects and symbols that represent these objects.

THE STAGE OF
CONCEPTUAL THOUGHT:
(*Age 11 to adolescence*)

7. Development of formal operations; thinking with abstract propositions; dealing with hypothetical possibilities.

The assumptions and implications of this explanation of natural growth of mental functions have been summarized by Hunt (1961) as follows:

1. The development of intelligence is essentially the continuous transformation of the organization and structure of perceived environment into inner schemata.
2. Lower-order forms of organization are incorporated into a hierarchical scheme ultimately including all kinds of relationships.
3. From a few basic operations, the child develops an increasing variety of skills until he possesses a great range of competencies.
4. The development of successive organizational schemes proceeds in accordance with a regular, if not fixed, sequence.
5. The attempt to repeat interesting encounters with environment stimulates intellectual activity, interest, and curiosity; motivation is inherent in the growth process.

These assumptions have, in turn, been applied to personality development (Erikson), the development of moral judgment (Kohlberg and Turiel), motivation theory (Maslow), and cognitive development (Bruner).

Erik Erikson (1963) suggests that personality development is also continuous throughout life. He views ego development as a series of stages in which the person establishes an orientation to himself and his social world. The stages are composed of positive and negative factors that influence the individual as he interacts with his environment. Each stage is influenced by the preceding one, but each stage contributes a new dimension. Even though earlier stages pave the way for later development, it is possible for an individual to overcome the effects of negative prior experiences if favorable experiences take place during the advanced stages.

Lawrence Kohlberg and E. Turiel (1971) have applied these concepts to explain how children formulate moral ideas, a particular form of organized patterns of thought. They have discovered that children, like teachers and other adults, have their own ways of thinking about values.

Kohlberg and Turiel identify three progressive levels in children's development of moral thinking. In the *preconventional level*, the child responds to rules and labels as good or bad and right or wrong. He interprets these labels in purely physical terms; punishment and authority support respect for moral order. Actions are right if they satisfy one's own needs and, occasionally, the needs of others.

At the *conventional level,* the attitude is one of conformity to the individual family or group social order. Loyalty is also present in the form of supporting and maintaining the order to which one belongs.

A clear effort to reach a personal definition of moral values is typical of the *postconventional level.* Generally, right action is defined in terms of individual rights and standards that have been examined and agreed upon by the larger group or the whole society. There is clear preference given to respect for personal values and opinions, and a corresponding emphasis on procedural rules for reaching consensus. Thus right is defined more consciously and in relation to self-chosen ethical principles based on some universal consistency. At this level the abstract principles of justice, equality, and respect for human dignity become meaningful to the person. Higher-level values are abstract and open-ended; they are also dependent upon the lower levels for support and concreteness.

From his study of gestalt psychology and anthropology, Abraham Maslow (1954) formulated a growth theory of human motivation. Maslow maintains that each person has an essential inner nature influenced by his environment. How the individual perceives himself in life situations involves continuous personal choice between safety and growth. The person in this process is never fully determined; rather, he grows into adulthood by discovering and uncovering what he already is. If his inner core is frustrated or denied, then his growth is restricted. When faced with choice, the individual naturally selects what he perceives as helpful to his personal growth and satisfying to his basic needs (Maslow, 1968).

According to Maslow, need gratification is the single most important principle underlying all development. As lower needs are fulfilled, new and higher needs emerge. From his study of mentally healthy individuals, Maslow proposed a hierarchy of needs that influence the individual's choice between deficiency and growth, from: (1) physiological needs for food, shelter, sleep, liquids, sex, and oxygen; proceeding to (2) the need for safety; (3) the need for belongingness and love; (4) the need esteem for self and others; and (5) the need for self-actualization, knowledge, understanding, and a sense of aesthetics (Maslow, 1968:chap. 4).

Jerome Bruner (1966) has developed an instructional theory based on a hierarchy of three successive stages of intellectual development in children. In the first stage, events and objects take on meaning in terms of the child's actions toward them. Bruner calls this the *enactive* stage. At about the age of three, *iconic* representation appears as a thought system utilizing visual and other concrete imagery. Around the age of eleven, a child is able to use language to translate experiences into images and as an instrument of thinking is called *symbolic* (Bruner, Oliver, and Greenfield, 1966).

Bruner's systems parallel Piaget's sensorimotor, concrete, and formal operational stages. Both regard mental development as influenced by maturation and experience. Piaget believes more strongly that even after a person has developed formal operational thought, he sometimes will revert to lower thought levels. Bruner believes symbolic thought is possible if deliberate opportunities are provided for its development before the age of eleven. Piaget, on the other hand, believes it is better to permit a child to have experiences at his own rate and in his own way, providing a maximum amount of concrete activity in his early environment. The nature of stimulation from the external environment must be matched to the stage of mental development appropriate to the learner's group.

Developmental psychology has been widely accepted, particularly in early childhood education. Piaget's stages of development offer a clear guide to the arrangement and presentation of objects and concepts to the learner and the introduction of symbolic language. As a learning theory, developmental psychology must be evaluated in other terms (Taba, 1962):

1. Is the development of intelligence dependent on a more or less rigid age scale, or is it more correct to describe a *trend* in the development of cognitive operations?

2. Do the thought processes of children differ essentially from those of adults, or are they essentially similar?

3. Does the development of intelligence follow a universal sequence, or is it subject to cultural variations?

4. Does the more or less rigid scale of intellectual development account adequately for individual differences in the opportunity for stimulation or in perception?

5. Must one wait for "natural" growth to occur, or can the process be altered by providing systematic experience in thinking and reasoning processes?

Existential Psychology

As Shermis (1967) asserts, "The precise implications of existentialism for education are far from clear." In terms of what we have said earlier about belief-systems theory, existential philosophy is represented by a great many widely divergent statements in many different literary forms, with relatively few substantive analyses. It is almost as though it eludes analysis or, more likely, does not see much merit in the more traditional modes of analysis. It is also likely that the existential beliefs which avoid or deny the appropriateness of analysis are also the premises which make it difficult, if not improper, to translate existential philosophy into a functional program of schooling. To demonstrate:

1. An essential condition of existentialism is that the individual must be free of all coercion as the means to his knowing fully the choices that lie before him. However, do not the efforts to bring the individual to awareness of this dilemma represent coercion? If this is so, how can we have imposed teaching?

2. An essential premise of existentialism is that consciousness and knowing are fundamentally individual and personal. Concern for the

verification of one person's conclusions in terms of another's is at least inconsequential, at worst destructive of the integrity of either or both. If this is so, how can we have a standardized, programed curriculum?

3. An essential concern of existentialism is the autonomous being. But what assurance is there that highly autonomous persons are better able to live and work together effectively and productively? (In becoming aware of my potentiality, I also became realistically and painfully aware of my limitations.) If this is so, how can autonomous individuals form a social group, much less establish a social agency called a school?

If existential philosophy has yet to produce clarity, what can we expect to find in existential psychology that is useful to teaching? There is even a lack of clarity in what to call the movement. The statement of existential psychology, most clearly related to the works of Abraham Maslow, Carl Rogers, and Arthur W. Combs, has been attached to such diverse groups as the human-potential movement, Third-Force psychology, confluent education, the free school movement, and various other humanistically oriented educational groups. The emphasis on the individual person, his self-actualization and his autonomous development as an appropriate ethic for education in a highly complex society, is admirable but not sufficient as a creative guide to the restructuring of the social institution we have described as schools.

Certainly we have to know what we want, and we have to want it badly enough to do something about it. We note with some dismay that the furthest Morris (1966) has progressed toward defining the methodological implications of existentialism is something of a warmed-over Socratic method. Recall that the Socratic method was born of philosophic Idealism and based on the a priori premise of absolute knowledge to be pursued and uncovered by man. Morris leaves too much to be clarified for this to be meaningful.

With regard to schooling, existential psychology appears caught in precisely the same dilemma that confronted the Progressive Education movement and led to disenchantment with it. The problem common to both is how to facilitate development of a responsible, competent, disciplined adult without imposing a restrictive organization. The free school movement appears to have its roots in, or at least strong support from, philosophic existentialism. It has yet to exert significant effect, either in numbers or by example, on schooling in general. Whether or not it does appears to be a matter of how clearly it demonstrates the efficacy of its precepts.

Existential psychology will need to demonstrate that man, when confronted by an unavoidable choice, freely and consistently chooses to persevere. This requires risk taking both individually and collectively. Indeed, a great deal of risk taking may be required, in light of the enormity of the problems of warfare and ecological, ethnic, social, and psychological suicide. But are the risks involved in absolute individualism any less than the risks of absolute socialism and social determinism?

Some will argue that something more than existential dread is required both for effective social action and effective classroom teaching. Existential psychology has yet to provide sufficient answers.

Cognitive-Field Psychology

None of the alternate psychological explanations that we have examined up to this point has been able to give satisfactory answers to the categories of questions we posed earlier. Although some of its simplistic notions persist, faculty psychology proved to be little more than folklore learning theory. The description of mind as a passive receptacle for fleeting ideas offered by the psychology of apperception seems laughably naive. Behaviorism's apparent inability to theorize much beyond the simplest knee-jerk reaction troubles a lot of people concerned with complex human activity. Few have been able to grasp gestalt psychology except as applied to simple visual patterning. Existentialists have difficulty agreeing among themselves as to whether man's future is dark and gloomy or bright and hopeful. Admittedly, these are intemperate criticisms, but the sum is that none of these has provided an adequate base for improved school practices.

The remaining alternative is cognitive-field psychology. As indicated in Table 9–1, cognitive-field psychology is founded in philosophic relativism. It treats the psychology of learning and organizing meanings as field-theory functions and operations. We should expect its treatment of the psychology of learning to be entirely consistent with the ontological, epistemological, and axiological premises of the philosophy of Relativism (Chapter 6).

Psychological Reality. If we are concerned with understanding why a particular person behaves in a particular way, our observation and analysis ought to be conducted on his terms, not on our terms. The focus of modern psychology and *hopefully* modern teaching is on finding ways to understand and work more effectively with other individuals. We have to begin with their reality; we have to find out what is real to them.

An individual lives and functions in the world of his own *psychological reality* (Bigge, 1971; Bigge and Hunt, 1968). This is reality as it is particularly real to the individual; it is psychological in that its dimensions and parameters are determined relative to what the individual person perceives, experiences, or senses is affecting him.

The person's psychological reality includes everything—immediate or remote—that in any way pushes or pulls him about. This world has a physical dimension, although at any given time the person may not be affected by every physical thing, nor by any particular physical thing in proximity to him. This world has a temporal dimension as well, although the person may not be affected by everything in his present or now-time, nor by *all* things in his past or the infinite range of future possibilities. This world has a social dimension as well; the person is affected by his relationships with other persons in the present, the past, and in the probable or possible future, although, again, certainly not by all of these at the same time or in the same way. The individual person's world is simply that: a world, multidimensional, multifaceted, but nonetheless holistic.

Learning.   Ordinarily, but not always, the person becomes concerned about what is pushing or pulling him about in a particular way (Bayles, 1960). He seeks to figure it out or understand it so that he can anticipate with some degree of certainty what will happen and behave in a manner that allows him as well as possible to do what he wants to do. He seeks to analyze what is happening and to understand why. As you recognize from the earlier discussion of philosophy, this is the basic ontological concern for knowledge by causes.

Bayles (1960:210) differentiates the general world of psychological reality into the more or less precise domains of the *world of effect*, what's happening, and the *world of insight*, or awareness, or why what's happening is happening in a particular way. The person seeking to know and to understand what these events are and how or why they affect him leads to the development of an "outlook on life," a configuration of thought patterns, or the development of *insights* (Bayles, 1960; Bigge, 1971; Bigge and Hunt, 1968). *Insight,* then, can be defined as a sense of, or feeling for, pattern (Bayles, 1960:40), and *learning* can be defined as a change of insight, a process of developing insight, of building new insights or modifying old ones (Bayles, 1960:46).

The person is able *to some degree* to find or impose order or meaning upon his world of effect, and to develop through this process a world of insight. Since the person's world of effect is dynamic rather than static, he must continually deal with a progression of new items emerging from his world of effect, pressing for awareness, comprehension, and meaningful order within the world of insight. The *growth principle* in this regard is to expand or enhance one's world of insight toward encompassment of one's expanding world of effect (Bayles, 1960).

To understand how a person learns, we must concern ourselves with the process he employs to treat new items that enter his psychological field. How does he go about giving meaning to the thing and establishing an order or structure to various meanings? Probably the central idea here is that the thing or item is acted upon *as it is perceived by the person*. An object or event or phenomenon does not possess meaning in and of itself; its meanings or qualities are formulated by the person in relation to the total situation or configuration in which the item appears (Bigge, 1971; Bigge and Hunt, 1968). A person *learns* what an item *means* from the relationship it appears to have to other things.

This learning about a thing is not the attachment of a fixed, final meaning, although there is a psychological inertia which sometimes inhibits our ability to alter these meanings and the way we have ordered them. The term "learning" must also be applied to the process of developing new insights or modifying old ones. Subsequent learning, that is, learning which occurs after the initial interactive experience with an item, may lead to a change of insight, either because the original meaning must be altered, or the original meaning is supported or enhanced (Bayles, 1960; Bigge, 1971; Bigge and Hunt, 1968).

Our definition of learning here is in direct conflict with the definition of learning as a change in behavior. A change in behavior may come after something has been learned, but the behavior change is the result; it is not the learning itself (Bayles, 1960).

Some persons are well able to verbalize some of their insights, but we can never assume that ability to verbalize is the same as ability to form insights, or that inability to verbalize this thought configuration is directly related to inability to form insights (Bayles, 1960). Some insights are preverbal, some verbalizable, some nonverbalizable (Bigge, 1971; Bigge and Hunt, 1968). Some insights are exceedingly simple; some exceedingly complex. Some are brilliantly profound; some relatively invalid. One person's insight may be completely unimaginable by another person (Bayles, 1960).

But because of what we *do* know about insights and how they are formed, we can conclude that each person has to create his own; no one else can do it for him (Bayles, 1960). In the context of teaching-learning, we need to know what we can do to help a person form a new insight, as well as help him test its truthfulness or accuracy (Bayles, 1960).

Verifying Insights.   We find in the continuing process of experiencing or interacting the basis for verifying one's insights. Simply, the person validates each new perception against those he presently holds—that is, against the psychological reality of his present insights. If the new perception "fits"—if the meanings attached to it appear to be functionally the same—the present insight is held to be valid. It is changed only to the degree necessary to encompass the new item. If it does not "fit," the existing insight may be altered to make it meaningful; a different insight may be formed to take care of the new phenomenon as a different item of meaning; or the new item may be rejected as without validity. Obviously, any degree of change may take place.

The test of accuracy of the person's insights is that of *anticipatory accuracy* (Bayles, 1960). Do the insights the person presently holds allow him to attach meaning or order to new items in the way he anticipated? Do the person's insights permit him to design behavior that allows him to accomplish what he predicts will be accomplished?

In more complex configurations, a more deliberate process of verification is required. The individual must take into account all "facts" available to him and treat them in such a way that they all make sense. The anticipated outcome, or hypothesis, would be verified or "proved" if it caused all available facts to fall together into a harmonious pattern in which the logic is so clear as to make further deductions readily possible. Thus the criterion of scientific validation is that *of adequacy and harmony of the conclusion in light of available or obtainable certainty* (Dewey, 1931).

Cognitive-Field Structure.   Taken collectively, a person's insights constitute what we may call *cognitive-field structure* (Bigge, 1971). This structure encompasses all aspects of his psychological reality, including personal, physical, and social phenomena which the person perceives and to which he attaches meaning. The structure ranges from simple perceptions of simple relationships to aspects which the person has deliberately considered, tested, and verified. This structure has one dimension —*clarity* (Bigge, 1971). In this sense cognitive structure *does not possess a time-space dimension.* What the person perceives as valid here and now will be taken to be valid at some other place at some other time. If not, the cognitive-field structure will be altered.

Along this dimension of clarity are distributed what the person takes to be the entire range from mere opinion to absolute fact, from simple belief to considered conviction, from the phenomena of effect to the insight of causality, from undifferentiated ground to precisely differentiated figure.

Cognitive-field structure corresponds to the *meaningful* knowledge of a person, knowledge being defined in the broadest sense possible (Wendel, 1971). A change of cognitive-field structure may occur in any part of a person's life space, including the psychological past, present, or future (Bigge, 1971). In this sense a person is not delimited by past knowledge because he may learn that this did not mean to him then what he takes it to mean now. New insights have caused him to reinterpret previous meanings.

Nor is the person condemned to an unalterable consequence of badly wrought insights about his future. He may, through the free invention of new hypotheses, alter what he anticipates. He has the right to "change his mind."

Cognitive-field structure may be changed through *differentiation, gen-*

eralization, or *restructuralization* of regions of the field. A region is a distinguishable, functional part of psychological reality. In differentiation, the process by which regions are subdivided into smaller regions, relatively vague and unstructured regions of a life space become cognitively structured and more specific. Differentiation, then, means learning to discern more and more specific aspects of oneself and one's environment.

Generalization is the process whereby one groups a number of particular objects or functions under a single heading. Thus one generalizes when forming a concept which includes previously differentiated aspects of oneself or one's environment. Generalization arises through categorization of subregions into a unified region of one's psychological reality (Bigge, 1971).

A person not only differentiates and generalizes his psychological reality into new regions but simultaneously restructures it, changing the meaning of respective regions in relation to himself and to one another. Restructuralization means that one defines or redefines directions in his psychological reality; he learns what actions will lead to what results through perception of significant relationships of different functional regions of his field. Consequently, restructuralization consists of separating certain regions which have been connected and connecting certain regions which have been separated (Bigge, 1971).

These three types of change in a person's cognitive-field structure are essential if he is to be able to deal with the ever-increasing meanings arising through his interaction. To avoid a cluttered conglomeration of meanings, a person attempts to economize the intellectual effort required in understanding by imposing order on his field.

On the basis of certain identities among different but related experiences of knowing, he forms unified regions of his field, or generalizations, or categories (Phenix, 1964). This categorization has as its main function the simplification of meanings or understandings (Foshay, 1962); the fundamental justification is to render experience intelligible. If we assume that an indefinite plurality of categorizing schemes is possible (Phenix, 1964), a person's choice of a scheme to structure his cognitive-field must be appropriate to him. An insight into how to structure one's field is subject to the same kind of verification as any other insight.

The Cognitive-Field View of Men and Their Knowledge.   What happens when two or more persons are in contact and attempt to communicate with each other? Although at first this may appear enormously confusing, our premise is simple: If we have an adequate description of how a single person functions psychologically, the same approach must also hold true in cases involving multiple numbers of singular persons.

We have said that each person must form his own insights and that insights are not necessarily verbalizable. However, one of the basic ways we attempt to verify our insights is to check them out, insofar as we are able, against those held by others. The process is neither completely efficient nor completely effective, but it is a means of verification that has become highly ordered, or formalized. I state my conceptualization, and you quickly give some kind of clue that may cause me to reaffirm or reconsider my initial conception: "Who was that chick I saw you with last night?" "That was no chick; that was my wife."

We have come to call those meanings which are more readily verbalizable and specifically ordered *formal knowledge*. Although this aspect of the total potential cognitive-field of a person is limited and incomplete, it represents a significant portion of it.

In the same manner that we may describe the fields of two persons as having similar items with similar meanings, i.e., items that both persons have differentiated or perceived in a similar way, we can by enlargement of this concept describe a cognitive structure, or more commonly a structure of knowledge, that possesses meanings shared to a greater or lesser degree by men in general.

The Cognitive-Field View of Formal Knowledge.   At this point we are close to a redefinition of the concept of *discipline* as described in Chapter 6.

We have come to differentiate one kind of knowledge from another, to order or structure similar items into categories of knowledge, and, as an intrinsic part of our search for understanding and clarity, to agree upon the nature and character of these categories. Some of these categories we have come to call *disciplines* of knowledge, because of the particular way we have agreed to treat a certain array of psychologically determined phenomena. Some categories are relatively unstructured. Quite a large body of commonly shared knowledge is simply called general knowledge; other categories, such as "fishing," may include fairly sophisticated items, such as what fly to use to catch what kind of trout under what specific conditions. This type of knowledge might fall into a *subject,* but it is doubtful that it be considered a discipline.

Again we must emphasize that these statements about general cognitive structure are *identical in character* to the descriptive statements we have made about the *cognitive structure* of a particular person. Basic to the concept of the structure of knowledge is the fact that it is fundamentally man-made. We can describe an individual's cognitive structure as a result of the ongoing communication of meanings. We can similarly describe the cognitive structure of the larger community of scholars.

Summary of Cognitive-Field Principles.   1. Cognitive-field psychology is based on the description of man's original nature as *neutral-interactive*. That is, man's moral nature is innately neither good nor bad but possesses the potential to become either good or bad—moral, immoral, or amoral—as these terms come to have meaning to him. Further, his actional nature is innately neither active nor passive but interactive—at a given point more or less active or passive. Man is neither absolutely determined nor absolutely determinant; he is a participant in an interactive process in which he may play an effective role. This assertion gives man a potentiality—not granted by other positions—for growth, education, development, becoming. It does not except man from the consequences of his acts, but neither does it condemn him to the consequences of unalterable actions.

2. Rather than attempt to define psychological activity or phenomena in terms of external criteria, cognitive-field psychology centers on the individual and the meanings he has made for himself through his unique interactive process. This requires considerable knowledge of the individual, the variables that have influenced him, and the manner in which they have influenced him. At the same time it avoids problems that arise should any description of the person differ from that which the individual holds to be real for himself. In considering the nature and causes of an individual's psychological activity, especially in matters of mental health, the question is "What is congruent with his psychological reality?" rather than "How do we make him conform to our judgment or preconception of reality?" The latter is destructive and coercive, not remedial.

3. The cognitive-field definition of *intelligence* as the span or scope of insights places emphasis on the meanings obtained through interaction/experience (Table 9–1) rather than the acquisition of factual information, or "correct" behaviors. Acquisition of a mass of data without some insight into what it means and what it is good for can be paralyzing rather than functional. The definition emphasizes the intelligent use of information in a meaningful context rather than defining intelligence as a thing in and of itself.

4. The cognitive-field concept of *transfer of learning* (Table 9–1) emphasizes the purposive application of what one has come to know to novel situations. Hence transfer is neither accidental nor arbitrary but an integral function of the act of learning. Educational purpose focuses on the development by the individual of intelligent solutions to perceived problems, a prerequisite to enlightened social participation.

5. Cognitive-field psychology defines *thinking* as the purposive process of clarifying and enhancing outlooks/insights (Table 9–1). It views thinking as something more than the mere addition of cognitive elements or the mechanistic linking of behavioral acts to form complex chains. The significance of this definition is that it directs deliberate attention to development of the ability to think with increasing clarity and dimension. It contradicts the notion that thinking is a native endowment or an ability that develops automatically with the accrual of information.

6. By definition, cognitive-field psychology makes consideration of the person central to any study or analysis of psychological activity, particularly the determination of appropriate teaching strategies and activities. It focuses the learning process on the most meaningful resolution of inadequacies and disharmonies of outlooks of the learner. Because it starts with what is "real" as the learner defines reality, what is addressed is fundamentally relevant. It requires that the learner continually verify the meanings he has derived from learning activities and consider the consequences and implications of each available solution to determine which most adequately fits conditions and resolves known discrepancies.

REFERENCES

Bayles, Ernest E. *Democratic Educational Theory.* New York: Harper & Row, 1960.

————, and Bruce L. Hood. *Growth of American Educational Thought and Practice.* New York: Harper & Row, 1966.

Bigge, Morris L. *Learning Theories for Teachers.* 2nd ed. New York: Harper & Row, 1971.

————, and Maurice P. Hunt. *Psychological Foundations of Education.* 2nd ed. New York: Harper & Row, 1968.

Bruner, Jerome S. *Toward a Theory of Instruction.* Cambridge, Mass.: Harvard University Press, 1966.

————. *Toward a Theory of Instruction.* New York: W. W. Norton, 1968.

————, Rose Oliver, and Patricia Greenfield. *Studies in Cognitive Growth.* New York: Wiley, 1966.

Burton, William H. *The Guidance of Learning Activities.* New York: Appleton-Century-Crofts, 1944.

Dewey, John, *How We Think.* Boston: Heath, 1910, 1931.

Dunwell, Robert R., "On Revisiting a Neglected Model," *Educational Perspectives* 9, no. 3 (October 1970):7–11.

————, et al. "The Assessment of Informal Factors Affecting Teaching and Learning in a Ghetto High School." Paper presented to the American Association of School Administrators, Atlantic City, N.J., February 24, 1971.

Erikson, Erik. *Childhood and Society.* 2nd ed. New York: W. W. Norton, 1963.

Foshay, Arthur, "Education and the Nature of a Discipline," *New Dimensions of Learning,* ed. W. B. Waetjen (Washington, D.C.: National Education Association, Association for Supervision and Curriculum Development, 1962), p. 5.

Hilgard, Ernest, R. *Theories of Learning.* 2nd ed. New York: Appleton-Century-Crofts, 1956.

Hunt, J. McV. *Intelligence and Experience.* New York: Ronald Press, 1961.

Kohlberg, Lawrence, and E. Turiel. *Research in Moral Development: The Cognitive-Developmental Approach.* New York: Holt, Rinehart & Winston, 1971.

Luchsinger, Robert D. "A Study of Student Teacher Perceptions of the Secondary Teacher Education Program of Colorado State College, Ph.D. dissertation, University of Northern Colorado, Greeley Colorado, 1969.

Maslow, Abraham H. *Motivation and Personality.* New York: Harper & Row, 1954.

————. *Toward a Psychology of Being.* 2nd ed. Princeton, N.J.: D. Van Nostrand, 1968.

Morris, Van Cleve. *Existentialism in Education.* New York: Harper & Row, 1966.

Perls, Frederick S. *Gestalt Therapy Verbatim.* Lafayette, Calif.: Real People Press, 1969a.

————. *In and Out of the Garbage Pail.* Lafayette, Calif.: Real People Press, 1969b.

Phenix, Philip H. *Realms of Meaning.* New York: McGraw-Hill, 1964.

Piaget, Jean. *The Psychology of Intelligence.* New York: Harcourt Brace Jovanovich, 1970.

Shermis, Samuel S. *Philosophic Foundations of Education.* New York: American Book, 1967.

Taba, Hilda. *Curriculum Development: Theory and Practice.* New York: Harcourt, Brace & World, 1962.

Weber, C. A. "Do Teachers Understand Learning Therapy?" *Phi Delta Kappan,* 67, no. 9 (May 1965):433–35.

Wendel, Robert. "Toward Meaningful Learning" *University College Quarterly* 16, no. 2 (January 1971): 18–23.

CHAPTER 10
Psychological Guides to Teaching

Although we are not yet ready to suggest an appropriate solution to the teacher's dilemma, we are now able to understand what the problem is and what has caused it to become a problem. Look at each of the sets of variables suggested by the system of psychological beliefs:

1. There are a number of psychological theories based on different notions of the fundamental nature of man. These theories define learning in fundamentally different ways and describe different sets of teaching practices, policies, principles, and techniques which, taken as a whole, appear contradictory. Consider "Punishment is necessary as a negative reinforcement to extinguish undesirable behaviors" vis-à-vis "The threat of punishment restricts and inhibits the ability of the person to interact with his environment freely and competently" vis-à-vis "Punishment contributes to the development of moral character."

2. The philosophical-psychological-instructional theories we have described are generalizations that can be drawn from a much wider range of individual belief systems. They indicate points on a continuum that represents the full range of possible psychological beliefs. Each major theory is actually a family of related psychological beliefs made up of central ideas and a few associated notions. We have restricted our examination to the major psychological groups, despite the appeal of all the rest.

3. The alternative psychological theories differ in their ability to generate effective guides to teaching practice. A given theory, by choice or by design, may provide a competent explanation of the learning of psychomotor skills, for example, but completely ignore the attitudes and values intrinsic to their successful employment. Understandings coupled with techniques are essential to assure practice that is ethical as well as technically competent. This is as true for teaching as it is for electronic

surveillance. Each theory is more or less capable of being translated into programs that make sense in terms of the realities of public education. The fact that some teaching practice may prove effective for a small number of students in a controlled laboratory situation does not indicate that such a program should be adopted on a broad scale. To the philosophic positivist, a psychological theory ultimately must be proved adequate to all kinds of learning of all kinds of things by all kinds of persons in all kinds of situations. If this is not possible, we will be stuck with a lot of unrelated theory fragments.

4. Psychological theories differ in their ability to relate appropriately to a particular social or ethnic group or to adapt to differing or changing groups. A particular psychological theory may appear to generate adequate descriptions of the activities, behaviors, motives, and values of middle-class America but be inept for the development of teaching strategies for other social-ethnic groups. To regard "talking" with departed relatives as an indication of mental illness is meaningless in a culture that holds this to be a unique religious experience. In the same manner, one generation may view the recitation of memorized passages from classical literature as evidence of learning; other generations may discredit form in favor of feeling and insist that we "tell it like it is." Differing performance expectations require differing teaching techniques and skills.

5. Individual practitioners will differ from one another in their knowledge and understanding of any particular psychological theory, and hence in the effectiveness with which it is employed. Teachers who do not understand a particular theory may nonetheless believe strongly in its value; teachers who *do* understand a particular theory may be less than fully committed to its practices. In the face of general confusion about psychological theories, it is not surprising to observe a general lack of commitment to technical competency. If the personality or teaching style of an individual inhibits, interferes with, or contradicts the achievement of desired ends, a different method is required. If the defect is due to a lack of knowledge, understanding, or teaching skill, we need wiser teachers!

What, then, would you expect to find among the various subject-area teachers in a modern American urban public comprehensive high school? A mixture of instructional practices with little relationship to a particular set of psychological premises? A contradictory set of approaches unconstrained by scientific verification? A system of education so diffuse and purposeless as to prohibit effective management or accountability? So it would seem to many who view the current state of education and see no reasons for it.

We have spoken of how this confusion must appear to the students upon whom it is imposed. Because teachers have not reached agreement on the purposes to be served, students are expected to be brilliantly inquisitive at one moment but are punished for opening their mouths the next. Because teachers have not reached agreement on which teaching method is more effective—even in something so basic as reading—students are expected to jump from one approach to another and achieve functional literacy. Because teachers have not reached agreement on what should be evaluated or how, students come to accept grading as inherently arbitrary, capricious, and irrational—which is true—and see teachers as punitive, vindictive, and discriminatory—as they frequently are.

From the point of view of the teachers, the situation presented by alternative psychological theories is no more certain or helpful. None of the learning problems described in the ed psych or methods texts ever seem to come up in actual practice. Conversely, the problems that do come up seem not to be within experience or remedial ability of the textbook writers. There is little or no relationship between the practices prescribed and the results to be achieved. When the sought for results are described, there are no clues as to how to achieve them.

Psychological belief systems, as the specific derivations of philosophical belief systems, preserve the essential distinctions that separate the philosophies. Some practices are apparently similar even though based on different interpretations, and other practices appear incredibly different even though intended to produce similar results. If it is difficult to justify the discrepancies among methods of teaching primary-grade reading, ask a neurologist, a psychiatrist, a naturopathic physician, and an osteopathic surgeon to explain their approaches to problems of physical health with any degree of congruence, except that they each begin with an individual and intend to make him better.

In the name of curriculum "policy," the teacher is frequently expected to follow certain guidelines with very little knowledge of what is being attempted. Efforts to uncover the rationale for these prescriptions are frequently resisted as a challenge to the originator's intelligence or met with an inordinate mass of impertinent data and ambiguous conclusions. Confronted by the necessities of day-to-day classroom operations, the teacher most often compromises, settling for a program that does not make sense by design. Compromise is by nature arbitrary and dictatorial, the antithesis of what seems rational to any of the protagonists. Certain matters may be arbitrated; when it is impossible to achieve agreement, a course of action must be worked out. But some matters—those that are central to the maintenance of the individual's integrity or humanness—may *not* be arbitrated or compromised.

What useful guides for teaching can be drawn from the preceding description of alternate psychological theories?

The Person as a Psychological Entity

Major psychological belief systems provide differing descriptions of the psychological nature of the individual person, the factors that determine or affect this nature, and the relationship between the individual and all that exists separate from this psychological entity. This relationship is viewed alternately as: (a) dependent; (b) independent; or (c) interdependent. This suggests that the psychological nature of man is: (a) determined by forces beyond the control of the individual; (b) freely determined by man acting in complete independence from any external force; or (c) determined through the interaction of man with external forces.

Alternate explanations of the nature of the person as a psychological entity are manifested in approaches to psychological growth and development, human needs and motivation, and mental health.

Psychological Growth and Development

Although alternate psychological theories describe psychological growth and development in similar ways, they differ in the description of the factors that cause or influence growth and development. This creates different explanations of how growth and development may be changed or controlled and the limits or potential of psychological growth and development. These alternatives suggest that in relation to external forces man is either: (a) *dependent:* human potential is determined by specific, describable factors or influences—such as genetic inheritance, chemical-physical environment, or social condition—which, after a period of effect, set or limit the potential for growth; (b) *independent:* human potential is not fixed or limited except by the individual's awareness of what he may desire to achieve; or (c) *interdependent:* human potential is a function of the interaction of the individual and his psychological reality—the individual cannot become aware of his potential except as he attempts and verifies what he may and may not achieve.

From the point of view of education, the teacher does not have clear evidence of the ultimate potential of any individual student, nor do we possess instruments capable of measuring the degree to which this *assumed* potential has been achieved. Even if we consider limits to be fixed by inherited or historic factors, these variables are outside the sphere of present teaching strategies. Accordingly, the teacher will emphasize what can be done to maximize whatever potential the individual possesses. The teacher demonstrates belief in the general improvement of all aspects of human psychological growth and development; the kind of teaching provided is not conditional on an individual's assumed status or potential. The teacher encourages each person to explore what he can do and how he can accomplish his desires. Recognizing the tragic loss of human resources that would result if potential were underestimated, the teacher creates a learning atmosphere that encourages individual growth through the cooperative planning and selection of meaningful learning inquiries (Bigge and Hunt, 1968; Hilgard, 1956).

Human Needs and Motivation

Alternative psychological theories differ in the description of the nature and source of human needs and motivation and of appropriate means to influence, change, or control human behavior by acting on personal desires or elements in the environment. These alternatives suggest that with regard to motivating forces for behavior man is either: (a) *dependent:* it is possible to control human behavior by controlling those factors which are motivating to all men because of their inherent and inescapable nature, or by the direct manipulation of the wishes and desires of the individual person; (b) *independent:* any attempt to control, change, or manipulate the individual destroys his ability to function autonomously and thereby is fundamentally immoral; or (c) *interdependent:* full realization of human motives is attained as the individual determines through interaction what produces the most meaningful satisfactions for him over time.

The teacher helps the learner to become aware of and sensitive to the factors that are motivating to him. The teacher helps the learner explore the meanings he has obtained from prior experience and those that may be obtained from further experience. The teacher encourages the learner to move beyond what was interesting or satisfying in the past to consider what may be interesting or satisfying in different circumstances. The teacher encourages evaluation of personal motives in the light of group motives and facilitates development of both personal and social conscience. The teacher helps the learner assess "motivators" (prizes, awards, rewards, grades) against criteria of pertinence and relevance. The teacher promotes consideration of short-run/long-run satisfactions as a means of encouraging independent judgment. The teacher guides the student to merge personal feelings of satisfaction into larger moral codes (Maslow, 1954; Goble, 1970; May, 1961).

Mental Health

Alternate psychological belief systems, in concert with social-ethnic belief systems, offer widely different—often conflicting—definitions of the mentally "healthy" person; of the causes of psychological "unhealth"; and of the therapeutic model most appropriate to the treatment or remediation of "mental illness." In this area, the primary triad of alternatives may be stated as follows: (a) *dependent:* mental illness is caused by the intrusion of external elements the person cannot control; hence treatment requires prescribed intervention to restore mental balance; (b) *independent:* mental illness is a culturally derived notion imposed on individuals in an effort to control and subvert their independence; individuals may require temporary supportive relationships to help them cope with psychological disruptions, but only as a means to reestablish their autonomy; or (c) *interdependent:* the continuing interaction between man and his environment can be facilitated by helping man to acquire more adequate coping mechanisms; although the primary purpose of schooling may not be therapy, learning is therapeutic and therapy is fundamentally learning (Rogers, 1951; Frankl, 1963; Perls, 1969).

The teacher is sensitive to indications of learning problems and dysfunctions. Although recognizing that these problems may be symptomatic of more fundamental personal dysfunctions, the teacher also recognizes the positive contribution of the learning situation as a supportive environment, and actively provides acceptance and support. The teacher systematically reviews current learning situations to ensure that they facilitate growth and are as free of threat, ambiguity, disruptions, and frustrations as possible. The teacher demonstrates how learning and education help individuals cope with life's problems *now,* as well as their potential contributions toward the mediation of possible future problems. The teacher assists individual learners in assessing the effectiveness of their own coping behaviors, in accepting the coping behaviors of others, and in designing more effective behaviors by arranging situations for both individual and group investigation. The teacher arranges experiences that help learners establish helping relationships with others as an instrumentality of mutual personal growth. The teacher demonstrates the potential for personal growth by sharing his current continuing growth and encourages others to be aware of their own growth (Combs, Avila, and Purkey, 1971; Bayles, 1960).

Psychological Data about Persons

The major psychological belief systems provide differing approaches to what is appropriately included in the psychological study of man, how psychological factors can or should be measured and assessed, and what kinds of appraisals may be made from these data. Alternately, these approaches view the relationship between human psychological data and other classes of "natural" phenomena as: (a) subordinate; (b) independent; or (c) interdependent. This suggests that human psychological phenomena: (a) should be regarded as no different from any other "facts" of nature; (b) are unique because of the fact of humanness, have an independent meaning, and must be treated as a special case for the purpose of inquiry and analysis; or (c) are functions of the interaction of man and his environment.

Alternate approaches to the treatment of psychological data about persons are evidenced in differing schemes for the classification of psychological data, psychological measurement, and the explanation of psychological differences.

Classification of Psychological Data

Different psychological theories do not mean the same thing when they speak of "psychology" or what is "psychological." Nor do they mean the same thing when they use terms like learning, intelligence, motivation, needs, interests, purpose, will, volition, and attitude. We should note as well that one approach may emphasize certain types of data, e.g., about self or self-concept, which another approach may consider unimportant to its concern for psychology. The three major alternatives may be stated as follows: (a) *subordinate:* all human psychological data may be classified in accordance with the same categorical scheme employed by all other behavioral sciences, and all terms appropriate to human psychological data are precisely congruent with other behavioral science terms; (b) *independent:* in the case of humans, much of what is central to the consideration of psychology eludes scientific classification or treatment; human psychology is more humanistic than scientific, more aesthetic and moral than objective and empirical; or (c) *interdependent:* adequate understanding of the interaction between man and his environment requires consideration of all pertinent factors and the full range of their variability; as the interactive process is dynamic rather than static, the appropriateness of any categorical scheme changes over time and requires continuing reappraisal (Bigge and Hunt, 1968).

The teacher maintains open consideration of a broad range of psychological data, becoming more and more aware of what categories are useful and valid and what data are significant but not readily attainable. The teacher avoids inappropriate generalizations, focusing instead on the most reliable information about individuals and their behaviors. The teacher determines what psychological data about humans are precise and what are ambiguous and judges the functional value of the information rather than its specificity or objectivity. The teacher recognizes that our knowledge of human psychology and the supporting data is incomplete and tentative, and that human behaviors, skills, knowledge, attitudes, values, sensitivities, and feelings are not discrete elements that can be treated functionally in isolation, but are aspects of individual humanness, functionally integrated, and functional only as integral (Maslow, 1962; Rogers, 1961).

Psychological Measurement

Alternate psychological theories offer different interpretations of kinds of psychological data that are important, and approach the question of psychological measurement from differing perspectives. Greater or lesser emphasis is placed on the importance of measuring psychological facts and events; greater or lesser reliability is premised in the measurement of psychological facts and events; greater or lesser measurability is assumed possible. These differing approaches may be stated as follows: (a) *subordinate:* psychological events, like all other natural events, are assumed to occur in accordance with a naturally prescribed order; precise knowledge of this order is possible, but only through the employment of highly sophisticated techniques under stringently controlled conditions; (b) *independent:* psychological "counting" has little pertinence beyond the integer that represents the individual person; the incidence, probability, and reasons for certain behavior are singular, personal, and of no importance whatsoever to any other individual; or (c) *interdependent:* because psychological events are integral parts of the ongoing interactive process, precise measurement of incidence, intensity, duration, or amount is far less important than determination of the meanings the person has made of *his* experience; data obtained from psychological measurement have importance only as they facilitate clarification for the individual.

The teacher uses available psychological instruments selectively and purposefully. The limited validity of current instrumentation requires the teacher to maintain continuing awareness of what can and cannot be tested. The teacher helps students become aware of the purposes of psychological testing. The teacher emphasizes the learner's understanding of the results of psychological tests as more important than the acquisition of results. The teacher is more concerned with the potential meanings of the results of psychological tests for the individual than for the group, and accordingly treats test results as privileged information. The teacher is hesitant to draw generalizations from test data. Where judgments are necessary, the teacher clearly states them in the context of the circumstances in which the data were obtained. The teacher is cautious about generalizing about the total person on the basis of information limited to a single aspect (e.g., "intelligence" test scores). The teacher involves the learner as quickly and as fully as possible in self-appraisal and self-evaluation. The teacher asks "What does this mean to you?" and "What do these data mean in light of other data we have obtained?" The teacher facilitates development of appreciation for psychological measurement, helping the learner sense what of himself can and cannot be identified objectively and, of these, what is most important (Allport, 1955; Jourard, 1968).

Explanation of Individual Differences

Alternate psychological theories treat the question of physical and psychological differences among individuals in very different ways. Here the infection of psychological belief systems by sociopolitical belief systems is most apparent, for justification of the former is designed and support obtained in terms of the latter premises with which one starts. Thus the psychological "proof" that supports "neighborhood" schools or grouping based on culturally biased tests is founded on racial bias and social apartheid.

The range of alternative approaches may be described as: (a) *subordinate:* individual psychological differences are *caused* by variations in the physical and social environment in which the individual finds himself by chance; bringing the variation back into line can be accomplished only through carefully determined intervention techniques, such as diagnostic-prescriptive teaching, behavior modification, or compensatory education; (b) *independent:* because a person *is* a person, the only significant individual difference is the degree of the individual's self-awareness; the responsibility for self-awareness or awareness of his human condition are the individual's alone; or (c) *interdependent:* individual differences are to be valued rather than discredited, encouraged rather than suppressed.

The teacher helps learners come to understand the degree to which all individuals are alike and the degree to which all are different. The teacher demonstrates the significance of both similarity and dissimilarity and provides opportunities for learners to experience, assess, and come to appreciate the functional values of both similarity and uniqueness. The teacher helps the individual learner obtain and verify meanings about himself, his uniqueness, and his similarity to others. The teacher assists the individual learner in understanding that his uniqueness is not something to be feared or flaunted but, rather, something to be used effectively in exploring aspects of a situation not perceived by others. The teacher assists the individual learner in understanding that his similarity to all others represents the basis for consensual action rather than consensual apathy (Frankl, 1963; Ginott, 1972).

The Psychologies of Human Learning

The major alternative psychological belief systems provide differing approaches to the description of the learning process, the objectives of learning, and the methods by which learning may be made more effective. Alternately, these different theories view the relationship between personally acquired meanings and externally established meanings as: (a) dependent; (b) independent; or (c) interdependent. This suggests that learning is: (a) the acquisition of meanings that exist independent of the individual person; (b) the development of personal meanings without regard for any external factors; or (c) the development of meaning through the interaction of the person with external factors.

These differing approaches to the psychology of learning are manifested in alternative ways of determining educational objectives, planning learning activities, and evaluating learning.

Determining Educational Objectives

Based on differing conceptions of the relationship between man and world, the alternative psychological belief systems arrive at differing sets of educational objectives and priorities. Needs assessment is obviously derived from axiological preconditions; that is, what we seek is based on what we "believe" to be important. What is taken to be important—what is seen as the ultimate purpose of education—depends upon how one perceives the total confronting situation. In classroom practice, if adjustment of one's life style, behaviors, and attitudes to harmonize with an intrinsic scheme of life is uppermost, it becomes possible to analyze each of the intermediate goals necessary to achieve the primary objective of education.

The primary objective of each of the three major psychologies of human learning may be stated as follows: (a) *dependent:* to survive, man must learn those behaviors required to adapt effectively to the externally ordered processes of Life; one seeks ultimately to possess complete knowledge of this system as instrumental to complete integration or oneness with it; (b) *independent:* to achieve complete autonomy, the individual must become intimately aware of his personal nature and potential; one seeks ultimately to possess complete knowledge of self as a system of personal forces to become an integrated whole; or (c) *interdependent:* to achieve maximum effectiveness, the individual must develop increasing ability to make sense of new problem situations and invent creative solutions that provide long-run satisfactions.

The teacher encourages the learner to assess emerging problem situations in terms of their causes and the requirements for their solution. The teacher helps learners understand the problems that confronted man in his historical past, how he attempted to deal with them, and how effective these solutions have been. Recognizing the importance of developing the skill of independent assessment, the teacher helps learners state, clarify, and analyze life-problems they perceive in their present circumstance. The teacher accepts these perceived problems as most appropriate for consideration now by these learners. The teacher assists learners to assess what skills, competencies, understandings, attitudes, and behaviors are necessary to solve these problems effectively and to determine how to develop desired outcomes. The teacher promotes consideration of the problems that may confront the learner in his perceived future, including occupational, social, and psychological needs. The teacher facilitates assessment of the personal capabilities this perceived future may require and the appropriate means of developing them. The teacher helps learners understand the degree to which they can affect the course of events to which their lives are related (Bayles, 1960; Rogers, 1969; Bigge and Hunt, 1968).

Planning Learning Activities

In a similar manner, the planning of learning activities is seen as a process involving the teacher and the learner in differing relationships. Because the degree to which learning depends on external-internal factors is treated differently by alternate psychological theories, the degree to which objectives can be predetermined and learning activities preplanned also varies. If the crucial variables were fixed by factors *external* to the teacher-learner dyad, learning activities could be designed to secure required objectives *separate from* the function of this relationship, and there would be no need for specific knowledge of variables within the teacher-learner dyad. If the crucial variables can be determined only through the process of teacher-learner interaction, educational objectives and learning activities can be planned *only* with reference to these variables.

The appropriateness of learning experiences is alternately determined as: (a) *dependent on external factors:* if learning is the acquisition of meanings that exist independent of the learner, the selection and planning of learning activities depend on factors external to the teaching-learning process: objective facts, principles, concepts, and so on, when all of these are treated as things separate and apart from persons; (b) *independent:* if learning is the development of personal meanings without regard for any external factors, the selection and planning of learning activities are determined by the unique requirements of the individual independent of any concept of an external structure of reality or teacher-imposed preconception of learner needs; or (c) *interdependent:* if learning is the development of meanings through the interaction of the person with external factors, learning activities can be cooperatively selected and planned as part of the ongoing process; in this instance, learning activities are seen as general opportunities rather than specific "lessons," and the validity of the outcomes must be assured by cooperatively established evaluative guidelines rather than by external standards.

The teacher, realizing that few particular learning activities are specifically suited for a number of individuals, plans a range of related initiatory activities and makes deliberate provisions for individual choice.

The teacher assists individual learners in identifying and selecting those alternatives that are most meaningful to them. The teacher makes a pre-assessment of learning activities that seem appropriate to the individuals in the class and is prepared to suggest a range of possible activities. The teacher assists the learner in becoming more effective in planning potentially valuable learning activities independently. The teacher encourages the learner to assess the degree of dependence-independence-interdependence with which he is able to operate in particular circumstances and to make predictable generalizations from these data. This cooperative process recognizes the dignity of the individual in the classroom and encourages individual growth in a democratic setting (Bayles, 1960; Bigge and Hunt, 1968; Parker and Rubin, 1968).

Evaluating Learning

The determinant of any learning is how effectively it advances the learner toward the desired educational goal; of any teaching activity, how effectively it promotes learning relative to the time, money, and effort required by it and other alternatives. The effectiveness of learning and of teaching can be determined rather specifically and objectively—*but only when the criteria being employed are clear.* A person who learns that lying is an effective means of protecting oneself against undesirable disclosure is obviously disadvantaged when a standard of absolute honesty is used. A person who learns that total recall of authoritative sources is the appropriate performance requirement is anxious and resentful if he is asked to provide a creative solution to an ambiguous problem.

Alternate approaches to evaluating learning demonstrate radically different standards: (a) *external standards:* if the goal of any educational program is taken to be the achievement of congruence with externally derived standards, the level of achievement and the effectiveness of any instructional activity in producing this level can be identified and compared in terms that are as valid and relevant as the adopted standard; (b) *internal standards:* if the goal of education is construed to be the maximum attainment of personally determined vetoes, the level of achievement and the effectiveness of any instructional activity in producing this level can be identified and compared in terms that are valid and relevant *only* to the individual person; hence self-evaluation and personal choice of standards take precedence over all other judgmental processes; or (c) *process evaluation:* if the goal of education is taken to be development of increasing independence (self-actualizing), the effectiveness of any instructional means can most appropriately be evaluated jointly by teacher and learner by the sensitive discrimination of variations throughout the interactive process.

The teacher recognizes that one of the purposes of education is to assist the learner to become a skillful evaluator of his own learning. The teacher helps the learner assess realistically where he is with regard to skills, attitudes, and behaviors. The teacher assists the learner in determining the skills, attitudes, and behaviors that appear to be desirable. The teacher encourages evaluation of both the effectiveness of the means chosen as instruments of goal achievement and the degree to which the value attached to chosen goals has been sustained. The teacher serves as a time reference to help learners realize that goals chosen and not achieved do not constitute failure but are indicative of ineffective planning. In a similar manner, the teacher helps learners recognize that the relative merit assigned to goals may change as perspective changes, and that this represents progress rather than inconsistency of values (Rogers, 1969; Ginott, 1972).

The major implications for teaching and learning as advanced by each alternate psychological position can be briefly summarized as follows:

1. When viewing the person as a psychological entity possessing growth potential, needs, and motivations, the dependent position holds that human potential is limited by both genetic and social conditioners; the independent view maintains that the person possesses unique potential for autonomous growth; and the interdependent position holds that human potential is realized through meaningful interaction between purposeful people and their environment.

2. In considering the psychological data about the growth of a person, advocates of the dependent/subordinate position hold that personal data are no different from other facts of nature and are subject to the limits and conditions of natural law; when the person is viewed from an independent position, psychological data must be treated as describing a unique human being; the interdependent view holds that psychological data about a person are relative to that time and as a function of interaction create opportunities for the enhancement of personal meanings.

3. Descriptions of the learning process also offer the reader a choice of interpretations. The dependent view maintains that learning is acquiring those behaviors required for adaptation to an externally ordered universe; the independent school strongly suggests that personal meanings are developed independent of external factors and the selection and evaluation of learning experiences are uniquely self-centered; learning is viewed by the interdependent position as individual involvement with problem situations that are cooperatively planned and evaluated.

The interpretations of psychological phenomena by these obviously different belief systems offer the prospective teacher a wide range of choice. Awareness of these alternatives is essential, but simply acknowledging that the differences exist is not enough. Without a functional understanding of the psychological rationale a teacher will not be able to translate beliefs into competent instructional programs.

REFERENCES

Allport, Gordon W. *Becoming: Basic Considerations for a Psychology of Personality.* New Haven: Yale University Press, 1955.

Bayles, Ernest E. *Democracy in Education.* New York: Harper & Row, 1960.

Bigge, Morris L., and Maurice P. Hunt. *Psychological Foundations of Education.* 2nd ed. New York: Harper & Row, 1968.

Combs, Arthur W., Donald L. Avila, and William W. Purkey. *Helping Relationships: Basic Concepts for the Helping Professions.* Boston: Allyn & Bacon, 1971.

Frankl, Viktor. *Man's Search for Meaning.* New York: Washington Square Press, 1963.

Ginott, Haim. *Teacher and Child.* New York: Macmillan, 1972.

Goble, Frank. *The Third Force.* New York: Grossman, 1970.

Hilgard, Ernest R. *Theories of Learning.* 2nd ed. New York: Appleton-Century-Crofts, 1956.

Jourard, Sidney M. *Disclosing Man to Himself.* Princeton, N.J.: D. Van Nostrand, 1968.

Maslow, Abraham H. *Motivation and Personality.* New York: Harper & Row, 1954.

―――. *Toward a Psychology of Being.* Princeton, N.J.: D. Van Nostrand, 1962.

May, Rollo, ed. *Existential Psychology.* New York: Random House, 1961.

Parker, J. C., and Louis Rubin. *Process as Content.* Chicago: Rand McNally, 1968.

Perls, Frederick S. *Gestalt Therapy Verbatim.* Lafayette, Calif.: Real People Press, 1969.

Rogers, Carl R. *Client-Centered Therapy.* Boston: Houghton Mifflin, 1951.

―――. *Freedom to Learn.* Columbus, Ohio: Charles E. Merrill, 1969.

―――. *On Becoming a Person.* Boston: Houghton Mifflin, 1961.

Suggested Readings

In addition to the items below, references listed in Chapters 4 and 7 may also be appropriate for the reader pursuing educational psychology and its application to classroom learning and instruction.

Ahmann, J. Stanley, and Marvin Glock. *Measuring and Evaluating Educational Achievement.* Boston: Allyn & Bacon, 1971.

Test construction and the use of testing and nontesting instruments to measure pupil achievement.

Ausubel, David. *Educational Psychology: A Cognitive View.* New York: Holt, Rinehart & Winston, 1968.

Deals with concepts from educational psychology that are specifically relevant to classroom learning. Stresses the various cognitive and affective-social factors that influence meaningful verbal learning. Distinguishes between reception and discovery learning, and describes the concepts of transfer, practice, motivation, and creativity.

Beard, Ruth M. *An Outline of Piaget's Developmental Psychology for Students and Teachers.* New York: Basic Books, 1969.

Describes succinctly Piaget's theories on the development of children's thinking and offers samples of his many observations and experiments with children. Implications for teaching are presented at the conclusion of each chapter.

Berman, Louise. *New Priorities in the Curriculum.* Columbus, Ohio: Merrill, 1968.

Designed to provide a framework for developing process-curriculum. Starting from the premise that the major emphasis in education should be on developing process-oriented persons, discusses eight processes and possible ways of centering curriculum on these processes. The processes discussed are: perceiving, communicating, loving, knowing, decision making, patterning, creating, and valuing.

Bruner, Jerome. *Beyond the Information Given: Studies in the Psychology of Knowing.* New York: W. W. Norton, 1973.

Combines Bruner's major works in the fields of perception, thought, childhood, and education. Elaborates on the concerns of how does one know, what does man do with information, and how he goes from experiences to insight, understanding, and competence.

———. *Toward a Theory of Instruction.* Cambridge, Mass.: Harvard University Press, Belknap, 1966.

From his own research, author advocates a method of teaching and curriculum construction patterned after human growth. Stresses structuring teaching as a developmental process. Available in paperback (New York: W. W. Norton, 1968).

Carswell, Evelyn, and Darrel Roubinek. *Open Sesame.* Pacific Palisades, Calif.: Goodyear, 1974.

A collection of excerpts from various humanistic publications presented in a humorous and easily understood format. Primarily for elementary teachers, elaborates on the characteristics of trust, understanding, love, living, expanding self, and their application to teaching and learning.

Combs, Arthur. *Educational Accountability: Beyond Behavioral Objectives.* Washington, D.C.: Association for Supervision and Curriculum Development, 1972.

Describes the dangers of the partly right behavioral objectives approach to instruction. The remaining chapters examine behavioral objectives as applied to assessment methods, skill development, intelligence, the nature of learning, professional accountability, and humanistic education.

Combs, Arthur, and Donald Snygg. *Individual Behavior.* New York: Harper & Row, 1959.

Describes a perceptual view of behavior and examines, from that viewpoint, values, learning, problem solving, emotion, and personal adequacy. Second part shows the implications of this view for the person as a teacher and member of society.

Dreikurs, Rudolf. *Psychology in the Classroom.* 2nd ed. New York: Harper & Row, 1968.

Applies a democratic philosophy and Adlerian psychology to behavior problems and learning deficiencies of students. The method advocated helps the teacher understand the motivation of each child and provides a means of changing motivation through practical illustrations of group dynamics techniques.

Erikson, Erik. *Childhood and Society*. 2nd ed. New York: W. W. Norton, 1963.

An outstanding leader in the psychology of human development details his theory of development and presents his popular concept of the eight dichotomous stages of human growth.

Gagné, Robert. *The Conditions of Learning*. 2nd ed. New York: Holt, Rinehart & Winston, 1970.

May be the bridge between neo-Behaviorism and Cognitive-Field psychology. Describes eight distinguishable classes of learning and identifies the conditions for learning associated with them.

Glasser, William. *Schools Without Failure*. New York: Harper & Row, 1969.

A widely read book which denounces the traditional school system for its emphasis in failure and offers suggestions for creating a success orientation.

Glines, Don E. *Creating Humane Schools*. Mankato, Minn.: Campus Publishers, 1972.

Suggestions for implementing needed revisions in schools, based on the extensive experimentation in the Wilson School of Mankato State College.

Gorman, Richard M. *Discovering Piaget: A Guide for Teachers*. Columbus, Ohio: Merrill, 1972.

The theories of Piaget approached through a workbook format in this paperback that stresses the application of Piaget to classroom instruction. Numerous problem exercises are illustrated and described, providing the reader with models for his own classroom experimentation.

Green, John A. *Introduction to Measurement and Evaluation*. New York: Dodd, Mead, 1970.

A comprehensive description of all aspects of educational evaluation. Especially good are the sections dealing with assessing social climate for learning, measuring problem solving, and assessing attitudes and opinions.

Green, John A. *Teacher-Made Tests*. New York: Harper & Row, 1963.

An excellent paperback describing the construction and use of several types of tests—objective, essay, oral. Stresses practical application rather than measurement theory.

Harvey, O. J., ed. *Experience, Structure, and Adaptability*. New York: Springer, 1966.

Examines the concepts of flexibility, adaptability, and creativity as psychological constructs influenced by personality, environment, manipulations, and social-political factors.

————, ed. *Motivation and Social Interaction: Cognitive Determinants*. New York: Ronald, 1963.

An excellent collection of essays by outstanding developmental psychologists such as Schroder, Hunt, and Harvey. Discussions center around conceptual organizing of perceived events and the cognitive aspects of self and motivation.

Havighurst, Robert. *Developmental Tasks and Education.* 3rd ed. New York: McKay, 1972.

A new edition of a work first published in 1948, when the author advanced his concept of developmental tasks as a theory midway between competing theories advocating individual freedom and societal constraint. Havighurst acknowledges the influences from Erik Erikson, another developmental psychologist.

Holt, John. *What Do I Do Monday?* New York: Dutton, 1970.

Holt combines his theories of education—the idea of learning as a growth process, a moving and expanding of the child into the world around him; a belief that we learn best when we feel the wholeness and the openness of the world around us, and our own freedom and power and competence in it—with practical, easy-to-use ideas and exercises in reading, writing, and mathematics. Available in paperback (New York: Dell, 1970).

Inlow, Gail. *Maturity in High School Teaching.* 2nd ed. Englewood Cliffs, N.J.: Prentice-Hall, 1970.

An excellent guide for the new teacher. Stresses the need for the teacher to develop personal adequacy, professionalism, and the abilities and attitudes to relate teaching sensitively to the learners' needs. Discusses lesson planning, instruction, learning aids, and evaluation.

Keen, Ernest. *Psychology and the New Consciousness.* Belmont, Calif.: Wadsworth, 1972.

Examines the Freudian movement, classifying it as a transition stage for developing a new consciousness typified by Berne, Szasz, and Laing. Phenomenology is discussed in depth and its meaning for the person also explored.

Kibler, Robert, Larry Barker, and David Miles. *Behavioral Objectives and Instruction.* Boston: Allyn & Bacon, 1970.

Very useful as a guide for analyzing, planning, and writing instructional objectives. Includes a large sampling of behavioral objectives in the three major domains.

Kirschenbaum, Howard A., Sidney Simon, and Rodney W. Napier. *Wad-Ja-Get? The Grading Game in American Education.* New York: Hart, 1971.

If schools are to emphasize the psychological development of children and are to place a major emphasis on feelings, creativity, communications, and so on, the issue of grades becomes vital. The authors present their case against grades in the form of a fictional account of one teacher and one class who decide to challenge the system. As narrative fiction the book leaves something to be desired, but as a practical and readable guidebook for bringing about change in the present grading system it should be extremely useful.

Klausmeier, Herbert, and Richard Ripple. *Learning and Human Abilities.* 3rd ed. New York: Harper & Row, 1971.

A textbook covering all aspects of educational psychology—growth and development, needs, motivation, individual differences, measurement, and teacher characteristics.

Mager, Robert F. *Developing Attitude Toward Learning*. Belmont, Calif.: Fearon, 1968.

Practical suggestions for improving a student's attitudes toward learning. Advocates a behavioral systems approach to instruction.

————. *Goal Analysis*. Belmont, Calif.: Fearon, 1972.

The latest thinking of one of the original thinkers in the behavioral objectives movement.

————. *Preparing Instructional Objectives*. Belmont, Calif.: Fearon, 1962.

An early and highly popular book describing the rationale for and the applications of behavioral objectives to instruction.

Maslow, A. H. "A Theory of Human Motivation." *Psychological Review* 50 (1943):370–96.

A frequently reproduced article outlining the author's concept of basic human needs and their influences on the psychological person. Also discusses motivation, metaneeds, and influences from the culture on the person.

Massialas, Byron, and C. Benjamin Cox. *Inquiry in Social Studies*. New York: McGraw-Hill, 1966.

Very thorough text dealing with inquiry, its applications and evaluation. Particularly good as a guide for planning inquiry learning activities.

Mayeroff, Milton. *On Caring*. New York: Harper & Row, 1971.

Paperback, deals with moral philosophy as applied to self and others through a helping relationship typical of teacher and student.

Phillips, John L. *The Origins of Intellect: Piaget's Theory*. San Francisco: W. H. Freeman, 1969.

Nontechnical summary of Piaget's research in developmental psychology, enabling the reader to comprehend more easily both the theory and applications of the theory to teaching and learning. Numerous illustrations are present, as are passages reproduced directly from Piaget's writings.

Piaget, Jean. *Psychology and Epistemology: Toward a Theory of Knowledge*. New York: Viking, 1971.

Excellent paperback provocatively presents Piaget's scientific basis for an entirely new epistemology. Sets forth the assumption that knowledge is not an accomplishment but a process; what is learned is not learned for all times but changes and grows with the learner.

————, and Barbel Inhelder. *The Psychology of the Child*. New York: Basic Books, 1969.

Translated from the original French, provides a comprehensive synthesis of Piaget's research, tracing the stages of cognitive development over the entire period of childhood.

Rubin, Louis J., ed. *Life Skills in School and Society*. Washington, D.C.: Association for Supervision and Curriculum Development, 1969.

Analysis of educational needs created by the changing times and speculations regarding the capacities of humankind, with practical implications for the school.

Saucier, Weems, Robert Wendel, and Richard Mueller. *Toward Humanistic Teaching in High School*. Lexington, Mass.: D. C. Heath, 1975.

An excellent book that examines psychological-social learning theory in order to extrapolate relevant applications of democratic-reflective teaching to the subjects taught in high schools.

Skinner, B. F. *Beyond Freedom and Dignity*. New York: Knopf, 1971.

Describes the author's belief that man must now take control of his evolution by consciously designing his entire culture so it will shape the behavior needed for survival. Chapters deal with such topics as a technology of behavior; freedom; dignity; punishment; values; what is man.

————. *Walden II*. New York: Macmillan, 1948.

A popular book proposing a utopia based upon the dependent behavior modification approach to learning and teaching.

Sund, Robert, and Anthony Picard. *Behavioral Objectives and Educational Measures*. Columbus, Ohio: Merrill, 1972.

Discusses the relevance and value of behavioral objectives, the criteria for their selection, some examples of how to write them for each domain, and examples of how to evaluate student achievement. Uses science and math as the subject matter for its treatment.

Wittmer, Joe, and Robert Myrick. *Facilitative Teaching: Theory and Practice*. Pacific Palisades, Calif.: Goodyear, 1974.

A fine book providing a systematic approach to acquiring the skills needed to be a facilitative teacher.

CHAPTER 11

Readings on
Psychological Foundations

Because teachers must interact with the people they teach, an understanding of the principles of psychology applied to learning is essential. Our discussion of psychology presented the most recent interpretations of each theory and a translation of those concepts into an outline appropriate for instruction. The purpose of this chapter is to elaborate certain learning concepts, such as insight development, motivation, stimulus-response learning, and facilitating meaningful learning.

Morris L. Bigge, professor of psychology at Fresno State College, discusses the relevance of psychology to the educational enterprise. This succinct treatment of the psychological views of mankind held by the Existentialist, the Behaviorist, and the Cognitive-Field theorist clarifies what each theory means for teaching. The significant concepts of each of these three major schools of psychological thought are discussed and compared in relation to their appropriateness in facilitating learning.

Research by Piaget regarding the growth of logical intelligence and the implications for educators is the subject of the article by Robbie Case, professor of education at the Berkeley campus of the University of California. He clearly presents Piaget's research on the properties of logical thought, the stages of intellectual development, and the factors that help to explain individual differences in children's performance.

How developmental psychology explains both intellectual and personality differences between men and women is the concern of David Lynn, professor of child development at the Davis campus of the University of California. In his article, focused mainly on women, Lynn reviews research describing the interaction of the biological, family, and cultural potentials and patterns which influence learning in both sexes. His hypotheses are carefully documented, which allows him to suggest several possibilities for altering those determinants that seem to have the greatest influence on intellectual growth in men and women.

In the fourth article Ernest Bayles writes about one of the most significant and most frequently misunderstood concepts in educational psychology: insight. His article is an examination of the process of insight development and the meaning the concept holds for teachers. Bayles also describes the key psychological concepts of practice, habit, and transfer, and their relationship to learning as an insightful process. The article gives some attention to the contrasting views of B. F. Skinner and Jerome Bruner.

The public is so familiar with the description of learning as a mechanistic linking of stimulus and response that the fifth article, also by Morris L. Bigge, provides a much-needed alternative point of view. A comparison is made of the two major descriptions of learning. The article also discusses motivation and interaction as both are advanced by Behavioral and Cognitive-Field psychology. For those who believe the difference between the two descriptions of learning is only semantic, this article points out the real differences and their implications for education.

The final article in this chapter addresses itself to the need for information that synthesizes diverse theories of learning into an acceptable and valid view. Carl Rogers reviews research and general statements about educational psychology and abstracts the most valid descriptions of the learning processes.

Significant in this discussion is the author's treatment of those concepts that occur simultaneously with learning. Rogers talks about change, self-concept, threats to learning, experiencing, creativity, relevance, and the ways a teacher might facilitate the positive development of these conditions through teaching.

From these readings one can begin to formulate a description of how a person best learns, what motivation is, and what appear to be possible applications of these concepts to the teaching process.

The Relevance of Psychology to the Educational Enterprise

Morris L. Bigge

Psychologists, in their attempt to study man with prevailing methods and techniques, have tended to oversimplify him. Thus, they usually have viewed man either as a subjective mind or person, as an objective body,

Reprinted, with deletions, from *Colorado Journal of Educational Research* 9, no. 2 (Winter 1970):27–32, by permission of the author and the publisher.

or as a combination of the two. Accordingly, on those occasions when psychologists have turned philosophical, they more often have asked themselves: "Is the proper image of man that of an active, autonomous being, is it that of a passively reactive recipient of stimuli, or is it that of a combination of the two?" However, a strong case can be made for the contention that no one of these three positions presents an adequate psychological image of man.

Now, how about man's being an active, autonomous being. Present-day emphasis upon the subjective nature of man is rooted in Roussellian natural unfoldment and various instinct and basic needs theories as exemplified by Freudian psychology. A contemporary position that champions autonomous development is existentialism. An existentialist harbors three basic awarenesses; they are I am a *choosing agent,* I am a *free agent,* and I am a *responsible agent.* However, his responsibility is only to himself and for how he lives his own life. To quote Morris, "The teacher's imperative is to arrange the learning situation in such a way as to bring home the truth of these three propositions to every individual."[1] Accordingly, an existentialist teacher always is searching for personal truth. In his teaching, he awakens awareness, freedom, and responsibility in his students so that they too will search for their own personal truths. But, each person's own feelings are the final authority for the truth that is gained through this process.

Current subjectivism takes the form of a psychedelic humanism within which a person, completely on his own, supposedly is sufficient for every situation. He arrives at decisions on all issues in accordance with the way he *feels,* and he is completely confident that he is right. Leaders in promulgating this subjective emphasis promote each individual's intuitive awareness of himself and the artistic expression of his self-actualization. To repeat, one's feelings are taken to be the only final authority for truth. . . .

For an existentialist, the function of teaching should be to provide conditions under which personal autonomy may emerge and be sustained, protected, and nurtured and to quote Herbst ". . . autonomy does not mean the principled rejection of authority but rather the ability to accept or reject it in the light of your own consistent standards."[2] Since teaching means to free people from their dependence on others, to stand them on their own feet, and to encourage them to walk for themselves, it must be free of all social and conceptual restraints. This means that students as well as teachers are considered to be autonomously proactive selves as contrasted with their being either passive or interactive ones.

[1] Van Cleve Morris, *Existentialism In Education* (New York: Harper & Row, 1966), p. 135.
[2] Jurgen Herbst, "The Anti-School—Some Reflections on Teaching," *Educational Theory* 18, no. 1 (Winter 1968):22.

Although the idea of autonomous expression presently is being promoted widely, for a social-psychologist a human person apart from a society is either a myth or a monstrosity. There is no such thing as a human person in total isolation from other people; a person is a psycho-social being, and an era of wholly self-determined men probably never did and never will exist. . . .

Next, let's examine the psychological outlook that is based on the assumption that man is a passive, reactive recipient of stimuli and emitter of responses. Within the behaviorisms man becomes an extremely well-designed, clever biological machine who learns through accumulating memories in an additive process. A human being is a biological organism with a history of conditioned behaviors. So, words such as foresight, purpose, and desire are literary, not scientific, terms. Behavioristic psychologists tend to consider any concept of goal direction or purposiveness to be teleological. To them "teleological" means deriving present behavior from the future. Consequently, it sounds mystical and superstitious. So, in their zeal to escape any commitment to future causation, they have emphasized past events as the cause of present behavior. Accordingly, they think in terms of stimuli being causes and responses being effects and of there being a time lapse between physical stimuli and organic responses. To quote Hebb, "Temporarily integrated behavior, extended over a period of time, is treated as a series of reactions to a series of stimulations. . . . Stimulus followed directly by response is the archetype of behavior. . . ."[3]

The most popular modern version of behavioristic teaching probably is that based on the deterministic operant conditioning theory of B. F. Skinner of Harvard. Professor Skinner's psychology is a strictly engineering type of science. He insists that psychology is a science of overt behavior and only overt behavior. Accordingly, he defines learning as a change in probability of responses. In most cases this change is brought about by operant conditioning, which is made more probable or more frequent; that is, an operant is reinforced. An operant is a set of acts that constitutes an organism's doing something—raising its head, pushing a lever, or saying "horse." Through operant reinforcement we supposedly learn to keep our balance, walk, play games, handle tools, paint pictures, and think about mathematics.

Skinner's basic thesis is that, since an organism, including man, tends in the future to do what it was doing at the time of reinforcement, one can, by baiting each step of the way, lead the organism to *do* very much what the experimenter or teacher wishes it to do. Using this thesis as a basis for his procedure, he has taught rats to use a marble to obtain food from a vending machine, and pigeons to play a modified game of tennis.

[3] Donald O. Hebb, *A Textbook of Psychology* (Philadelphia: W. B. Saunders, 1958), p. 46.

Skinner is convinced that operant conditioning, so fruitful when applied to animal training, promises equal success when used in schools. He feels that the most efficient control of human learning requires instrumental aid. He recognizes the first task of teachers to be to shape proper responses, to get children to pronounce and write responses properly. But he sees their principal task as bringing proper behavior under many sorts of stimulus control. Accordingly, he writes, "Teaching spelling is mainly a process of shaping complex forms of behavior. In other subjects—for example, arithmetic—responses must be brought under the control of appropriate stimuli."[4] To achieve this task, Skinner recommends the use of programmed instruction. This may be accomplished either with or without the use of teaching machines.

Programmed instruction is a system of teaching and learning within which preestablished subject matter is broken down into small, discrete steps and carefully organized into a logical sequence in which it can be learned readily by the students. Each step builds deliberately upon the preceding one. The learner can progress through the sequence of steps at his own rate and he is reinforced immediately after step. Reinforcement consists of his either being given the correct answer or his being permitted to proceed to the next step immediately after he has registered the correct response.

A teaching machine and its system of programmed instruction, when left to itself, tends to make students into its own image, to place a machine at each end of the handle. To quote Rollo May, "We then tend more and more to ask only the questions the machine can answer, we teach more and more only the things the machine can teach, and limit our research to the quantitative work the machines can do. There then is bound to emerge a real and inexorable tendency to make our image of man over into the image of the very machine by which we study and control him."[5]

Now, in what direction should scientific psychology advance in order for it to benefit by the great mass of valuable psychological thinking and research that has been accomplished, and become an appropriate guide for the improvement of school instruction? Cognitive-field psychological theory represents a possible answer to this question. The meanings of the tenets of this position are sharpened when they are compared with those of the tenets of the behaviorisms, which also constitute a scientific approach to the study of man.

Within an enlightened outlook, learners could well be considered neither passive recipients of stimuli and emitters of responses nor au-

[4] B. F. Skinner, *Cumulative Record* (New York: Appleton-Century-Crofts, 1959), p. 165.
[5] Rollo May, *Psychology and the Human Dilemma* (Princeton, N.J.: D. Van Nostrand, 1967), p. 173.

tonomous beings, who engage in free choice completely independent of their environments. Instead, they could be viewed as purposive persons interacting with their unique psychological environments, and this is the basic paradigm of cognitive-field psychology.

Cognitive-field psychology promotes the idea of man's being purposively and perceptually interactive, but it in no way sponsors the concept of autonomous human activity. Its being a purposive psychology means that it assumes that intellectual processes are deeply affected by an individual's goals and that learning activity, including habit formation, is goal directed. So, ideas concerning goals and purposes become central to cognitive-field learning theory. This contrasts sharply with the practices of adherents of conditioning theories, who either ignore learners' goals and purposes completely or make them only peripheral and incidental.

Cognitive-field theorists challenge behavioristic statements that imply that propositions of psychology must likewise be physicalistic ones. As they view matters, men cannot, in terms of physics, chemistry, and biology, adequately explain themselves as persons. So, they need a psychology that is a science in its own right. Although they do not assume that significant human behavior is determined by prior causes, they do think that it can be scientifically predicted. Accordingly, they seek understanding of contemporaneous causal relationships, not of a sequential cause-effect order of human behavior.

To be scientific, one need not necessarily be physicalistic or reductionistic. Although, from a physical point of view, a denial of mechanistic causation may well be foolhardy, an educational psychologist as such should not be concerned primarily with mechanistic, physical causation of human behavior. Whereas behaviorists center the understanding of an individual in his past pointed toward the present, cognitive-field theorists center their study of an individual in the present projected into the future.

The life space metaphor of cognitive-field psychology provides a pattern for thinking as contrasted with a picture of any absolute existence. It cuts through any splitting off of man into body and mind, and deals with him in terms of his unique distinguishing characteristics.

The purpose of cognitive-field psychology is to formulate tested relationships that are predictive of the behavior of individual persons in their specific life spaces. In order to understand and predict such behavior, one must consider a person and his psychological environment as a pattern of interdependent facts and functions. Accordingly, cognitive-field psychology is an interpersonal, social psychology that constitutes an effective vehicle for characterization of man. It integrates biological and social factors and treats respective persons as interacting with them. . . .

In the interactive process a person and his psychological environment are construed as interdependent variables. Thus, a person is neither dependent upon, nor independent of, his environment. Likewise, a person's environment is neither made by him nor independent of him. Whereas behavioristic psychologies are biological-organism centered, cognitive-field psychology is psychological-person centered. "Organism" suggests a mechanism and human passivity; "person," in contrast, suggests purposiveness and interactivity.

Cognitive-field theory contrasts sharply with the behaviorisms in regard to the manner in which adherents of the two respective positions use observable behavior of persons as psychological data. Behaviorists use observable behavior and only observable behavior as data. Consequently, they restrict learning objectives to those expressible in terms of observable behaviors. In contrast, cognitive-field psychologists also study observable behaviors, but they infer from them the changing personalities, environments, and insights of the persons being studied. So, whereas for behaviorists one's physical behavior also is one's psychological behavior, for cognitive-field theorists psychological behavior is something quite different from mere physical movement; it is change in the way a person perceives both himself and his psychological environment.

Whereas behavioristic educational psychologies have emphasized overt behavior, cognitive-field psychology contrastingly concerns itself with outward behavior only insofar as it may provide clues to what is transpiring psychologically or perceptually. Thus, *psychological* is understood to mean in accordance with the logic of a growing mind or intelligence. So, to be psychological in his pursuits, a cognitive-field psychologist must look at the world through the eyes of the learner. To describe a situation psychologically, he, to the best of his ability, must describe the situation that confronts the individual under study. Such a situation is viewed as a pattern of personal-environmental relationships that provide and limit opportunities. Once the person-environment structure is established, the problem is to use constructs and methods adequate to deal with the underlying dynamics of behavior and to do this in a scientifically sound manner.

Cognitive-field psychology describes how a person gains understanding of himself and his world in a situation within which his self and his environment compose a totality of mutually interdependent, coexisting events. This psychology involves the kind of generalizations about learning that may be applied to actual persons in school situations. It is associated with the knowing and understanding functions that give meaning to a situation. Also, it is built around the purposes underlying behavior, the goals involved in behavior, and persons' means and processes of understanding themselves as they function in relation to their goals. Factors of a life space acquire meaning as a person formulates his goals and develops insights into ways of achieving them.

A functional interpretation of psychological life opens the way for extensive use of systematic constructs. Whereas a behaviorist supposedly restricts his generalizations to those based on the use of "objective" data, a cognitive-field psychologist knowingly uses constructs that go beyond the observable data. His employment of such constructs provides a means for bridging the gap between general principles, which cannot be observed, and the functions of individual persons, which can be gathered as data. Thus, through the use of a few constructs the essence of an individual case can be adequately represented.

The *meanings of all the constructs of cognitive-field psychology are mutually interdependent.* Each depends for its meaning upon the meanings of all the others. Thus, there are no independent, dependent, and intervening variables as in the behaviorisms. Instead, *all the variables of cognitive-field psychology are interdependent.*

Cognitive-field psychologists establish order but they go about it in a different way than do behaviorists. A sizable amount of psychological research has been conducted within a cognitive-field frame of reference. However, cognitive-field theorists base their psychological principles upon research that has been conducted by behaviorists as well as upon their own. So, along with benefiting from the experimentation done under other banners, they develop their own unique type of scientific research. Field theorists note that, provided either lower animals or persons are credited with being genuinely purposive, the results of most psychological research supports cognitive-field psychology. For example, the results of experiments, such as those developed by B. F. Skinner to test operant conditioning, also support cognitive-field theory; it is only necessary to assume that the individual being studied is attempting to take care of his welfare the best way he knows how. Accordingly, Skinner's pigeons behave the way they do because that behavior is what gets them food (there is no suggestion here that lower animals "think" verbally or abstractly, but they do size up their situations).

Experimentation within cognitive-field psychology involves the study of such matters as cognitive processes, recall of uncompleted tasks, relationships of levels of achievement and levels of aspiration, psychological ecology, group dynamics, action research, concepts of self, personality rigidity, individual and social perception, and reflective processes.

For cognitive-field theorists, terms such as purpose, foresight, and desire impart scientific as well as literary expressions. But, they in no way imply the reality of a sheer isolated individuality of persons. A principal source of basis of each personality consists of the customs, beliefs, attitudes, values, and habits of the social groups within which an individual lives. So, what a person actually is in his life experience—his succession of life spaces—depends to a large extent upon the nature and purposes of his associated living. Accordingly, the idea of absolute autonomy of individuals is a completely inadequate guideline for the direction of human affairs. The course of the cognitive structures of a person's life spaces, which are in continuous psychological movement, can be predicted accurately only within the ecological–physio-social–environments in which it proceeds.

To summarize the cognitive-field theory of learning we may say that a person learns through differentiating, generalizing, and restructuring his person and his psychological environment in such way as to acquire new or changed insights, understandings, discernments, or meanings concerning them, and thereby achieves changes in motivation, group belongingness, time perspective, and ideology. In this way, he gains greater control of himself and his world. So learning, concisely defined, is a process of one's gaining or changing his insights, outlooks, discernments, or thought patterns.

Cognitive-field theorists, in thinking about the learning processes of students, prefer the terms *person* to *organism, psychological environment* to *physical* or *biological environment,* and *interaction* to either *action* or *reaction.* Such preference is not merely a whim; there is a conviction that the concepts *person, psychological environment,* and *interaction* are highly advantageous for teachers in describing learning processes. They enable a teacher to see a person, his environment, and his interaction with his environment all occurring at once; this is the meaning of "field."

For a teacher to teach other persons in a significant way, he should have sympathetic understanding of students as persons and should strive to develop an accurate idea of what actually is transpiring in the life spaces of those whom he is teaching. To gain an understanding of each person and his cognitive world, a teacher needs to develop a sort of disciplined naivete; he must see the student's person and environment as the student sees them. In order adequately to see a student through, *he must see through him.* In other words, a teacher should strive to construe his students' construings.

To accomplish his purpose a teacher should have an extensive background of varied knowledge; he should be alert to the attitudes and outlooks that students are developing; and his ideal should be to promote an atmosphere that fosters maximum insightful growth. This means that he should be able to judge which attitudes or insights are conducive, and which are detrimental to continued growth.

Advocates of cognitive-field psychology think that a teacher should teach; neither baby-sit nor dictate. A babysitter usually performs a custodial function but teaches children little. A dictator imposes the "right" answers. A teacher, in contrast with both, should perform his democratic teaching role in a process of student-teacher mutual inquiry. Teaching for insight or understanding can be either reflective or nonreflective,

but democratic teaching should always strive toward reflective procedures. . . .

Piaget's Theory of Child Development and Its Implications
Robbie Case

Should the elementary school curriculum be overhauled? Should formal instruction in reading be delayed until the third grade? Is didactic pedagogy at all suited to the natural reasoning processes of young children? Are conventional IQ tests invalid?

Questions such as these are not new in education. What *is* relatively new is the extent to which educators are basing their answers on the work of Swiss psychologist Jean Piaget. The purpose of this article is to summarize Piaget's research and theory, and to take a critical look at its implications for education.

Philosophical Foundations

In order to put Piaget's work in perspective, it is worthwhile to point out that it stems from a very different philosophic position from the work of many American psychologists. The latter, particularly the behaviorists, draw heavily upon the philosophy of the British empiricists, Locke and Hume. Both Locke and Hume were concerned with formulating ideas about the way in which man comes to acquire knowledge of the world. They both came to a conclusion that, although somewhat heretical at the time, seems almost commonplace now: Man acquires his knowledge of the world not from God or from logic but from the impressions he receives through his various sense organs. At birth, man is essentially a "blank slate," but as sensations are etched into this slate, he acquires knowledge of the world. The process by which this knowledge is ac-

Reprinted, with minor deletions, from *Phi Delta Kappan* 55, no. 1 (September 1973):20–25, by permission of the author and the publisher.

quired is essentially that of association: the association of one set of sensations or stimuli with another.

By contrast, the work of Piaget was based on the writings of the German philosopher, Immanuel Kant. Although Kant was impressed by much of what Locke and Hume asserted, he decided that their conceptualization of the knowing process was incomplete.

One of the main dimensions of human knowledge on which Kant focused was its organization. He concluded that, while it is true that human beings cannot acquire any knowledge of the world *without* their sense organs, it is impossible to explain the universal organizational properties of their knowledge by assuming their sense organs to be the *only* source of this knowledge. All human beings have certain basic notions—of space, for example, and of time—which they do not simply "receive" from their senses but which they in a way possess already, and which they use to give order and meaning to what they *do* receive. Consider the simple fact that objects have a permanence independent of our own sensations. For Kant this truth could not simply be "etched in" to our minds by sensation, since it refers to something which must by definition always lie *beyond* our sensation. Rather than being a perceivable fact, then, it is a precondition which is necessary for what *is* perceived to have any meaning, or coherent organization. The human mind does not accept the registration of total chaos, as a blank slate might. In effect, it *demands* that the world be organized, and it has the inherent capacity to make that demand come true.

When Piaget began his pioneering studies, it was with this basic philosophic perspective. Like Kant, he assumed that human beings are not blank slates which passively receive the world; rather, that they actively structure it. Like Kant, he assumed that the structure of man's knowledge depends on certain universal notions which he is never explicitly taught: notions concerning space, time, causality, the permanence of objects, and so on. What Piaget became interested in was the *development* and *origin* of these basic notions. As he himself described it, what he became interested in was *genetic epistemology*.

Perhaps because the notions Piaget was interested in *were* so very basic, and were so "taken for granted" by adults all over the world, the results of his investigations were often quite surprising.

Experimental Findings and Theory

The Sensorimotor Stage

From the first days of life, the infant exhibits basic reflexes when confronted by certain stimuli. If a nipple is placed in his mouth, he will suck;

if something enters his hand, he will grasp; if a shape moves into his field of vision, he will track it. But his appreciation of causality, or of the permanence of objects, does not appear to be as inborn as these basic reflexes. In fact, it does not appear to be really *finely* developed until he is about two years of age.

Consider the following simple facts. If an interesting object enters his field of vision, even the youngest infant will track it. However, if it goes out of his field of vision repeatedly and then immediately returns, he will not wait for it: His glance will move to other things. Time does not appear to be represented the same way for a child as it is for an adult. When something is out of sight, it is out of mind.

When he is somewhat older, the infant's glance *will* linger in a situation such as that mentioned above. In other situations, however, he will still act as though that which is not immediately present does not exist. For example: Hold a rattle out to a six-month-old child. Then, as he starts to reach out, conceal it behind something he could easily move, such as a handkerchief. All his signs of intention will vanish and he will not try to retrieve it. In fact, he may not try to retrieve it even if it is only *partially* hidden.

When one thinks about it carefully, one can appreciate that a half-hidden object does not look exactly the same as one that is completely in view. How is the child to know it is not "half-made," as it were? When one thinks about it carefully, one can appreciate that a covered object is not present to sensation at all. How is the child to know it has not been completely *un*made? Piaget's interpretation is that this is exactly how infants do see the world—things are made and unmade, and a half-hidden object is only half an object.

Consider another example. There is a stage in the first year of life when a baby will make no attempt to rotate a baby bottle that is presented to him bottom first instead of nipple first. Once again, how is he supposed to know that they are the same object? The bottom certainly doesn't look like the top. The knowledge that an object looks different at different times but is actually a constant thing seems to be one that the infant has to *develop*. In short, the world as we see it is not something that is automatically *given* to the infant by sensation at all; it is something that he has to construct.

In constructing his world, the small child seems to follow a definite series of steps, or successive approximations, to the world we know. When he is just beginning to toddle, one can hide his favorite toy under a bright red handkerchief (in his full view) and he will remove the handkerchief with great glee. Aha, you say, he has learned that an inanimate object continues to stay where it was put. But has he? After you have played this game a few times, place the favorite toy, again in full sight, under a yellow handkerchief. Then watch as he looks under the red one again and appears baffled that the toy is not there. What he appears to have learned is only a first approximation—that when someone causes something to disappear, it will always continue to exist under a red handkerchief.

Piaget invented a number of these sorts of "trick" situations, and he found that it was not until about the age of 18 months to 2 years that the child ceased to be fooled by any of them. Piaget's inference was that it is not until this time that the child has a really strong intuitive notion of the fact that objects have a permanence independent of his perception and that cause and effect can operate independently of his willing them.

How does the child acquire this knowledge? If you watch an infant, you will note that he is continually exploring things with his mouth, his hands, his eyes, and so on. At first these explorations occur independently of each other; later they are coordinated; and finally they are extended to include shaking, throwing, and other actions. Such exploration and testing may not be too easy on parents, but the indications are that it is universal.

For Piaget, this activity is the key mechanism by which an organized view of the world is constructed. An action, even if it is a reflex, is represented in the brain by some sort of plan. You could call it a program. You could call it a neural impulse: the firing of some cells in the brain. It doesn't matter. Piaget calls it a *scheme*. Consider what happens when the child looks at his bottle or a matchbox. The visual configuration of the top activates something in the brain, called a *schema* by Piaget, and the child then acts on the object himself by manipulating it. Presto! A brand new visual configuration appears. Furthermore, when he manipulates the bottle again the first configuration reappears.

In Piaget's terminology, the first schema, or the representation in the brain of the top of the box, is assimilated by (or actually incorporated into) the scheme representing the child's action. Then the reciprocal event occurs: The second schema or visual pattern is assimilated by the same action scheme. As this happens time and again, a compound schema is built up, composed of all the various ways the matchbox can look (all the various schemata) and bound together, as it were, by all the ways it can be acted upon (the schemes). Thus the top of the box is no longer a floating, isolated pattern. It becomes part of a series of patterns, which are intimately connected by virtue of the fact that any one can be produced from any other by simply acting on it. It becomes part of a coordinated whole. Because Piaget sees the product of the child's first two years of life as the result of this sensorimotor integration, he labels this first phase of the child's development the sensorimotor stage.

Preconceptual and Intuitive Thought

The toddler now uses the achievements of the first stage of his life as building blocks to reduce the chaos of the world even further. Now that objects are perceived as entities, and reflexes are integrated into coordinated movements, they can be given names. A little later they can be grouped together in different ways and the whole group can be named.

However, once again, none of these accomplishments occurs overnight. To begin with, the child's language reflects that his psychological units are still objects very different from adult units, which tend to be concepts. At first he seems very uncertain as to the difference between particular objects (for example, his brother), and whole classes of objects (for example, boys). He is not always sure if objects are actually in the same group. When he does build rules about general categories, they tend (as with the rules built in the sensorimotor stage) to be only first approximations to the ones used by adults. They tend to focus on only one attribute of a class and then not necessarily on the adult one. We are all familiar with the child who delights his parents by labeling a dog as "doggie," and who goes on to label a cow as doggie, a cat as doggie, and maybe even his younger brother as a doggie too. By degrees, of course, the child's organization and classification of the world becomes more refined. By the age of 5 or 6, although he cannot yet answer such tricky questions as whether there are more red roses or more white roses in a flower bowl, he does appreciate that all the flowers are roses, and that some are red and some are white.

According to Piaget, the mechanism at work is very similar to that in the first stage. By forming things into classes and dividing them again, by calling a certain pattern a cow at one time and an animal at another, the child's mental activity begins to tie together the separate labels and the separate groups into an organized hierarchical framework. At first, during the preconceptual stage, a moving object is gradually tied together with other similar moving things until they all may be called cows. Then, in the intuitive stage, cows are tied together with cats and put into the category of animals, and the whole classification system is bound together as a whole.

In short, between the second and seventh year of his life, the child builds on objects to form concepts and on concepts to form classes of concepts. He does this by grouping things together, regrouping them, naming them, and continuing to explore. By the age of 7 or 8, he is capable of making some remarkably sophisticated observations about the world. His thinking begins to take on quite a logical character. However, it still depends heavily on interacting with the concrete world and it is still different from adult thought in many interesting respects.

Concrete Operations

The building blocks are now not just individual objects or people but classes of objects or people. Not only does a lump of Plasticine remain in existence when hidden but it remains Plasticine, able to be differentiated from other similar objects such as mud by certain properties, and itself containing subcategories depending, say, on whether or not it will harden overnight.

Once more, by acting on the world, the child begins to reduce the remaining chaos. He begins to extract higher-order features of groups that do not change, even though the groups change drastically. For example, having learned by the age of 5 or 6 to classify objects as long or short, heavy or light, and so on, and to relate perceptual properties of objects by using categories like more and less, he begins to appreciate that there are such higher-order categories as length and amount, which remain constant even though the perceptual input (on which the classification is originally made) may change drastically.

Probably the most famous of Piaget's experiments concerns just this sort of achievement. Take your bright-eyed little 5-year-old daughter who has just learned to count. Have her count out five beads in one row, then five in another row right beside it, and ask her if there are the same number in each row. She will tell you—perhaps proudly—that there are. However, spread out one row a little farther so it looks longer and ask her if there are still the same number in each row. Again, perhaps proudly, she will tell you that there are not, that there are more beads in the long row of five than in the short row of five. What we see once more is that her first understanding is only an approximation of the adult one and that it is based more on changing sensations.

By age 7 she will no longer make this mistake. However, her understanding will not yet be complete; once again is will proceed in definite steps. If we take two balls of Plasticine that she agrees are equal in size, and roll one into a sausage, she will not think that the long one has more Plasticine than the short one, but she *will* still think that the long one weighs more.

Although the kind of activity taking place is no longer one of sensorimotor manipulation, or of grouping and naming, Piaget sees the mechanism by which these higher-order adult constancies are introduced as essentially the same as the mechanism operating in the first two stages. The child learns that although one can always transfer two arrays of five into states where they appear different, the number you get by counting each array will still be five. Furthermore, you can always conduct the reciprocal operation: You can always transform them back into a state where they *are* in one-to-one correspondence. Once again, then, the various possible perceptual configurations of "five" all get tied together into an organized whole, connected by the internalized operations, the mental schemes. The result is that one label can eventually be applied to any array of the same number, no matter how different they look.

Formal Operations

With such higher-order concepts of the properties of objects as number, quantity, and weight, with a good intuitive grasp of causality, and with an understanding of the various possible ways things can be transformed, the child is ready to begin creating an order that is more formal. He is ready to begin relating things—for example, such concepts as mass and number—in terms of invariants which are of a higher order still, such as scientific laws. In addition, his activity in noting the things that actually happen in the world and in producing changes appears to enable him to begin thinking about what *might* happen and to envision all the changes that are possible. It enables him to reason without visual props. This in turn enables him to deduce an appropriate method for scientific procedure.

Consider the following problem: A spinning wheel has holes of various sizes in it and marbles of various sizes on it. A child is asked to figure out why some marbles fall off before others and then to test to see if he is correct.

The child who is in the concrete stage can classify the holes quite accurately and can even cross-classify them. He can see that there are big and small holes and that in both categories there are some near the center and some near the edge. He also has an intuitive notion of causality. However, he appears restricted to noting what actually occurs. If you ask why the big one fell off first, he will say, "Because it's bigger." Then, if you arrange them so that a small one falls off first, he will sometimes say, "Because it's smaller," without being overly upset by the contradiction. If you ask him to *prove* that big ones fall off first, he will not always bother to keep other things constant.

For Piaget, this child has not internalized a system in which *any* relevant attribute may vary and in which many different combinations of possibilities can all produce the same result. The child sees a big marble in a small hole near the edge and concludes that it fell off so soon because it was big. He does not imagine that one could put a small marble in a small hole near the edge and that it might fall off too, so he does not see the need to control other factors before he draws a conclusion about size. In short, although he has an internalized classification system, it is still bound to the concrete things he sees before him. The organization of his knowledge is not yet complex enough to represent conditions of the world accurately which are not before him.

In describing the sequence of stages, I have been referring with confidence to *the* child rather than to *some* children. This is because a remarkable uniformity has been found in the things children can and cannot do (the knowledge they have and don't have) and in the order in which they learn to do them. The exact age at which an individual child may begin to appreciate that weight does not change if nothing is added or subtracted may vary, but it never occurs before he learns that objects have a permanence or after he learns that all other things must be equal in a scientific experiment. Within substages the same is true; a child will always learn the conditions under which weight remains constant before he learns the conditions under which displaced volume remains constant and after he learns the conditions under which number and amount remain constant. We may thus talk about *the* child, since in these most basic interactions with the world and in the constructions of reality, all children achieve an identical series of accomplishments in an identical order.

What Piaget has described, then, is a series of stages through which all children develop. What he has postulated is that the process which propels them through these stages is a highly active one: At each stage the child starts with a world that is ordered in some respects and chaotic in others. And at each level, by acting on the world, by executing transformations, by reversing these transformations, and so on, he builds some further element of order into it. He constructs something that remains unchanged in the face of change—a coordinated whole.

I would now like to turn to the influence Piaget's theory has had, or is having, on education.

Educational Applications and Influences

Basis for the Content of New Curricula

One of the first applications of Piaget's theory, dating back almost a decade, was to suggest the content for new curricula. The reasoning of the curriculum developers probably went something like this: If these are the stages of development through which a child passes, if the abilities he acquires are really the crucial ones from a cognitive viewpoint, and if one of our jobs as educators is to assist in intellectual development, then maybe we should start providing some assistance to the child in precisely the processes and achievements which Piaget has concentrated on. Furthermore, since one stage appears to be built on the prior stage and to incorporate its achievements, maybe we should start this assistance at an early age. Whether or not this has been the precise reasoning, a number of different curricula have been developed, all aimed at providing activities to assist the preschool or elementary school child in representing number, space, and time, or to help him in classifying the world around him. Curricula have also been developed for elementary and high school students to better prepare them to understand formal and experimental reasoning in science. Particular attention has been paid to making these programs suitable for disadvantaged children. It is felt that such children may benefit more than others from programs aimed not at specific rote skills or the acquisition of factual knowledge but at broader cognitive development.

Exciting as it may seem on the surface, however, the attempt to make Piaget's stages the basis for new curriculum content is not one which, in my opinion, should be accepted uncritically. When one sees how painfully inadequate (by adult standards) is the knowledge of some children, there is a great temptation to rush out and prove that one is a really good teacher: that one can teach the child what he doesn't know or, at least, "help him in his attempts to teach himself." There is an equally strong pull to take something new and exciting and clearly intellectual and, because it *is* all these things, put it in the classroom. But, even if we assume that intellectual development is important—which I *do* assume—I submit that this extension of Piagetian theory into classroom practice can be justified only on the basis of one of two further assumptions: that children would not achieve the stages of development unless they had our help or that (if they *could* achieve the stages without our help) they could not achieve them as early.

Let us consider these assumptions separately. There is some evidence to suggest that not all adults reach the stage of formal operations. Estimates of adults who do not reach this stage vary between about 30 and 90 percent. The people trying to teach formal operational skills would seem, then, to be on the right track. Assuming that these skills are important and that 50 percent of the people in the world never achieve them, here is a definite task in which the schools might help.

But what about concrete operational activity and the insights about the world that result from it? Here the evidence (literally, from around the world) is very different. Children appear to acquire these insights and skills on their own almost universally. Why, then, should we expend effort and money teaching them these skills in the classroom?

The only possible justification I can see is the second assumption: that for some reason children should learn these things a little earlier. But this assumption cannot be accepted simply on faith. What reasons are there for rushing a child toward a goal he will reach in a year or so anyway? The only reason I can think of is that the skills in question are somehow necessary for success in the *other* things that the school must teach and that the child who is missing them will therefore be handicapped. Yet, although I stand to be corrected, I know of no evidence to indicate that this is the case or that any conventional elementary school subject cannot be taught until children have reached the stage of concrete operations. I have seen studies quoted which suggest that children often learn to perform certain kinds of arithmetic problems at the same time as they learn to solve certain concrete operational problems, but this is obviously not the same thing.

A crucial study would be to take a group of children who were low in general development, to accelerate or broaden their development with a Piaget-based curriculum, and to show not only that they could *now* learn the required material or generalize it to the required variety of situations, but also that they could do so with less effort than a group for whom the same amount of time had been spent teaching the specific lower-order subject skills prerequisite to mastering the later material. Until such a study is done, I see no reason to support the investment of money in Piagetian elementary school curricula other than in the hope that they *might* help the children and might be fun. But similar reasoning could support the abolition of curricula completely.

Basis for New Assessment Procedures

A second school-related use to which Piaget has been put has been the development of a new intelligence scale. So far, the results have correlated well with those obtained on regular intelligence scales. The Piagetian items, although they probably can be influenced by specially enriching experiences, are said by those developing them to have the advantage of being linked to a theory of intelligence, which normal IQ tests are not. Also, they are said to draw on experience which varies less widely from subculture to subculture; they do not appear to depend on linguistic sophistication, for example, or on any particular knowledge unique to middle-class North Americans.

The attempt to construct and validate an intelligence scale based on Piaget's tests seems to me to be a basically worthwhile one. The only comment I would offer is that any decision as to which sort of test should actually be used in a school should depend on which sort of test proves to be the most useful. This means that criteria other than those of academic or developmental psychologists have to be invoked. Is the test any better at predicting school success? Does it arouse any less hostility in the community at large? Does it provide any more clues as to what help should be given to a child whose poor school performance is associated with a low IQ, and so on?

Justification for a "Readiness" Approach

A third educational influence I feel Piaget is having is that of providing people who believe in "readiness" with some additional ammunition for their arguments. This influence is not so easy to demonstrate as the first two I mentioned. I cannot point to particular teachers or particular programs and say, "There. They are doing that because they believe in readiness, and one of the reasons they believe in readiness is clearly Jean Piaget's work." Yet in the discussions I have had with teachers and have seen in the literature on Piaget's discussions with teachers, his developmental findings are often cited in precisely this connection.

The argument generally goes something like this: The stages of intellectual development have been discovered across a wide variety of tasks. Furthermore, they have always emerged in a definite order; the consolidation of activity and knowledge at one stage is clearly a prerequisite for the progression to activity and knowledge at the next. Since the base of the stages *is* so broad, since one stage *is* the prerequisite for the next, and finally, since the child must actively restructure his world at each stage *for himself,* one should therefore not try to lead the child too much. The best that a school can hope to do is to offer an environment that maximizes readiness-related experience; then, when the child appears to be ready, the teacher can introduce him to those activities that will produce the desired learning. "We can get more mileage from five minutes of teaching at this time than from five hours of teaching before he is ready" is the kind of argument put forward by proponents of readiness.

However, once again, arguments using Piaget to support a laissez faire approach should not be accepted uncritically. Ironically, one can uncover exactly the same unsupported assumption in them as is present in the arguments of those who advocate acceleration. That the achievements of one stage normally depend on massive general experience is probably true. That the achievements of one stage are prerequisite for those of the next stage may also be true. One can even assert the opposite of that which is claimed by those who have developed Piagetian curricula: that the school cannot provide a program which is much superior to normal general experience from an intellectual point of view. However, even if one assumes all three of these propositions, it does not follow that one should avoid teaching a child some specific subject (for example, reading) until he has reached a certain developmental stage—unless one also assumes that some general level of intellectual development is vital to achievement in this subject. And, as I have mentioned already, there is really no strong evidence either way on this point.

Given the pressures inherent in our present system—the stigma and frustration, for example, that are attached to not being able to read until grade five—it would seem that the greatest short-term payoff for our children would be to adopt a chain of reasoning something like this: If some children do not appear "ready" to profit from our current teaching methods, let us not stigmatize them by waiting four years to teach them. Let us find out what specific skills they can be taught so that they *will* be able to profit from our methods. Either that or change the methods.

Justification for Activity-Learning and Self-Discovery Approaches

A fourth use to which Piaget's theory has been put is similar to the third, in that it is not easy to demonstrate and also represents an attempt to justify a teaching method in which—perhaps for other reasons—people already believe. Since early in the century, "progressive" educators have believed that children should learn from their own spontaneous activity, that they should discover facts about the world for themselves, and that education should not be some tight little ticky-tacky compartment set off from the rest of children's experience. Renewed life has been added to this philosophy recently, with student unrest, with liberal criticism of our mechanized, uncreative way of life, with the advent of open plan schools, and so on. One of the bodies of evidence to which people interested in alternative education have turned has been the work of Jean Piaget.

Their reasoning has been roughly as follows: Piaget has shown that the child's own activity is what is responsible for his intellectual development, that he has to rediscover what the adult world already knows. It is therefore a mistake to make him enter a classroom, sit down in one of five rows of eight desks per row, and absorb facts for 15 years, as though he were a blank slate. In so doing, conventional education, like conventional psychology, is employing an understanding of human knowledge that has not evolved since the time of Locke and Hume. What we should be doing is encouraging activity or discovery learning.

The only comment I would make on this point is that one must be very careful about what one means by "activity" and "discovery," and one must be very precise in one's thinking about goals, before one can come to a decision as to whether Piaget's work is even relevant to this argument. Piaget's point, as has been stressed by Vinh Bang (his colleague most closely connected with education), is that when school children do learn something that really becomes a part of their view of the world or their way of thinking, it is by internalized activity. In the early years this activity must have a concrete base, but, nevertheless, it is still internalized, i.e., thinking. This would certainly imply that if one's goal was to produce such learning, one should not merely talk to young children or have them recite rules. However, this probably happens (even in traditional schools) much less often than liberal educators think. Teachers have got the message that rote learning is not the most desirable kind. Rote learning is not at issue.

What is at issue is whether, by setting tasks for children, especially tasks that are done at desks and in which the goal is not to discover something but to demonstrate or apply it, one can really bring about this sort of "constructive" mental activity—whether one can get the child to rediscover what one has just told him and to make it a part of himself.

What is at issue is not the *nature* of thought, which would certainly appear to be active, but whether children can genuinely be stimulated to think about being left on their own, taken to the zoo, told to choose a project, or asked to discover a principle. My suspicion is that they *can* be stimulated to think and that this is what good traditional schools have always attempted to do. However, what is needed to answer this sort of question is a Piaget-type study about concepts that are taught in school rather than concepts that are never taught in school.

Even if this type of study were conducted, however, the implications for education would not be automatic. Let us suppose it was discovered that a proper mix of didactic instruction and interaction with concrete props produced a greater amount of mental activity and a greater depth of conceptual understanding than an activity or discovery method. This finding could still not be used as sufficient evidence to argue that traditional methods are more desirable than progressive ones. A question of desirability like this—like the one about IQ tests—simply cannot be answered purely on the basis of psychological investigations. All that can be shown is that A does or does not produce X, not whether X is or is not desirable. It could well be, for example, that although a discovery method turned out to be inferior at eliciting scientific understanding, it might nevertheless be more desirable than a lecture method from other viewpoints—perhaps motivation, recall after 30 years, training in independent work, absence of anxiety, sense of controlling one's own destiny, and so on. And these other standpoints might well be more important to parents, students, and teachers alike than scientific understanding.

Questions of desirability do not depend only on empirical facts about their consequences. They also depend on value judgments about the desirability of those consequences. And one simply cannot ask psychology—or, for that matter, science—to make these value judgments for one.

Summary

The research and theory of Jean Piaget takes as its point of departure the philosophy of Immanuel Kant—in particular, Kant's proposition that some knowledge of the world is universal and inborn in the human species and not stamped in by sensation. Piaget has shown that, while a certain kind of knowledge is indeed universal, it is not present at birth but is, rather, constructed in a series of stages over the course of the first 16 years of human life. Piaget has also theorized that the mental process through which these stages are achieved is a highly active one, with origins in the first reflexes that the human infant exhibits.

Since one of the universal functions of education is to ensure that the younger generation does not lose the knowledge and perspective that the older generation went to so much trouble to acquire, it would be hard to argue that any theory related to the nature of that knowledge or the processes by which it is acquired could be dismissed as irrelevant. However, what I have attempted to show is that most of the current "applications" of Piaget's work actually go a good deal beyond what he has established empirically, or even what he has theorized. At a deeper level, most of them depend for their justification on an additional set of assumptions, which are either untested as yet, or inherently untestable.

Determinants of Intellectual Growth in Women
David Lynn

This paper postulates that the intellectual development of women is based on an interaction of: (1) biologically-rooted potentials which predispose women toward some roles more than others; (2) parent-child relationships, seemingly inherent in the typical family pattern, which predispose toward certain cognitive styles; and (3) both blatant and subtle cultural reinforcement of traditional feminine-role prescriptions. It also suggests areas of research for improving the quality of the education of girls and women.

But why should the education of females be singled out for special consideration when girls average higher grades than boys throughout the school years?[1] True, the gap in grades between boys and girls gradually narrows toward high school graduation; even so, if grades were the only criterion there would be little justification for giving special attention to the education of females.

Nevertheless, there are a number of reasons for concern. Grades are not always a valid measure of actual scholastic achievement: girls receive better grades than boys even in subjects in which boys score higher on

[1] Eleanor E. Maccoby, "Sex Differences in Intellectual Functioning," in *The Development of Sex Differences* (Stanford, Calif.: Stanford University Press, 1966), pp. 27–28.

Reprinted, with deletions, from *School Review* 80, no. 2 (February 1972):241–60, by permission of the author and the University of Chicago Press. Copyright © 1972 by The University of Chicago.

standard achievement tests.[2] For another, males, on the average, score higher than females in measures of comprehension, verbal reasoning, mathematical reasoning, mechanical aptitude, and analytic and problem-solving ability. There is small comfort in the superiority of females in measures of verbal fluency, correct language use, spelling, articulation, manual dexterity, perceptual speed, clerical skills, and rote memory.[3]

Most people would agree that the skills in which males surpass females are those essential to scientific, technical, professional, and administrative excellence. On all measures of abilities there is considerable overlap in distribution of scores between the two sexes, but sex differences are substantial in some aspects of analytic ability, in mathematical reasoning, and in mechanical aptitude.[4] In addition to surpassing females in measures of high-level intellectual operations, males also surpass them in almost every aspect of actual intellectual achievement—books and articles written, artistic productivity, and scientific achievement.[5] . . .

My position, to be discussed in more detail later, is that conditions have changed, that producing and rearing children can no longer be the sole basis for the meaningful existence of women.

Certainly women are superbly qualified by nature and reinforced by nurture to produce and care for babies. If such functions were not bred into the species and supported by social institutions, this animal would not have survived. In addition to the obvious biological capacities to give birth and to nurse, there appear to be other potentials which predispose women toward some roles more than others, potentials not only biologically rooted but reinforced and institutionalized by cultural prescriptions. There are sex differences, seemingly biologically based (e.g., they appear in earliest infancy), that should contribute to keeping the female closer to the nest than the male. Staying near the nest seems functional both for child care and for protecting against attrition of females, the less-expendable sex for the survival of the species. Her smaller size, lesser muscle mass, lower metabolism and energy level, and less restless and vigorous overt activity should make her more likely than the male to remain near the nest. The greater restless and vigorous overt activity of the male occurs in such early infancy that it seems clearly biologically based. . . . The lower pain threshold and greater tactile sensitivity of the female from birth on should discourage her from venturing out where

[2] E. S. Carter, "How Invalid Are Marks Assigned by Teachers?" *Journal of Educational Psychology* 43 (1952):218–28; J. S. Coleman, *The Adolescent Society* (Glencoe, Ill.: Free Press, 1961); E. H. Hanson, "Do Boys Get a Square Deal in School?" *Education* 79 (1959):597–98.

[3] Josef E. Garai and Amram Scheinfeld, "Sex Differences in Mental and Behavioral Traits," *Genetic Psychology Monographs* 77 (1968):169–299.

[4] Maccoby, "Sex Differences in Intellectual Functioning," p. 28.

[5] Ibid., p. 66.

she might expose herself to painful stimuli.[6] Her lesser interest in novel or highly variable stimuli, evident as early as five months of age, should also reduce the temptation to explore.[7] A woman's interest in people, essential for raising babies, had its origin when she herself was in the cradle. At the age of 12 weeks, girls looked longer at *photographs* of faces than at schematic line drawings of normal or distorted faces, whereas boys failed to discriminate between these stimuli.[8] By 24 weeks, boys paid more attention to geometric forms than to faces, whereas girls preferred photographs or drawings of human faces.[9] Girls also vocalized more to the faces than to the forms; boys vocalized equally to each.[10] . . .

Most cultures reinforce those potentials which would keep females at home—by training in nurturance, responsibility, and obedience, and allotting women tasks at or near home that minister to the needs of others and involve responsible discharge of established routines rather than high-level skills.[11] In the past it may have been functional for survival of the species to keep women docile, subservient, at home, and pregnant. Today, however, a new adaptation may be demanded for the species to thrive. With the population explosion, having more children than needed for simple replacement of one generation by the next may stigmatize a woman rather than symbolize biological fulfillment. As a result of medical progress, a woman should have many vigorous years ahead after she has produced and raised those children necessary for replacement. By the time they are 35 or 40, for many women the responsibilities of motherhood consume only a fraction of their energies, leaving them relatively free for other pursuits. Our society has generated few (if any) roles for either men or women that offer prestige and fulfillment other than vocational ones, barren as work can sometimes be. So it would seem that society must confer prestige on women as well as men for work, since women can find only partial fulfillment through producing and rearing

[6] Garai and Scheinfeld, "Sex Differences in Mental and Behavioral Traits," p. 191.

[7] See William J. Meyers and Gordon N. Cantor, "Infants' Observing and Heart Period Responses as Related to Novelty of Visual Stimuli," *Psychonomic Science* 5 (1966):239–40; Anne H. Stevenson and David B. Lynn, "Preference for High Variability in Young Children," *Psychonomic Science* 23 (1971):143–44.

[8] Michael Lewis, Helen Campbell, B. Bartels, and D. Fadel, "Infants' Responses to Facial Stimuli during the First Year of Life" (Paper delivered at the American Psychological Association, Chicago, September 3, 1965).

[9] Michael Lewis, Jerome Kagan, and John Kalafat, "Patterns of Fixation in the Young Infant," *Child Development* 37 (1966):331–41.

[10] Jerome Kagan, "Continuity in Cognitive Development during the First Year," *Merrill-Palmer Quarterly* 15 (1969):101–19.

[11] Herbert Barry III, Margaret K. Bacon, and Irving L. Child, "A Cross-cultural Survey of Some Sex Differences in Socialization," *Journal of Abnormal and Social Psychology* 55 (1957):327–32.

children. It also seems obviously unfunctional to restrict opportunities for productive contributions to society for women who are prepared to contribute, want to, and *need* to.

Society has a long way to go in adapting to these new demands. There are biases in vocational counseling, prejudice against hiring women for responsible positions, discriminatory promotion practices, lower pay for women doing the same jobs as men, and many other barriers, including inflexible schedules and inadequate day-care facilities which make it difficult for women with children to further their education or to work. Even if the nation were not legally and morally committed to equal opportunity for all its people, it could be damaging to the fabric of society itself, not simply unsatisfying to women, for them to face years without a meaningful role. One can imagine all kinds of mischief resulting in addition to an unwelcome and destructive overinvestment of mothers in their children.[12] If the Women's Liberation movement did not exist, society would have to invent one to help awaken the nation to the necessity of undertaking the new adaptations demanded of it.

Feminine Identification and Learning Style

Let us hypothesize ways in which nature contributes to the process of acquiring feminine identification to produce a style of thinking and learning for females which differs measurably from that of males. We have already described sex differences appearing early in infancy, suggesting a biological origin. That biological differences could, in theory, underlie sex differences in style of thinking and learning is suggested by the fact that differences have been reported in almost every physical variable, including body build, anatomical characteristics, physiological functioning, biochemical composition,[13] and even in the structure and function of areas of the brain itself.[14] But postulating biological differences underlying at least some of the sex differences in style of thinking and learning is not meant to minimize the powerful forces operating in family interaction, and in the culture as a whole; to foster masculine and feminine role differentiation. Sex differences in style of thinking are postulated as multidetermined.

An almost universal experience in the human condition is that of the mother as the primary caretaker of the infant. The first and principal

12 Bruno Bettelheim, "Women: Emancipation Is Still to Come," *New Republic,* November 7, 1964, pp. 48–58.

13 Anne Anastasi, *Differential Psychology* (New York: Macmillan, 1958), p. 462.

14 See H. Lansdell, "A Sex Difference in Effect of Temporal-Lobe Neurosurgery on Design Preference," *Nature* 194 (1962):852; and "Sex Differences in Hemispheric Asymmetries in the Human Brain," ibid., 203 (1964):550.

person to whom the baby forms an attachment is usually the mother.[15] *It is hypothesized that both male and female infants also usually establish their initial and principal identification (as contrasted with attachment) with the mother.* Initially, she is the principal person on whom they model themselves, so that they internalize some of her characteristics and often react in a fashion similar to her without being aware of doing so. This almost universal condition of the mother as the major caretaker demands that the boy make a shift from his initial identification with her to identification with the masculine role, while no shift is demanded of the girl. In our culture, certainly, the girl has the same-sex parental model for identification (the mother) with her more than the boy has the same-sex model (the father) with him. Much incidental learning which she can apply directly in her life results from the girl's contact with her mother. We tend to assimilate characteristics of those with whom we associate, whether motivated to do so or not. In the absence of his father and male models, a masculine role is spelled out for the boy, often by his mother and women teachers. Through reinforcement of the culture's highly developed system of rewards for typical masculine-role behavior and punishment for signs of femininity, the boy's early-learned identification with the mother weakens. The latter-learned identification with a culturally defined, stereotyped masculine role is impressed upon this weakened mother identification. This leads to another hypothesis: *Males tend to identify with a culturally defined masculine role, whereas females tend to identify with their mothers.*

We suggest that the task of achieving these separate kinds of identification for each sex requires separate methods of learning. These separate identification tasks seem to parallel the two kinds of learning tasks differentiated by Woodworth and Schlosberg—the *problem* and the *lesson.*[16] With a problem to master, the learner must explore the situation and determine the goal before his task becomes clear; with a lesson, exploration and goal seeking are omitted or minimized, as when someone is instructed to memorize a poem or a list of nonsense syllables or to examine pictures and recognize them later. The female's task of achieving mother identification is considered roughly parallel to the learning *lesson,* and the task of achieving masculine-role identification for the male is considered roughly parallel to the learning *problem.*

We can assume that finding the goal *does* constitute a major problem for the boy in acquiring the masculine role. When the boy begins to be aware that he does not belong in the same sex category as the mother, he

---

[15] H. Rudolph Schaffer and Peggy E. Emerson, "The Development of Social Attachments in Infancy," *Monographs of the Society for Research in Child Development* 29, no. 3 (1964).

[16] Robert S. Woodworth and Harold Schlosberg, *Experimental Psychology* (New York: Henry Holt & Co., 1954), p. 529.

must then find the proper sex-role identification goal. Hartley[17] says of the boy's identification problem that the desired behavior is seldom defined positively as something he *should* do, but usually negatively, as something he should *not* do, and that includes any behavior that people regard as "sissy." The boy must learn to set the masculine role as his goal from these largely negative admonishments sometimes made by women and often without the benefit of the presence of a male model during most of his waking hours. He must also restructure the admonishments, often negatively made and given in many contexts, in order to abstract the principles defining the masculine role. He is assisted in his quest by his high energy level, his vigor, and his curiosity, all probably biologically rooted.

It is assumed, on the other hand, that finding the goal does not constitute a major problem for the girl in learning her mother-identification lesson. Since the girl, unlike the boy, need not shift from the initial mother identification, and since she typically has the mother with her a relatively larger proportion of the time, it is postulated that the question of the object of identification (the mother) seldom arises for the girl. Remember, we have postulated biologically based mechanisms which increase the likelihood that the girl will remain at home much of the time, increasing the probability of her modeling the mother. She learns the mother-identification lesson in the context of an intimate personal relation with the mother, largely by imitation but also through parental behavior selectively reinforcing her mother-similar tendencies. Similarly, abstracting the principles that define the mother role is not considered a problem for girls, since any bit of behavior on the mother's part is of potential importance in learning the mother-identification lesson. The girl needs to learn, not principles defining the feminine role, but, rather, an identification with her specific mother. . . .

It is in the context of a close personal relationship with the mother that the girl learns the mother-identification lesson. This process is reinforced by appropriate rewards for signs that she is learning this lesson. Since she is rewarded in the context of the personal relationship with her mother, she should become highly motivated to maintain this relationship. By generalization, a strong need for affiliation should develop in other learning situations. This need is thought to be superimposed on an existing preference for faces over other visual stimuli, which emerges in early infancy. The boy has fewer opportunities than the girl to receive rewards for modeling himself after the adult male in a close personal relationship. His rewards result from learning the appropriate principles of masculine-role identification as they are abstracted from many contexts. Therefore, the need for affiliation in learning situations does not

---

[17] Ruth E. Hartley, "Sex-Role Pressures and the Socialization of the Male Child," *Psychological Reports* 5 (1959):458.

become as strong for him. The lesser need for affiliation is consistent with his early failure to differentiate a preference for faces over other stimuli. . . .

Since girls do not have to shift identification from the mother, they are not motivated by their identification task to assert themselves as vigorously as is necessary for boys. From the earliest age boys are described as more vigorous, restless, and aggressive than girls. It is not surprising, then, that *in learning situations females often show greater docility, passive acceptance, and dependence,*[18] and that in motor tasks, where one has to react with speed to various stimuli, *they show a "reactive response set" whereas males show an "active response set."*[19] That is, women seem to wait for the appearance of a stimulus before they prepare to respond, whereas men seem to have a motor-response set available for instantaneous reaction prior to the appearance of a stimulus, whatever it may be.

In learning to identify with the mother, the girl may find that any bit of behavior on the mother's part might be of potential importance. The mother-identification lesson does not require the girl to restructure the situation or abstract principles of femininity, but, rather, to learn the lesson as presented. She is thereby gaining practice in lesson learning that is not available to the male, who is struggling to solve the masculine-role identification problem. Therefore *females surpass males in rote memory*. Indeed, females generally surpass males in rote memory demanding exact repetition of a group of digits, the copying of geometric figures or pictures from memory immediately after presentation, and the recitation of a story, a paragraph, or a poem read to or by them.[20]

Physiologically, girls mature faster than boys. There is an earlier maturation of the speech organs and probably an earlier maturation of the cortical structures relevant to speech, so it is not surprising that girls talk sooner than boys. There is much evidence that the amount of contact between a child and adults enhances the language development of the child. We have presented arguments supporting the proposition that girls spend more time with the mother than boys do and experience more verbal interaction with her. We have also developed the proposition that from an early age they have a greater interest in people than boys have.

[18] See Garai and Scheinfeld, "Sex Differences in Mental and Behavioral Traits"; Laberta A. Hatwick, "Sex Differences in Behavior of Nursery School Children," *Child Development* 8 (1957):343–55; Herman A. Witkin, H. B. Lewis, M. Hertzman, K. Machover, P. B. Meissner, and S. Wapner, *Personality through Perception* (New York: Harper & Row, 1954).

[19] See F. M. Henry, "Influence of Motor and Sensory Sets on Reaction Latency and Speed of Discrete Movements," *Research Quarterly of the American Association of Health and Physical Education* 31 (1960):359–68; and "Stimulus Complexity, Movement Complexity, Age, and Sex in Relation to Reaction Latency and Speed in Limb Movements," ibid., 32 (1961):353–66.

[20] Leona E. Tyler, *The Psychology of Human Differences* (New York: Appleton-Century-Crofts, 1965), p. 246.

It follows that *females surpass males in verbal fluency and language use.*[21] This is not to say that they surpass males in verbal reasoning and vocabulary; in fact, the reverse is true. Vocabulary is related to curiosity and a wide range of experiences, both more common among males. Verbal reasoning relates to problem-solving skills, which we have postulated to favor males also. Females do surpass males in verbal fluency, correct language use, sentence complexity, grammatical structure, spelling, and articulation. Their verbal skills seem to be utilized more in the service of affiliative motives than in the solution of problems other than interpersonal ones. Their more personal use of speech was found in a study showing that women used more words implying feeling, emotion, or motivation, and made more references to the self, whereas men used a greater number of words implying time, space, quantity, and destructive action. These sex differences, however, tended to disappear in the higher ranges of intelligence.[22] . . .

In the process of solving the masculine-role identification problem, the male acquires a cognitive style that should be applicable in solving other problems. It is hypothesized that he is thereby accumulating practice in problem solving. On the other hand, the feminine cognitive style deriving from the process of learning the mother-identification lesson, is not well geared to problem solving. Consequently, *females are surpassed by males in problem-solving skills.* Sweeny reported studies that support this proposition, including experiments of his own demonstrating that men solve certain classes of problems with greater facility than women do, even when differences in intellectual aptitude, special knowledge or training, and special abilities are controlled.[23] In general, the results confirmed the hypothesis that sex differences will favor men in problems that involve difficulties in restructuring (i.e., discarding the first approach and reorganizing the task in a new way), but not in similar problems that involve no such difficulties. Another study found that female college students were surpassed by male students in problem solving even when the characteristics of the problems were altered so that they were inappropriate for the male but appropriate for the female role (e.g., cooking or sewing). Moreover, the male superiority was not reduced by giving both males and females a chance to warm up and become familiar with the material.[24] On the other hand, Milton had previously found that al-

---

[21] Garai and Scheinfeld, "Sex Differences in Mental and Behavioral Traits," pp. 198–200.

[22] Goldine C. Gleser, L. A. Gottschalk, and J. Watkins, "The Relationship of Sex and Intelligence to Choice of Words: A Normative Study of Verbal Behavior," *Journal of Clinical Psychology* 15 (1959):182–91.

[23] Edward J. Sweeny, "Sex Differences in Problem Solving" (technical report no. 1, Department of Psychology, Stanford University, Stanford, Calif., 1953).

[24] Samuel Roll, "Sex Differences in Problem Solving as a Function of Content and Order of Presentation," *Psychonomic Science* 19 (1970):97.

tering the content to make it more feminine did reduce male superiority but did not eliminate it.[25] . . .

Cultural Reinforcement of Traditional Femininity

. . . The pervasive patriarchal foundation of society is an example of a cultural reinforcement of traditional feminine-role prescriptions. Brown noted that the superior position and privileged status of the male permeates nearly every aspect of our lives, from the prizes in boxes of breakfast cereal to God as "Father" rather than "Mother."[26] The double standard of sexuality has by no means disappeared, nor has lower pay for the same job, nor stereotypes about what is appropriate woman's work.[27] Advertising presents a demeaning image of a childishly sexy housewife, apprehensive lest husband reject her coffee, and the children her cookies. It is not surprising that in one study[28] both men and women, *especially* the women, rated men as more worthwhile than women, and in another study[29] both boys and girls with increasing age had a better opinion of boys and a worse opinion of girls. Goldberg demonstrated women's contempt for their own capabilities when he asked them to rate the scholarship in an essay signed, alternately, John McKay and Joan McKay.[30] Women generally agreed that John's article was scholarly and Joan's was commonplace, although it was the same article.

Feminine-role prescriptions are reinforced in the family. Girls are treated less permissively than boys and more conformity is demanded of them. . . . The American father, even more than the mother, encourages his daughter to behave in a feminine way, even when she is still a preschooler.[31]

Reinforcement of the traditional feminine role pervades our schools, from the image of females presented in school readers to discriminatory vocational counseling. When Child, Potter, and Levin analyzed the content of third-grade readers, they found that girls and women are shown

[25] G. Alexander Milton, "Sex Differences in Problem Solving as a Function of Role Appropriateness of the Problem Content," *Psychological Reports* 5 (1959): 705–8.

[26] Daniel G. Brown, "Sex-Role Development in a Changing Culture," *Psychological Bulletin* 54 (1958):232–42.

[27] Kate Millett, *Sexual Politics* (Garden City, N.Y.: Doubleday, 1970), pp. 39–40.

[28] John P. McKee and Alex C. Sherriffs, "The Differential Evaluation of Males and Females," *Journal of Personality* 25 (1957):356–71.

[29] S. Smith, "Age and Sex Differences in Children's Opinion Concerning Sex Differences," *Journal of Genetic Psychology* 54 (1939):17–25.

[30] Philip Goldberg, "Are Women Prejudiced against Women?" *Transaction* 5 (April 1968):28–30.

[31] Evelyn W. Goodenough, "Interest in Persons as an Aspect of Sex Difference in the Early Years," *Genetic Psychology Monographs* 55 (1957):287–323.

as sociable, kind, and timid, but inactive, unambitious, and uncreative.[32] The person who is nurtured is usually female, and the person who supplies information is male. Seventy-three percent of the central characters are male, leaving only 27 percent female. Cursory perusal of current readers will substantiate these findings. Teachers also give girls differential treatment. They are likely to reward girls for dependence, friendliness, and conformity, while rewarding some boys at least for autonomy, independence, and creativity.[33] The vocational counselor may be tempted to encourage girls, whatever their talents, into traditional feminine fields for their own protection against future discrimination, or because they believe the girls will probably later change their minds and marry and raise a family. In addition, girls are genuinely difficult to counsel because, compared with boys, they are unrealistic in appraisal of their abilities, so that there is essentially no relation between their scholastic achievement and intelligence and their vocational aspirations.[34]

Suggestions for Research

If social demands for conformity and passivity in girls contribute to any of the sex differences in intellectual functioning described above, research attempting to change such attitudes should result in improved intellectual performance. Surprisingly, little research of this sort has been done. One study found that men had a consistently more favorable attitude toward problem solving than women, and that group discussion aimed at improving this attitude increased the problem-solving performance of women but not of men.[35] In another study, Torrance observed that boys made many more suggestions than girls about how science toys might be used.[36] He discussed with parents and teachers how misplaced emphasis on stereotyped sex roles could interfere with later potential and advised them to encourage girls to experiment more freely

[32] Irvin L. Child, Elmer H. Potter, and Estelle M. Levin, "Children's Textbooks and Personality Development: An Exploration in the Social Psychology of Education," *Psychological Monographs* 60, no. 3 (1946), whole no. 279; Betty Miles, "Harmful Lessons Little Girls Learn in School," *Redbook*, March 1971, p. 86.

[33] See H. H. Davidson and G. Lang, "Children's Perception of Their Teachers' Feelings toward Them Related to Self-Perception, School Achievement, and Behavior," *Journal of Experimental Education* 29 (1960):107–18; Pauline S. Sears, "The Effect of Classroom Conditions on the Strength of Achievement Motive and Work Output on Elementary School Children" (final report, cooperative research project no 873, Stanford University, 1963); E. Paul Torrance, *Guiding Creative Talent* (Englewood Cliffs, N.J.: Prentice-Hall, 1962).

[34] Garai and Scheinfeld, "Sex Differences in Mental and Behavioral Traits," p. 213.

[35] Gloria L. Carey, "Sex Differences in Problem-solving Performance as a Function of Attitude Differences," *Journal of Abnormal and Social Psychology* 56 (1958):256–60.

[36] Torrance, *Guiding Creative Talent.*

with scientific toys. After this, the girls demonstrated and explained as many ideas as the boys. Other experimental procedures for overcoming the narrow definition of femininity might be: (1) introduce sections in social science on the changing role of women; (2) bring achieving women (professors, executives, scientists) into the schools in the early grades as resident scholars, leaders of seminars and workshops, etc.; (3) eradicate feminine stereotypes from school readers; and (4) have workshops geared to eliminating discrimination against females in vocational counseling.

Play for boys seems to be preparation for entering the objective, ordered, rule-regulated vocational and public life of a masculine-oriented adult world. Piaget could find not a single collective game played by girls with as many rules and with the fine and consistent organization and codification of these rules as the game of marbles for boys. Tyler observed that boys' recreational pursuits in the first grade were related to their mental ability, with brighter boys preferring paper-and-pencil games and activities. Brighter girls showed no such preference.[37] Young girls often play house; young boys engage in fantasy activities outside the house (e.g., flying airplanes and driving trains). Evidence has been accumulating that boys who want to become scientists crystallize their interest between the ages of 10 and 14,[38] and one can only assume that their play often influences their choice. With all this in mind, research might be done to test the effects of encouraging changes in the play of girls to foster greater preparation for the vocational and public life of adults, including both broader interests and the objective reciprocity which comes from applying rules in collective games.

There are some changes which might be introduced into experimental classrooms to test their effectiveness in enhancing intellectual functioning in girls. Teachers could reward rote memorization and superficial language skills less and teach and construct tests so that grades depend more on thought. When the girl starts to school she is in advance of boys in many ways, including language development, and her greater success with rote responses and superficial language skills in the early grades may so habituate these responses that it is difficult for her to switch when more thought is required later. Why not demand thought at the appropriate level of complexity in every grade so that children do not become "spoiled by success" in superficial tasks? In addition, more attention might be given to classroom discussion on the cognitive styles of prob-

[37] See Jean Piaget, *The Moral Judgment of the Child* (New York: Free Press, 1965), p. 77; Leona Tyler, "The Relationship of Interests to Ability and Reputation among First-Grade Children," *Educational and Psychological Measurement* 11 (1951):255–64.

[38] Garai and Scheinfeld, "Sex Differences in Mental and Behavioral Traits," p. 260.

lem solving, such as breaking a set; that is, to approach a problem in a new way when the first approach proves unproductive.

Since there is considerable overlap between the distribution of scores of the two sexes in all measures of ability, a simple solution suggests itself; just group students by ability. Besides the problems inherent in such groupings, however, two people may score high on the same ability but approach it with different cognitive styles. So why not group by cognitive style, the different ways by which individuals approach intellectual tasks? This is difficult because so many elements are involved. An individual may resemble another in his approach to mathematical tasks but differ in approaching verbal reasoning and other tasks. Personality also enters into styles of tackling intellectual tasks. Grouping by cognitive style, disregarding sex, is difficult also because there are systematic sex differences in cognitive style in equally capable males and females. Even so, the possibility is still open to research on grouping by an interaction of cognitive style and ability (rather than sex). The first task would be to develop genuinely sensitive and meaningful tests of cognitive styles in approaching a variety of intellectual tasks.

I flinch at the thought of "Female Mathematics" or "Female Science" in parallel to "Black," "Native American," or "Chicano History," but experimentation along these lines should not be summarily ruled out. Perhaps a more practical solution would be to try Garai and Scheinfeld's suggestion of having textbooks and teachers present to mixed classes the approach considered to be most easily understood by males *and* that considered to favor females.[39] Probably both sexes would gain, since presenting a variety of approaches to the solution of problems usually enhances learning.

There is some evidence that girls tend to be more timid and more confused by failure and criticism. A negative relationship has been found between anxiety and cognitive development in females. Experiments might be tried to raise frustration tolerance in girls, perhaps using behavior-modification approaches. Before frustration tolerance is built up, a relaxed learning atmosphere with reward for success rather than punishment for failure should facilitate learning for girls. Since impulsive, active, and even aggressive behavior may be associated with intellectual development in girls, testing the effectiveness of reinforcing (or at least not dampening) such behavior in girls seems appropriate.

In conclusion, I hope that women can add much that is uniquely theirs to our vocational and public life. I join with Erik Erikson in the wish that when women gain full participation "they will add maternal concern to the cares of world governing."[40]

[39] Ibid., p. 275.
[40] "Erik Erikson: The Quest for Identity," *Newsweek,* December 21, 1970, p. 87.

Insight: Its Nature and Its Place in Education

Ernest E. Bayles

Insight is a widely familiar term whose meanings in common usage are not strictly confined to [dictionary] . . . definitions. . . . I am, in fact, following the lead of the Gestaltists, such as Kurt Koffka, in using it as I do. Hence, as long as I take pains to specify what I mean when I use the word and thereby give my readers or hearers reasonable notification, I believe it justifiable to use insight as meaning *a sense of, or "feel" for, pattern.* Let me elaborate.

In *Pragmatism in Education* (1966), I wrote as follows:

> . . . We use it [insight] to designate whatever pattern actually is sensed, whether deeply perceptive or undiscerningly shallow. An insight may be comprehensive and widely generalized, or it may have only a single experience as referent. An insight may be true or it may be false; it may be vague or it may be clear; it may be thoughtfully derived or it may represent merely a snap judgment. It is always one's *sense of pattern, what one takes* a situation to be. It is never to be confused with any set of words that may be used in connection with it; it is what lies back of words, the meaning that words are designed to convey. Yet the word *meaning* is not quite satisfactorily interchangeable with insight. In common parlance, meaning is a word that seems to be tied too exclusively with words. One's "feeling for" or "sensing of" the weight of an object is not quite what would commonly be considered part of its meaning, yet "getting the heft" of a thing is exactly what we mean by the word *insight,* whether it is getting the heft of a table that is to be moved or "getting the run" of pragmatic thought. *Whatever sense of or feeling for pattern an individual possesses we wish to designate as his insight* (p. 19, ital. in orig.). . . .

Conveyance of an insight is not like passing an object from one person to another, for in so doing the giver no longer has it; the object is then possessed solely by the receiver. Instead, successful conveyance of an insight leaves the giver with perhaps even more than he had and the receiver with what he previously did not have. This is something that a would-be public speaker needs to comprehend fully. He must empathize

Reprinted, with deletions, from *Colorado Journal of Educational Research* 9, no. 2 (Winter 1970):14–20, by permission of the author and the publisher.

with his hearers, watching them keenly to sense what *they* are making of what he says and to keep them active and alert in the *formulation* of what he is trying to "get across." And a writer, to be successful, has first to envision his reader-audience then keep *talking to them* as he writes and in imagination watch their reactions (or actions?) to see whether they are *doing* what he is hoping they will do—"doing" in the sense of comprehending, whether they believe or agree or whether they do not and whether they are "taking it to act upon it" or whether they are not. . . .

. . . [I]t seems obvious that human behavior can be interpreted in no way other than by taking into account human goals or purposes, human surroundings, and human insights. The interpretational (or predictive) principle then is that a person will design action and attempt to carry it out in such a way as to achieve what he is wanting to achieve (goal) in the quickest and easiest way (least action) that he senses or comprehends (insights) under the circumstances (confronting situations). This is the *principle of least action,* and is experimentally or scientifically verifiable on the basis of its efficacy in enabling one (who employs it authentically) to anticipate or predict behavior with accuracy. . . .

If we posit behavior based on the three factors, goal, insight, and confronting situation, what seemingly do we have to take learning to be? When we say that a person has learned something, what do we refer to or mean? Do we mean that his goals have changed? It is indeed true that, after one has "learned a thing or two," he may modify in greater or lesser degree what he may be seeking to accomplish. If, for example, after contemplating a pleasantly quiet evening at home, my wife reminds me that this is the night for the Dean's reception, my purpose for spending the evening may radically change. But the change in purpose is not the learning; it is a *consequence* of the learning. A change in goal may be an entailment of having learned something, but the goal-change is not the matter learned. The learning is that a goal-change is necessary.

Again, the reception may have been called off—a change in the situation for the evening. If I know of the cancellation, I'll switch plans accordingly; if I do not, I'll probably go, then suffer the embarrassment of showing up where I'm not expected. In either case, it is not the change in the situation that constitutes the learning. Rather, it is my *becoming aware* of the change; the change is in my insight.

From the foregoing, it seems clear that learning must be taken as a *change in insight.* There are those who assert that learning is a change in behavior. But behavior-change may be entailed by a change in goal or a change in confronting situation, with no insight-change involved. Or behavior may change solely as an outcome of a change in insight. The point is that learning is not to be equated to or identified with a change in behavior. I am often *with* my wife, but that does not mean that I *am* my wife.

If learning is not to be taken as a change in insight, then what can it possibly be? Those who call it a change in behavior, if they have considered the matter at all, tend to have strong behaviorist or connectionist learnings. If one assumes that learning a given act or set of acts is purely the outcome of a sizeable number of repetitions, then it probably is easy to take the next step of saying that learning *is* those repetitions. But this is pretty loose thinking, even if one should be inclined to grant that exact repetition is humanly possible—which I am not. . . .

Taking learning then as change in insight, what follows? Perhaps first and foremost is the notion that *practice* is to be taken as complete denial of repetition. It is not the number of times a given action is repeated, because repetition is a biophysical impossibility. And, if it were possible, it would defeat the end sought—to make what is learned transferable, useable in myriad ways never previously employed. Hence, what constitutes practice?

Practice needs to be inventive, innovative, creative. It is not a random, Thorndikean-trial-and-error procedure. It is action that is distinctly purposive; an end is sought and ways to achieve it are tried and tested. It is basically experimental, whether virtually instantaneous or long-drawn-out. Tentativity is never relinquished; one never is deemed justified in thinking he has IT, beyond shadow of doubt.

This precipitates us into the matter of reflective thinking and reflective teaching, the latter carrying the implication of handling classes so as to promote the former. My experiences with students make it seem unavoidable to keep people from identifying learning as change in (or development of) insight with reflection, at least on first introduction. When shortly afterwards I'd ask members of my classes to tell me how to handle a class so as to develop insight, almost invariably they would describe reflective teaching.

I am, and have long been, insistent that one can develop insights *non*-reflectively as well as reflectively; that insightful practice and insightful learning *do not necessarily* promote the independent learning ability that reflective teaching means, if it means anything. I grant that Dewey wrote that "thinking is the method of an educative experience" (1916:192; 1966:163). But he immediately followed with, "The essentials of method are therefore identical with the essentials of reflection." That word "essentials" is vital. We can (and do) grant that the essentials are identical, but we must keep in mind that both explanatory and exploratory teaching can be insightful yet lead to very diverse outcomes.

In actuality, it is doubtless true that no one can learn anything except insightfully—though teachers from time immemorial seem to have done their best to keep students from doing so. Indeed, they may have had the best intentions to the contrary, but that may have made for more of a bungle rather than less.

Explanatory teaching is the kind in which the teacher, as quickly and effectually as possible, illuminates or clarifies a proposition that appears to need it. This is developing an insight, but a particular one, known beforehand by the teacher and presented to the class, not for contemplation or consideration but for acceptance and employment.

On the other hand, exploratory teaching has built into it the purpose of helping students develop not only particular insights but concomitantly promote or foster the capacity to develop insights on their own, independently. The teacher seeks to develop *independent learning ability*. Hence, though teacher-explanations can and will be admissible as occasions seem to warrant, such explanations will always be offered, not as finally authoritative pronouncements but as grist for the mill of further thought. They are brought in so as to furnish another dimension to the picture, another hypothesis which is to be evaluated along with the rest. The teacher, in explaining, does not pontificate; he illuminates. And many are the occasions in reflective teaching when the requirements of formal education make this highly desirable if not necessary. After all, in fifteen to twenty years our schools have to help students develop life outlooks that it has taken mankind as a whole twenty-five thousand years (and more) to develop.

The difference between explanatory and exploratory teaching is not in the devices employed; it is in the enveloping atmosphere, the overarching purpose, that contributes immeasurably to the overall design of instruction. The teacher, instead of being a mere purveyor of insights already possessed by him, becomes the chairman of an investigational body, responsible for seeing that the investigation moves forward to an educationally justifiable end but one that was not *fixed* in advance. In so serving, the teacher may anticipate with considerable accuracy what the end or outcome will be (he has been through it before), but he doesn't *require* it. It is the investigation itself that determines the outcome, not preconceived notions whether of teacher, of community, or of an entire culture.

Let me therefore repeat, and urge upon you, that insights may be developed both reflectively and nonreflectively. But let me add that insightful learning and learning by rote differ vitally from one another. Of course, it is perhaps impossible for anyone to learn strictly by rote, as Katona (1940) brought out long ago. He observed that, even in learning nonsense syllables, his experimental subjects either formulated some sort of pattern for the syllables or did not learn them at all. Witness the Puritan schoolmaster's device of fitting the ABC's to a tune, for the very purpose (though perhaps not consciously realized) of supplying a pattern—a musical one—by means of which the letters would become configurational. When teachers try by repetitious "drill" to make children learn, the children may finally "learn," but probably in spite of teacher rather than with her help.

As I said before, the process of learning something—of practice if you have that kind of learning situation in mind—is inventive, innovative, creative. The learner has to "get the feel" for it, which, being basically cognitive, ideational, or conceptual, tends to come in a wave of comprehension. This is the "Eureka" phenomenon—"I have it! I have it!" And, as with Archimedes, there often has to be a period of contemplation or practice beforehand. But the practice is, as Bode expressed it, a matter of "finding and testing meanings." It is not the number of times an act is performed or an idea expressed, it is the advent of *closure* that counts; of *Pragnanz,* as the German Gestaltists called it, the congealing or jelling of a comprehensive insight that causes a diversity of lesser insights to fall in place and become parts of a single, encompassing whole. Once closure is genuinely achieved, further practice serves only the functions of testing to see whether one really "has it," of making minor adjustments or trimming and smoothing off unnecessary roughness, and of developing confidence in the efficacy of one's new possession. All of this, you see, is a far cry from repetitive drill. But we must go on.

Speaking of closure, it should be noted that the advent of each and every insight is a matter of closure. But insights may be small or large, true or false, widely generalized or narrowly particular. Making a forty-cent purchase at a store, I hand two quarters to the cashier and she immediately hands me a dime in change. Insight into the single event closures at once. But the final closure on how to transplant human hearts with dependable success has not yet arrived; only partial success has come, due to closures that seemingly take into account only parts of what is needed.

What we have just noted, however, illumines the seeming nature of habit, or habit-level behavior. We can never repeat, hence habit has to be interpreted on some basis other than establishment of fixed sequences of acts. Instead, we interpret habit as any case in which a person's insight into each successive confronting situation closures instantly and accurately, so he can proceed with what he is doing without halt or hesitation. We get *a steady flow of efficacious action*—habit-level behavior. And this interpretation does indeed explain successful behavior the first time; there never is any second time.

To the question of how nervous systems work in achieving the kind of behavior we call human, the answer is that we do not know. But we do have convincing evidence that the reflex-arc concept is woefully inadequate, to say the least; in fact, it is quite misleading. Animal organisms without nervous systems behave in about the same way human beings do;

the only seemingly basic difference is in the very limited reach of their insights, a difference that is quantitative but not qualitative, and one for which we certainly do not need to posit some soul-substance or substantive-mind stuff.

For a moment, let us take a look at *transfer*—the *using* of an insight as opposed to the getting of one. And, on this matter, I expect that I can reasonably admit to having done a bit of pioneering work. Up to the thirties, considerable attention was given to what was then called "transfer of training." In our parlance, it can of course be called *transfer of insight,* for it is insights that are shifted in such ways as to enable us to use previously learned ideas so as to handle distinctly different (or novel) situations. There is no need here to review the history of thought on transfer. . . .

Our transfer theory is based on the three factors of our overall goal-insight theory, since transfer is simply one aspect or kind of human behavior. The theory is that we transfer a learned insight if and when: (a) the confronting situation offers an opportunity; (b) we sense or comprehend the possibility of its doing so; and (c) we wish or decide to take advantage of it. Thus, confronting situation, insight, and goal are taken to be at work. In the employment of this theory, it is not necessary to make the qualification, "other things being equal," because it posits all that is taken to pertain.

The failure during the past three decades to pay much if any mind to the question of transfer is, I think, due to oversight rather than to its lack of importance. The very purpose of education is to foster transfer-capacity—else, there would be no point whatever to the continuingly widespread criticism that in-school training involves little carry-over into out-of-school living. Moreover, since we never behave twice in exactly the same way, day-to-day living is nothing but transfer. Our theory of the nature of habit-level behavior is merely a slightly different way of expressing our theory of transfer; and reflection is another. It's all cut off of the same bolt of cloth.

What, then, should conscious recognition of the educational desirability of teaching for transfer require in terms of curricular offerings? Simply that the insights that accrue from them should be basically of the widely useful, transferable, generalizable variety. Every unit of instruction should be designed to foster generalizations as widely useable as the minds under instruction are maturationally able to grasp. Moreover, under properly designed instruction, capacities for generalization can be made to mature more readily and rapidly than without it. Therefore, curricula should be designed: (a) to promote development of insights that are as widely generalizable as possible or feasible; and (b) to help youngsters learn the values of widely useable, carefully authenticated generalizations. Such policy helps lift people to enhanced capacity for dealing with life on the basis of progressively higher levels of intellectual abstraction—in other words, it helps human beings become more human. And, when we incorporate also the methodology of teaching reflectively, is there any question as to the reaches of further achievement that education—both formal and informal—has the potential of accomplishing? When Robert M. Hutchins envisions a "learning society" and the education that will foster it, is he not logically bound to posit a kind of education such as this? . . .

Lastly, I'd like to take a very quick look at the proposals of two widely publicized writers as they impinge upon the present topic—those of B. F. Skinner and of Jerome S. Bruner. I feel it legitimate, and very important, to ask just what of innovation or progression these proposals embody; legitimate because neither writer registers any real acknowledgment of the two-thirds century of prior work by John Dewey and company and important because it would seem that such acknowledgment would not only support and strengthen their efforts but would likely do much to make clearer the propositions that both are sponsoring.

To put it bluntly, if Skinner's *operant conditioning* means anything, it means development of insight. Yet Skinner (1968), though expressing distrust of theory, acknowledges the priority of Thorndike's so-called "Law" of Effect and makes generous use of the connectionist terms stimulus, response, conditioning, and trial-and-error learning. . . . My feeling in that regard is that calling something operant conditioning does not help either. Where does Skinner ever define his term, or ask what is "fed back" in order to cause a subsequent act (picking up a food pellet) to reinforce a preceding one (pecking at an illuminated disc)? Even with machines, as shown by Wiener in *Cybernetics* (1948), feedback represents the conveyance of information whether by radar-scanning or by some other device. Given a goal or objective, either a mechanism or an organism must have continuous and continuing information as to goal-location or it cannot guide itself. Skinner's pigeons didn't "get the idea" the first time or the tenth but, once they got it, requisite action followed and was subsequently employed.

And, with Bruner, the "intuitive understanding" to which Chapter Four of *The Process of Education* (1960) is devoted is certainly not the intuition of philosophical "revelation." It can be nothing other than the closuring of an insight, tentatively or hypothetically held until examination can verify or disprove it (interaction?). And the whole burden of both *Process* and *Toward a Theory of Instruction* (1968) is simple recognition of the efficacy of reflective teaching. Thus, regardless of whatever other comment should be made, it seems clear that both Skinner and Bruner are in reality working on the idea of learning as development of insight. . . .

REFERENCES

Bayles, Ernest E. *Pragmatism in Education.* New York: Harper & Row, 1966.
———. *The Theory and Practice of Teaching.* Harper, 1950.
Bruner, Jerome S. *The Process of Education.* Cambridge, Mass.: Harvard University Press, 1960.
———. *Toward a Theory of Instruction.* Cambridge, Mass.: Harvard University Press, Belknap, 1966. Available in paperback (New York: W. W. Norton, 1968).
Dewey, John. *Democracy and Education.* New York: Macmillan, 1916. Available in paperback (New York: Free Press, 1966).
Hutchins, Robert M. *The Learning Society.* New York: Praeger, 1968.
Katona, George. *Organizing and Memorizing.* New York: Columbia University Press, 1940.
Skinner, B. F. *The Technology of Teaching.* New York: Appleton-Century-Crofts, 1968.
Wiener, Norbert. *Cybernetics; or Control and Communication in the Animal and the Machine.* New York: Wiley, 1948.

A Relativistic Definition of Stimulus-Response

Morris L. Bigge

Stimulus and response are terms which have become deeply embedded in the vocabulary and the ideas of educational psychology. In recent years the ideas represented by these words often have been made to correspond to the concepts of cause and effect as used in the physical sciences. Psychologists, in their attempt to avoid assumption of any metaphysical purposiveness, have posited a mechanistic behavior devoid of purpose in any sense, teleological or otherwise.

Current mechanistic educational psychology shows the influence of attempts to derive directed activities without assuming directed dynamic factors in human behavior. Behaviorists and connectionists have attempted by means of concepts, such as "goal gradient" or "law of effect," to recognize directed factors in behavior without surrendering a basically mechanistic position. Inasmuch as it is coming to be generally recog-

Reprinted, with deletions, from *Journal of Educational Psychology* 46 (December 1955):457–63, by permission of the author and the American Psychological Association. Copyright © 1955 by the American Psychological Association.

nized, in educational psychology, that an atomistic stimulus-response idea is not adequate for describing human behavior, the tendency of many contemporary psychologists who continue to hold to a mechanistic outlook is to speak of "molar behavior" and of "total responses to patterns of stimulation." Educational psychologists may recognize behavior as molar, speak of situations and patterns of response, and emphasize "belongingness"; yet, as long as they maintain their allegiance to some modern version of associationism such as behaviorism or connectionism, they are clinging to a frame of reference fundamentally different from, and incompatible with, that of a truly relativistic field-theoretical approach. . . .

A prevalent current practice among educators of defining learning as change in behavior reflects or implies mechanistic definitions of stimulus and response. Observable *results* or *outcomes* of learning are interpreted to be the actual learning. It is true that when a person has learned or is learning, his behavior probably changes. However, it does not follow that, for learning to take place, there must be an observable change in behavior. Change of behavior is an indication that learning has been or is taking place, but the change of behavior is not the learning. Learning is more adequately defined as development of insight or understanding. . . .

A relativistic field theory differs from any mechanistic theory of human behavior in that it assumes that intelligent behavior is purposeful. This assumption, however, is accompanied by no attempt to assert or deny existence of teleological forces. It simply means that a person, behaving intelligently, acts as if he were trying to do something; and that, if one is to predict accurately what a person will do in a given situation, he must envision what that person is trying to do. . . .

A relativist in educational psychology assumes that intelligent human action is purposive and must be interpreted in light of the goals it is designed to achieve. An individual acts in such a way as to achieve his goal or goals—satisfy his wants or desires—in the quickest and easiest way that he comprehends or senses as possible under existing conditions. When a person behaves intelligently, he acts as if he is pursuing a purpose and as if he has some foresight as to how the purpose is to be achieved. When one has a purpose, he displays a capacity to refer present conditions to future results, as well as future consequences to present conditions.

Man's ability in abstraction and conceptualization enables him to define his purposes symbolically, through use of articulate speech. When a person is motivated toward doing something, his description of the situation is that he wants or desires to do it. He consciously carries activity forward to a goal through a process within which he constantly searches out conditions for the next step, all along the way. Moreover, a relativist who takes his relativism seriously sees continuity in the nature of learning throughout the animal kingdom. He observes purposefulness of behavior in adults, in children, and in lower animals, each on his own intellectual level. . . .

A relativist, in defining psychological terms such as stimulus and response, assumes a bipolar relationship of person and environment. Instead of thinking of an environment (stimuli) impinging upon a physical organism, he assumes that in any situation a person acts in accordance with the psychological field which he perceives. This field is not defined in "objective," physicalistic terms, but in the way it exists for a person at a given time. A thing is perceived only as a relationship among an object, a viewer, and the background of the situation. In a psychological field, rather than passive behavior as a mechanistic response to an activating environmental factor called a stimulus, there is postulated an actively interactive experience—conscious behavior. Experience consists of a person trying something and simultaneously undergoing or noting the consequences of his attempt. "To 'learn from experience' is to make a backward and forward connection between what we do to things and what we enjoy or suffer from things in consequences" (Dewey, 1916).

Interaction is a popular term in current treatises on educational theory. When one searches for an incisive definition of the concept he finds that, in describing person-environment relationships, the word is used in two quite different senses. It may be used to denote a passive process within which a person or an organism is stimulated or modified by the environment and, in turn, the environment is modified by the organism. Each, organism and environment, is assumed to be passive while it is being acted upon by the other; e.g., a man is bitten by a dog, then the dog is kicked by the man. A stimulus from an object impinges on the end organs of a passive organism. The organism then responds. The temporal sequence is stimulus-organism-response. Since it is recognized that a human organism can modify its environment—change something outside of itself—the process within which the environment influences is called interaction or the interactive process.

Interaction has been used in a second (relativistic) sense by John Dewey and others to describe a process in which a person actively appraises his environment as contrasted with his being passively stimulated by it. "An experience is always what it is because of a transaction taking place between an individual and what, at the time, constitutes his environment" (Dewey, 1938:41). One's environment consists of those conditions which interact with personal needs, desires, purposes, and capacities to create the present experience. Experience includes an active and a passive element peculiarly combined. "On the active hand, experience is *trying*. . . . On the passive, it is *undergoing*. When we experience something we act upon it, we do something with it; then we suffer or undergo the consequences. We do something to the thing, then it does something to us in return: such is the peculiar combination. The connection of these two phases of experience measures the fruitfulness or value of the experience. Mere activity does not constitute experience" (Dewey, 1916).

The concept of active interaction in experience involves a description of situations. For a person to live in a world he must live in a series of situations. One experiences through acting and perceiving the consequences of his acts. Every experience both takes up something from those experiences which have gone before and modifies in some way the quality of the experiences which follow. It influences in some degree the objective conditions under which future experiences are had. When a child learns a thing, he determines to some extent the environment in which he will act in the future. . . .

A relativist, taking available data into consideration and harmonizing it to the best of his ability, concludes that a concept of active interactions is highly fruitful in a scientific study of human behavior. He recognizes that there are incidents in which one is passively influenced by an object from outside his organism; e.g., when a man not cognizant of any danger is shot from the back. However, whenever there is intelligent behavior, active interaction is highly descriptive of the situation. One cannot derive behavior teleologically from the future, neither can one derive it from the past. A psychological event is always a result of the interaction of many factors and is to be explained in terms of apparent relations.

Psychological person and psychological environment function as sub-wholes of a psychological, contemporaneous field or life-space. If stimulus and response are to be retained as descriptive terms in this frame of reference, stimulus suggests environment-centeredness whereas response refers to the functioning of cognitive and manipulative abilities of a person.

A relativist does not insist on discarding the terms, stimulus and response; neither, however, does he use them in the mechanistic sense of their origin. Behavior, for him, is not a passive response to an activating environmental factor called a stimulus. He sees little basis for assuming that "a crucial interval of delay occurs" (Cole and Bruce, 1950:53) between the psychological stimulus and the psychological response. He redefines stimulus and response to mark a distinction within a larger field. Since an entire field operates as a unit, stimulus and response cannot be separated from each other temporally; they can be contrasted only in terms of function. To repeat, for a stimulus to be a stimulus a response must be going on. One does not first see objects and then respond to them—he sees objects in terms of the response he makes to them. "The reason why we speak of a stimulus at all is that the coordination or situation is *inadequate;* there is a drive or pressure towards a better coordination or adaptation. The stimulus is that phase of the situation which requires to be made more definite or explicit; the response is constituted by the reactions which create the need for a more adequate determination of the conditions for further activity. A stimulus, then, is a stimulus, in a psychological sense, only as long as there is this need of greater definiteness. When this definiteness is achieved, there is no longer any purposiveness at this point; the resultant action becomes an element in the next coordination" (Bode, 1940:230). Events such as seeing and hearing take place because, already, action is going on. The response is not a consequence of a sensory experience but is an antecedent or condition of it. Thus the reflex-arc hypothesis, in which the activity is a pure sequence, seems inadequate to explain intelligent human activity.

Stimulus and response, insofar as they are related to intelligent behavior, operate concurrently and simultaneously. In any perceptual situation, the whole field, including the organism, is actively interactive from the start. The existence of neural couplings need be neither affirmed nor denied. The point is that the concept of couplings or connections is inadequate for describing the function of learning in the most fruitful manner. There is a certain definite set of the motor apparatus involved in hearing just as much as there is in subsequent running away. Movement and posture of the head and tension of the ear muscles are required for "reception" of a sound. It is just as true to say that a sensation of sound arises from a motor response as that running away is a response to a sound.

When behavior is viewed mechanistically it is assumed that a stimulus merely activates or starts an activity of an organism, whereas, if intelligent behavior is assumed to be purposive, a stimulus undergoes continuous reconstruction throughout the whole course of the activity. A stimulus is a continually changing directive factor—directive in the sense of acting as a tool for achieving a goal. It changes cooperatively with the organic response as a person progresses toward his goals.

REFERENCES

Bode, Boyd H. *How We Learn*. Boston: D. C. Heath, 1940.
Cole, Lawrence E., and William F. Bruce. *Educational Psychology*. Chicago: World Book, 1950.
Dewey, John. *Democracy and Education*. New York: Macmillan, 1916.
————. *Experience and Education*. New York: Macmillan, 1938.

Regarding Learning and Its Facilitation

Carl Rogers

Here are a number of the principles which can, I believe, be abstracted from current experience and research related to this newer approach:

1. *Human beings have a natural potentiality for learning.* They are curious about their world, until and unless this curiosity is blunted by their experience in our educational system. They are ambivalently eager to develop and learn. The reason for the ambivalence is that any significant learning involves a certain amount of pain, either pain connected with the learning itself or distress connected with giving up certain previous learnings. The first type of ambivalence is illustrated by the small child who is learning to walk. He stumbles, he falls, he hurts himself. It is a painful process. Yet, the satisfactions of developing his potential far outweigh the bumps and bruises. The second type of ambivalence is evident when a student who has been absolutely tops in every way in his small town high school enrolls in a superior college or university where he finds that he is simply one of many bright students. This is a painful learning to assimilate, yet in most instances he does assimilate it and goes forward.

This potentiality and desire for learning, for discovery, for enlargement of knowledge and experience, can be released under suitable conditions. It is a tendency which can be trusted, and the whole approach to education which we have been describing builds upon and around the student's natural desire to learn.

2. *Significant learning takes place when the subject matter is perceived by the student as having relevance for his own purposes.* A somewhat more formal way of stating this is that a person learns significantly only those things which he perceives as being involved in the maintenance of or the enhancement of his own self. . . .

Another element related to this principle has to do with the speed of learning. When an individual has a goal he wishes to achieve and he sees the material available to him as relevant to achieving that goal, learning

Reprinted, with deletions, from *Freedom to Learn: A View of What Education Might Become* (Columbus, Ohio: Charles E. Merrill Publishing Co., 1969), pp. 157–66, by permission of the author and the publisher.

takes place with great rapidity. We need only to recall what a brief length of time it takes for an adolescent to learn to drive a car. There is evidence that the time for learning various subjects would be cut to a fraction of the time currently allotted if the material were perceived by the learner as related to his own purposes. Probably one-third to one-fifth of the present time allotment would be sufficient.

3. *Learning which involves a change in self-organization—in the perception of oneself—is threatening and tends to be resisted.* Why has there been so much furor, sometimes even lawsuits, concerning an adolescent boy who comes to school with long hair? Surely the length of his hair makes little objective difference. The reason seems to be that if I, as a teacher or administrator, accept the value which he places on nonconformity, then it threatens the value which I have placed on conforming to social demands. If I permit this contradiction to exist I may find myself changing, because I will be forced to a reappraisal of some of my values. The same thing applies to the former interest in "beatniks" and the current interest in "hippies." If their rejection of almost all middle-class values is permitted to stand, then an individual's acceptance of middle-class values as a part of himself is deeply threatened, since to most people it seems that to the degree *others* are right, *they* are wrong. . . .

4. *Those learnings which are threatening to the self are more easily perceived and assimilated when external threats are at a minimum.* The boy who is retarded in reading already feels threatened and inadequate because of this deficiency. When he is forced to attempt to read aloud in front of the group, when he is ridiculed for his efforts, when his grades are a vivid reflection of his failure, it is no surprise that he may go through several years of school with no perceptible increase in his reading ability. On the other hand, a supportive, understanding environment and a lack of grades, or an encouragement of self-evaluation, remove the external threats and permit him to make progress because he is no longer paralyzed by fear. This is also one of the great advantages of the teaching machine, when properly used. Here the poor reader can begin at his own level of achievement and practically every minute step he makes is marked by reward and a feeling of success. . . .

5. *When threat to the self is low, experience can be perceived in differentiated fashion and learning can proceed.* In a sense this is only an extension of, or an explanation of, the preceding principle. The poor reader is a good illustration of what is involved in this principle. When he is called upon to recite in class the internal panic takes over and the words on the page become less intelligible symbols than they were when he was sitting at his seat before he was called upon. When he is in an environment in which he is assured of personal security and when he becomes convinced that there is no threat to his ego, he is once more

free to perceive the symbols on the page in a differentiated fashion, to recognize the differing elements in similar words, to perceive partial meanings and try to put them together—in other words, to move forward in the process of learning. Any sort of learning involves an increasing differentiation of the field of experience and the assimilation of the meanings of these differentiations. . . .

6. *Much significant learning is acquired through doing.* Placing the student in direct experiential confrontation with practical problems, social problems, ethical and philosophical problems, personal issues, and research problems, is one of the most effective modes of promoting learning. Illustrations range from the class group which becomes involved in a dramatic production, selecting the play and the cast, designing and making the scenery and costumes, coaching the actors, and selling tickets, to much more sophisticated confrontations. I have always been impressed with the fact that brief intensive courses for individuals on the firing line facing immediate problems—teachers, doctors, farmers, counselors—are especially effective because the individuals are trying to cope with problems which they are currently experiencing.

7. *Learning is facilitated when the student participates responsibly in the learning process.* When he chooses his own directions, helps to discover his own learning resources, formulates his own problems, decides his own course of action, lives with the consequences of each of these choices, then significant learning is maximized. There is evidence from industry as well as from the field of education that such participative learning is far more effective than passive learning.

8. *Self-initiated learning which involves the whole person of the learner—feelings as well as intellect—is the most lasting and pervasive.* We have discovered this in psychotherapy, where it is the totally involved learning of oneself by oneself which is most effective. This is not learning which takes place "only from the neck up." It is a "gut level" type of learning which is profound and pervasive. It can also occur in the tentative discovery of a new self-generated idea or in the learning of a difficult skill, or in the act of artistic creation—a painting, a poem, a sculpture. It is the whole person who "lets himself go" in these creative learnings. An important element in these situations is that the learner *knows* it is his own learning and thus can hold to it or relinquish it in the face of a more profound learning without having to turn to some authority for corroboration of his judgment.

9. *Independence, creativity, and self-reliance are all facilitated when self-criticism and self-evaluation are basic and evaluation by others is of secondary importance.* The best research organizations, in industry as well as in the academic world, have learned that creativity blossoms in an atmosphere of freedom. External evaluation is largely fruitless if the goal is creative work. The wise parent has learned this same lesson. If a

child is to grow up to be independent and self-reliant he must be given opportunities at an early age not only to make his own judgments and his own mistakes but to evaluate the consequences of these judgments and choices. The parent may provide information and models of behavior, but it is the growing child and adolescent who must evaluate his own behaviors, come to his own conclusions, and decide on the standards which are appropriate for him. The child or adolescent who is dependent both at school and at home upon the evaluations of others is likely to remain permanently dependent and immature or explosively rebellious against all external evaluations and judgments.

10. *The most socially useful learning in the modern world is the learning of the process of learning, a continuing openness to experience and incorporation into oneself of the process of change.* . . . A static kind of learning of information may have been quite adequate in previous times. If our present culture survives it will be because we have been able to develop individuals for whom *change* is the central fact of life and who have been able to live comfortably with this central fact. It means that they will not be concerned, as so many are today, that their past learning is inadequate to enable them to cope with current situations. They will instead have the comfortable expectation that it will be continuously necessary to incorporate new and challenging learnings about ever-changing situations.

So much has been presented . . . about various methods of facilitating and various qualities of the facilitator that only the briefest summary of some of the guidelines which can be abstracted will be presented here.

1. *The facilitator has much to do with setting the initial mood or climate of the group or class experience.* If his own basic philosophy is one of trust in the group and in the individuals who compose the group, then this point of view will be communicated in many subtle ways.

2. *The facilitator helps to elicit and clarify the purposes of the individuals in the class as well as the more general purposes of the group.* If he is not fearful of accepting contradictory purposes and conflicting aims, if he is able to permit the individuals a sense of freedom in stating what they would like to do, then he is helping to create a climate for learning. There is no need for him to try to manufacture one unified purpose in the group if such a unified purpose is not there. He can permit a diversity of purposes to exist, contradictory and complementary, in relationship to each other.

3. *He relies upon the desire of each student to implement those purposes which have meaning for him as the motivational force behind significant learning.* Even if the desire of the student is to be guided and led by someone else, the facilitator can accept such a need and motive and can either serve as a guide when this is desired or can provide some other means, such as a set course of study, for the student whose major desire

is to be dependent. And for the majority of students he can help to utilize the individual's own drives and purposes as the moving force behind his learning.

4. *He endeavors to organize and make easily available the widest possible range of resources for learning.* He endeavors to make available writings, materials, psychological aids, persons, equipment, trips, audiovisual aids—every conceivable resource which his students may wish to use for their own enhancement and for the fulfillment of their own purposes.

5. *He regards himself as a flexible resource to be utilized by the group.* He does not downgrade himself as a resource. He makes himself available as a counselor, lecturer, and advisor, a person with experience in the field. He wishes to be used by individual students, and by the group, in the ways which seem most meaningful to them insofar as he can be comfortable in operating in the ways they wish.

6. *In responding to expressions in the classroom group, he accepts both the intellectual content and the emotionalized attitudes, endeavoring to give each aspect the approximate degree of emphasis which it has for the individual or the group.* Insofar as he can be genuine in doing so, he accepts rationalizations and intellectualizing, as well as deep and real personal feelings.

7. *As the acceptant classroom climate becomes established, the facilitator is able increasingly to become a participant learner, a member of the group, expressing his views as those of one individual only.*

8. *He takes the initiative in sharing himself with the group—his feelings as well as his thoughts—in ways which do not demand nor impose but represent simply a personal sharing which students may take or leave.* Thus, he is free to express his own feelings in giving feedback to students, in his reaction to them as individuals, and in sharing his own satisfactions or disappointments. In such expressions it is his "owned" attitudes which are shared, not judgments or evaluations of others.

9. *Throughout the classroom experience, he remains alert to the expressions indicative of deep or strong feelings.* These may be feelings of conflict, pain, and the like, which exist primarily within the individual. Here he endeavors to understand these from the person's point of view and to communicate his empathic understanding. On the other hand, the feelings may be those of anger, scorn, affection, rivalry, and the like—interpersonal attitudes among members of the group. Again he is as alert to these as to the ideas being expressed and by his acceptance of such tensions or bonds he helps to bring them into the open for constructive understanding and use by the group.

10. *In his functioning as a facilitator of learning, the leader endeavors to recognize and accept his own limitations.* He realizes that he can only grant freedom to his students to the extent that he is comfortable in giv-

ing such freedom. He can only be understanding to the extent that he actually desires to enter the inner world of his students. He can only share himself to the extent that he is reasonably comfortable in taking that risk. He can only participate as a member of the group when he actually feels that he and his students have an equality as learners. He can only exhibit trust of the student's desire to learn insofar as he feels that trust. There will be many times when his attitudes are not facilitative of learning. He will find himself being suspicious of his students. He will find it impossible to accept attitudes which differ strongly from his own. He will be unable to understand some of the student feelings which are markedly different from his own. He may find himself angry and resentful of student attitudes toward him and angry at student behaviors. He may find himself feeling strongly judgmental and evaluative. When he is experiencing attitudes which are nonfacilitative, he will endeavor to get close to them, to be clearly aware of them, and to state them just as they are within himself. Once he has expressed these angers, these judgments, these mistrusts, these doubts of others and doubts of himself, as something coming from within himself, not as objective facts in outward reality, he will find the air cleared for a significant interchange between himself and his students. Such an interchange can go a long way toward resolving the very attitudes which he has been experiencing, and thus make it possible for him to be more of a facilitator of learning.

CHAPTER 12

Resolving the Dilemma of Education

American public education is in the midst of a dilemma. It is confronted by problems that make increasing demands on the system at the very time that the system is becoming less and less able to respond. Education is facing an energy crisis just as perplexing as the oil shortage, but even more crucial because of the implications it holds for the very future of American society. What happens when society is no longer able to educate effectively? What happens when society can no longer create the skills or understandings or beliefs necessary to maintain essential societal functions?

Part of the problem, as we see it, has been that too many "educationists" have proposed patent remedies and too many educators have willingly bought the package without examining the contents. Not only has education not been improved, it has become less able to obtain improvement. We are not proposing a solution, for none is available that is adequate to the problem; we are proposing the means to a plausible solution.

We choose to address ourselves generally to everyone who is concerned with improving education, because we believe that the process is fundamentally the same for any individual or group of individuals. It involves (1) determining what needs to be done; (2) selecting appropriate objectives; (3) finding out what can and cannot be done; (4) determining the requirements of the job; (5) figuring out how best to do the job; (6) continually evaluating the success of our efforts; and (7) developing new methods and practices as necessary.

Determining What Needs to Be Done

If the dilemma of education is to be resolved, the process by which program requirements are obtained for all educational operations must be made more comprehensive, more open, and more honest.

The adequacy of any attempt to identify and resolve program discrepancies depends upon the availability of good hard data about what is going on in education. This is a technical problem of data acquisition and control; however, from the perspective of organizational improvement, it is also a problem of choosing what you want to look at.

The person who chooses to become a prospective teacher, for example, emerges from a fairly orderly and extended process of education. He or she has obtained a particular set of meanings about what needs to be done in "education," what "learning" requires, and what a "teacher" can reasonably expect to have to do. Typically, the teacher-preparation program supports these meanings or at least does nothing to contradict them. Result? a person who operates from a particular point of view, frequently limited in the scope of hard data considered, usually unable to transcend the acquired restrictions of a particular set of meanings, often unable to read and process discrepant data, and definitely limited in the ability to reconstruct outlooks independently.

But our analysis also suggests that the system is not fixed. It suggests that individuals must be sensitive not only to what the situation is *now* but to any change that may be taking place. And they must become progressively more sensitive and more skillful in constructing new outlooks. The teacher-education program should start with "what meanings do you have now?" and move quickly and in a nonthreatening fashion to "how can we verify these meanings?" not to "your meanings are unsuitable; please adopt these meanings instead."

Teacher-education programs have to become a lot more honest and realistic. This means, first, that the prospective teacher will be required to look at a lot of different kinds of learners in a lot of learning situations before anybody starts drawing conclusions or generalizations about what is taking place. It means looking at substantive notions from sociology, psychology, and philosophy (as we have suggested in earlier chapters) and verifying the function they have for learning, if any.

Second, it requires opening the dialogue to a much broader range of participants—practitioners, learners, parents, and teaching candidates. Passivity and silence should be discouraged as noneducative. Techniques should be developed that will allow us to process widely divergent and sometimes discrepant data efficiently.

Third, this requires acquisition and consideration of many kinds of data about proposed teaching activities and behaviors, their effectiveness, and the beliefs and attitudes prospective teachers develop about them. A great deal more than "talking" about what teachers are supposed to do is required: what is needed is honest appraisal of how the teacher "feels" about teaching activities as well as what the teacher "knows" about them technically.

Almost every curriculum text has something to say about the gap between what society needs and what the schools provide. General systems theory suggests that we have to develop monitoring systems that are quickly responsive to changes if we are to make adaptations before the system is unduly affected. A real question is whether or not we can continue to tolerate "culture lag," whether we can continue to tolerate any educational program that is fundamentally unrealistic or irrelevant. The question is provoked by our declining fiscal revenues and by the increasing credibility gap in education.

In American society, to become an effective teacher one must also become a concerned student of sociology, political science, economics, and whatever other disciplines may lend some perspective on the relationship between education and the general social concern.

In American society, each teacher must become aware of the social significance of all the data obtained through these disciplines. It is increasingly clear, for example, that "science" teaching and learning cannot be confined to a classroom or a biology workshop, and that "scientists" cannot be allowed to become soulless automatons in a social vacuum. It is becoming increasingly clear that teachers, as members of the community of discourse, and education, as a social agency, need to be increasingly sensitive to the effect knowledge has on society and the effect society has on knowledge.

Our analysis suggests that it is wiser to treat observations of the larger system as tentative or conditional, certainly not as final and reliable over time. This allows us to work meaningfully and honestly on the problems at hand without becoming concerned with whether or not these are the most crucial or the most persistent problems confronting the profession. Realizing that our initial considerations will be followed by another and yet another has a number of salutory effects: (1) If we do not want to be faced by the same problem the next time it comes around, we will deal with it now. (2) If the problem we are working on now is *not* the most pertinent or significant, the next round will clearly demonstrate that. (3) If problems of real significance have eluded us, we will have several other opportunities to ferret them out and identify them. Clearly, we are not branded forever by the misfortune of our earliest efforts; we are not obligated to make the same mistake over and over again.

Selecting Appropriate Objectives

If the dilemma of education is to be resolved, the process by which educational objectives are selected and endorsed must be made clearer and more effective; at the same time, it must be made more responsive and more responsible.

If the prime trait of American education today is that it is "mindless," as Silberman has suggested, the obvious solution is for it to become "mindful" of what it is about. But that is a lot like saying to a child, "You are irresponsible; you must become responsible!" Or to teachers "You are poor teachers; you must become good teachers!" The assertion is both judgmental and redundant; the emphasis does nothing to advance an understanding of what needs to be done to alleviate the problem. The statement is simply not subject to analysis.

Let us use teacher preparation to exemplify the more general problems of the educational system. Again let us start with some rather discrepant views:

PROSPECTIVE TEACHER: Education courses are dull, dull, dull! And they don't even tell you how to teach!

DIRECTOR OF PERSONNEL: We expect all our teachers to be proficient in using the video-tape recorder; if you don't teach your people how to use it, we won't hire any more of them.

ELEMENTARY TEACHER: Most education profs haven't been in a school classroom in twenty years! What do they know about teaching?

COACH: Long hair on boys is the sign of a sissy and should be banned from American athletic fields. A good hair code is necessary to get the abnormals out of athletics before they become coaches.

EDUCATION PROFESSOR: After those kids have been out teaching for five or ten years, they'll begin to realize the importance of what I covered in my basic concepts class.

PARENT: I'm more interested in having my child learn respect for the American way of life and discipline than in any of these "progressive" education notions.

ACADEMIC PROFESSOR: It's no wonder the public school teachers are so bad. Every year our weakest majors wind up in education.

SCHOOL PRINCIPAL: The problem of drug use has been greatly inflated by the newspapers. Anyway, it can be traced directly to a small number of very undesirable students.

SECONDARY TEACHER: When this school started to turn black, we decided we'd hold the line in our Algebra classes. The people who pass now are every bit as good as the ones who used to pass—there are just a lot fewer of them.

STUDENT: Man, you wouldn't believe how bad school really is!

How can we get any sense of direction from this range of views (and we have heard each of them stated)? How could one persuade these people to agree on what should be done to improve teacher education?

Often we are urged to accept an answer for reasons that have nothing at all to do with the rationality of the answer. We should become very sensitive to those feelings within ourselves, to our own anxieties about vagueness and ambiguity.

Determining the objective of a particular enterprise actually breaks down into a series of conditional inquiries: (1) How much sense of direction is necessary before we start out? (2) How much agreement about our objective is possible? (3) How reliably can we specify an objective on the basis of the information that we have at hand? (4) If consensus is not possible, what provisions must be made for alternate objectives? (5) If reliability cannot be assured, how shall we check ourselves to be certain we're not too far off the track we want to follow?

In teacher education as in other areas, there is no reason to fear student involvement in the planning of course or instructional objectives if the teacher knows enough about the subject and the process to provide skillful direction. The best question a student can ask is "Why do we have to study *that*?" The usual response is a defensive "Because I say so!" or a pretentious "You'll need it when you get to (whatever the next highest level of education is)." The most uncommon response—and the one with the greatest learning potential—is "Why indeed? Let's see if it *can* be eliminated from our consideration. Let's see if we *can* prove that it is irrelevant. Let's devise a set of criteria for *what* really makes sense and then see if dropping this topic makes more sense than keeping it."

Several advantages accrue from this approach. Immediately the learner is invested in the difficult task of assigning priorities to objectives that are at least competitive if not contradictory. Discrimination of the value of alternate topics is placed at the beginning, where it receives more attention. The teacher obtains immediate evidence of the learner's perceptions of program priorities. The learner obtains immediate evidence of the usual lack of agreement and the need for further consideration. Motivation for learning is usually obtained as a function of the problem situation; it does not have to be contrived.

It would probably create too much consternation if one were to begin a teacher-education course by announcing, "There is no clear agreement on what it means to be a good teacher" (a valid statement). "Therefore, there is very little that I can tell you that will make you a good teacher" (an honest statement!). We would suggest the desirability of asking prospective teachers "What do you see as the objectives that should guide the improvement of teaching? How do you go about obtaining these objectives? How do you go about verifying these objectives?" They may not start with very enlightened points of view, but they will become enlightened very rapidly by this process.

It would probably create too much anxiety among the students if you were to begin a teacher education course by announcing: "There are no real authorities on what it means to be a good teacher" (a not invalid statement). "Therefore, we shall accept our own views, beliefs, perceptions as authoritative until proved otherwise" (a valid proposition). We suggest that it is desirable to initiate consideration with that which is basic but not absurd. We are interested in involving learners at the level most appropriate to *their* experiences and *their* meanings, rather than expecting them to become engaged with second-level propositions and generalizations others have drawn. We propose a shift from the study of what authorities have said about education (product) to the study of what is authoritative about education (process). In many instances, to be sure, the two will be similar or congruent in substance. What differs—and here the differences are significant—are the values and attitudes and feelings and beliefs the prospective teacher develops.

It would probably create too much resentment if you were to begin a teacher-education course by suggesting, "There is a wide range of acceptable objectives; hence, the choice of program objectives is an arbitrary one made solely on the basis of the instructor's preference." We would suggest that there is a choice to be made, and that it is a choice that the teacher will have to make sooner or later. Because the objectives of improved teaching eventually becomes the teacher's, the focus of the teacher-education program would better be directed to wise choice making from the beginning. Our concern as teacher educators ought to be with granting responsibility to prospective teachers, not with substituting institutional responsibility for personal responsibility. The individual must choose whether he wishes to become an ordinary teacher or an extraordinary teacher. His choice of goals should be encouraged but never usurped.

Finding Out What Can and Cannot Be Done

If the dilemma of education is to be resolved, we must develop a much clearer understanding of how educational systems are influenced by various forces, and we must become more skillful in assessing limits and constraints, including personal limits and constraints.

Given a situation in which the system has sufficient resources so that the uneconomical expenditure of some does not constitute a threat to the system, we are not really too concerned about what we do. If we have an unlimited expense account, we do not worry about the price of dinner while on a business trip. If there are no time limits or deadlines related to a specific task, we do not worry about when it has to be finished.

The same logic seems to apply to educational systems, whether we are thinking about individual schools or large district or state organizations. At any given time, a system is made up of the interrelationships among the particular elements of the system. At any given time, a system has a certain energy reserve, which can be used to alter the elements or the relationship among them. The problem, then, is to figure out whether we can bring about the changes we have decided are appropriate, or what else we must do to produce desired changes.

The American educational system has enjoyed the advantage of sufficient resources to ensure its persistence. It has had sufficient success to warrant the continuing availability of energies for change, development, and experimentation. America's separation from England was seen to require the ability to educate citizens in the practical skills of commerce and governance, independent of the institutions that formerly had contributed this resource. After World War II, the political, economic, and military security of America was seen to require certain personal skills and knowledge as a part of our national strategy. (Lest anyone resents our noting the complicity between education and the military-industrial complex, let us point out (1) that service in the armed forces is now seen as a means of earning the right to a cost-free "civilian" education, (2) that industry and the military have demonstrated their strong belief in the value of education by their continuing expenditures in that area, (3) that the largest federal participation in education to date is labeled the National Defense Education Acts, (4) that continuing federal involvement is highly politicized by socially and economically deprived minorities seeking to use education as an instrument to achieve personal and group ascendancy and (5) that the primary motivation behind current federal involvement is the advantageous manipulation of the labor market and economic productivity through direct infusion of the school curriculum with career-education programs).

We have evidence, then, of factors in the larger socio-political-economic situation that have enabled education to acquire resources in excess of a maintenance level, producing an educational "growth economy." The effect of this is that more people see an opportunity to fulfill personal goals and become willing to contribute personal energies, a broader range of alternative goals is taken into consideration, a larger number of alternate means is developed, people come to believe more and more in what education can do, and the goals of education are accorded greater and greater social value and credibility.

All this happens in an educational system during a growth cycle, but obviously the net system economy can change, and the cycle of expanding energy can become a cycle of diminishing energy. As soon as the question of credibility is raised openly, other forces are altered and realigned. Stringent accountability becomes a systems ethic. The psychology of plenty, of optimistic growth, of the expansion of opportunities becomes a psychology of poverty, of pessimistic retrenchment, of the restriction of opportunities as an inevitable fact of systems future. At the worst it can become a national neurosis such as the American Depression and the aggressive nationalism of both America and other nation states.

Knowing this about systems, about education both generally and particularly, and about persons collectively and individually, our major concern becomes one of determining what we can and cannot do.

What happens if this assessment is inaccurate is all too obvious. A system can devote all available energy to the strict accounting of financial elements and become a tightly controlled operation with little or no growth potential, creativity, or imagination. An organization can devote so much energy to research and development that it never masters the technical skills necessary for effective production. We may spend more time defending current practice than might be required to develop more effective practice, a dilemma American automobile manufacturers appear to have created for themselves in the "clean air" controversy.

Applying these systems principles directly to teacher education provides clear direction for resolution of the dilemma. Prospective teachers have to obtain valid information about what they can and cannot do as teachers. In terms of the individual, initial career commitment is crucial. If the prospective teacher finds that teaching requires more energy than he is willing to contribute—and this must include both physical and psychic energy—he had better decide not to teach. This decision, however, must be based on a realistic self-appraisal and an understanding of teaching. Both require considerable time and meaningful experience; this is precisely what the teacher education program should provide.

The prospective teacher must obtain valid information about what he can and cannot do about learning. It would probably be well, for example, for him to learn that he can never create learning for another person, that learning is something that takes place *within* the person, frequently unobtrusively, usually autonomously. The prospective teacher should learn that he can create conditions that facilitate and enhance the learning of others. The prospective teacher should learn to utilize his energies so as to have the greatest effect on the largest number of people. He must learn as well to encourage the most efficient use of the learner's energies to achieve the most meaningful learning with the least expenditure of energy. If teachers came to appreciate this fact of classroom "ecology," think of the conservation of energy that would be achieved simply by eliminating time-filling busy work. *Then think of what could be done by redirecting that energy toward productive learning!*

The prospective teacher must obtain valid information about what he can and cannot do to improve the quality of the classroom program for which he is responsible. In an absolute sense, teachers are not restricted by the subjects they have to teach or the textbooks or curriculum they have to use. They are not limited by the students assigned to their classes, certainly not in the way limits are imposed on students by the arbitrary happenstance of achievement test scores frequently used in grouping and scheduling. The teacher is not expressly constrained by available physical facilities and equipment. The teacher is not limited by the lack of skill or contrariness of the school principal either, for we have yet to find an administrator so skillful, so energetic, so omnipresent that he could possibly *prevent* good teaching from taking place.

It would probably be well for the prospective teacher to learn quite early that the most insidious and damaging limits to good teaching and learning are those he imposes on himself, often unwittingly. Most teachers are limited by their own conception of what is possible. Imagine the loss of potential contribution when learning is never attempted because the learner does not have a chance to know what possibilities exist! Imagine the loss of potential when a teaching act is never attempted because the teacher is unaware, insensitive, unnecessarily cautious, easily discouraged, or worse, unwilling to make the effort! *Imagine the loss to mankind for all time when a teacher underestimates the ability of a learner and never attempts to teach him what in actuality is possible!*

The prospective teacher should become aware of the realistic constraints on good teaching. The prospective teacher should be prepared to make a maximum contribution. The prospective teacher should be prepared to be surprised, excited, fascinated by accomplishing what he may have thought was not possible.

Determining the Requirements of the Job

If the dilemma of education is to be resolved, we must become much more skillful in determining the tasks required to achieve our stated objectives and much more effective in acquiring the skills to perform these tasks.

The discrepancy between man's desires and his ability to design behavior that is effective in meeting those desires is more than a technological gap or a culture lag. Central to the question of the system's ability to succeed is how well it can analyze the mission it seeks to accomplish into the essential work functions and job tasks and the energies it has available to accomplish them.

It is useful to regard the individual person as a system of energy forces. However, we frequently oversimplify the analogy and regard man as a simple mechanical input-output system. Certain foods are essential to "fuel" the system, and the proper combination of vitamins and minerals will produce champions and even rehabilitate 97-pound weaklings. Too often we inappropriately limit our concept of man's energy output to a physical notion of work performed: how many bricks can a bricklayer lay, how much effort did the person put into an assignment, how many units of work are produced per unit of time, how many years do you put in to earn retirement benefits. Too often we inappropriately limit our concept of what can go wrong with man to a physical notion of "catching a disease," "wearing out," or "breaking down": what germs produce the discernible symptoms of what illness, how much of which biochemical agent is necessary to "medicate" this system imbalance, how long will it take us to discover and control the biochemical agent that produces mental illness.

We really know a great deal more about the individual person as an energy system than these simple analogies indicate. We have firm evidence that chronic physical conditions are sometimes caused by psychological factors. We know that men who are apparently similar in every physical factor differ widely in their outlooks, behaviors, capacities, and wishes. We know that some individuals apparently can withstand incredible physical and psychological shocks while others are unable to cope with apparently minor disruptions.

From the basic concept of individual man as a holistic system of related forces, we can draw some generalizations about interpersonal and intergroup relations. The analysis of the nuclear family as a system of personal forces provides a useful framework for understanding the interaction among parents and children. When we try to help the family work through disruptions, this approach comes to grip with more of the factors involved than do therapeutic efforts directed to getting a divergent member to conform to the neuroses of the rest of the family. Applying it to other interpersonal groups, even as large and complex as societies and industrial organizations, provides us with a more adequate basis for analyzing our objectives into necessary tasks and functions.

In even the simplest situations, the individual does what he deems necessary to achieve his goals. In situations with which he has a degree of familiarity, he moves without much deliberation to fulfill those functions that he knows will meet his purposes. If one is at home in the evening and wants a cup of coffee, it does not require a great deal of conscious deliberation about what jobs he will have to perform to satisfy his wish, as long as things proceed according to expectations.

In situations that are not familiar, that involve other persons whose activity is not predictable, or that are highly complex, a great deal more analysis is necessary. The initial phase of problem-solving, then, is to determine the requirements of the job to be done. Analytically, these are work functions and tasks rather than techniques for the performance of work. A simple example can be found in the recipe for roast duck: First, you get a duck. We could analyze the functions and tasks required to meet the objective "make old-fashioned home-made ice cream" into equipment, materials, the personal knowledge and skill necessary to prepare the mixture, the nonintellectual work energy required to turn the crank, and the experience necessary to determine when and how to pack the ice cream so that it will "set" properly. It is not surprising that only a few people are interested in making old-fashioned home-made ice cream, usually on special occasions when the effort (energy) required appears warranted.

What functions and tasks would have to be performed to meet the objective of placing a man on the moon? Let us acknowledge the fact that the work to be done, including the necessary knowledge, skills, understandings, and attitudes, can be analyzed into larger functions and more specific tasks. Let us acknowledge, as well, that this mission was attained with a high degree of effectiveness and a level of expenditure of system resources that generally was quite acceptable to the persons whose contributions were essential.

Although there may be agreement on the purpose, potential contributors in complex situations may still disagree over the functions and tasks that are necessary. We may agree that it would be "fun" to spend the evening playing poker and still argue about whether to play draw or stud, what the ante ought to be, or a host of other particulars, until everyone comes to believe that spending the evening playing poker—at least with this bunch—is not worth the trouble.

Although we may perform a highly sophisticated analysis of our objective, we may find that subsequent performance of the described functions and tasks does not result in the complete fulfillment of the objective. We may find that we can achieve the objective in this way, but that doing so requires a greater expenditure of energy than we anticipated. We may find that the requirements are not available in sufficient quantity to provide a satisfactory level of effectiveness. (Haven't you ever seen a basketball team whose members knew what they had to do to win and had all the necessary skills, but happened to be up against a team that was an awful lot taller?)

We may have an adequate notion of what we want to accomplish and the tasks and functions necessary to do so and not possess the skills to verify that proper performance is taking place or is, in fact, achieving what it was designed to achieve. We may assume that the system outputs do not require monitoring or appraisal. But we may expend all available energies before making adequate provisions for examining the actual products to see if they are the anticipated products.

We can apply this notion directly to the dilemma of education. First, most students enter teacher education with less than complete understanding of all the functions and tasks actually involved in teaching. This fact is not a discredit to their abilities or experience; rather, it points out the disadvantage imposed on learners by our educational system. Their experience has almost exclusively been that of the subordinate in an authoritarian teacher-student relationship. This does not necessarily mean that the teaching to which they have been subjected is harsh, cruel, and punishing. Teaching does not have to be physically abusive to be characterized as authoritarian. All we have to do to be authoritarian is to exclude the recipient of the action from participating in the process of determining the course of action; all we have to do to be authoritarian is not to give someone a choice. The most inhumane device of the authoritarian teacher is not corporal punishment, but psychological coercion like "If you will not do this for me, I will withhold my affection, support, warmth, and respect for you as a person." In their lower division "liberal" education and their academic majors, prospective teachers generally experience the same kind of authoritarianism. Since liberal arts faculty pick their most successful students to follow them as teachers, and the most successful students are those who are most accepting of traditional academic authoritarianism, whatever liberalizing value competent teaching might promote is quickly subverted to the demand for academic conformity. Teaching in our colleges has become traditionally bad, and bad teaching has become accepted as a characteristic of higher education. In general, the total experience of prospective teachers has been exposure to the *products* of learning carefully extracted and separated from involvement in the *process* of learning. Academic types have become successful in manipulating these learning products; they accept this situation as reasonable and valid and resist efforts to change what their cumulative experience has already verified. We do very little to intervene in this progression. Thus the expectations of the prospective teacher are transmitted to the next generation of learners in pure and unadulterated form.

Teacher education could better be directed to the analysis and examination of the prospective teacher's experience. He should be asked to clarify the meanings he has acquired that relate directly to the nature of learning and the dependent conduct of teaching. He should be asked to audit his prior experience carefully to discriminate commonness from uniqueness, the ordinary from the extraordinary, peak experiences from plains and valleys. He should be asked to recall those occasions, few though they may be, when learning really "blew his mind." He should be asked to identify the factors or circumstances that seem to be related to that kind of learning. He should be asked to develop a tentative set of new meanings for his own experience, not to distrust his prior experience but to realize the full meaning that can be drawn from it.

The prospective teacher should then start examining a great deal more data about learning than his own experience. He should immerse himself in situations in which learning is supposed to be taking place to discover the particularities of these situations, as opposed to the random, purposeless, unstructured observation of classrooms and school children that is common now.

The prospective teacher should be brought to the realization that his prior experience with learning did not take into account all pertinent factors such as context and syntax, intent and content, substance and strategy, because at that time he was a learner, not a teacher. Purpose dictates that our accumulated meanings about learning now be translated into meanings about teaching. Our objective becomes that of developing the most adequate set of meanings about what we can possibly do to facilitate learning.

Since the prospective teacher will at some point have to come to know the skills and understandings and attitudes required in teaching, and since we know that he will appropriate for himself those meanings that will exert the greatest influence on his teaching behavior, the most efficient approach seems to be to require him first to make a complete determination of the requirements of the job, then to assist him in verifying and improving the adequacy of this task determination.

Most of the things learners do in schools produce little or no valid, meaningful learning. Still, most of it passes for learning. Teachers, administrators, parents, and even students become convinced that the activities being carried out have some value that some day will become apparent. Unfortunately, we rarely get around to checking that out, so we keep repeating the same insufficiencies.

Figuring Out How Best to Do the Job

If the dilemma of education is to be resolved, we must broaden the consideration of alternative means to accomplish educational functions and tasks and become increasingly skillful at selecting and preparing alternative instructional means.

A lot of people have trouble accepting the systems notion that for a given objective there is an infinite number of possible ways to achieve that purpose. In almost all situations, we have learned to look for and accept the answer that "works." We may realize that it has some imperfections but feel that the further refinement necessary to eliminate them would not be worth the effort. So we wind up with ways of doing things that are usually less than perfect, and we learn not to expect to meet our objectives fully.

After the individual has accepted a way of doing things, he seldom spends much time considering any other possible means. The accepted way becomes habitual. There is a resistance to altering the pattern, even in the face of less than complete satisfaction. The suggestion that a better way exists may elicit a defense of the accustomed pattern rather than an examination of its insufficiencies. A person may even accede that the proposed means is better but still exhibit preference for the familiar pattern. "I know your way is better, but I'd rather do it my way!"

Transportation in the American scene presents a convenient example of the general systems approach to the identification and selection of alternative means. At some point in the past, the transportation needs of the individual American could have been met by a number of alternative means. In early America, the horse was not the only available means of transportation, nor is it likely that it was ever a completely adequate or satisfying means. But it was a means that attained acceptance, and was elaborated to fantastic proportions, such as the breeding and training of matched hackney ponies with exaggerated gaits. As conditions changed and the needs of the system changed, the values and meanings attached to the accepted means also changed. As changes took place, they were also resisted, just as the last horse owner resisted buying his first automobile.

Had anyone been clairvoyant enough to anticipate all that occurred because of the selection of horses as a means of transportation, many would have scoffed. The same would have been even more true for the American automobile, but of course it was no more possible to predict all that would happen because of the internal combustion engine than it is to predict reliably any other uncertain future. If you doubt this, imagine yourself a member of the First Continental Congress being asked to accept or reject some research engineer's proposal for a system of personal transportation that included these specifications: Each American will equip himself with a chrome-plated "vehicle" weighing nearly two tons, costing from $2,000 to $35,000, consuming large quantities of expensive liquid fuel and requiring a network of "filling stations" to supply it, requiring conveniently located and highly technical repair facilities, necessitating the paving of eight-lane wide strips of concrete across the country on which to operate the vehicle and multistoried garages in urban centers in which to park it while we go about our business.

All this has come to exist in its present form, of course, but *it was not inevitable.* And having come to be, it in turn created another set of problems and objectives to which possible alternate solutions must be proposed. Still we exert considerable resistance to any effort to control or alter the situation to which we have become accustomed, despite all the problems and inefficiencies associated with it. The last car owner will resist buying his first whatever-it-is vigorously. The alternatives are infinite; we could even go back to horses. The alternatives and the ability to develop the technology to make other alternatives possible are part of the situation that must be assessed sensitively and accurately if new means to goal achievement are to be selected wisely.

The prospective teacher faces much the same perplexity in the selection and preparation of instructional means. There is an overwhelming array of alternative instructional means available, including: physical components (texts, films, workbooks, slides, materials, objects, instruments, equipment), instructional activities (reading, discussing, writing, observing, viewing, and many other instructional techniques), and instructional strategies (lessons, units, plans, patterns, sequences, meta-method).

But that is only the beginning of the problem. In some way the selection of means has to be related back to instructional functions and objectives, in the broadest sense. We have many techniques available—for example, a whole body of literature on classroom simulation and games theory. But nobody has bothered to find out what all this is supposed to accomplish or whether it is accomplishing anything except to fill up available time.

There are those who believe that there is one "right" way to teach something—division of fractions, for example—and traditional teacher education consists of the acquisition and mastery of all the appropriate techniques and tricks. There are those who believe it does not make any difference, that all sorts of instructional means can be employed interchangeably, arbitrarily, even capriciously.

The prospective teacher, then, is confronted by a great many available means, each with its advocates. Principles from systems theory provide some reassurance that the perplexity is not insurmountable, can even be treated in a rational way.

First, let us recognize that the selection of instructional means is governed by the relationship they have to learning functions and teaching tasks specifically and to educational mission or goal generally. We need to realize, as well, that many differing interrelationships exist within the system of forces to which we need to be sensitive. Some instructional techniques may be more appropriate to some teaching tasks and learning functions. Some may be closer to the accepted practices of a particular group and hence easier to employ as part of a larger strategy. Some means may be more economical than others in terms of expense, time, and energy—and just as effective. Some instructional techniques may initially seem inappropriate when further examination might reveal them as being precisely appropriate. Some assumed limits and constraints on the use of some instructional means may be shown to be invalid. Some instructional techniques will probably need to be invented.

The prospective teacher ought to come to realize that the effective teacher is less a skillful technician than a skillful tactician. This suggests that the creative arts of teaching have to do with bringing about an effective relationship between the learner and the means of learning. This suggests that the prospective teacher should provide potential learners with an opportunity to choose among apparently equivalent means in order to determine if there are any real differences. This suggests that the personality, adaptability, intelligence, and humanness of the teacher is an instrumentality for learning—an instrumentality to be perfected and polished and employed—and that teaching is more an art than a science, more creative and inventive than mechanical and objective.

Continually Evaluating the Success of Our Efforts

If the dilemma of education is to be resolved, we must develop a broader and clearer image of how our efforts relate to the larger system, we must become more skillful in assessing and verifying our own effectiveness, and we must become more aware of and committed to meeting these needs.

It should be obvious that the general systems concept is concerned with more than the elements in an organization and how they are arranged. The general systems concept is concerned about organizational elements and how they are arranged, but it is concerned about a great deal more.

We have learned that the usual descriptions of an organization are very important and very useful. We have also found that their usefulness is limited. Any description is useful only so long as it is a valid representation of the actual situation. Anyone foolish enough to try to drive from Dallas to Chicago with the aid of a ten-year-old road map could attest that the map was just great as long as the roads were still there. The usefulness of any description, then, is limited by whether the situation described is static or may change, and if the latter, in what direction.

We can get along quite well with road maps that are brought up-to-date every year or so. If our physical system is in pretty good shape generally, we usually feel that we do not need a thorough physical examination more often than once a year. We may have our teeth checked every six months and our car checked every two or three thousand miles, to determine if any change has taken place that might otherwise go undetected. Obviously, if we became aware of change—a knock in the engine of the car or a toothache—we would act on the basis of that information.

But there are other kinds of situations to which we respond differently. A racing driver continually checks the operating temperature of his engine, because any change might be indicative of a very serious problem. A stockbroker maintains constant surveillance of the tickertape while the market is open because he is looking for even fractional variations in prices as possible indicators of a trend. In the intensive-care units of major hospitals, the blood pressure of cardiac patients is continuously monitored, for obvious reasons.

The need for a more effective way to deal with change or the possibility of change led directly to the development of general systems theory. If elements are not static, they are subject to change; change is not necessarily constant, change is not necessarily constant, it does not always follow in the same direction, and it does not always occur at the same rate. But if the elements are dynamic and subject to change, then how can we keep track of what is going on in even a fairly simple system? If we have trouble keeping track of the changes in a fairly simple system, how can we keep track of a complex system with a large number of elements, each possessing a wide range of potential variation and an infinite variety of possible interrelationships?

It quickly becomes obvious that the systems concept requires a great deal more information and a much more sophisticated means of acquiring and analyzing it just to know what is going on and to identify possible trends.

If our intent is to change or influence the way the system is working, if we wish to discriminate what alterations ought to be made and whether or not these are having the desired effect, we need sufficient control of the information systems process to enable us to evaluate management strategies. Without adequate information, management can be effective only by chance. An adequate information system alone does not guarantee effective management. Effective management is not a technical process but a moral process requiring that responsibility to the achievement of just ends be exerted.

The prospective teacher must become able to discriminate among available objectives to select the most relevant. He must become able to analyze objectives to determine program requirements and become skillful in assessing systems and personal limits and constraints. The prospective teacher must become able to analyze the instructional tasks required by education objectives, to select among alternative instructional means, and to prepare needed means. He must become aware of the full scope of the system and effective in evaluating his own efforts. The prospective teacher must become committed and responsible.

This requires a prospective teacher who has acquired a great deal of information about himself and the way in which he interacts with his environment, and about other persons and how they interact with their environment. The prospective teacher must come to realize that this information is not valid for all time but that he must remain continually sensitive to the changes taking place if his effectiveness as a teacher is to keep pace with changing system requirements.

Developing New Methods and Practices as Necessary

If the dilemma of education is to be resolved, we must accept the need to revise current practices, we must acquire the skills needed for the continual development of new outlooks, and we must accept the responsibility to engender and guide discerning choices without attempting to manipulate the outcomes.

Our analysis of the recent history and present state of the American social order convinces us that America's ability to respond constructively to social problems and issues is severely threatened by the increasing complexity of society. Our analysis of current alternative belief systems convinces us that we must develop intellectual abilities that will allow us to comprehend and process increasingly complex phenomena about man and his world. Our analysis of current approaches to learning and teaching convinces us that these means must be employed a great deal more sensitively and deliberately if the potential of teaching is to be realized.

We are convinced that effective means are possible and available, but that their realization may not become possible. If adults are expected to believe and participate effectively in democratic decision making, they must be educated to do so. If effective participation in democratic decision making must be learned and practiced, it is incumbent on schools as an agency of society to prepare young people to do so. If students in schools are to become skillful in democratic decision making, they must be taught by persons who themselves possess the requisite knowledge, attitudes, and skills. If teachers are to acquire these requisites, they themselves must be educated in such a manner. If one is to teach democratically, one must believe in democracy; if one wishes to teach reflectively, one must become reflective.

The knowledge, attitudes, and skills of democratic teaching and learning are not discrete traits that can be transmitted by glib but unconvincing means. Democratic teaching requires a conviction of the basic humaneness of man.

Name Index

Subject Index

absolutism
    axiological, 132, 158
    epistemological, 130
academic freedom as yardstick of
    democracy, 80
accountability, 16, 18, 27, 32
    business's role in, 29
    classroom practice and, 30–31
    "educational auditors" and, 31
    evaluational methods and, 31
    leadership and, 29
    management of educational sys-
        tems and, 27
    performance contracts and, 31
    quality assurance system of, 28–29
    school budgets and, 27
    teachers' status and, 30–31
    "zero reject system" of, 28
achievement as human motivation,
    95–97, 102
activism, see militancy
activity learning, 268–69
Adams State College (Alamosa,
    Colo.), 75
Adlerian psychology, 242–44
administrators
    as managers, 28
    organizations of, 23
    teachers' associations and, 3, 23
adult education, 20–21
aesthetics, 157
    concept of, clarified, 134
    see also axiology
affiliation, sex difference and, 275–76
AFL–CIO, 23
AFT, see American Federation of
    Teachers
alphawaves, 179

altered states of consciousness, 179
American Association for Humanis-
    tic psychology, 179
American Federation of Teachers
    (AFT), 22–23, 25–26
analysis-centered activities, 80
anarchistic academic freedom, 80
anarchistic educational system, 78
anarchistic testing, 81
animal learning, 212
Ann Arbor (Mich.), 106
anticipatory accuracy, 223
apperception, 128, 209–11, 212
    in psychological taxonomy, 206
apprenticeship, 52–53
Archimedes, 286
Aristotle, 48
Association for Supervision and Cur-
    riculum Development (ASCD),
    6
athletics, sexism and, 106
attitudes
    of college students, 147
    student, 55–56
        internationalism and, 59
        on schooling, 17–22
        self-concepts and, 41–42
    teacher
        to learning process, 199–200
        philosophy of education and,
            123–24
Auburn University, 162
audio-visual techniques, dangers of,
    191–92
August Martin High School (N.Y.),
    98
authoritarian education, rationalized
    system as, 147–48

73